Doris

an anthology of
Doris zines from 1991-2001

Cindy Crabb

Microcosm Publishing / Portland Oregon

Microcosm Publishing
5307 N Minnesota Ave
Portland, OR 97217

text: Royal manual typewriter and some other typewriter which have long since broken and been thrown away.

1 3 5 7 9 10 8 6 4 2

Crabb, Cindy.
Doris - an anthology of Doris zines
from 1991-2001

ISBN 0-9726967-8-4

printed 2005

for Wyette Hertz and Ernie Gulner

Introduction

People sometimes ask me, why the name Doris? but it's part of a story that I can't really explain. It has to do with a restaurant I worked at for awhile, and how one day the other waitress pointed to herself, and then to me, and then to Dan, and she said, "My name is Doris, your name is Doris, his name is Doris. Doris, Doris, Doris!"

The restaurant was a place I had hung out at when I was younger. It had grease in the air, orange, hard benches, bubble-gum under the booths. I would order eggrolls, rice and tea, and eat slowly, hoping it would sustain me. I didn't recognize hunger then, but my joints ached and sometimes I fainted.

Strange things happen when your insides are screaming and your outsides are trying to look cool and calm: When you can't hold in the secrets of your life, but to tell them in plain language would kill you: When you can't trust your trust and you can't stop loving and wanting no matter how much you wish to make yourself dead. If you can find a path through it all, no matter how fucked up it is, you are lucky.

Not lucky like: Let's pop the corks and celebrate. Not lucky like: "What are you complaining about, you're lucky." I mean lucky like the luck that is steeped in sadness and has questionable outcomes: that sometimes feels like "Lucky? Why me?" and sometimes fills you with such relief you cry.

No. Not as sad as that.

Doris is about finding a life worth living and creating a world that will allow us to live: Creating a world full of meaning, that we can thrive in, that we can come together in, where we will be heard, where we will be able to believe in ourselves, where we won't think our thoughts and emotions are crazy. A world where we will know for real that we are not alone.

Printed here is the first ten years of Doris. I cut out a little, but not very much. If you've never read Doris before, you might want to start in the middle, because the beginning is kind of beginningish. If you've never read a zine before, what they are is small, self-published magazines, and they come in all kinds.

I'm still writing Doris. The end here is not the end at all.

The weird thing about putting these all together into one book is that each zine is really meant to be read on its own, with long intervals of time between issues. So maybe you might want to just read a little bit and then put it down for awhile, and then pretend a long time has passed, and then pick it up again.

I want to apologize to G.W. for writing the cynical story, because that's not really how I felt, and you were a good friend.

I want to thank everyone who has written to me, who has helped stave off my hunger, who has sustained me.

this is a
window
this is an
animal.

My friends in Vermont knew about art. They knew about how great temporary art is, and they're all still around, but this country/world is too damn big and I hardly get to see them.

One friend is in New York now, and he draws things in chalk. You know how electric companies and sewer fixers are always making strange cryptic letters and numbers and arrows on the street and sidewalk, and you never really know what they mean? He does that. Random numbers and letters and sometimes maybe a 'do not enter' on the side of a wall, or a lopsided coffee cup, and if you watch him while he does it, it looks like he's painting some amazing painting, his face gets that look, and the 7643 68 ⟶ becomes one of the greatest things you've seen in Brooklyn in a long time.

This other friend, she knew about polaroids, and when we lived in Vermont, we used to go down to her apartment and drink tequila and take polaroids. Pictures of Jody standing at the open fridge, wearing a bra and holding three eggs, or weird abstract pictures where you rub on the back when it's developing and everything gets all distorted.

There was one picture we took, outside at night, and Paula's goddess like dead dog appeared in the photograph, but only when you look at it from a certain angle. Paula makes alters, simple ones that don't attract too much attention, but make her house amazing.

And then there's Casey, she makes cake art. Crazy cakes with dolls sticking out of them, or cakes that look like big boobs, and it's the best kind of art, she says, because you get to eat it, and she's right.

And then there's my one friend who's living in Portland too right now, and I've gone out walking with him on one of those horrible days when everything is grey and not quite raining, but more than drizzling. They are sometimes his favorite kinds of days, and we'll go walking down in the old industrial traintrack areas, looking for window frames or digging in the stained glass dumpster.

I love this kind of art, this everyday, found stuff on the street art, this don't care if I see it again art, or if anyone else sees it or if it lasts more than a minute art. And it makes living in acrappy city somewhat bearable. And you can't make it if you always drive and never walk down alleys or talk to ratty haired kids who stare at you from their doorsteps.

the end. ♡

I'm a little afraid of people these days, of people being really intolerant and not knowing how to work with other folks without compromising their own politics. I ran away a few weeks ago. It's kind of weird because I don't live with my parents or anything. I hit the freeway with my backpack. All I packed was a pair of shorts, my blanket and two hats. Oh, and my tent, and my taxes which I never bothered to do. I got a ride in this VW bus, but it wasn't a hippie. It was this guy who'd been in Alaska and was heading back down to Texas. His best friend had just died and his dog was dieing too. He smoked camel straights and offered me one every time he had one, so I started smoking again. The bus broke down in Yreka. I think there is something weird about a town called Yreka right near a town called Eureka. We got it to this little garage where this guy helped us out, but wasn't too into it. At one point, I was sitting against the wall, trying to be very i invisible, reading Wide Saragosa Sea, and the garage guy yelled "fire". I heard him, but didn't really register what that meant. I get really into books when I read. Then the guy whose bus it was yelled at me to move and I saw that there were huge flames coming out of the engine, about three feet from me. I moved. The bus didn't blow up though, and after about 3 hours of working on the thing, it was fixed, and the garage guy only charged us 30 bucks. The guy whose bus it was and me got to be really good friends in the two days of traveling, and his dog started to get better and play with my dog and all that kind of stuff...eating and drinking water again. And the whole thing was just exactly what I needed. Some stranger getting me breakfest because I didn't have any $, and listening to my stories about my friends wanting to kill my other friends, and all that, and not thinking that I was totally crazy or something. I'm not sure how to tell you exactly. It was encouraging. Especially because the last time I hitched, this gross guy was trying to feel me up the whole time. There was a baby seat in the back seat too. It was bad. There was this other time when I was hitching in Vermont, and this guy picked me up. He was an enviornmentalist. That's what he did for a living. Tested levels of toxicity in landfills and tried to figure out how to manage them better. I worked for the Institute For Social Ecology, so I was telling him about that - about needing to change the whole base of society, create a new ethics, get rid of hierarchy all together, recreate community and see ourselves as part of nature rather than it being a tool to manage. stuff like that. He kind of flipped out, but in a good way. Like he didn't know other people thought like that. He knew life-style change wasn't enough, that new and better landfills wasn't enough, and that there wasno way to make corporations be environmental in this crazy capitalist society. Fuck. Even Ben and Jerrys dumps their waste into the river on occation. He told me his life story. He took me out to dinner and told me about growing up in El Salvador when it was a military dictatorship and how he got arrested for talking informal speech to a police officer and of having a gun put to his head to make him sign his release papers and then getting sent right back to his jail cell. People were disapeared a lot then, but for some reason, they let him go, and told him that if they ever saw him again, they'd kill him. So he left the country. He said he hadn't told anyone about it in 7 years. He cried and everything.

the end

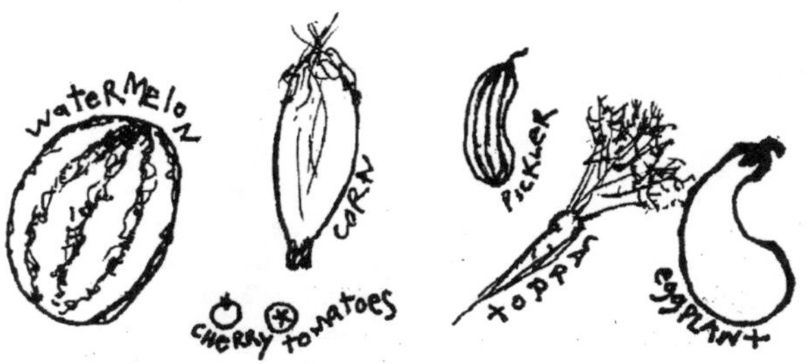

Did you know that asparagus can grow two to three inches in an hour? It's true! And it sucks when you have to harvest seven acres of them, hunting through the weeds just to try to find the stupid stalks and there are about a million deerflys in every square foot. It can make you hate asparagus really quick. Well, I've always hated it, but this other woman I worked with swore she'd never be able to buy asparagus again, knowing what hell whoever had to pick it went through. I worked on this crazy farm last summer, in Maine. The farm was supposed to be organic, but it wasn't totally. The summer was hell, really, and I loved it.

The man I worked for was a minipulative asshole who treated his family like shit, and on top of that, he was a rotten farmer. I mean, the farm was big - we grew thirty acres of vegetables or more, and only three people worked on it full time, and all three of us were interns. Well, I guess we worked way more than full time - 70 hours per week.

But even though I had to work for an asshole and got eaten alive by bugs and worked so much that I couldn't do anything else, I still loved parts of it. It's just that I love farming. I love the work, pushing down long rows of corn, hauling buckets of cucumbers, peppers, tomatoes, Growing callouses on my fingers, my muscles getting stronger with each step. And one of the best things about working so hard so long is that you get to eat so much! And I could just walk right out the barn I lived in and think - What do I want for dinner tonight? - and then go pick it. And I love going to sleep with mud caked to my ankles and feet and not even noticing. It would stay there for days. And I love the acid sweet smell of tomatoes and how my hair sticks up in every direction, and how I could see so clear every crack in my fingers cuz the dirt was so soaked into my hands so that even when I scrubbed them it wouldn't come out and I love the smell of carrots as I pull them out of dirt and how my feet were the permanent color of dust.

And I love to help things grow.

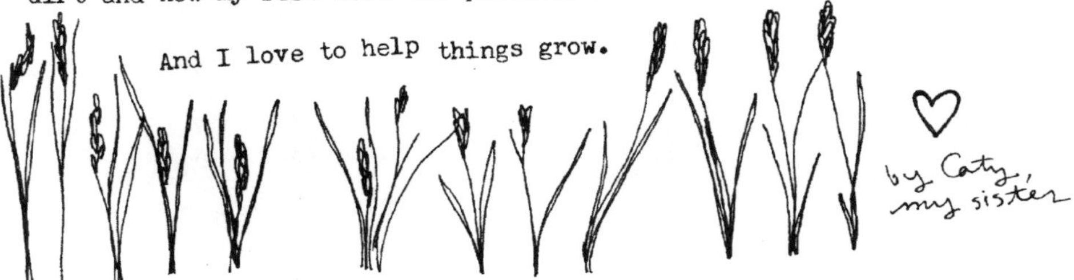

by Caty, my sister

first page

My sister is amazing. She helps me figure things out. Like why I'm writing this thing. I mean, I don't have it all figured out or anything, and some of it is just because it's fun. but part of it is something else. It's that I'm really interested in people's stories, you know, what their families were like and weird stages that they went through, and fucked up things that they did and thought, and crazy fun things that they did. how they got where they are. that kind of stuff. and I like to tell those things too, but it doesn't happen in my life enough. Like maybe people don't talk about it because they don't think the other person will be interested or because they don't know how to talk about it or just how to bring it up, and I don't ask because I'm afraid they won't want to tell me, or it will make them too vulnerable or too invested in me and also because I don't know how to bring it up. Like, I don't really think anyone will be interested in this doris thing, and I don't want it to be some stupid weird ego thing because it's not. and then there's this whole thing I have about strangers. I wrote about it a little bit later on in this doris, but not enough. it's not quite developed, my thoughts on it, but it's something like I think there's something really subversive about giving secrets to strangers. like look at these things that are important to me and we're not really supposed to talk about, and there's too few people who really know us, and we're supposed to be so shut off from eachother. And here I am, handing you this thing full of my life, and I want it to break down those barriers, and I want it to make it so people talk about their lives and secrets aren't secret anymore, and we're not all shut off and selfconscious and scared and cool and tough and alienated and quiet. I want the range of what we talk about to be so much huger than what it is now. and I know this doris isn't gonna do all that, but that's what I want. part of what I want anyway.

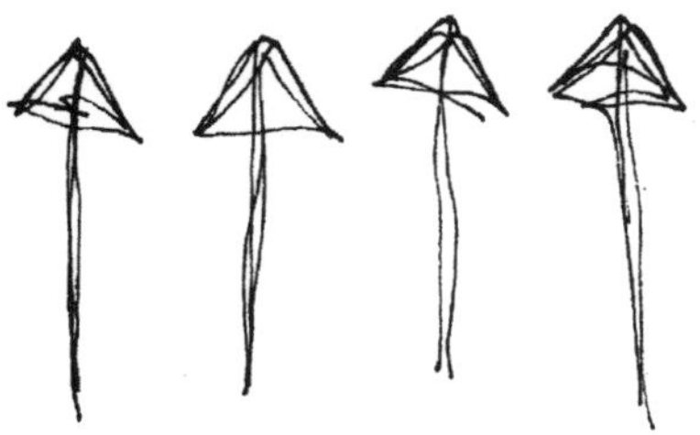

this is the more important part.

next story

I started handing 'this is a window this is an animal' out to strangers on the bus. I'd get all nervous before I'd do it, like there was something very furitive about it, like I was giving them something very secret and important, like I was breaking some big taboo, giving strangers something I helped make. I don't really know exactly why it felt like that. It seemd like a very goofy way to feel, but it really made me want the thing to be full of secrets, maybe it's because I like telling things and I haven't

really figured out how to do it. I have too much invested in speaking aloud - expectations and whatnot. like I expect the person I'm talking to to listen and think about it and remember. you know, high expectations.

There is something about public transportation I really like. I get kind of attached to people on buses and I really want to know about them. like one time there was this guy sitting in front of me one night, and he looked so damn sad and he had short fuzzy hair, and boy, i really wanted to reach up and rub his head in a comforting kind of way, and rub my thumb across his eyebrow, but I couldn't, you know. and that made me really fucking sad. and there's this weird thing that happens when I'm on the subway and it comes up into the outside after being underground for a long time, there are about 2 seconds right then, when I see the neighborhood I'm in and the daylight. There's these 2 seconds where I really want to cry. and I'm not a depressed person. i don't know what it is either. sad about the fucking desolation of cities, or happy cause there's some really beautiful art on the side of the bridge or some great old house with geraniums and falling down porches. it's hard to say. and I think if I rode the subway more to try and figure it out, the feeling would probably go away forever. ♥ end

---

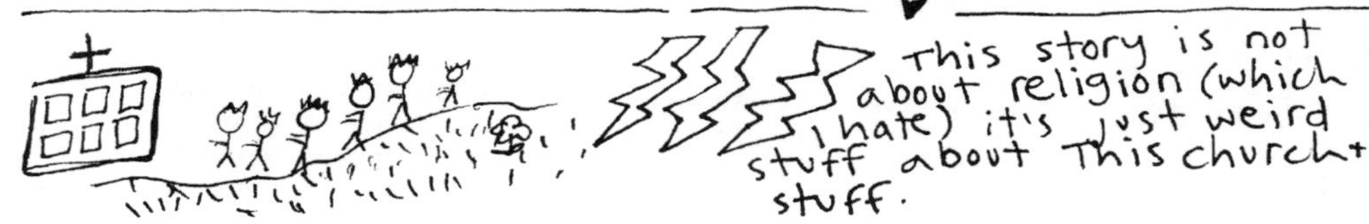

This story is not about religion (which I hate) it's just weird stuff about This church + stuff.

I never really had to go to church. I have all these friends who had to go to church school and church every sunday or whatever, and it sounds very very scary. But I've been thinking a bunch lately about when I moved in with my mom when I was in seventh grade and this church I went to sometimes with her. It was really cool for a church and I had my first political debate with my dad because of it. See, we had this refugee from ElSalvador, our minister did all this refugee work and got arrested and all that stuff. and this guy who we were harboring had been in the army or something and they made him kill people and he didn't want to, so he fled, and he couldn't go back because they'd kill him and his family. Well, it was in the newspaper or something and my dad thought it was totally Bad. and that this guy had killed people and so he deserved to go back to his country and die for it. and I tried to explain that it was really complicated and that he hadn't had much of a choice, and that it was a military dictatorship and stuff, and my dad said that if the government asked him to kill someone he certainly wouldn't do it. Well, I wasn't a very good arguer yet (I'm still not) I also had one of my first really embarassing puberty related experiences at that church. It must have been the summer before 7th grade. We were putting on this 'Peace Child' play/musical thing. It was one of those - if people in Russia and the US could just make friends with eachother there would be an end to the arms race and we wouldn't have to die in a nuclear war. (yep. totally ignoring powerhungry government and all the real reasons war and arms build up happen that have nothing to do with fear of another society fear is just what they try and instil in us to justify it all) Anyway. I felt pretty stupid practicing for this play, having to dance and sing and all that, but I did it anyway because both of my sisters were. Then we got to dress rehersal and we had to wear turtlenecks. oh christ. and I had these tiny little boobs that were totally unhidable. i even cried about it. it was very tramatic. Well, this last and most exciting thing about this church experience was this weird youth group that I went to a couple times in early 9th grade because I had a crush on the leader of it. I mean, I hardly ever went, but boy was he cute. This one time we had a church lock-in, with both boys and girls. It was very weird. We watched Watership Down and The Meaning of Life. I was in my sleeping bag trying to watch the movie but really watching this cute senior boy Scott who was in his sleeping bag next to me. and we got talking and yep...kissing. it was my very first kiss and I went home the next morning and thought I would never brush my teeth again, just to keep the flavor of his mouth in mine. ♡the end

title: When I thought my cunt was the only part of me that was worth anything, and only because boys could stick stuff in it.

It's crazy to me how at I6, freak girl, ratty hair smelling like skipped
school city lakes and sex, I totally bought in to this fucked up notion of
what makes girls worthy. crazy sexist crap. selfworth depending on boys
wanting to fuck me stuff. I was reading this old diary and it was worse than
I remember. feeling good or shitty depending on whether they liked me.
spending all day kicked back, drinking tons of coffee, waiting for some
boy to show up who probably wouldn't. My best friend bugging the shit out of
me because she was so emotional and talked about things like highschool and
parents around these boys who were 23 24. oh, very uncool when we wanted
them to Like us. There was this one guy and I really can't quite believe it. He was 27 or something and a record store manager and boy did i have a crush on him, andhe knew it but said he didn't want to do anything til i wasI6 because I was jailbait, yep. no joke. I thought that was kind of fucked up but these other things he would say - crazyhead brainwashed girl, I would feel flattered. Like there was this time i walked into the store and he was

eating a peice of cake and he said "wanna lick my cream" and i said sure and took a bite of his cake. yech. and the (un) funny thing is, I thought he cared about me. weird assumption. and after i turned I6 and we fucked I thought we had a relationship.

But the crazy this is, I can't fucking imagine being in those older boys shoes. seeing this I5 year old babygirl crazy in need and thinking really just fucking her would be a fine thing to do. did they not have Brains, those boys? didn't they Think? i used to go back to the record store to see the man I used to crush on because i didn't have a crush on him anymore and I thought that gave me power. but if I ever go back to that city again, I'm not going to drop by. after reading over those old diarys, now I just hate him. Yep Ryan, I'm talking about you.

boy oh boy did all that shit make me hate myself.

and

this is about my most excelent friend PETER ♡ hi. wherever you are i miss you ♡ ♡

I have this amazing friend Peter who I've completely lost touch with and it bums me out. I lived with him in this house in Plainfield. the house was falling in to the river, the whole thing was slanted. the floors were painted puce green and mauve. and Peter was a genius. I'm not even sure where to begin or how to make you understand. he was an inventor. He was having problems getting up out of bed so he made this huge wire extention thing from his alarm clock so that it would ring in his room but he'd have to go all the wayto the kitchen (where the coffee was) to turn it off. He was really in to Buckminster Fuller and Rilke. Sometimes we'd stay up late reading eachother the most pathetic parts of old diarys. He had the worst taste in house hold objects. One day he brought home an owl lamp and one of those clocks that have plastic or tin or something painted gold and glitsy all around it - with pressed butterflys in it. He was depressed a lot and one time he put a note in a bottle that said "Help me. I'm stuck in Plainfield".

HELP

he corked the bottle and threw it off our porch into the river. He built a paddleboat. The best thing about it was he didn't know a thing about building or anything about boats. He decided to build it in the winter and he got lots of books out from the library. He would draw lots of complicated plans and consult me about them. He'd say "do you think if I made this joint bend at a 38 degree angle and this one at a 55 degree angle and then got them welded together and put them here, that would work better than what I had planned before?" and I'd never really know what he was talking about and I never really knew what the previous plan had been, but I tried to be encouraging. finally after many months of planning, hand sawing and many trips to the hardware store, it was built. We launched it and Peter sat in the back, paddling as hard as he could but the boat still floated down stream, slowly, but still, down stream, heading straight for the waterfall. He paddled and paddled and I screamed and yelled, but the paddling part of the boat was, well, a little bit inefficient. Eventually he took the paddles off and just poled up river to Maple Valley (the store we worked at).

It was a really nice boat.

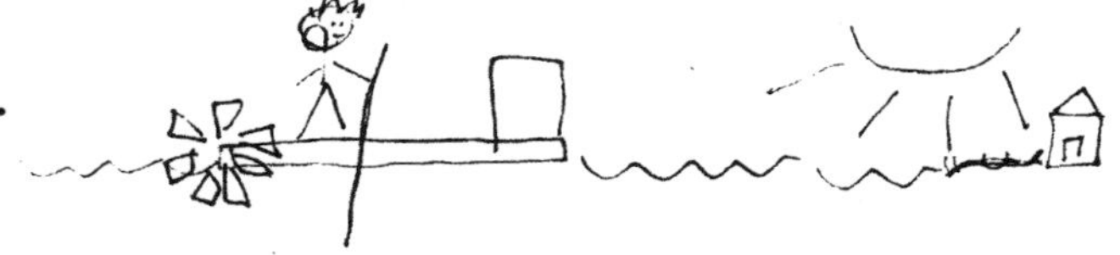

He had this really great friend Michael and they started having tea parties. They would wear wigs and old housewife dresses and drink tea or mixed drinks and play cards. They mostly played crazy 8's, i think, but maybe they were really playing some kind of poker, I don't really remember. and Peter always lost because they played with girly cards and Michael was gay and Peter wasn't and no matter how hard he tried, he got embarrassed and distracted by the cards.

One time, I went away for a week in the winter and Peter took care of my dog, who I love more than anything in the world and never leave her side and never trust anyone with. But I trust Peter. While I was gone, him and Michael invented a game, where they got dressed up in thick clothes with lots of padding and went to an icy hill. They held on to Anna's leash and would throw a stick down the hill and she'd lunge after it, with them holding on, and they'd get pulled straight off their feet and go flying down the hill after her. When he told me about it, he was worried I might be mad, but not at all. I wanted to play it too.

Peter was obsessive and interested in spontanious combustion. I miss him a lot.

♡the end

i lived in a house full of homosapiens

Hey, you wanna know where I am right now? I'm in a park playing fetch with Anna (my dog).

I put my typewriter in my bike basket and have been riding around all day, going over bumps and practically crashing trying not to dump my Smith-Corona and trying not to fall on Anna. There's something really great about typing in the sun. it's still weird being in a new city, and I've been thinking about portland alot today. I had these neighbors across the street who lived in a pink house and had a pet pig. The pig would make crazy loud noises when they tried to get it to go down the stairs and even crazier louder noises when they lifted it into the car. The pig was huge and named Charlotte. There was this girl who lived in the house and when her mom wasn't home, she'd play music really loud and practice dance moves on the porch and the boys would come over and hang out.

oink squeel oink squeel oink

the next door neighbors were kind of a mystery. Like, maybe they were a family but it was hard to tell. There were 2 women who looked a lot alike and this old man who smoked a pipe and Icould hear him hacking late at night. He'd sit out in the back yard with the dogs and the women would sit out in front. It seemed like none of them ever left the house. Then there was this son who was 40 or something. He was pretty quiet. My roommate Sarah was cool because she was alot more friendly than me and she'd talk to the neighbors a lot. This one time she was hanging out with the son. He started talking about the girl across the street and was saying that she was a slut and stuff. Sarah got all in her defence, saying you can't say that about her or judge her like that! Plus, she was really nice to me". and the son said "she's not so nice to you." "What are you talking about?" said Sarah. And the son said "She called you and your friends a bunch of homo... homosapiens!" Sarah knew what he meant, but said "So what. You're a homosapien too". "What!" the son said "What are you talking about? You can't say that about me!" *the end*

DRAWING

In case you hadn't noticed, I can't draw. In fact, this is the first time anyone's really seen anything I've drawn. Actually, it's practically the first time I've drawn anything. see, my older sister, when we were kids, she could draw, so I didn't because it would just look bad compared to her. For a long time, all through highschool, the only thing I would draw was this big tree with big roots. I drew it a lot. Then in Vermont, I started making collages with my friend Miss Casey, and then in Portland, I got some oil pastels and started colorying. I make really fast colorings in my journal and sometimes show them to people and laugh. One time I colored a picture of my bed, and a week later I couldn't figure out what it was supposed to be a picture of. But my excellent friend Kyle, he loves my colorings and won't let me get away with just laughing them off and saying I suck. He even said the coloring I made of my red velvet couch was good, and all it was was two rectangles on top of eachother. Kyle said "let's make a comic" so we started, and all I drew was a stick figure and her pet turtle, but somehow he made me feel like it didn't really matter if you could tell what my drawings were of, as long as...I don't know. But it got me drawing in this and I like it. My sister Caty is a great help too. She has influenced my style, like the people on bikes with their hair flying backwards, that's justhow she draws people on bikes. Every time I draw something, I ask her if she can tell what it is and usually she can. It is very encouraging. She loves color more than most things, if you ask her what her favorite color is, she'll list off about twenty million colors before she even knows what she's doing.

You know what I saw yesterday when I was riding around on my bike with my Smith Corona typewriter and Anna? I saw my maybe gonna be friend Chris, who I don't really know. I stayed with him in Eureka for a few days when I was trying to hitch back up to Portland but it was raining. He let me drive his van all around and took us to this great amazing flea market. Well, I was just on this back street and there he goes, riding by on someones bike. He was sitting on the seat, holding his crutches in one hand. and his friend was standing up pedaling. It was very great. *the end*

I just remembered that I wanted to put Stuff I Think in here, not just stories. In a way, I'm afraid I haven't been thinking enough this past year, since I left Minneapolis and my group of friends who had the same basis of politics I have. Or maybe I've been thinking more because I don't have their critique to fall back on. I don't know, but I do know that my life is much more difficult without an affinity group, and I want one.

I want friends who are committed to talking out a common politic; who want to meet and plan and do action and who are as committed to process as they are to action - you know, making sure gender dynamics are in everyone's minds and that all the fucked up shit that goes on is confronted and changed - and that people know it can and will be changed because people are up for it and aren't too full of their own ego and don't need to be purged. These are the people I want to be with, but I can't find them, partially because I am scared shitless to express myself, so I never really find out what other people think that much and so I never really know if we have a common enough base to work on this kind of project together.

Oh boy, but more and more it seems that people I do talk to think really differently than me, when it comes down to the nitty-gritty, and I think that stuff is important. You know, like we both want revolution, or freedom or something, but when we talk about how it will come about, or what kind of stuff is valid and what stuff is crap, well...it get frustrating. and forever I've been noticing how people don't really seem to want to know how you think, especially men. It happens with women too, but a lot more often with men.

they'll just talk and talk at me telling me everything they think, and saying it all like it's fact and they're experts. I don't get it. I don't want to be an expert on everything. I want to learn dialectically (I mean, like I say "I was thinking blah blah blah" and you say "hmm. that's interesting, because I was thinking of it like this..." and then we find whole new great ways of thinking. well, anyway, my sister and me have been thinking about identity lately, and the more I think about it, the more confused I get, but I'll write about it later.

— the end —

my family

I used to think it was normal that my parents wear robes - bathrobes - all the time. I mean, from the minute they wake up to the minute they have to leave the house, than as soon as they get back home, the robes go on again. But the more I thought about it, the more it got weird. I mean, if I went over to any of my friends houses, and their parents were sitting there on the couch in their bathrobes, I would think maybe they had just gotten out of the shower. but if every time I went overe there, their parents were in their terrycloth bathrobes, it would start to seem a little weird. But what I'm trying to say is this: my mom and stepdad are the most incredibly great people in the universe. I mean, they're totally fucked up, but that's not what I want to talk about. I'm not sure when to begin. My god. okay, my stepdad is a total alcoholic and he tells the funniest jokes every time he's drunk, which when I was growing up, seemed to be about every other night. The thing was, he always told the same three jokes, but they were so funny every time. He told the one about the guy with the wooden eye, and the one about this kid who was born just a head, and he told the Henway joke all the time. I can't even tell you how many times I fell for the henway joke. Like, he'd be outside, suntanning, and I'd be going inside and he'd say "as long as you're going in, will you grab me a henway?" and I'd say "What's a henway?" and he'd say "oh, about 3 or 4 pounds." I fell for it so many times. And when we all wouldn't fall for it anymore, he started telling it to strangers, check out ladies at the supermarket, long lost friends he'd find walking down the beach. He also used to get my mom to look down her shirt and spell attic all the time. I swear, she just never got it. and he wouldn't tell her what was so funny, he'd say 'look down your shirt and spell attic' and she'd let out a big sigh, like 'Oh jeez, not this again!' and she'd do it, and he'd laugh andlaugh, and she'd look at him like 'What's so funny?' They are in love. He is not a sleezoid. He is very funny. He makes specialty item toast. He wakes up at 6 in the morning and butters bread and puts it in the oven at a really low temperature, and say about 9 o'clock, it's hard as a rock and ready to eat.

And speaking of rocks, when he's out on the rocks of Lake Superior, and laying out Sun Tanning, he says, just out of the blue "Nope, I don't need a pillow, just give me a rock. All I need is a nice Rock, no pillow for me." Sometimes during dinner he pretends he can eat through his ear. I'm serious. He paid his way through college by playing cards, and now he won't even touch a deck of cards. I mean, he won't even hand a deck to you if they're near him and far from you. He's an elementary school teacher, and is the best teacher ever. I know because he was my teacher for 3 years. That's how my mom met him. For awhile he was teaching 3rd and 4th grade, and he is totally obsessed with this one cat we have. And one year he convinced most of his class that the Cat Could Talk! He'd just bring it up. "Oh, the cat told me the other day..." or, "I was reading about so and so and so, andthe cat said..." and the kids would say "Do you really have a talking cat?" and he'd say yes. So, one time, a parent came in to talk to him. She was really mad. She said he was a bad influence, teaching kids it was ok to lie and deceive. My step dad said "what are you talking about?" the mom said, "my kid keeps telling me you have a talking cat!" My stepdad just looked the mom in her eyes and said, "my cat does talk".

the end

UG UGH UGH UGH

My Biggest Secrets:

Right now, sitting in this little grove of redwood trees, I'm not sure my secrets are so secret or scary, but last night, when I wrote the title, the title was as far as I could get. I'm all wired on coffee now, and I'm not at all sure I know how to explain, I'm not even sure that I know what they are. There are the secrets about my body, how I am scared and distrustful of it, how I feel diseased and sometimes everything inside of me becomes so removed, and I think if I tell people about my past, they wont want to be with me. I have about five million secrets about my mom, but they're not really the stories that are the secrets. I could tell you them all, about the times I sat by her bed and she kept her face buried in the pillow the whole day, not letting me see her swolen face from crying, and I couldn't understand half the slurred words she said, but she handed me the pills to take home with me so she wouldn't take them all. and I could tell you about how I had her locked up and how she passed out in the driveway and knocked out two teeth and the whole side of her face was black and blue, so even when she felt emotionally better, you couldn't ignore what was happening to her. All this is not a secret, but the emotion behind it is very secret, even to me it is secret. It scares me. It is the first locked up thing I've had since I learned to unlock

(I feel stupid and dramatic and boring telling you these things.)

Well, another secret has to do with being scared to sleep with girls. duh duh duh. I mean, the idea is great, but I get worried about what girls think of me, and worried that they won't like me and they'll judge me a lot ... I guess because that's how it was in my sick group of friends growing up. But I think I simplify it and that it's way more complicated than that - like, so much of the basis for friendships I have had has been sexual, and I don't really want it to be like that. I always seem to end up kissing boys, because it's comfortable and stuff, and lately it's been pretty much fine. but still, I deal in this sexual realm because I feel secure there, but also I think it stops different kinds of friendships from emerging, like slow, sneak up on you kind of friendship. Or friendships founded on really common political ground. So I get worried about sleeping with girls, even though I know it's a stupid way to process all this crap and a fucked up way to deal with it, but sometimes it seems like girls are my biggest break from having to be a sexual being, and boy do I need that fucking break.

Another secret is I don't like menstruating. I don't hate it or anything, and it doesn't make me feel bad about myself or any of that creepy stuff like it used to, but it annoys me. Most of my women friends are really into their periods and I think that is so cool, but I never did have the guts to say I don't like it.

The most rediculous secret of all, and sometimes the most overwhelming one to me, is that I am a girl with strong needs. I like to think I'm not. That I don't need shit, which is lucky because there's hardly ever anyone around who could give a fuck about what's up with me. But even if they are around, well, I don't want to burden them and blah blah blah, they'll probably blow me off anyway and then I'll regret telling them, blah blah blah. So I am a girl with strong needs that never get met because I refuse to even admit that they're there. dorky stupid patheticness.

I love sucking on tootsie roblpops getting dragged down the sidewalk of city streets on a skateboard with my dog and climbing apple trees in alleys picking apples and trying to not eat the worms, missing riots because of picking blackberries and music. dancing crazy with my sister in the sweaty attic and listening to the same songs. putting up posters of poetry and swimming in any water, ocean or pond. but I do love the ocean and I've only been there a few times. It is still overwhelming to me. I still see it and go Yikes, There it is! and I love the taste of salt on shells. sometimes I keep the saltiest tasting shells to lick later when I am landbound again. I love this girl Neva who had the biggest eyes in the world and would come over to my house and ask for pieces of rounded colored glass and ask where were the grits when my sister and I ate scrambled eggs. The girl had laughing eyes more than anyone I've ever seen. I am afraid I wouldn't recognize her now. I make wishes on eyelashes and clocks and sometimes stars. I skip rocks when I am near a lake. I love the way the sun feels on me and I love diving in snowbanks and eating snow with syrup. I want to be able to do back flips again and to ride my bike naked with only a cape the way Giles did in Plainfield, superhero child. and he came to my house one day when I was in the backyard, fixing the things on scardy crab's grave, and Giles came over and asked what I was doing Timmy's hermit crab died, I said, and I'm just arranging things on his grave. Giles looked at me very seriously and said, Scardy died but his spirit didn't die. We should make him an X. So we wove an X out of sticks and river grass, and it was more beautiful than any cross. I love expressions like Give me a break, and Take it or leave it, or You can say that again, or Bop down to wherever, Toast and Geez, Rotten and Hold on to your hats! There was one time my sister and me were driving through wisconsin and we were eating pizza somewhere, and the waitress spilled something and said "Call me Job I have so many mishaps" but we thought she said Joe, and we have a friend Joe who has many mishaps, like one time we were all standing around in the kitchen and Joe caught on fire and no one really knew quite what to do. Some people were fanning his shirt, and someone was trying to splash water on him from the sink and my sister was yelling "Stop Drop and Roll, StopDrop&Roll" and finally he turned around and stuck his shirt under the running water. So we thought the waitress said Joe, because neither of us knew much about Job, and we thought it was very very weird. I love avocadoes and the color orange. I love the sun and the way it feels on me, and iceskating on the street after freezing rain storms. I hate white guild and cultural appropriation and the stupid things rich people do to make themselves feel better - like they aren't so bad, like they're not killing people with every dollar they make because they wrote a letter to a congressman or went on an eco-tour and got to see poor people and learned from it to live more simply, bullshit crap. I hate people not being critical of their lives and of the world and I hate simplicity. None of this shit is simple. I love barefeet and the way my dog nuzzles up to me in the mornings and how she's almost a horse. I drempt about sunflowers last night. *the end*

I LOVE MY DOGS LIPS

There are two other secrets I forgot to tell you. One is that I shaved my mustache for years. From the time I was 14 to 21. It was very embarassing, but now I love it. I want to dye it pink but I think it would just dye my skin mostly. The other secret is that I got pregnant on purpose to see what it was like to have an abortion. I mean, it wasn't totally on purpose, but I was wondering about it a lot, because I didn't think it should have to be a big deal at all, and it was the first time I'd really felt that way. So I was pretty uncareful. I thought I was being careful kind of, but really, I just didn't care. And it wasn't that big of a deal, but it was bigger than I thought it would be, partially because I found out while I was traveling, and it fucked up all these plans, and I caught it late, so even though I drank a ton of herb tea, I didn't induce abortion, and I felt pretty rotten. and I don't know, there was this weird thing inside of me sometimes going Keep it keep it. Even though it was totally removed from what I wanted, and that was weird, but I don't think it was any biological impulse or something, it is just pretty damn hard to get rid of all those years of conditioning, and so I had a medical abortion. It was at this amazing great place, the Feminist Women's Health Center, in Vermont. and this rad woman did it, and this cool woman held my hand and told me what things would feel like and it hurt but was way less tramatic than tons of gyn visits I've had, stupid fucked doctors who don't tell you anything about what they're doing. And, well, that's it. It was weird afterword, seeing kids was a bigger deal, more sad or more of a relief, but it's not any more.

Sometimes I am amazed with how little I get by on. the woman I passed by, she was dressed all in pink, and I thought to myself, If she asks me for money I'll give her everything I have, because she was the only thing I'd seen beautiful all day, and she turned to me and handed me a wreath of yellow and red carnations. "A flower garden for you" she said. I too it in my hands. Thank you so much. And riding around for hours, sore and lost in Oakland, and this man with bad english talks to me about my dog and where he came from he had a dog like her and he had cows and I swear he said buffalo, and his dog herded them, kept them close by. I rode away thinking Buffalo! Sometimes it is only strangers who don't disappoint me, and I worry that even though I eat plenty, usually. I worry that I will wither away. and I'm surprised I haven't yet. I want to meet boys and not have to worry about w whether or not they're thinking about whether or not I'll fuck them. I want to have friends who I don't need to make conversation with. I want to walk around my house without my shirt on. I want my friends to come visit me instead of me always going out, me always hunting them down. I don't think these are big wishes.

the end

Last Page

This is the last page. I want to know what other people spend their time thinking about. I spend far too much time thinking about why other people do the things they do. I want to know what other people would do if they could do whatever they wanted and I want to know the things that keep you going and the projects you would be involved in if only there were the people to do them with. I want to know the games you play. Whether you like to dive in bushes or jump on park benches or climb trees or sit in rivers. I want to know if you have brothers and sisters and if the sun feels good on your back or if it worries you. I want to know what made you rebel and whether or not you've ever broken any bones. I want to see your scars and I want to show you mine, see here, on my head, from the car accident, and here on my finger from carving, and here on my face from being a clutsy child who wouldn't listen to my grandmother. I want to hear you play piano and trumpet and I want to laugh at the way our lips feel when we try to make that trumpet make noise. and I want to bake a cake with you. but only if you know things and only if I like you. *the end!*

THE DAY ONLY THE TABLES SHOWED UP FOR THE STREET SELLING STUFF YO DON'T NEED FAIR

Remember to dance

What was I thinking? I tried to write Doris #2 and I hadn't danced in a month. I swear, what was I thinking? I didn't even know what was wrong, why it wasn't going right. I had even given up for the night when I remembered this tape I checked out of the library and I slapped it in the tape deck for a listen. Me and my sister, my most greatest sister, we danced and slapped our bellys and sweat and stunk, and now I know, that's what was missing from doris. So I'm starting over. Maybe you want to know what the tape was, but I'm not telling. It's a secret. Doris is about secrets, if you got #I you know that already.

doris is about secrets in a way I can't explain. It's about giving strangers something real, something shitty and beautiful that I hand to them with shy smile. It's about how sometimes when I walk down the street, this particular street that's all tables with stuff to buy and people buying stuff and incense making my head hurt and people dieing and I can't get around and get through to where I'm going and I hollar at the top of my lungs, and a small girl in front of me turns around and says "I know just how you feel" and maybe she does, and maybe she doesn't, but maybe next time, she'll be the one yelling.

and I wanted

If we could fly, I could take you places. The treehouse 20 feet up with the spiral staircase and the tree through the middle that moved in the wind. I could show you where it was where I laid down in the road, lost and frozen in the snow and rain, and I could show you where the best blackberry bushes are and the gravestone that my sister likes to lay on. I saw this dance last night, this crazy beautiful and angry dance, with crashing and falling and a violin player in a shopping cart and businessmen with ladders for cars, and there was pulling and pushing and slaming into eachother just like real life and music so loud it was uncomfortable, just like it is. And I want everyone to be able to move like that, to know the extent to which we can push our bodies, and to be able to express ourselves like that, just at any time, just on the street, Can you imagine what it would be like? If our responses to every little thing were opened up completely? and screaming and whistling and dancing and hollering, small movements and big ones, if we closed our eyes when we didn't want to look at someone any more. If this is what we did instead of words and expressions and little gestures? Yesterday I saw a girl who looked like I did once. She had a motorcycle helmet and quick strong gestures, sharp tough movements, threw her cigerette down on the table, drank her coffee black, looked out the window when her boyfriend wasn't across from her, slapped her elbowpit when he fed her a bite of cake - good as junk - and I slipped her a doris when I left. She is the only one I never made eye contact with, never said anything and never looked back. and I know I'll never see her again, and she'll probably hate doris.

I'm sick of feeling like prey like boobs and a cunt and ears maybe ears after the fucking is done I'm tired of feeling like lips like tounge like choking and moans. of having to wonder who is talking to me because they want to fuck me who is smiling at me because they want to fuck me, who is becoming my friend because they want to fuck me. I am tired of women coming into my house and seeing vultures come out. and them having to deal with the prey they have become. and we deal with it we deal with it in different ways and I resent it all I am bitter about it all. every guy we fuck because we need to survive, every time we laugh at their jokes -

I am sick of having to second guess, i am sick of having to doubt intentions, of having to question everyone who is nice to me, of having to mistrust everyone who smiles at me are they thinking about my cunt. are they thinking about whether or not i'd suck them off. are they thinking about patriarchy and what we are put through every day what has been put into our heads, what has defined our worth, how our bodies have defined us as bodies. What we have to go through every day even if we don't leave the house and walk down the street jeered at, even if we wear blindfolds to keep away the advertisments, even if we wear earplugs to keep out the words. even if we become crazy because it is the only option left the only way maybe the only way out. the only thing left to give in to. I am tired of having to deal with being prey when I think I am just around maybe gonna be friends and all of a sudden something happens and I know all of a sudden I know that they see me like a mouse like a melon like something they want and maybe they don't even think it outloud to themselves, but they do, and I hate it i hate it and i hate what we do to survive. I hate what I do to try andget myself back, how I act crazy to ward them off, to make them not want me, how I make myself ugly, how I hide in my room, how I fuck them sometimes because then maybe when I blow them off again, they'll understand. they'll think it's breaking up when really I was just prey to begin with and I was just holding my ground in the only way I could right then.

THERE'S SO MUCH TOO MUCH TO TELL JUST HERE ♡

I love when I've only walked down a street once and then I walk down it again with my sister and I can say - last time there was a woman standing on that porch, here comes a park I found, oh geez, this weird window painting, check it out, it's lighted from behind tonight. - I love how I point out all these small changes nand how, in Plainfield, every small change was noticed. Like when the dog with the invisible leg wasn't tied up in the yard anymore, or when the green house on routh 2 put up lace curtains. Plainfield is full of amazingness. There's Willis who brings his screaming red guitar down to the stone church wall and plays in amazing no time no pause rhythm like only Willis can play. There's Louie who has radio antenna filling his apartment and who takes pictures of everything that has ever happened in that town. There's Paula, most wonderful beautiful Paula, with her lawn ornament eco-pig and her concrete angels she stole from the Baptist church. Great things happened in Plainfield. Megan took poloroids, Casey made art cakes, Peter jumped off the bridge and chased his bathtub boats down the river. There was Carter who saved every scrap of paper he found that had red on it. Kurtis projected movies out of his bedroom window onto the wall of the building next door. Tim and William played bluegrass on the porch and my boss/father figure would put on red lipstick with me when we were closing the store, mopping up the cafe, and I'd get that New Zealand cynic family man dancing to Sweet Transvestite. You could count on things in Plainfield. You could count on the people who had a big concrete horse and two matching horse heads to decorate the shit out of their lawn ornaments every holiday. There was the perpetual yard sale, rain or shine, and usually it was self service, just drop your coins in the tin can. Fresh bread got delivered Tuesdays and Friday, and you had to pick up your mail at the postoffice.

plainfield oh my plainfield

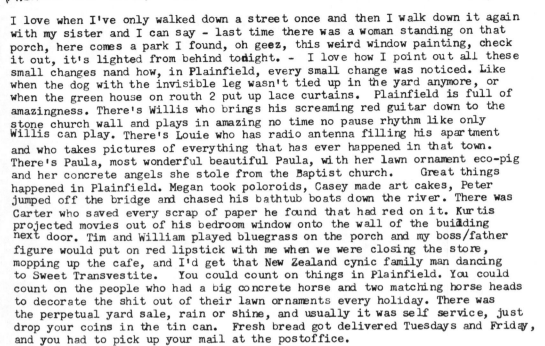

Plainfield is also where I've been the closest to death. There was the time I was sleeping in the yellow house and in the middle of the night we heard screaming, and thought - fucking drunk townie kids - and it turned out it was people dieing. crashed on their motorcycle, these friends of friends, and they died right there, on the side of the road. And then one winter night when I lived in the riverhouse, my most favorite woman in plainfield, the quiet crazy woman with scars covering her face, my most beautiful burnt faced woman, did a swan dive off the bridge and landed head first on the ice river. They pulled her off, Michael and Joe, and her skull bled on my stair step. A big candy colored stain that never went away. My sister and me almost died once. There was this huge rain storm, big lightning and thunder and we went out to the river, waded across and sat on the big rock getting pelted with raindrops, laughing like crazy until the thunder was deafening and we started to worry about electrocution. But by then the river had risen and we couldn't cross back over, and we almost died climbing up the edge of the shore with the ground falling away underneath us, the water trying to rip us off our feet. I caught her and she caught me andAnna would slip and knock us over. We came up behind the yellow house, where I thought there were stairs but there weren't any more. We came out when the storm was just passing and we were bruised and tired and scared and relieved, dirty and cut up and drenched. We walked down the street thinking everyone should scream - Thank God you're alive! - but they were standing stoned in Manuels doorway and we laughed that they could be oblivious to what we had just been through.

XXOXX OOOXO XXXOOOXO XXXXOOOXO XXOXXXOOOXO

BEAUTY SHMOOTY

Somehow, somewhere along the way, I got this standard of american beauty. I don't know what part of me it is, especially today and yesterday because I'm having ugly days. I don't know if it is maybe my eyes, which I hide behind big unhip tortiseshell glasses. I don't know, but I've had really mixed feelings about it. Usually I hat it. I don't want to fit this standard. I don't want people to look at me and think beauty. for a long time I did not think anyone saw beyond that. and still, I try to hide it, but at the same time that I hate it, I am terrified of not being desirable, and I want to be big and strong and beautiful. And so I hide it and flaunt it at the same time. Sometimes it makes my stomach hurt. Sometimes I am long limbed and gangly and I think I will knock everything over. Sometimes I am very very small and will fit inside any little crack, any doorway. ▫

THIS IS GONNA MAKE FRIENDS OF MINE MAD AT ME

I'm sitting on a no cushion couch under the freeway bridge, drinking my refil and thinking about theory. I was reading Foucault, me & my sis are reading it together, and I love it

I don't understand half of it & it frustrates the hell out of me, but it also gives me life. I love being challenged & learning to look at things in a whole new way; checking out perspectives & histories & explanations of how our thoughts and assumptions & actions are formed by the way things have been represented and the way things have been discussed publically. And what I love best is the writers who embrace complexity & try to make sence of it. It makes me feel like there's so many more possibilities for fundamental social change when I'm looking at how complex everything is, and trying to fit it all together. Because simplifying seems like a huge boring trap to me & I feel so surrounded by it; by people trying to make struggle understandable by making it simple, like people suck and should all die, like men suck and they should all die, like rich people suck and they should all die. It is not that easy.

I've been frustrated by veganism lately. So often it turns into this easy set of rules - this way to become more revolutionary than everyone else, without having to really be challanged, without having to confront andbreak down power dynamics. ugh. And the logic gets so faulty when you look at other industries that destroy & torture humans & animals in ways that may not be clear cut, or maybe are. like fruit pickers getting sprayed all the time with pesticides, and corporate farms diverting water sources from native lands. Communities being completely destroyed by being forced into producing export crops. And where do you draw the line? How do you decide that plastic vegan boots are more humane than leather when plastic factories are entirely toxic, and the people (poor people) who have to live near the factories are getting all kinds of diseases. And cotton - the crop with the most deadly pesticides in the world. If you look at it this way, you end up confronting so much more - looking at imperialism, the need for decentralization & community reliance. You look at genetic engeneering & how terrible biotechnology is. And maybe you get overwhelmed by it all, maybe it seems like too much to deal with, or maybe it makes you grab some friends to discuss it with, maybe it gets you angry enough & thinking enough that you plan strategy & action & go blow stuff up, make friends with your neighbors, call your pals on their shit, talk & read & write & make theater, take over the streets and learn from eachother. And you end up creating crazy, far reaching strategy, intense coalitions, that bring people together and make real, for real changes. Because when you think about it, lifestyle change is the minimum you can do and isn't necessarily revolutionary at all.

---

this is not exactly about my dog

I did the stupidest thing yesterday. It was really great. see, I've been worried that my dog hasn't been getting enough nutrients. I cook for her usually, and it's usually rice & beans with some stolen canned dog food mixed in. She's skinny, skinier than me, so I aquired some money to buy her a big old bag of high quality dog food. Me in my rust wool tanktop dress, in my red corduroy baseball cap, me in my - I'm not wearing my rockridge shoplifting disquise, nope, just my usual, everyday disguise. I hopped on down to the pet supply store. I was wired on coffee and laughing at how depressing the Ernie Pook's Comix was that day. I walked in the big glass doors into the room that smells like leftover toxic waste they pass off as flea repelent. I walked in and there was no one there, not a shopper, not a worker in sight. So what could I do? I stuffed as much as I could in my baggy tights, and picked up the 40 pound bag of dog food in my buff girl arms, my arms that can pick up my 80 pound dog and spin her around. I picked up the dog food and went to the counter. There was still no one there, and something happened, do you know what I mean? I swung the bag over my shoulder and went outside to see what it looked like down the block. and I was making my way down the block at a good pace, and I was just about to round the the corner, when this Golds Gym nerd style guy came running after me, and for the weirdest stupidest reason, I didn't drop it and run. I turned to him with a confused look on my face.

"Excuse me, did you pay for that?"
"No, my sister did."
"What?"
"My sister, she, didn't she come in a minute ago and pay for it?"
"You can't just go walking out of my store with a bag of dog food without paying for it"
"It wasn't paid for?" my voice all purity and innocence.

but the guy brought me inside to talk to the manager, and I explained the whole situation to them. "You see," I said, "I have this sister and she's a little bit crazy and sometimes she does these things to test me to see if I trust her. She has big trust issues, and sometimes I do trust her when I really shouldn't. I'm really sorry. She told me she had bought this dog food but it was too heavy for her to carry and she asked me to come get it. "

I paid for the dog food andwas heading out the door. "You better have a talk with your sister" he says.

this is not exactly a secret.

There are stories I like to tell that I hardly ever do because I think people will think I'm trying to prove how cool I am or something. So I just sort of mention them in passing, all casual, and then they say, "wait, back up, what was that? You lived in a treehouse?" "Yeah," UI say, "yeah, it was half a mile from the road and 20 feet up in the air between three trees. It was great. really cold though. I lived there in the winter." and if they push me a little, I'll tell them about it, how I'd haul out tanks of propane on a little red sled to fuel the stove and the heater, and how it hardly got above 40 degrees, but I'd sit at the table in my sleeping bag and write in the patch of sun that came in through the window. I'll tell about the spiral stairs going up to it and how my dog fell out of it once and didn't even get hurt. and how sometimes I would stay there for a few days without leaving, and no one to talk to except my dog and the coyotes, and the squirrels. How sometimes I'd run away from my house and sleep on couches at friend's houses and at the college student lounge, because that aloneness would get so overwhelming. But it was perfect, that house, the way the tree that went through the house by the head of my bed would sway back and forth in the wind, and in storms, the whole house would move like crazy and I'd get a little bit worried that the whole place would fall down. I could talk about it for hours, but I never do. I talk about it under my breath. I tell bits and peices and never the whole story.

The other story is about how I almost had my step brother killed. It was all set up, with someone who was going to do the act, and let him know just what it was for too, graphically, and all I had to do was get my little sister out of the state so she wouldn't have to deal with it. But I couldn't tell her. I couldn't tell anyone. and I'd come back to Minnesota, tried to get custody of her, tried to talk her in to running away or letting me kidnap her, but it didn't work out, she didn't want to leave like that. They wouldn't let her go, and she said, how about next year, when she turned 16, then she'd go. But by then, the next year, I'd changed my mind, and I was glad, in a way. He could have been 9 months dead and I'd have the biggest secret in the world to think about forever.

real secret.

When I was I3, I fell in love with my stepbrother. I thought maybe someday we'd even get married, and I knew we could, because we weren't really related, even if it would be kind of weird. We had really nice times, getting glass bottles of soda at this little store on this big island where there were red and grey foxes and waves of the coldest water crashing around the shore. We told eachother secrets like how he someday wanted to find his real mom who put him up for adoption. We talked about placęs we wanted to go and things we wanted to do and how crazy our lives had been. We'd slepp out on the shore of Lake Superior, me and him and my older sister and some friends, and we'd play this game - hop around in our sleeping bags and tackle eachother. and sometimes when he'dtackle me or I'd tackle him, we'd end up kissing closed mouth kisses. Those were my first kisses. We'd go camping with the family and trade backrubs in the musty plastic tent. His hands would sneak down and touch the sides of my hardly there breasts. and I thought maybe he did that to my older sister too, but I still loved him. I was in love. I'd listen to cheesy songs like For Your Eyes Only from that James Bond movie and I'd think of him. I listened to Ozzy Osborn and Black Sabboth and I'd get jealous of the girls he'd hang out with. It was so real, he was my first guy friend and it was so perfect. I was in love but I wouldn't tell anyone because I thought they would think it was too weird, but it wasn't. It was perfect. We'd watch falling stars and make wishes on them, and I'd wish that we would always be together forever and always, and he'd hold me tight for real. And then it started. Him sneaking into my room in the middle of the night and touching me while I was sleeping in the place I'd never touched myself. and he watched me take showers and him and his friends wrote porn about me, hid vibrators in my bed. He ruined it all. everything I had wanted. everything that I was. he fucked it all up. He ruined it all.

There are perfect places, like the place Ivy took me where everything happens perfect. Like bread and water appearing just when you're wishing it, and the amazing girls handing me this magic column set typewriter like it was nothing, like it wasn't exactly what I'd been looking for for weeks. Where there's ocean and crappy city shit and big bushes, wide expanses, and you see two radio towers with red lights flashing. There's my bush for in the weird naturyist place near all the underpasses and bridges, where you can wake up in the morning and pick blackberries growing above your head, and no one can see you even if they walk right by. Kyle's closet the night I left Portland when it was empty, not even a bed, and that was all I wanted, a tiny space with my typewriter at my feet and one change of clothes for when it was hot out. There's the side of the road when I'm angry and the tops of trees when I'm not. I want to be able to jump high on concrete, as high as I can on my bed. The smallest things make me fall in love with people for a minute. like sweeping the crumbs off the table and putting them

in your shirt pocket, singing at the top of your lungs, riding a bike that's 20 times too small. laughing crazy at the church of elvis and wanting to put stale donuts around the sidwalks at the cop station. running to this chair in this alley to watch the sun go down. lending me a pen, shy and quiet. having good things in your pockets. playing cards and getting for real excited about stupid things. eating a pop tart when I give you one. I like it when people have idea, when they have something to say other than 'I don't know, what do you want to do?'
A stranger told me she liked my bonnet. Someone I know told me I look like a psychopath. I like being a strong girl and crying in public when I want to. I don't cry easily. Not these days. We used to go to parties to bait commies, argue drunk about the Russian Revolution. We used to wear buttons, us girls, that said "Talk to us about politics". We had paint on our hands and sang the International, made jokes that no one understood but us.

I used to want to be the tortilla lady, walking around my blocks early in the morning with a basket of warm tortillas on my back. 'Tortillas for sale' I would yell, loud and crisp, 'tortillas'. Now I want to be the cake lady, delivering cakes to people I don't hate yet, people who live down hill from me so I can deliver them on my skateboard. Bunt cakes, carrot cakes, and cakes with cracks in the middle and plastic animals covering the tops. For awhile I wanted to have a junk-yard, I wanted to be the traveling squat repair lady, I wanted to be a punkrock singer, I wanted to live on a farm. Now I want my house to be full of bags of flour, sugar, bins of cocoa and peanut butter frosting. And when people would see me walking down the street they'd say 'There's that girl that's always baking cakes'. and I'd hum to myself and laugh.

Doris #3

My sister is back! My sister, there is nothing in this world better than her returning to me. Not avecados or wet dogs or loveletters. nope. My sister makes everything be just the way it should be. One month she was gone, and it's been a decade. She says "My life is totally different. I think i'm gonna end up living in cities and doing city gardening with kids. I'm gonna do real stuff to change things, and figure out how to live, not just get by, in cities." I say, "My life is really weird and different. I have some friends. I've been swimming and getting 5 million things done in a day." She sits on my lap in the kitchen. "Oh, what am I going to do with my life?" she moans. "I don't know" I say, "but do you want to organize disco parties at the Long Haul?" She gets up and kisses me and sits back down. I get to use my best expressions around her, and she has great ones too. She told me she laughed her pants off. I can't believe how much I laugh when I am with her. We laugh at the same things that no one else would get. Today we layed down in bed to take a nap and ended up talking. She was telling me about her homeopath and she said "So Jenkins said..." and I looked at her, astounded, "Jenkins?" and I swear, we could not stop laughing. We drank water laying down out of bendy straws she got me after the day I said "God, my life would be so much easier if I just had bendy straws." I made her laugh and practically drown on a mouthful of water. One time, we were at this place, dark and outside at this party, sitting in the corner, just me and her, laughing. My cruxh came up to us and couldn't believe it was just me and her. He thought there was a whole crowd, laughing. This is what it's like, having my sister back.

ch. 2

It's fall today, fall in that way where the air is crisp and feels clean no matter what. I could wear a tanktop or a thick jacket and I'm not sure which would be right. I'm out in my garage and there's this beautiful broken bike with me, this amazing white bike that's really two bikes welded together - a bike build for 2. I am in love with it already, and it's only been here one day with its rusty chains. I can hardly stand to look at it. Do you know what I mean? When something is so beautiful it breaks your heart just to know it exists? Like orange berries on bushes and white pumpkins for sale at payless. It's fall, and I want a pair of those gloves with the fingers cut out. I used to think those gloves were for poseurs who didn't know about real cold, but I want them now, with my palms getting sweaty and my fingertips pounding on these keys. This fall stuff makes me miss Minneapolis like crazy. I miss the cold and the way people aren't as friendly out there. I don't know, I feel like I've had this conversation about Minneapolis and east coast people a bunch in the past couple weeks, and I never really knew what it was I thought until I was walking up to this little lake with

Jesse late one night and I started talking and it came out right. I thing that's so weird when that happens. See, I don't really get it here. Where I'm from, maybe people are less likely to trust you, to open themselves up enough to even talk. They kinda test you and weird stuff like that, but once you're friends, there's something real there. I'm not so sure about here. People are too damn friendly. They make friends easily, so if something goes a little bit wrong in a friendship, oh well, they have a million other friends anyway. And you just never see that person any more, except maybe in passing on the sidewalk. I know, you're saying 'yeah, right, it's not like that at all', you're thinking, 'god, can this mopey girl overgeneralize a little bit more?' I know, enough already.

Do you ever wonder about going crazy? Not WORRY about it, just sort of wonder? I do I think it's funny. Actually, I don't buy into the definition of insanity, but you know what I mean? Like I did LAUNDRY a couple days ago, and I was standing on my bed sorting it out and holding up these long underwear I've had for about ten years, and it really looked like the giant hole in the knee had disapeared. This hole is huge and I really couldn't find it. And I thought to myself, "boy, that is so weird when that happens. You put your stuff in the washer and it comes out repaired!" I really thought the hole was gone and that this kind of thing was a regular type event in my life. Like maybe if I washed my clothes more than 3 times a year, none of them would have holes any more. yikes. the thought of it!

I'm always making up plans. Like when I was riding in the back of the van with Kyle and we were talking about how in a year we were gonna get this band Anna going, that will be all songs about my dog, and we'll buy a van somehow and tour, playing all shitty highschool dances. And then I was telling him that when I'm sixty, I'm still gonna have the same van and just live out of it and I'll sit around in my van or in some fold up chair right outside it, me with my grey or white hair. I'll knit socks and sell them at church sales for a living and it will crack me up, to be an old lady, knitting! It's hard to explain. Like, just going down to the bagel shop to get my millionth cup of scammed coffee, I'll put on my roller skates and maybe my big brown wig and red courduroy hat, just to make it more fun. I don't even really think about it, that's just what I do.

I CAN'T LIVE WITHOUT A

I've been pretty bummed since yesterday because I had this great plan for the day. I knew I could not survive another day without a file cabinet. In fact, I'd written I CAN'T SURVIVE ANOTHER DAY WITHOUT A FUCKING FILE CABINET in big letters and taped it to my wall with duct tape, just to remind myself. Then I set out on my bike with my dog. The plan was, I'd ride around and look for one on the street and then I'd go to this big house full of students to meet this woman who I'd known for 2 years but never met, who was here for the weekend visiting her brother. Then I'd drink coffee and ride down to Urban Ore and buy a file cabinet, find a shopping cart, stick the cabinet and my bike in the shopping cart, tie my dog to it, and push it all home, four miles, uphill. It was such a great, perfect, beautiful plan, full of excitement and frustration and exhaustion and cursing myself for not being more practical, but finally arriving home, stinking and triumphant and hungry. I hadn't thought it out like that, but that's what it would have been like. And it started out right. I rode up Claremont in all the rich neighborhoods, laughing because that was probably the last place I'd find anything discarded on the side-walk. I passed by the hotel and thought about going in for a quick swim, but was too anxious to really get going on my plan. I stopped by thebig house and found the woman right away, lounging under the basketball hoop. She gave me strong coffee and was even cooler than I had imagined her; talking about compost and millions of other things. there were people sitting with us and 3 or 4 conversations and interruptions everywhere, I couldn't really get words in, and really I just wanted to be talking to this one woman about specific things. I'm not so great in that kind of situation. I get kinda nervous and shy and when I talk, I talk too loud. Someone asked me what I was doing that day, and I started explaining, all wild eyed and excited, but I hardly got in to it when I could see all of a sudden what it was. Impractical. Crazy. Waste of time. Impossible. What if there was no shoping cart? What if my bike and file cabinet didn't fit in the shopping cart? What if I couldn't push it all that way? What if my dog keeled over from heat exhaustion andI had to ballance her precious body on top of everything? Oh, hmmm. The million things that could go wrong. Well... I said, "on second thought, maybe one of my housemated would lend me their car." So I used the phone, rode back home, crawled into the toyota through the window, Daisy Duke style, turned on the radio and headed west, with my dog beside me. And it was nice driving a car again for the first time in months. I pretended like I was going to Albuquerque and sang loudly to songs on the radio I didn't know. But it wasn't the same. I had given in. Shit. I had given in.

ch. 3 ♡ ⟶ ⟵ ♡

I have this crush, this crazy crazy crush. It's gotta be the biggest crush of the entire century. It keeps me up at night and makes me want to sleep really late because maybe I'll dream about him. It's a boy. A boy crush. Sometimes I think about him so much I think I should just slam my head into a wall. But I love this crush, the way I get excited about life in different ways than usual, see things in new ways, see new potentials, like the back of my garage, freight elevators, rooftops. They take on new dimentions. I was walking to downtown Oakland the other day and saw this field and just wanted him with me so I could chase him through the field and tackle him and we could get leaves in our hair and I'd kiss the freckle on his ear. I think of what it would be like to go to new cities together. We'd get there, grumpy from hitchiking and sunburnt. We'd split up, me on my rollerskates, him on his broken shoes, and later, full of coffee and new things in our pockets, we'd bump into eachother, laughing, and we'd run around town, showing eachother what we'd seen. I want to make fry bread at three am in my garage on my sisters camp stove. I want to wake up at dawn and see him stumbling groggy up my driveway. It's the kind of crush that scares me, that makes me act like a coot tough girl to ward it off. Because I am a romantic and I hate the ideal of romantic love. It makes things very confusing, this conflict. I hate the way couples become couples and that's the only thing in their lives and they expect one person to fulfill them, no friends, no community, ugh. I never want to fall into that kind of coupledom again, and actually, I know I couldn't. I hate what people have expected of me; to give them meaning in their lives, to figure everything out for them and take care of them. Yeck. stupid. but enough of that. See, this crush, it is crazy. Ir ide my bike around singing loud songs for him and looking for places to take him when he gets back, because he's not even in town and I don't know when he'll be back. I stuff the ends of my cigerettes into theholes in my floor, counting down the unknown number of days. And you know what? You know what's great? This is the first time in forever that I don't have control over the whole situation. Usually I like people who are safe, who need me or something dumb like that. But I quit that. done with that forever. and this crush, I doN't know, it's out of my hands. It inspires me and makes me do more art. I think about how I was always walking too close to him so my tanktop arm would brush against his. And how I want him to get back here so I can haul him into my new dusty room, so my hands can get stronger getting knots out of his back, so I can chew on his soapy hair.

but then... I don't know if he would want that at all.

ch. 4 new york 1990

There was the day we tried to shut down Wall Street, me and a fucking million other people. There were baracades in the street burning, people running, getting thrown to the ground; flyers and banners and drums and slogans and a zillion cops in full riot gear, on horses and motorcycles, vans and cars. But first, wait, first I was in Vermont, I was living in Vermont when the whole thing was being planned, living in the tree house and working at the Institute For Social Ecology. It was 1990, and the green movement was the new thing to co-opt. Exxon was spilling oil all over the place, but putting out enviornmental products, and people were buying it. Buying Toms toothpaste by the truckload, buying Ben and Jerry's rainforest crunch. anything that they could purchase to save the earth, they got it. They'd done their part. And the radical potential of the ecological movement was being drowned out by a massive green buying frenzy. They weren't looking at the way ecological destruction and capitalism connected. They were placing the blame on life style instead of multinational corporations and a society based on the domination of nature by humans. So, Earth Day was coming up and people were organizing like mad. Plans to protest the whole thing and place the blame where it lays, Wall Street, stock exchange. I was living in my treehouse, just me and my dog, and sometimes I wouldn't see anyone for days, and then I was in New York. I was passing out flyers for the action, standing on this huge street that had been shut off from traffic for stupid tables full of crap. There were earth products everywhere and the smell of gas generators heating up some meat to see to all the millions of people passing by. Everyone was walking down the strip, checking it out and being pleased about all that was being done to save the earth. A million people passed me in an hour. More people than lived in the state of Vermont, I swear. It was crazy. I talked to tons of people, explaining the whole action, and finally it was time to quit for the day, rest up for tomorrow. We stayed in this nice squat full of great people, and I wandered around the lower east side with my affinity group. There's this funny thing about Plainfield Vermont. It's so cut off from mass culture, we didn't even get TV and only one radio station. Pretty much evenyone I knew worked at the radio station, including me, and we'd sometimes find these really horrible or just really weird albums that we figured no on in the world knew about except us. They'd become sort of our theme records. A couple months before we went to NY, we had been really into this one song by this really awful singer Bizmarke. He sung in the most off key voice and had the stupidest lyrics. Even his rhymes were sucky. and we used to yell the song at eachother from across the street, especially if we ran into each-other in Montpelier or someplace other than Plainfield. If you heard someone yellin "Oh baby you, you got what I need", then you knew a true friend was near. So damn if we weren't surprised to be walking down Ave C and hear these kids bust out into our fucking BizMarke song. It blew us away completely. I mean, not only were there people other than us thatknew the song, but the song was fucking famous! Yikes!

We went back to the squat, laughing, and fell asleep. Woke up late. See, we were all supposed to meet at different places at the same time and converge on the stock exchange building. The whole thing was amazingly well planned out. very impressive. The anarchists having our blazing glory of a kick off and meeting all the other folks, the hundred or so groups that were all organizing it coalition style, for speakers and whatnot, but I missed most of the burning glory part. got there a few minutes too late, after Palula was already dragged away into the van of pigs shouting "Unarrest me you fuckers!" to her comrades. (If I had been there, I would have saved you, girl) The whole thing was amazing. Cops like crazy and people in their faces. The business suits all had to be escorted through police barricades with people screaming and screaming at them. It made them very nervous. And a couple of comrades dressed up like suits and got in the escort line. They acted completely freaked out by the whole thing, all terrified style, and that made the suits even more scared than ever, some sort of terror sweeping through them. It was great. We were there for hours, days, years, with the zillion cops and everyone fucking shit up and passing out good information. And then it was home. The long car ride and hike through the woods. The squirrels had scammered into my house and eaten my bread. I crawled into my sleeping bag and slept with my hand touching the tree bark, my dog at my feet and the coyotes howling a few miles away.

ch. 5

My first comic.

It's not really very funny.

ch. 6

Sometimes it seems like half my friends here have only three things to talk about, tattoos, piercings and traveling. So I try to avoid talking about those things as much as possible. but...see, this thing happens. My dog gets the travel itch. I swear to god. She has seen more of this country than I have because her and my sister went on a three month road trip, leaving me behind to ward off the cockroaches in my Minnesota apartment. So it happens, my dog gets restless. It starts with her running away from home. Sometimes I'll be sitting out on the porch, right where she knows I can see her, and she just takes off down the street. Very bad. And if I don't get the hint, then she just starts grumping around the house and generally being a pain in the ass, so I'll get mad at her and then feel bad for being mean to her and then decide that what we really need is some time together in someplace new, just me and her on the road. Just me and her against the world. I kinda like hitchiking when it's just me and her. I mean, half the time I get picked up by pretty sketchy people and have a hard time restraining myself from punching their teeth out, and I swear I start feeling like I'll never get a ride after about forty minutes of holding my sign up, and I feel like I should just give up. But ever since I hitched with Kyle and Zeb, and they taught me this side of the road game, I play it when I'm feeling hopeless. What you do is, say outloud all the reasons a car didn't pick you up and all the resons you didn't want it to anyway. Car phone, mustache, big hair, red car, tinted windows, too much room, too clean, daughter at risk. This time it was pretty lonely out there on the on ramps. My sign said Eureka. I think there's something really great about a sign saying Eureka, but still, I was lonely. I'd been feeling pretty lonely since my sister left and my crush left, so I made up conversations I would have with different friends if they were there with me. I caught up with about 5 people who I haven't seen for years. Just made up what they would have said and what they were up to these days. But mostly I thought about my crush and how it would be to have him sitting next to me getting sunburnt and grumpy.

The things I like about traveling are the weird little things. Like when I was stuck at this shitty SantaRosa on ramp and this woman holding a gas can came up to me and told me she used to live in Eureka but she had to move because she got cancer, and how she'd met someone down here who told her that they give mastectomys to women way more often than they need to and that she should just eat a lot of grapes and stuff. I like getting to a new place and doing things kinda different but kinda the same. Exploring for awhile, drinking coffee and writing letters and stories and stuff like that. Eureka was good for sneaking into the backhouse with Kyle, drinking warm beer and trying to play the drums. We'd argue about who sucked worse at it. I love Kyle because he thinks. He confronts shit and isn't afraid to disagree with his friends. But he's not all defensive and self-righteous about it at all. I love Kyle because he's nuts and will laugh at stupid things just like me. We walked to the ocean together, across these crazy long bridges, the longest bridges in the world, I swear, and these giant logging trucks would go wooshing by, and we hardly had any room to walk and we held tight to Anna's leash as the trucks tried to blow us away, and we held onto the side of the bridge because the whole thing would shake when the trucks went by. And then there was ocean, all huge and right there with the biggest, weirdest looking jellyfish washed up on shore. We played the toe game and I went swimming. I love cold water and the way it takes my breath away and makes me feel all alive, alive. Way better than coffee. Way better than anything, the way everything is tingly and real when I come out on to land. One night there was a thunderstorm! A Thunderstorm! I'd been thinking I would not be able to live much longer without a thunderstorm. I'd been thinking of traveling somewhere where I thought they might have one, and then waiting around for one to come, like Montana or something, but my sister said thunderstorms are unpredictable and it wasn't very likely that one would come if I went out looking for one, and then, in the last place I would have looked, a thunderstorm came to me in Eureka!

Eureka was good. Kyle and I got a crush on the same girl. I went into her work and asked if she wanted some of the cake we'd been given."It's not vegan though", I said. and she said "oh, I'm vegan", rubbing her belly. I got nervous and left. Sometimes it's the small things that I feel are the fullest of adventure. Like, I walked around and saw places that friends of mine had explored when they were passing through; cool, spooky places, but I did little things, like walking around in the fog with this stranger guy, rollerskating in this dark warehouse full of old stoves and fridges and a box making machine. Cooking stirfry on the campstove in the backhouse with a switchblade for a spatula. Going up to a stranger's studio and watching home movies of his kids, throwing his unfired ceramics out the window. Drawing comics with Kyle. And now I'm home, in my garage, and everything is the same, just like how it was before I left, and everything is different, entirely different.

ch. 7

Sometimes I can't believe I live through this life the way I do, with everything intense and swinging around. Obsessing and laughing, being grumpy as hell and not crying enough. Yesterday I spent an hour in the laundry mat. I wasn't doing my laundry, just writing and drawing pictures of the washing machines and feeling sick from the strange laundry chemicals. I rode on my bike as fast as I could, yelling high, strange noises. I cooked eggplant and ate icecream. listening to bad music with friends. But one thing I can say, one thing that confuses me, in a way, I really don't understand boredom. I don't get it. There is too much to do. Too many things to explore. Beautiful and ugly art to make, dictonaries to read, and history and theory to study and everything. I don't get apathy. How people can give up like that. In a way it seems crazy selfindulgent. So what if we can't obtain a utopian society, there's still so much crap we need to take responsibility for. So much to struggle for, and the hard part is finding what it is that will sustain you. You know, what speaks to your experience, has to do with your own life and wont be just doing something to appease some sort of guilt. Oh... not doing something martyristic. And I haven't figured it out either, but let me tell you, it's a hell of a lot more interesting to be always challenging yourself and challenging this fucked up world and changing things, than it is to sit around and feel like everything is hopeless. Right now boredom is the thing I can tollerate the least. Boring is my worst insult.

ch. 8

new york again

There was this other time I was in New York. The only time I spent days there. I flew in on a plane, with no one to pick me up, which is how I like arriving. Stranded someplace new and having to figure it out myself. It gives me time to adjust and feel like in a small way I have conquered this new town. New York. By the time I got to the city from the airport, all my friends were at work or school or still asleep and I spent the day eating my rice and lentils I'd brought from home and wandering around. Wandering in the right directions and the wrong directions and always looking like I knew just where I was heading. I loved New York, the way there were millions of different things and people and culture right there in front of me. Places where I was an outsider in ways I'd never really experienced. Colors and filth and pidgeons and cheep Indian food. Friends who I missed like crazy and finally found. For three days, everything was amazing. I sat on this strange sundeck roof with Michael and looked at all his plants that had died in the heat.

Listened to Chuck talking about how grateful he was for places with airconditioning. A.C., he called it. I hung out with this boy I had kind of loved for a long time. his poetry in piles on the floor, ten million baseball hats on his dresser. We ate cake in strange cafes in Brooklyn where all the customers knew the waitress by first name. And it was a little too crazy, a little to intense. Do you know how it is when you want to do everything at once, see everyone, talk and dance and sleep. And then you don't want any of it, you just want to be wandering around alone and you wish you had no ties to anyone and no responsibilities to your friends and that you didn't have to rely on them for a place to sleep? New York started to get creepy. The way people bought tee shirts and sunglasses and the whole money transaction was done very secretly, like they were trying to make sure no one saw their money. There were these guys sitting under one of those walkways they put up when they're doing construction on a building and you have to sort of walk in the street because the sidewalk is being all used up. These guys sitting there had this very real looking rubber rat, sitting out in front of them, right in everyone's path, and no one seemed to notice it at all. I loved it, those guys and their beautiful rat.

I didn't really realize that the whole place was getting to me until this one morning. I woke up in Brooklyn and was walking down to the subway. There was this pidgeon on the curb in front of me. It was all discolored. It's feathers were falling out and it was hobbling around. I stood there stareing at it and waiting for the light to change. It was pretty sad to look at, that pidgeon. Then there was this nice car at the stop light. The guy in the car leaned over to the passenger window and unrolled it so he would talk to me. I thought he was going to ask me for directions, but instead he just said "It's not going to make it", in this really sad voice, and he looked towards the pidgeon. I must have looked confused because he offered further explainnation. "The pidgeon. I don't think it will live." I shook my head, no I don't think it will either. And the light changed. And it made me really sad. A fucking pidgeon and some stranger and me bonding over it's fate, and no one ever said anything to me about the people I passed by dieing on the sidewalks, or the kids playing in puddles covered with the rainbow colors of spilled oil. I hated New York. I caught the first train out I could, up to Vermont and Paula's porch, where I could listen to the creek slipping away beneath me and hear Willis playing his guitar all crazy and loud, just like it was when I lived there.

ch.9

When I was I7, I moved out of my mom's house into my beautiful apartment looking over the freeway off ramp, where kids rode their bigwheels down the sidewalks and cops drove screaming by every hour. I moved out of my moms house, where the laundry was always piled up on the couch unfolded and the cats made their beds in it. Where I had sat at the kitchen table, eating cereal and poptarts, watching my mom and stepdad do the crossword puzzle, watched them dance in the kitchen when no music was playing. where I'd watched them drink their vodka and o.j.. watched my mom cry over how much she loved me and - how was I going to function in this world - she would wonder - when I looked crazy and every injustice broke me, too much made me angry and too much made me cry. I would come home too late, smelling like the cigerettes my junky friends smoked, and mom would be there, asleep on the couch, waiting and worrying about me. And all I could figure was she didn't trust me.

I left the school where I'd walk down the halls and people would yell "Dyke". and I could pass all my classes without even trying. I moved into my beautiful apartment where I would hardly get to spend any time because I'd work all day and take classes all night. But this is what I was trying to get to. This small story I was trying to tell. When I moved, my mom helped me bring a few of my things there. It was the only time she came to my house and she didn't actually come in, not that I remember. And like all good mothers, she had some advice. You know, the kind of life advice that they feel is urgent to pass on to their kids if they're going to survive this crazy world on their own. She looked at me, all wide eyed and serious. "If you are ever broke, and all you have in your refridgerator is moldy cheese, you can eat it and you won't get sick." This was her last advice to me.

ch. IO

I love wheels. the kind that roll beneath me and make me travel in different ways. My rollerskates that I stumble down the street with, leaning too far forward still, still I don't quite have the hang of it and sometimes I fall down when I'm standing still. I love the way people look at me when I'm on rollerskates, blue sneaker rollerskates. and you know what? this weird thing happened.when I was in Eureka I was a little bid drunk and roller-skating around with my dog, and she was being bad and I was leaning down and scolding her and out of the corner of my eye I saw someone rollerskate by with rollerskates Just Like Mine. I have never seen rollerskates just like mine before. Just like a movie, I though, Out of the corner of my eye like that.

I love wheels, the way they make everything look different and the different speeds they take you on. My small skateboard. "Yeah, I had a skateboard just like that when I was a kid", Eli says. It makes me look at the street, and now I know which streets, which back streets are smooth and which are bumpy. I know the sidewalks from rollerskating, I know which ones are crowded and which go downhill, and then the wheels on my bike that need pumping up every few hours on the road. and that bike, it can take me anywhere, anywhere I tell you. I love wheels so much that sometimes I forget to walk.

Sometimes my feet forget what it's like to be on the ground, and then everything moves by so slow that I have to skip or run. Sometimes I am so happy it makes me mad. I feel like I might spontaniously combust and it's hard to get much of anything done. And then, then it is good to walk slow down the sidewalk, to draw hearts hearts and cats and messages with chalk, in front of shoe repair stores and places your friends might see. It's good to walk slow and pick up things, pidgeon feathers marbles, drawings dropped by kids.

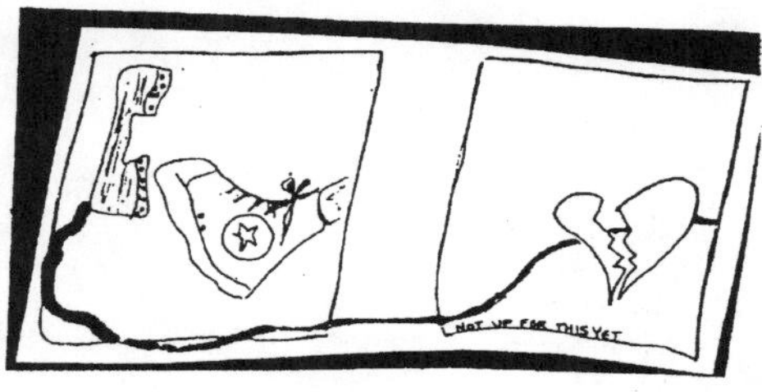

← people

lemmings →

A FEW WEEKS AGO MY SISTER TOLD ME ABOUT LEMMINGS,

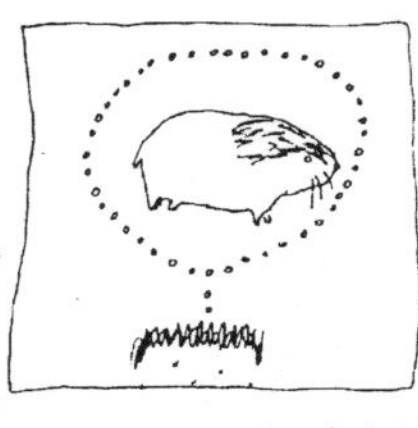

AND SINCE THEN I CAN'T STOP THINKING ABOUT THEM WITH A STRANGE RESPECT.

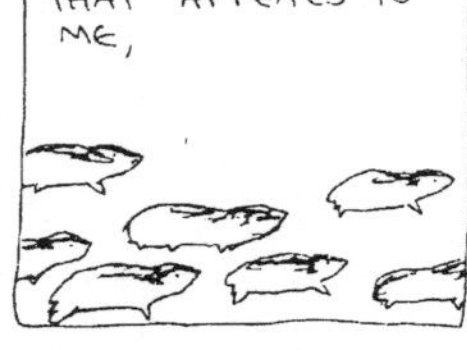

IT'S NOT THE MINDLESS FOLLOWING THAT APPEALS TO ME,

OR MASS SUICIDE. IT'S NOT ABOUT DEATH AT ALL.

BUT I UNDERSTAND THE SIMPLE DESIRE TO WALK TO THE SEA NO MATTER HOW LONG IT TAKES. AND ONCE YOU GET THERE

TO WALK IN TO IT. NEVER TURN BACK. JUST KEEP GOING.

When I'm making Doris I don't need anything. I don't need food or sleep or company. (that is a lie, but that's what it feels like) and when I'm done, it becomes something else. It becomes photocopy stores and staplers. It is something strange. something sad. And now I just want my dead friends to come over and sit on my cardboard funniture and drink tea. I have a lot of dead friends. I want my sister to be healthy and my mom to be sane. I want my neck to stop hurting and my feet to warm up. I want to swim in the ocean for hours. just me alone, cold and drenched and floating.

doris #4

sometimes doris sleeps

this is doris, typed up in 3 different houses and a cold shed in another city. typed up with these sore fingers of mine. on desks and floors and beds and tables made out of milk crates and splintery wood. 4 months and 2 different typewritters. sissors, wax, tape and glue. and i still have hardly been to the ocean. my sister sees it every day when she walks out of her tent and into the farm fields. 4 months, and here is my advice to you; never drive a hot car too slow on the highway. never go to uhkiah.

theres t his plaee in my new neighborhood i love. the sidewalk cafe. it has donuts and coffee and ethaopian food. its a tiny place, off the main road, and i think i am the only one who has ever ordered food there. last tim e the guy behind the counter said they were out of bread, but 5 minutes? he asked. and i said alright. he called up the other guy, and he brought down the injera, fresh and warm. the guy behind the counter doesnt know much english, but we say what we can to eachother, and i go in and spend my last dollar on coffee just to see him.

its summer again, and my bike is broken. usually when something breaks on it, i just end up taking that peice off. i took off the thing you use to shift gears. i dont hardly have any brakes. but its the tire thats broken this time, im trying to figure it out and fix it. toasters, rollerskates, b ookshelves, i can fix them. but my bike, i dont know.

like always, doris is about strangers and secrets and stories. if you want to write me, my address is: cindy ovenrack, ~~po box 4279, berkeley ca 94704.~~ doris I & 2 are still available for 50¢ each plus some stamps

table of contents

Reduced Print of a Page of the Score of the *Coffee Cantata* by Johann Sebastian Bach, bearing the Refrain "How Sweet is the Taste of Coffee, more Charming than a Thousand Kisses, softer than Muscatel Wine." (See p. 201.)

i like things to be small to fit in my pockets. magazines, paperback books, strings and rocks, gum and photographs. i want this thing here to be smaller. may be you could fold it twice and it would fit snug in the back of your blue-jeans like doris #one did, getting dirty and ratty and torn.

i was on the bart train the other day and there were these four girls, highschool girls. three of them looked just like t.v., long hair that they would brush back with their fingers. all these practiced facial expressions, small noses, lines drawn around their eyes. but one girl, she was too tall and gangly and it looked like she just got her braces off, the way she kept feeling her teeth with her tounge. her backpack had paintings of suns and moons and flowers that you could tell she painted on there and you could tell her friends made fun of it behind her back. she was the one i watched. her backpack was unziped part way and i snuck doris number one in. number one, full of my secrets. i couldnt hand it to her because i knew she wouldnt take it, not with her friends watching. i snuck it in to her life for her to find later, alone, in her bedroom. the people on the train who saw me do it glared at me mean and suspicious, like i'd stolen something from that girl, and may be i had. i got off at the next stop.

but the truth is, i dont hand it out like i use to, watching people on the train, on busses, on the street - handing one to this girl who is laughing with her friend, one to that girl sad and alone on the last train of the night, the girl with the red boots, the one sitting on the wet curb, the boy who pulled his hair in front of his eyes and chewed on the ends. i still want the same things. to break-with this one small gesture-the crazy things we are taught; to keep distant and distrustful, alienated, lonely and safe. i still want to know stories whispered and yelled and coughed out between too much laughing. but i live in these cities now and i know too many people, all ½ way and california style.

and i never got winter

cold sun and thick blankets of snow. a warm room to hibernate in. time to sleep and read and swim around inside my head. this place is not condusive to that and i still spend my days running around like crazy. every day feels like ten. sometimes i say to my friends 'god i havent seen you in weeks' and then i realize its only been two days. everything is changing faster than i can follow. my sister is leaving.

my home away from home was evicted. i have all my things packed in milk crates and boxes ~~but i dont know where im going yet~~. ive climbed fences and got drunk in the abandon school yard. i sat out on the grill outside the train station with a broken heart in me and a broken heart drawn on the sidewalk with chalk. i rode my pink bike double, wobbly and laughing. i rode the bicycle built for two all alone, feeling shitty and beautiful and lonely and good. filling up the front tire at every gas station and walking it when the gas stations were too far apart. i set up office hours in a coffee shop so far out of the way i know no one will come visit me there. i pound on things and pretend to sing. i've found short cuts that take twice as long. i've made this city mine.

HOUSES THINGS

somehow i fall in love with every f ucked up crazy place i live. the garage with everything damp and molding, filled with broken bikes, window shades, and a whole pile of doors. there was the hot attic where you could hardly move without getting drenced in sweat, hardly move without knocking over a box of something noone had looked at for years. there was the house that overlooked the freeway, the one by the river, one house with ghosts, one in the trees, one with kids swarming through it, yeah, and thats not it. there was the storage space where i couldnt tell if it was day or night. if it was raining or sunny. i'd work on my projects all night and then buzz up to marcs office on my intercom. "hey boy? you got coffee for me up there?" and now theres this new house. where it rains inside like faucets. an alarm going off for hours above me. someone playing violin on the back porch. the raido blaring true stories of runaway trains, and then the drumming starts. drums and buckets and pots and pans, and just when it gets loud enoughto drown out the alarm, just when it gets so loud there's nothing you can do, there's an earthquake and the dogs start barking. two of them barking, and i laugh along with it.

its unexplainably the way i fall in love with things sometimes. people i hardly know. they say one thing. tell me one horrible nightmare, one secret, one expression, and i swear, something in me is dedicated to them forever in some smallway. and no matter what, istand up for them. i worry about them. my face lights up when i see them on the street. this morning i opened my front door, comming in from the thick rain, and there's Colby on my stairs with his backpac k and his blankets rolled up and tied. i hold him and he doesnt let go. we sit down and he rests his head on my lap. "what's wrong?" i say, he says "i've been sad all day". i look at his dirty soft boy face and my tears fall right into his eyes.

i fall in love with things, and i think they're perfect even when i know they're not. me and my friend Shoes, we drove to junction city to look for the girl who's in my skin. we brought back a bike and a typewriter, the two things i fall for hardest. and there, in the cold shed, i watched the bike. mustard yellow it was. JC Penny one speed it's stickers said. but it had 3 speeds and a flatt tire. i was sure that in the morning the tire would be fine and i could ride it for days on end. take it anywhere. the typewriter, $5.00 because the cap's dont work. my first electric typewriter. youplug itin and it hums. i know thatwith my fingers on those charged buttons i will write in new ways. its tactile to me, writing is. the way the pen fits into my fingers. the way the lettered keys collide.

AND SECRETS

words get stuck in my head. cabbage. albatros. years. secrets. i've been talking to my sister about how thesedays im scared of peoples secrets. i have never been the type to take words lightly. i listen to peoples stories. i bring them home and mull them over. i use to think it was the task of the revolutionary to redefine commmnication. to make every sentance valuable and push every encounter beyond its usual limits. and to be honest, i never could understand the people

who hardly listened. you could tell them part of your life and the next day they'd have forgotten. i never understood interuptions, that calous kind of listening. i remembered everything and asked questions people were afraid to answer. and now. im not sure what to do with it all. i get worried when someone openes their mouth, that i'll listen too hard and wont let go. i dont want things to go in one ear and out the other. im not that casual and dont want to be. but secrets, secrets, they get stuck in my brain. this stranger girl says to me "ive spent 12 years wrapped up in rage", and i think "what girl, what else?" i want to turn her hands over to seeif her knuckles are bloody from punching walls. i want to hear her yell and i want to look her right in the face. 3am and i want to figure it all out for this girl i dont even know. i know its not expected, that if i said a word she'd be surprised.

---

all the time i hear these secrets, spit outlike broken bones. "i'm afraid of bathrooms" "my friend was dumped in the river" "my mom's crazy" "i've never slept alone". i use to take all these stories, everyones secrets, the bits and peices i could gather. i shoved them under my fingernails into my skin and too sonn, you know, too soon my hand s were tired and full.

in portland i decided i didn't need sleep. i was sick of sleeping. i had too much to do. fuck it. 4 hours was plenty.

julia and i had decided to be best friends. we hardly knew eachother but it seemed like a great idea. we went to this worst coffee shop in the world. everyone we knew refused to go there, but we decided to love it anyway. they put our own Dennys style pots of coffee right on our table next to us. there was this totally fucked bus boy. we called him bondage head and gave him killer glares every time he walked by. He had a skanky green mohawk and a bad tattoo of a woman in bondage on the side of his head. i told Margo about him later. "oh yeah', she said, 'i know the guy. i beat the shit out of him at some show last week.' julia got a crush on the round faced waitress. i got a crush on the matty hair junky girl. neither of them noticed we were alive.

we came home at 9am. julia headed upstairs to go to bed. i put beans on to soak and was pulling on my boots to get ready for the day of dumpstering big boxes of produce, washing and cutting, cooking and packing up the car to drive down to the park and serve to practically no one. the tuesday Food Not Bombs servings sucked because i usually did half of it alone. Why the hell did everyone else sleep? there was too much to do. I was in the kitchen trying to plan it all out when Julia came screaming down the stairs. 'the ice cream truck!' I could hear its bell song rolling down the street. 'they never stop', i tried to tell her. 'I swear, every time when i was a kid, we'd go running after them and they never stopped for us'. 'what are you talking about' she said, and dragged me out the door. We ran after it laughing and the fucker didn't stop. We chased it down 2 blocks and around the corner. She was screaming 'stop you fucker', i was yelling at her 'I told you so'. Finally it pulled over right in front of this house where a girl and her little brother were playing. The boy saw the icecream truck and fell on his butt crying because there it was and he didn't have the money to get anything. His sister stood back watching us while we ordered our icecream sandwiches. Julia called the crying kid over. 'You want something? What do you want?" 'Mario' he said, solid and sure with his thumb in his mouth. Julia bought him his ice cream and i bought the girl a bomb pop. Julia went home to sleep. I went to go conquor the world.

When i came home there were two kittens in the house. Skinny white things with messed up ears. 'Can I keep them?' she asked, like i was her mother. 'I'm crazy alergic' i told her, 'but if you vacuum maybe it'll be okay.'

Julia did everything in weird fucked up ways just like i did, only different. Her ways didn't follow any sort of logic at all and they never seemed to work out. She had moved to Portland on money she

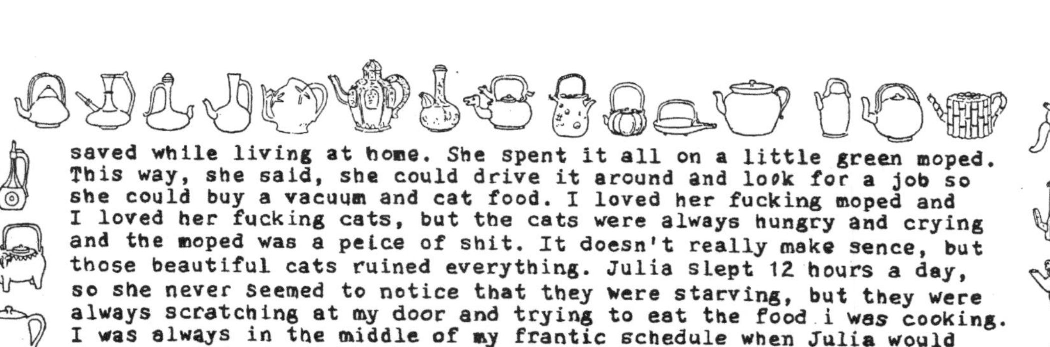

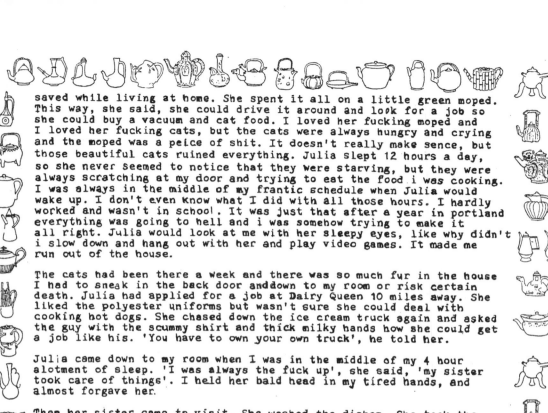

saved while living at home. She spent it all on a little green moped. This way, she said, she could drive it around and look for a job so she could buy a vacuum and cat food. I loved her fucking moped and I loved her fucking cats, but the cats were always hungry and crying and the moped was a peice of shit. It doesn't really make sence, but those beautiful cats ruined everything. Julia slept 12 hours a day, so she never seemed to notice that they were starving, but they were always scratching at my door and trying to eat the food i was cooking. I was always in the middle of my frantic schedule when Julia would wake up. I don't even know what I did with all those hours. I hardly worked and wasn't in school. It was just that after a year in portland everything was going to hell and i was somehow trying to make it all right. Julia would look at me with her sleepy eyes, like why didn't i slow down and hang out with her and play video games. It made me run out of the house.

The cats had been there a week and there was so much fur in the house I had to sneak in the back door anddown to my room or risk certain death. Julia had applied for a job at Dairy Queen 10 miles away. She liked the polyester uniforms but wasn't sure she could deal with cooking hot dogs. She chased down the ice cream truck again and asked the guy with the scummy shirt and thick milky hands how she could get a job like his. 'You have to own your own truck', he told her.

Julia came down to my room when I was in the middle of my 4 hour alotment of sleep. 'I was always the fuck up', she said, 'my sister took care of things'. I held her bald head in my tired hands, and almost forgave her.

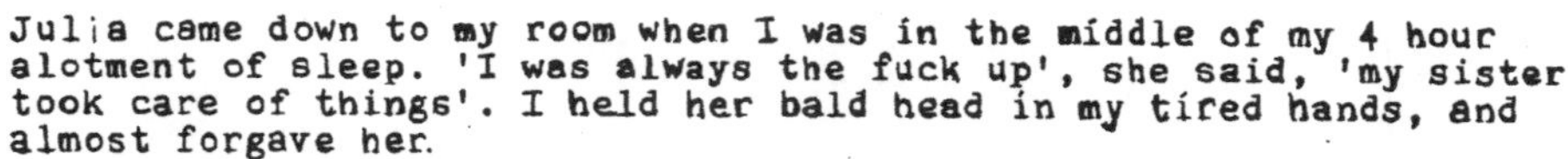

Then her sister came to visit. She washed the dishes. She took the moped out at 3am to try and find a hospital that would let her donate blood. She took the moped to the other side of town to the Saint Vincent thrift and bought a ten dollar vacuum, tried to ride back with it in one hand but she kept almost dropping it and almost crashing. Somehow, with her long haired, sweet girl ways, she got the drive through coffee place to hold on to the appliance while she went back to the house to borrow my car. I wasn't home so she grabbed some rope and went back to the coffee shop. She tried to tie the vacuum on to the back of the moped using crazy made up knot configurations. A few blocks from the house,the vacuum fell off and broke. She left it on the side of the road. This was Julia's sister who always took care of things.

A few weeks later there was a punk show at the Winery. Me and Julia went there together. It was like old times. We danced until we were sore and sweaty. we got drunk on too much wine. 'Fuck everything', I said, leaning into her and holding her hand, 'let's forget it all. I'll get a vacuum, I'll feed the cats, let's listen to the oldies station, bake rice crispy bars, drink coffee, climb on roofs and

run around town'. She kissed me and puked out my car window. I almost fell asleep in her bed.

it seemed like everything could get better. like everything could be just fine. but i'd been living in portland a year and the whole place had turned into a nightmare. i only slept 4 hours and i still didn't have time for anything. i remember now what i did with those hours. i tried to peice together all my broken friendships, and find time to play with my rad kid friends who lived in the house i had deserted. i tried to take care of my new friends, buying them coffee, bringing them food, hiding in the bushes and talking things through. i tried to make sure the 2 new food not bombs days were going okay and tried to make something good out of our new womens only space. i was writing and cooking and realizing how different my politics were from the politics of the people i was working with

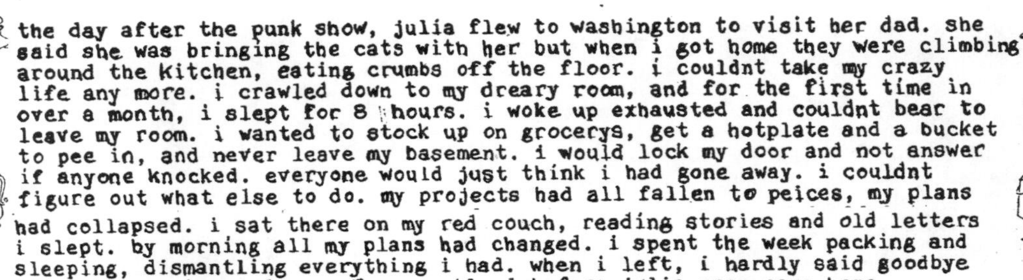

the day after the punk show, julia flew to washington to visit her dad. she said she was bringing the cats with her but when i got home they were climbing around the kitchen, eating crumbs off the floor. i couldnt take my crazy life any more. i crawled down to my dreary room, and for the first time in over a month, i slept for 8 hours. i woke up exhausted and couldnt bear to leave my room. i wanted to stock up on grocerys, get a hotplate and a bucket to pee in, and never leave my basement. i would lock my door and not answer if anyone knocked. everyone would just think i had gone away. i couldnt figure out what else to do. my projects had all fallen to peices, my plans had collapsed. i sat there on my red couch, reading stories and old letters i slept. by morning all my plans had changed. i spent the week packing and sleeping, dismantling everything i had. when i left, i hardly said goodbye to anything. i moved away from portland before julia even came home.

letter

* I'm at my job right now- lifeguarding at a condominium pool. Mostly boring, but it has it's exciting moments. Like today there was an odds and ends sale in the rec. room beside the pool (there's a big window dividing the two, so I can see what's going on) This one table was selling a pair of binoculars and people kept on looking through them at me. I was like "What are you doing? I can still see you y'know." I think sometimes people forget the first hide and seek rule they ever learned. Remeber, there was always the kid who would always just stand there and put his hand over his eyes. Then you would have to explain to him the principle of "even though you can't see them, they can still see you." Either there are people who never quite grasped that principle, or who just like to conveniently forget every once and a while.

They're are a whole bunch of kooky characters living here. But I think that's mainly because there are a lot of single retired people who are lonely and do strange things. Or, I'm sorry, I don't know why they're strange, they just are. There's this one man I love though. His name is Mr. Middleton and he's the cheeriest man I've ever met. He comes through the change room door, walking this jaunty walk and swinging his arms. As soon as he sees somebody in the office he'll throw up an arm and shout "Hi there!" Then he'll come over and chat about whatever. He is the only person I have ever known who uses the expression "the rascal" For instance (i'll put it into context for you) Me- "Mr Middleton, they've found that Nestle is paying doctors to sterilize women in Africa." Mr. Middleton- "No! The rascals!" I can't help it, it always makes me smile. Mr. Middleton has been around. He joined the Foreign Legion when he was 18 (because he didn't have any family) and did quite a few wars. He's not proud of it, but at least he knows everything there is to know about the army. When he was 40 he was teaching a grade 10 class. This was during the sixties, just after Cuba had started to settle down after its revolution, and

Mr Middleton decided to write Fidel Castro, telling him how interested he was in how communism was working there. Fidel wrote him back saying "why don't you bring your students and come and see." So he and the class went, visiting projects, and doing all sorts of stuff. One day there was a baseball game organized between the the canadian students and Cuban students. The canadians were losing Terribly so Fidel stood in and pitched for them. Mr Middleton has slides of him playing baseball with Fidel Castro! I wish I had a grandfather like him. He's such a great role model. He's always coming down saying "So when are we going to start the revolution?!" I love him! He's the only old person I know who never told me I'd lose my ideals. If I had a revolution Mr. Middleton would be there, Larry Edwards would *not* be there, Rush Limbaugh would *not* be there. Like throwing a party, I sometimes think of throwing my own revolution. Making up the guest list is so much fun. Actually, making the list of things and people who can't come is even better. There's so many people I know who think they have their political stuff together, but who just don't know how to apply any of that stuff to people, who I'll never let darken the doorstep of my revolution. They're the very worst kind!

i love doing things i suck at and doing things all wrong. like riding my bike no handed. somehow ive never learned the trick. and i ride around on back streets screaming songs all off key and letting go of my handlebars and practically crashing every minute. its better than coffee the way it makes my heart beat fast and wakes me up and makes me laugh and see everything more clearly. i love building things. and really, i know the right way to go about making shelves and whatnot, but when i get around to it i usually make them all fucked up anyway. cutting the boards crooked. and i never measure anything. my rooms always look like they'll fall apart at any moment. and sometimes they do.

i had this thing with the garage i just moved out of. it took me forever to climb up on the roof and see if there was any possible way to make it not leak quite so much. i mean, there was a huge hole with vines growing through it, and when it rained, it rained all over everything, especially my bed. i finally decided to climb up there and check it out, only i was wearing these huge golashes my sister had gotten me at the dayton thrift. you have to wear shoes under these golashes, otherwise they fall right off

your feet every step you take. i wasnt wearing shoes under them. so there i was, climbing a tree to get myself up on the roof. i had a shovel in one hand because there was about a half foot of dirt on the flat part of the

better than coffee

roof. i had this big hedge clipper thing sticking out of my back pocket to cut the ivy down with, and my golashes were falling off my feet. but somehow i made it up there without loosing my shoes or impaling myself with the fucking hedge clippers. i cut all the vines and shoveled off the dirt. but back down in the garage, all i could find to cover the holes were a couple old rotten peices of wood and this weird plastic thing that looked like it had once belonged to the back seat of a car. i threw all that junk over the holes, and then, when it started raining again, the place leaked more than ever.

finally, like a month later, this friend of mine was gonna come stay in the garage for a few days to get some work he needed to get done, done. i figured what better time to actually waterproof the place. tarps. thats what i needed. and it was crazy luck. the first alley i walked down, looking for a tarp, there one was. i grabbed it, but one tarp was not enough. i rode my bike all around looking for more tarps. only i ended up going to the dumpster instead, finding a bunch of pineapples, and going to my home away from home. it was their last night and all the knives had all ready moved out, so we couldnt even eat the pineapple, but i threw one at the boy who was sleeping. and i told them all my plan. "ive seen a lot of tarps covering cars up, so i think i might just grab some of those".

the sleeping boy said he didnt think that was such a great idea. "people get really possessive over their car tarps", he said. "and you know", he said, "you can get huge rolls of clear plastic for really cheep, like under 3 bucks".

"really? under 3 dollars?"

"yeah", he said, "plastic's hella cheep. that's why they make cars out of it".

Rain.

so the next day i got this big roll of plastic at the hardware store. 250 square feet of it. and idont know what i was thinking. i brought it up to the top of the roof and just unrolled it all to seehow big 250 square feet was. there was more plastic than i could have ever imagined and i couldnt get it all unfolded unrolled and flatened out. plus i didnt have anything with me to pin it down with. no nails, no staple gun, nothing. i had to climb back down, find my staple gun and staples. i had to tell my sister to listen for my screams because there was no telling whether or not id be able to find stable enough places on that roof to climb on. in fact, chances were pretty good the whole thing would cave in under me and id go crashing down to the concrete floor of the garage. i crawled around the edges of the holes, stapling the plastic down, reloading the staple gun, stapling more. and when i was done, the place was water proof. thenext time it rained, not a thing got wet. and finally i could sleep out there, on my bed made out of a door and some scraps of foam. i could sleep under my plastic covered roof and listen to the rain fall.

found things

Candice Willis

In America people tend to say "Normal" but what is normal? I don't think there's an exact thing as normal. What is weird? Is it when you don't look or dress the way the next person looks or dresses? Now and days people are becoming apart, making new styles, so to me there's no such thing as different or same.

Dear Beutiful Karen
that Bag of socks you wanted is in Back i went for Bike ~~test~~ Ride But will Return shortly its 8:35pm ill Be Back By 10:30pm please wait for my Return
Love D

People can destroy their culture.

How does people can destroy their culture?

People who doesn't accep their own culture most of yungh people who comes from another countries, they try to be like somebody else and also people who likes to be envolved in drugs.

I Know one perso of my native country, he doesn't accept that he is mexican, because of his parent came to U.S.A whe he was 7 years old, he started to go to school and there he was changing little by little until he complitily changed his mine even his faces looks like mexican, his skin's color. But I know another person who lives with an American when she is at home she acts like american but when she is with her family or friends she acts like them, she did not loose her culture, but she has learned another culture.

For me to Keep my culture is one of the most important thing, because if I loose it little by little my culture will be loose for ever and nobody will live same customes as we do.

SEX & POWER

feeling of power and sex

ive been reading this book by Dorthy Allison calledSkin. its got me thinking a lot about sex and power and how the two have been all intertwined in my life. i never talk about sex. ive always seen myself as devient even though i dont think my desire is out of the ordinary. i dont talk about sex because i think ill be judged, condemned, pitied. i think my sexuality will be simplified, catagorized and my friendxs will feel all alienated from me. that illbbe held at arms length, looked at out of the corner of their eyes thatmysex choices willbeseen as a betrayal. it makes me pretty confuxed, and kind of protectivie. even though i feel secure in my body now, in how i see it and how i use it, and i feel like my choices are real choices now. i know what im doing and what i want. before it was more questionably - what i did was half choice, half necessity. more muddled. had more control over me. yeah, stuff like that. somehow, i think its important to start talking about some of it. some of this stuff. but here i am, sitting in bed witha fever and chills, blowing my nose on amy peice of clothes i can find. drinking hot water because i ran out of tea bags. and i dont really know where to begin.

learn what is acceptible

there's the simple things. like when i was sixteen and theone thing i knew i could do well was flirt. i did it in that cool tough girl way. looking too long in someones direction. i loved sex and the way it gave me power over these boys, when usually, just walking down the street or something, my body was what made me vulnerable. and i had been taught so precisly that sex could be used to take everything away from me. i loved sex and the way i could lose myself in that taste of skin. my life could be a huge hell of depression, but for those hours, warm with another body nothing else really mat ered. sex gave me power. power over my own self in a way i never felt in my usual, by myself, life. when i was fucking i could feel as much as i wanted. it was all about the ways i learnad to move and breath and think. there was someone with me, but for those hours, my body was mine. it was just about the only time i felt strong and in control of my life. sex wasnt so much wrapped up in love for me, not like it was for my friends. sure i wanted someone to love me or something, i was lonly as hell, but i didnt at all think sex and love had to go together. sometimes it got confusing, sure, that close to another body thinking somehow emotions should go along. but in my head, no, that wasnt how i thouhgt. i liked sex in the beginning, when i hardly knew the person, when they were a stranger still. but i could really never resolve it all. the way i wanted to fuck, wanting that power in my body, and then feeling all crappy about the way i was viewed. feeling like my body was the only thing that held any worth. that the rest of me was powerless and worthless.

some nights my mom would come down to my basement room, drunk and slurring her words. "sex can be really great" shed tell me, "really amazing, but only if you're in love. you should wait til youre in love". her voice would lower to a whisper, like she was telling me some girl secret. "johnny and i have sex every night and it's great. but i never enjoyed sex with your father". she'd been married to my father for thirteen years. she told me this same thing, in this same way, at least ten times. it was her only advice to me. that what was true for her would be true for me. i would look at her all sad and cynical. i wanted other kinds of advice. like could you buy the pill at the drug store or did you have to go to the doctor. i wanted to tell her that when i started really liking someone, that's when sex got complicated. thats when i started feeling vulnerable and things came up in my head that i didnt want to think about.

years later, when i was moving away from minnesota for the second time, she gave me her favorite books from college. two volumes of anais nin's erotica. i thought theyd be cheesy love stories, and when i read them i couldnt believe it. these well worn pages. stories of threesoms and exhabitionists, seduction and all that stuff. every story full of sex, detailed and graphic.

i'd never read erotica or porn or any of that stuff. i'd never been much into fantisy. there were a few weeks when i was eleven and living with my dad and i found his huge stash of playboys. id look at those girls with their big tits and thin legs spread. i'd read about their hobbys, their height, where they grew up. I d lay in my bed, this small room under the stairs. i wanted to be like the Fonz. he'd just snap his fingers and girls would swarm to his sides. no question about his desireability. i'd lay on my bed and pretend like i had a whole file cabenet full of phone numbers, like the fonz did. id call up one of those numbers, all innocent like, just inviting them over. but i would be naked in my bed with the sheet pulled down just below my nipples. and when they walked in and saw me there like that, they'd be shocked and speachless, but there was nothing they could do. they'd want me like no one else. gender was unimportant. i could never get it clear in my head. was i a boy inviting over girls? a girl inviting over boys? a girl with girls? gender was a minor distraction. it was about shock, power, unquestionable desire.

(already typed on other page) where is it?

when i was seventeen everything started sort of exploding in my head. i was taking this womens studies class at the university and they were trying to get me to look at my life within a social context - to see my explotation, oppression and self image within a wider context than just my own personal thing. and maybe i was getting it, i dont know, but i decided i was sick of being fucked over by boys who i wanted to care about me. i decided to live out my perception of myself - good for sex and thats it. unworthy of being cared for. i think it was the first time id gone out specifically to pick some boy up. id neger really been the agressor. but i was good at it. and it didnt take long before i was on the back of steves motorcycle heading down to his warehouse. this relationship would be about power, i thought, no emotion, just this simple thing. i would have full control over my own objectification by objectifing myself. there would be no blurred lines like with other boys, where i was one minute human, one minute body. whith this boy i would know exactly where i stood. everything i knew taught me these desires were fucked up. that i was fucked up for wanting this, for pursuing it and living it. the problem was, steve wouldnt play out his role. he was the sweetest boy i'd ever hung out with. he touched me like i was something breakable, slept with his hands on my face. we rode his bike through the country to his small home town of farms and forests. i could have loved him, yeah, but i resisted it all and resented him for making it so hard. he took me to that movie Blue Velvet. it made me cry and dig my fingernails into my palms. but when he brought me to his house that night i whispered "hit me, hit me". maybe i was too quiet. maybe he didnt hear. i said "you can tie me up if you want to". he said "you'd have to teach me. i dont know how". i didnt know how either. i never brought it up again. the more i expressed and lived my desire, the more crappy i felt about myself, and the more guilty i felt for rejecting what was suppose to be healthy - the search for true love.

i did this performance peice for my art class. i didnt know what it was about until i was performing it - until the end of it - when it was so clear. how i hated myself for my sexuality, how i bound myself to this one image of myself and how it all tied in to being abused. i hadnt thought much about my abuse before. it gave me a good reason to break up with steve - and it was probably half the reason. the other half being that it just wasnt working, the no emotion idea, playing out sex and power. i felt kinda crazy, wanting what i wanted.

then i met lisa. she wasin my class Sexuality and Self Image. A small tough italian girl who wrote in her notebook the entire first day of class, paying no attention to the teacher. we'd go outside together to smoke during breaks, and half the time we wouldnt return to class. wed just sit out there on the steps talking about incest and our histories and how crazy we were now. id never talked about it before and she had just started talking. her stories were huge and violent - so i lied about mine. compared to hers, i didnt think mine were bad enough to matter, so i lied.

"do you have flashbacks?" she asked me. "sometimes" i said. which was half true. i didnt flash back like she did to a huge father above a small girl body. i had weird flash moments where i felt a loss of control - and with that came a crazy intense fear. i had times of disengaging myself - feeling nothing. i dont know how mush of that had to do with my abuse and how much was a reaction to the daily terror of growing up a girl. Lisa spoke about her desire in raw language i had been looking for. there was one day in class where we all had to sit in a circle and talk about what we considered erotic. "icecream", one woman said, "flowers", "silk". The two of us sat huddled into ourselves, not saying anything outloud. but lisa leaned over and whispered to me "whips and stones and broken bones", and i nodded my head. it was so simple, theway she scorned people who's sexual imagination fit within the realm of accepted desire. she knew that the specifics of her desire were informed by her abuse, ~~that she wanted her boyfriend to call her names because that's what her dad had done,~~
t didnt think this made her desire wrong. i finally began to stop condemning rself for my desire.

over thenext five years i was in a million different kinds of relatiohships. long term boyfrinds, onenight things. manogamous, nonmanogamous. i learned all ab out my own body and all about boys bodies. i spent forever talking through dynamics, emo tional and sexual. trying to break out of roles, make things equal. i fucked boys i loved and boys i never wanted tossee again. and somehow, amongst it all, i got rid of my dependance on sex relationships to give me self worth and i finally felt powerful in a million ways, not just in my body. and now i make my choice instead of falling into things for reasons i dont exactly understnad. i make my choices consciously. sometimes dumb choices, sure. im no magic girl who always gets everything perfect. but even dumb choices, im usually pretty aware of their stupidity and why im doingit anyway.

~~fuck fuck fuck fuck~~ poem.

You like to give and watch me my
pleasure. Machete me in two.
Take for the taking what is yours.
This is how you like to have me.

I'm as naked as a field of cane,
as alone as all of Cuba
before you.

You could descend like rain,
destroy like fire
if you chose to.

If you chose to.

I could rise like huracán.
I could erupt as sudden as
a coup d'état of trumpets,
the sleepless eye of ocean,
a sky of black urracas.
If I chose to.

I don't chose to.
I let myself be taken.

This power is my gift to you.

-sandra cisneros

i wasnt sure how i was going to end this, how to tie it together into some sort of conclusion. i thought i would say something about dorthy allison and how she says write what youre most scared to say. how i dont talk about desire, and why. when i started writing this, i thhought maybe i should start trying to talk about sex. sex and power and all that. i thought maybe that was a good idea. yeah, right.

now here i am outside in the cold night air with a stream running next to me,a lamp light making my paper clear. coffee, donut, sprained wrist, confused head. it's happened again. same old thing. i feel like im suppose to choose aliance - between gender, the boys i love and the girls i know who think my boys are fuck ups. who've been fucked over by my boys. i feel condemned again. like they dont understand that my experiance could be different than theirs. that what was bad for themcould be good for me. i didnt know how to talk about it. i told half truths because i dont even know the whole truth. i say one thing and then it feels all wrong. i didnt want my perspective to invalidate my girl friends experiance. so i told half truths, all simplified. i said 'i like fucked up boys. i like weird dynamics all out in the open and clear. i like being the aggressor. i like boys who dont want anything from me so i dont get sucked in to taking care of them.' i didnt say 'i tell my boys when i think things are fucked up, when im confused and dont get whats going on, i bring it up. i tell them what i want.' i didnt say any of that because i thought it would look like i was blaming the girls for the ways they were fucked over. because, yeah, i think they were fucked over. but i dont think my boys are fuck ups. not exactly

i think they're sweet tough boys, and that's exactly what i want. i'm sick of talking everything through. i'm sick of boys telling me all their problems i don't want to help them through all their shit. I'm sick of boys hiding their fuckedupness behind accepted language. my tough boys, they are not so afraid of hurting me that they lie about how they feel. and the ways they are demand that i be strong enough to ask difficult questions, and be ready for their crazy answers. "do you like kissing me?" i said. and he aaid "well, sometimes, for a little bit. but then it starts to feel weird". this answer, yeah, it would have destroyed me 5 years ago, but now girl, now it makes me laugh.

my sweet tough boys make me stronger. i can swear at them and punch them, laugh at them when i think they're dumb. i can say exactly what i think. i can hunt them down and rest my head on their shoulders. tackle them from across the room, say 'i walked all over town looking for you'. my face can light up when i see them. and they take it just for what it is. dont read into it, dont freek out scared. they dont try and figure out how i feel. dont push me for more words. if i have something to say, i need to make myself say it. ididnt use to be able to, nope. and i dont thing there was anything wrong with that. nothing bad about helping eachother learn to say what we need to, build confidence, feel strong.

so yeah, here i am, cold coffee, aching hand. i know what i want. i want relationships that take my strength for granted, andi dont want to have to explain why this good for me. i want to fuck and play with power. pull hair. hold eachother down. i want to lick my sleeping angels eyelids and have my heart break just watching him sleep. i want to talk about sex. i want to blow the lid off the whole closed up subject. have conversations like where one person says "it creeps me out when i'm fucking someone and it seems like they dont even care who i am. i could just be any old girl. it makes me feel like shit". and the other person says "i can see how that would totally be fucked up. but you know, i like that. i like feeling annonymous sometimes. it turns me on." i want to talk about sex and not feel judged
~~i want to explore out differences in experience and desire, and learn from~~
~~i want to talk about sex and not feel judged and fucked up. to explore~~
~~differences~~

~~i want to talk about sex and not feel judged and fucked up.~~

~~that instead of it being dev~~

~~that instead of it being divicive~~

i want to explore our differences in experience and desire, amd learn from that instead of it being divisive.

on nights like this i let my dog take me for a walk through the 3am streets.

i follow her. i look at peoples porches. there's logs for my wood stove, hanging plants for my sisters window. a chair for mydesk. i dont take any of it. my body is bruised and sprained from an angry game of basketball. ~~my beautiful earthquake girl is mad at me.~~ nights like this, anna drags me around town. i always think what we really need is some calm house. someplace with a clean kitchen, full shelves, a big back yard and calm. but me and my dog, we end up seeking out chaos. tonight she takesme to the boarded up house. we haventbeen there in a year, but she runs up to the door like it's home. she loved that place, packed with people and puppies and rats with missing limbs. that'swhere i went when charlene died. i crawled into a loft and woke up my matching body friend. i swear every month that i'll break back into that house and takephotos of the murals for my boat girl. my dog wants back in there. she wants a room full of up all night punks. buttonight the house is empty and so is the park.

there's this one guy who's at the park a lot. this older guy who sits over by himself and spends all afternoon yelling out sports scores. sometimes they're current scores, sometimes they're scores from 20 years ago. he never talks to anyone, but he'll yell all the information about every sports hero you ever heard of. he knows everything. I'd never seen him anywhere but in the park until this one day when i was walking around downtown with my dog, it was 5:00 and the streets were swarming with people, and all of a sudden, before i even saw him, i heard his sports-caster voice yelling out "and there's the dog that loves to play ball"! my stepdad would love the guy.

• • ♡ • • •

i've been thinking lately about family stories, and how few stories i know. there's great grandma bessie bell. all i know about her is that she was horrible and mean and strongheaded. and that she saved this tree in northern minnesota. it's this huge old pine tree on the side of this kinda back road. its all knarled and twisted and old, and everyone in thefamily is proud of it. whenever we'd drive by it someone would point and say "there's bessiebell's pine". see...back in her days they were just starting to put in power lines or telephone lines or something and they were going to cut down that tree to make room for them. but bessiebell, she went out there every day and climbed up into it and just sat there, wouldnt budge. and the powerline people, there was nothing they could do. they had to give in to her.

they had to cross the road with the power lines, and cross back to the other side of the tree.

i have driven by That tree a million times and have never once gotten out of The car to touch it's base.

dad

there's my dad's story. when he was a kid and sick of his little brother always comming into his room without asking. so my dad put this hammer up on thetop of his door frame, ballanced there. then his mom called him down to dinner. he snuck out carefully, but then completely forgot it was there. after dinner he went charging back into his room and the hammer came crahing down right on top of his head. knocked him right out.

MOM

my mom and her sisters locked their youngest sister out on the back padio when their parents were gone. the sister pushed and pushed on the glass door, trying to open it, until the glass shattered and her arms want right throughit. blood everywhere, through the back room into the kitchen, filling the kitchen sink, out the frontdoor, they all piled into the car and took her to the hoppital, and when my mom's parents got home, all the girls were gone. all that was there was this trail of blood.

all the stories i know are heroic feats and great mistakes. and i know these are the kind of stories that are suppose to get told. but somehow i hope, when i have new family to tell stories to - like my sisters kids or something - that i give them something more. sure i want to tell them the heroic stuff, tearing down the fbi fence, spending the night in the student occupied university but i want to get the small stuff in there too. riding broken bicycles, writting poetry on walls with chalk. finding pizza in the dumpster and drinking coffee until you cant stand it any more. i want to tell them about the amount ofstuff in my bed. library books and wigs, my bass, my belt, all my clothes. dirty dishes, toast crumbs, my 90 pound dog, tapes and rubberbands. notebooks, letters and me. once i saw a photograph of my mom. twelve years old with jeans and cowboy boots. sitting on a fence and staring straight into the camera. sometimes i think this picture is the only thing i know about her childhood. and its kind of amazing to me, that i have no idea how my family lived.

cheese bread

•

i use to be really addicted to this cheese bread that was made at this bakery in montpelier. it was like a big braided loaf of soft white dough with some sort of creamcheese junk all braided into it. its hard to explaine, buttherewas somthing crazy about this bread, and sometimes, even though they made weekly deliverys of the stuff to the store in plainfield, i'd find an excuseto go to montpelier just so i could stand in the bakery and look through their fresh baked racks of cheesebread. i'd pick out theloaf witht he most cheese in it and eat the entire thing in the car on the way home. every time it made me feel sick.

SICK SICK SICK

•

it was one of those days, i wason my way back from the bakery, wh en i picked up john derry hitchhiking. i'd never seen him before in my life, but he had one of those stylie haircuts that came up close around the back of his head except for one little peice hanging down the side. it was a stylie haircut that had been out of style for years. so i pulled over. he talked in this quick, articulate way, and was really really polite. he introduced himself and all that. and his way of talking was that kind where at first you dont think you understand at all, but a second later all the words catch up to you so that right as youre asking him to repeat himself, you know exactly what he said. he was going to plainfield too he told me, his friend's sister lived there and he was going to meet the both of them and wander around town. he'd never been to plainfield before. he moved his hands when he talked and made more facial expressions than i'd ever seen anyone make in my entire life. he made me a little nervous. i thought he was probably nuts. see, i had this theory about vermont. it has pretty much the best mental health services of the entire country. there's tons of halfway houses. and i pretty much thought that everyone i met either lived in a halfway house or, if the were old enough, had done too many drugs in the 60's. john derry was too young and to quick to be a drug casualty. all of a sudden, out of the blue, he goes "where's your dog today?" i had no idea how the hell he knew i had a dog, and i must have looked at him with some sort of nervous shock because he laughed and said "there's dog hair covering your entire interior". and it was true. my car was covered with dog fur. there was probably enough fur in there to build a whole new dog. we drove in to plainfield. "that house", he said. it was my house. "who's your friend's sister?" i asked. "Casey."

•

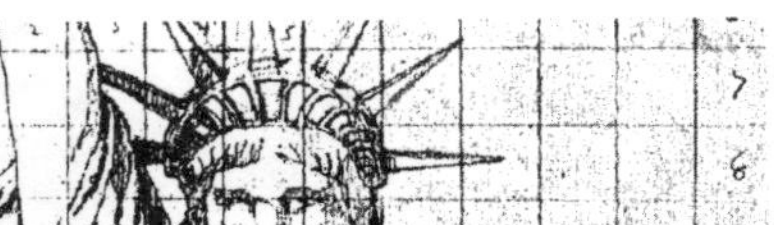

casey

casey and i both moved into the river house around the same time. i lived in the upstairs poarch floor with my genious inventor friend peter and a couple other folks who sort of came and went (my sister even lived there all summer! yes! my sister!) casey lived in the basement apartment with her smoochcat gerard. gerard and casey both knew how to make any small scrap something beautiful and huge, only gerard was more quiet and shy about it than casey. when i first moved to plainfield i had a huge crush on gerard. i use to stand under his window at night looking up at his miles davis poster in the window and i'd half hope that he would somehow know i was there and come down to seeme. i half preyed that he wouldnt. the two of them lived in the river house now with timmy, the irish mandolin player, and scardy, the hermit crab. Megan, little megan, lived on the ground level apartment and a crazy suicidal women who we didnt know lived in the attic. she was always comming home with broken legs.

before the river house i moved every three months or so,from one shack to another. from a doomed roomate to a doomed relationship to the middle of the woods and back. i had plainfield covered. but for some reason, the river house held me there. when i picked john derry up, i'd been living there a couple months and casey and mewere just starting to be friends. i'd go down to her apartment and we'd make mashed potatoes and talk about cake. i'd alwys wanted to be friends with her. she was six feet tal andhad a copy of tom jones singing that prince song Kiss. she had thirty small figureines of the statue of liberty, and she always refered to statue of liberty as "the lady". one time she told me a story about her friend lee. i'd met lee a couple times but hardly knew him. the story went something like this:

7-11

you know how you're suppose to get a car for your sixteenth birthday or something like that. well, fucking lee did. and so him and his best friend go out to drive it all around town. first thing they did was go to the seven eleven. lee pulled into theparking lot, pulled right up to the store, went to step on the brake only hit the gas instead and they drove striaght into the store, right through that huge glass window. everything was flying everywhere all the customers were loosing their minds screaming, lee's friend was freeking out, the manager or someone ran through all the broken glass, right up to their car, yelling his brains out. but lee, he just rolled down the window of his car, stuck his head out a little bit, and said "can i have a Slurpee?"

the river house

the river house was perfect in so many ways. we all lived in the same house but were seperate enough that we didnt want to kill eachother all the time. it was a quiet looking house, but everything happened there. each floor was good for different things. casey's floor was good for inspiration. there was junk everywhere, a big pile of wood and metal and bits of statues outside the front door. magazines and paper, paint and glue. and a good kitchen for baking cake and drinking coffee. it was just right for early evening. you could sit out on the front stoop and watch the river slink by and listen to timmy and william and josh play bluegrass. you could climb through the back yard bushes onto peter's paddle boat and take it up the river for a sunset spin. megans floor was good for late at night, when it was pitch black outside and about once every hour a car would pass by and lights would shine through her window. we'd stay up late, drinking tequila and taking polaroids. we were on a mission to break polaroids out of their traditional role as family snapshots. and boy, did we ever. megan and i had tried to be friends a few years earlier when neither of us were doing all that great. we'd sit up on this hill by the highway and talk about our fucked up relationships. i'd say "everything's falling apart. i keep fucking up and i dont know what i'm doing wrong. i suck". she'd say "hmmm. i have the opposite problem. my boyfriend sucks". or it was something like that. she told me about her phobias. like she was scared her car was going to blow up, and every time she drove it she had to stop every ten minutes and look under the hood to make sure it wasnt on fire. by the time we lived in the river house, she was over that. we'd meet at her apartment at night. she'd gotten an entire case of this crazy candy peanut brittle stuff from some weird contest. we'd eat it until we were more wired than we could stand and then we'd pile in her car and drive to burlington to go dancing. megan was suprising. she looked sweat. like she'd always been this sweat, small, curly haired clean slothes beautiful girl. but she had stories and stories about living in l.a. and getting all drunk and fucked up and how her friends would just throw her out the car door on to her parents lawn. she taught us the L.A. dance. cigerette in one hand, drink in the other. you stand still, just moving your head slowly, checking out everyone in the room. she had that dance down.
um. right. so then there was my floor

my floor of the river house was sort of early afternoon. there was room to stretch out and make plans and sit in the sun. the front porchlooked down onthe main street. we knew everyone who walked by. paula would walk by with stacks of mail in her arms, on the way to the postoffice. jody would come flying down the street and flash us her tits. everyone waved at us. my floor was where we came when the gulf war started. we made collages and fliers and tried to figure out what the hell to do. we stole flags. they were plastic. so we spraypainted duh on them and layed them down in the street. we made a giant cake that said fuck you george bush on it, and passed out peices at the cold, windy demo. we took over some government guy's office. but really, we knew none of that was enough.

and then it happened. the moves came. megan moved out to a new house down the street. then casey and gerard left. they went to mexico, and gerard left me all his books. books and books and books. more books than you can imagine. the plan was he'd write me and tell me which ones to send to which new towns he'd be in. he couldn't really bear to just pack them up. and he couldn't possibly bring them with him. but here's what i was trying to get to, okay. John Derry moved in to the basement.

i never really got to know john derry all that well and i have no idea how he ended up in vermont. he'd been a bell hop for awhile, and he fit that image perfectly. he was courteous. courteous to the hilt. he shaved his eyebrows to a thin pointed slant, and changed his name to fit his job. when he was in cooking school his name was basil. when i knew him he was a farmer. john derry. he was the cleanest guy you've ever seen, and if you've ever known anyone who worked on a farm, or even gardened for that matter, you'd know his cleanliness was impossible. he'd spend all day out there in the fields, digging in dirt. then he'd come home and spend hours scrubing. two hours at least. getting every speck of dirt off his ankles and out from underneath his fingernails. he had a picture of lenin as a baby in a locket he kept on his dresser, and when he left plainfield, he moved to holland to become a tulip farmer. on days like this, when the tulips are just starting to open up to the sun, i wonder about that boy, and i wonder if he's out there in those flower fields.

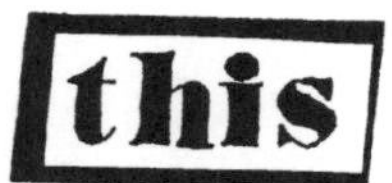

this city

sometimes i cant believe i live in a city. where's the smell of pine trees? mountains, wide fields and open sky? in vermont i would walk home in the pitch black night to my tree house. and sometimes it was so dark i couldn't even see the path. i'd have to look up and see where the tree tops parted to the sky. that's how i found my way home. following the sky path. now i walk on concrete, pavement, median strips. but i love it here. i love watching Pacific Bell guys climb the telephone poles with their big spiked boots. and the welders underneath the bart train tracks, in their yellow body sutis and big face masks. sparks fly everywhere and there's this purple and yellow glow. i never thought i would like it here, bbut i do. i like how there is city, but after midnight it's like a small town. i mean, not exactly, but sort of. like tonight, walking home from my uncles house, meand my dog on the back streets. we hear a gun shot,and then 4 blocks later someone opens their door when we walk by "be careful out there", the man says "i heard a gun". yeah, me too, i say. but im not worried. with my dog i am invincable. on shattuck i see the same guys i always see on shattuck. i dont know them, but they're familliar in that small town kind of way. and down a few blocks, my friends are out drinking tea and smoking cigerettes in ther truck. then down to adaline, 3 punks walking down the middle of the road. "what are doing" i yell. and one of them answers "going to eat oatmeal". one time i was walking through the empty downtown streets. 2am, eating donuts and drinking coffee, and my earthquake girl ran up behind me. it was before i knew her, really, and we decided to have our own 24 hour coffee shop that night. we went up to my house, made coffee and sandwidhes, loaded my shopping cart up with a folding table and chairs and candles. wheeled it all down the street to the corner and set it up. drank coffee all night there on the dark street, at our own table, talking an d writing until sunrise.

i love my friends here. how i came to this town withmy sister and we just hid out, made friends slowly. and they're the right kind of friends. the kinds i dont need to talk to all the time. i can show up at that house by the tracks and just sit on the floor, making art out of their garbage and writting letters. i can go by carolyns and, of course, neither of us ever get enough sleep, so we tell eachother our plans and then fall into nap. i can stop my marcs and pace around his room while he draws, and every on ce and awhile we mumble something at eachother. i love comming home and finding ian asleep in my bed, waking up to kyle knock ing at my door. i love how this town swings around crazy just like my moods one week everyone is here and there is too much to do, i cant figure out how to cram it all in. and the next week, my sister is gone, aaron and kyle and ian are gone. all thats left is me and my dog. carolyn, marc, and the house by the tracks.

one night me and aaron were riding bikes, 2am, with logs under our arms for my wood stove. we saw the lights behind us. cops pulling us over on our bycyles. 'is there a problem officer' i said. and he mumbled, in that low voice of authority 'we couldnt tell what you had there under your arm'. 'it's a log' i said, and he looked like he had never heard the word. had no idea what i was talking about. 'logs. for my wood stove'. he hasseled us a little, and then left, still confused.

upstate

it's kind of suprising to me that i've never been to jail or even harrased by cops much. there was one time, me and my sister were driving back from vermont. me and my sister and the dog and all my sisters wordly possessions loaded up in my falling apart car. we ran out of gas in the middle of the night in the middle of nowhere. and i was delerious from lack of sleep. we left anna in the car with the window cracked. 'guard the stuff' we told her, and she wagged her tail, happy to do just that. caty and me, we walked down the deserted freeway, looking for an off ramp, an open gas station. but we'd only gotten a mile or tow when cops stopped behind us. 'our car ran out of gas', i explained. the cop put his hands on his loaded hips. 'ooh', he said, all knowingly and smartassed. 'so that's your car back there'. 'yeah'. 'so that was your dog we had to shoot'. my jaw hit the ground. there were no words in me, i couldn't say a thing. i could picture how it happened, one of the cops reached in the window, anna bit him, the other cop shot her. 'you didnt' caty said. he paused a long time and then shrugged 'no'.

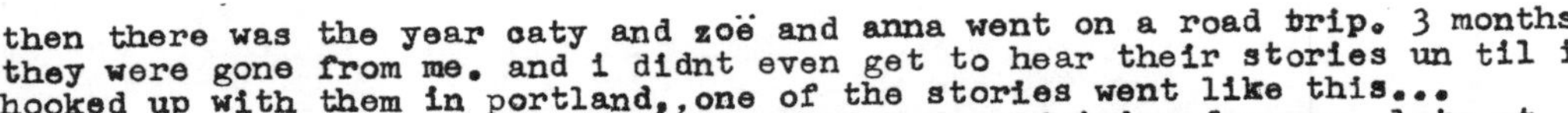

then there was the year caty and zoë and anna went on a road trip. 3 months they were gone from me. and i didnt even get to hear their stories un til i hooked up with them in portland,,one of the stories went like this...

caty and zoë had been driving forever, late at night through louisiana, and not a single gas station was open. they drove and drove until finally they were almost out of gas and they couldnt go any further. they pulled the car into a gas station parking lot, decided to wait there until it opened. but before to long, cops came to check them out. caty and zoë explained their situation, and the cop grumbled and glared and told them they couldnt park there. they'd have to come with him down to the sherifs office and they could wait in the police parkinglot until morning. morning was still a ways away, and the car was too cramped to sleep in, so they opened the car doors, set up their tarp, and fell asleep out there on the pavement. two freek girls sleeping in the sherrif's parkinglot. when they woke up, groggy, there was a new cop on duty. he couldn't believe they'd been sleeping out there. 'i thought you were just sitting out there talking. if i'd known you were sleeping i'd have invited you in. there's a couple empty beds in the jail. you could have slept in the jail instead of out there in the parkinglot. i just didnt know you were sleeping. sorry. do you want some coffee?' it was all a little too much for the girls. luckly they dont drink coffee. they hightailed it out of there.

its not about any of this shit, this bright hair of mine, this cat collar around my ankle, the thick green and oragne of my jacket. its not about the way i sit slouched on the sidewalk, metal through my body, ink in my skin. its not about any of that.

its the way we dance strong and fast, climb buildings and fences and scream when we want to. the way we carry eachother home, sleep next to each other with our faces covered. its every small genious thing we do. words we put down in pencil, in paint, scratched into cement. all we need built out of rusty bolts, old car parts, bottles and milk crates. its sleeping in the rafters with a door for a bed. stealing pianos off front poarches. swimming in cold toxic water because your dead friends ashes are somewhere in there.

its about how we can learn everything from each other which trains to take, how to play this guitar and this violin, how to break in, break things down, wire them back up the way wewant them. its being awake when everyone else is asleep, looking in their windows, running through the streets, walking seven miles to the next town for coffee, building bonfires in closed down landfills and having enough time to want everything.

i know a boy with his toothbrush around his neck. i know a girl who always spits on her shoes. i have a teeshirt that belonged to my great grandfather. i have a patch that someone made me. its these small things that hold us together. these invisable things they dont see.

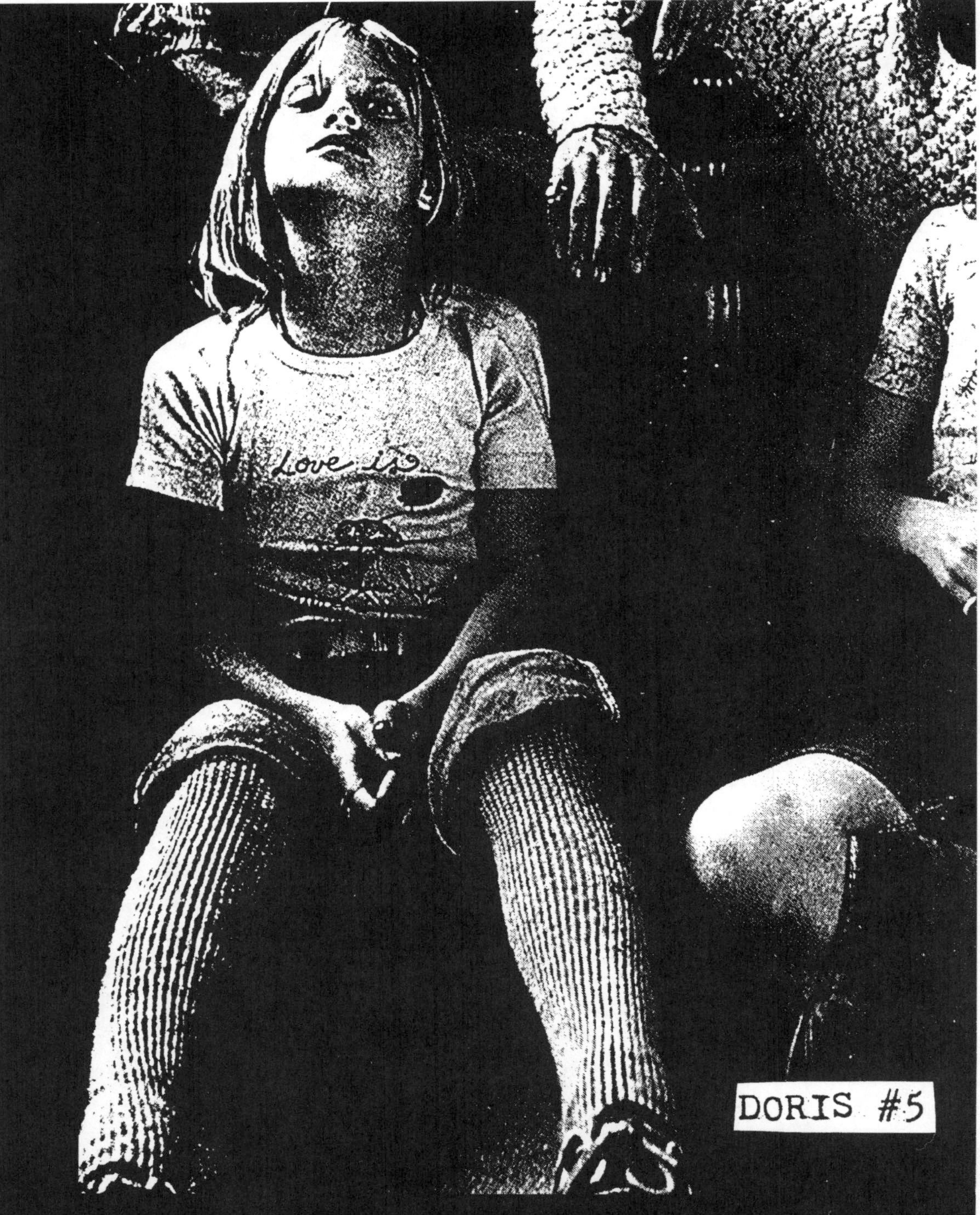
Love is
DORIS #5

This is Doris #5, typed up in the hot days and cool nights of late summer, where the cats hide under parked cars to keep cool and I ride my bike barefoot with brakes that fail constantly so that each intersection I come to, I prey to make it through.

Me and Marc, we walk down to the Ranch House for afternoon breakfest and dig through allthe big trash on the way home. I have a table and small shelves and a book all ballanced on my head. He is carrying a VCR that I'm sure is broken. And he says to me something, something about my sad life. and I think it's strange, you know. Because I'm one of the happiest people around. 'you think I have a sad life?' I say to him. And he sighs at me 'yeah girl, you have buckets of sorrow coming off you all the time'. And I guess he is right. I just didn't think anyone would notice.

So yeah, I've been blue lately. That set deep into my jawbone kind of sad that I don't know how to get rid of. And it doesn't help that my wisdom teeth need to get pulled and hurt like hell. I've been looking for distraction and forgetting to do all the secret things I usually do. Like getting coffee to go and holding it in my hand while I ride fast down University and listening to the way the wind blowing over the coffee cup lid makes this strange whistling noise.

Somehow it's autumn already, and I'm typing this up in the cold wind. This is Doris. about secrets and strangers and sidewalks and shoe shops. Big cars and small wishes and as much as I can fit. Abrupt endings because that's the way things are these days.

this issuehas a story by my uncle in it. its the one about the truck and the broken arms The back cover and this drawing here are by Zeb, who holds my head in his hands when he greats me. so thanks to them and to paula and wade and my sister and aaron who are all consistant even when I'm not. You can write to me: Cindy Gretchen O. PO Box 4279, Berkeley CA 94704. and if you are looking for back issues, you can send 1.50 in money or foodstamps or stamps or whatever for #4 or for numbers 1&2 together.

1995

kansas or kalamazoo

I love sitting on the corner, the cement church steps drinking my coffee cold from the long trip across the bay. and watching the girl walking up with her hair bigger than her big healed shoes. and the city bus goes by, the one that says "to Kansas". I know it's a street, not Kanasas for real, but I think forget work I'm getting on that bus to see where it takes me. and it takesme somewhere but not the Kansas I've been before when i was still a girl kid tomboy not aware of my body except my skinnyness and my new shiny gold through my ears. In Kansas we made gingerbread houses and Beth took me on a horse and buggy ride. You know the ones where you ride huddled under a thick wool blanket and watch the street lights pass by you like each one is the moon. and the leaves fall fast and people rake em up quick. We use to live across the street from a family who had only evergreen trees. no maples or birch, or aspen or oak. No piles of leaves, no kids to jump in the piles. So we use to sneek them big bunches of leaves, when it got dark out we'd bring over some of ours. They never said anything about it, but the leaves never stayed in their yard for more than a day. Maybe they blew away, we thought and we'd bring them more. We lived by train tracks then and I leared to wiggle my ears.

Today Caty found a 5 dollar bill, laying there flat on the sidewalk like it was a trick. 5 dollars and Carolyn. and when I came home on my bike with my basket full, the girls were there in the kitchen eating toast like we use to and my sister, she handedme a piece half eaten with peanut butter.

If you take peanut butter and mix it with a little honey and crumple lots of Ritz crackers into it and mix it good. Then you take a big pinch and roll it between your palms until it's a ball.That is agood snack. It'll gross your mom out. You can lock yourself in the bathroom and take everything out from under the sink. Plug the sink with the stopper and pour alittle of everything in. Toothpaste and bleach andhairspray and perfume and shampoo. This you can do for hours. It's agood distraction.

I want to find arecord player with aneedle that works. a chello and an old trombone. I want to slide a red sled down a long hill of snow. Or even a small hill and refridgerator box would do. Cause when I think of snow I dont think big hills. I think prairie. flat roads, long horizon. and I want to go to Kansas or Kalamazoo. Somewhere where farm houses sit there freezing in the wind. you can almost see them move and no one ever comes out, hardly. I've been over to that side of the Mississippi once already this year, but standing here on Kansas street in the hot sun and people in busses, it feels like so long ago already, and so far away again, and like I went there, sort of, but there was something I missed. Something small maybe, I'm not sure, but something none the less.

I went to this college onee. it was really fucking weird. This tiny school called Goddard and I was there for a year and a half. There were only about 60 students all together and it was suppose to be super radical, and in a way it could have been. like the students decided what classes were going to be off ered and had a lot of say in running the school or whatever, and clases were very student centered. and that, really, is where the problem was. cause by the time i got there the school was basically going under and they'd stoped trying to recruit older students who knew what they were doing and had some sort of direction, and they were pretty much just recruting anyone they could find. especially if they were young and had money i guess. I wasnt recruited. I found it all on my own, And I drove my big white studabaker full of stuff all the way to vermont before I was even sure I was getting accepted to the school. The floor boards fell out somewhere in upstate newyork, but I still made it.

The place was pretty much a disaster but I lovedit. Half the buildings were old farm buildings and really beautiful in this noncollegit way. And the dorms were these small houses. They were actully totally crappy and I think they were built as temporary structures. That's what everyone said anyway, they were built in the late 60's and were only suppose to last 10 years. but it had been 20 years and they were still all there.

They stuck us new students in one dorm together and we were all pretty confused and lost and fumbling around. Then Zen moved in. He had been at Goddard for a couple years, so a bunch of us figured maybe he knew what was up. I didnt think so. I mean, he had this horrible personality and he woke up at 6am and walked down the hallway on his way to the shower singing "Dont Worry, Be Happy" really really fucking loud, every morning. I wanted to kill him. But he himself thought he knew exactly what was up at the school and so people listened to him. He said the place was totally corrupt and there needed to be immediate action. Students had been trying for years to get things changed throught the traditional channels and it wasnt working so it was time, he said, for a student takeover! There was this one guy, Dan, who right away became Zens sidekick. They were completely serious about everything they were doing, and started wearing black and redarmbands, no joke. All the new kids were pretty rialedup, I was even going to join their mad scheme cause it kind of seemedlike the thing to do, but all the older students ignored Zen andDan, and as the days passed they both started to seem more and more paranoid and self important and deluded, and I started to get pretty suspicious of the whole thing.

So then the really crazy thing happened. They decided it wastime to type up their demands and sort of pres ent them to campus, right. But they were having this typing problem. See, their electric typewritter needed athree prong outlet and

their rooms only had twoprong outlets. and they didnt have an adaptor. They only 3prong outlet in the whole dorm was in the common room. They were worried but they got an idea. They calledall of us around and said it wasup to us to protect them while they typed. To stand guard against anyone who might try and come in and stop them.

They were actully serious. It was done in dead earnest. They carried the typewritter out all ceremoniously and put it on the table in the corner, then in a frantic whirlwindthey grabbed every chair and peice of furniture in the room and piled it around the table. Barricaded themselves into the corner. "Bring your bedframes!" Zen yelled, "they will never stop us from typing!" and he raised his clenched fist.

They typed all night and b y the morning their demands were complete. Five pages ranging from "full student access to goddard financil records"(which we already had) & "make Lisa accountable for the bra she bought on Goddards charge card" to "Free Nelson Mandella" and "End Homelessness in America". It was all typed in capital letters with lots of exclamation points and it was basically impossible to read. The next night, Dan andZen and about 5 new students all broke in to the administration building and barricaded themselves in, armed with fire

extinguishers. And if anyone came near them, they got squirted. They said they wouldnt come out until every single demand was met. So for days and days the administration building was occupied and classes were canceled to deal with the situation even though these was really nothing that could be done. Eventually they came out. I'm not sure why. Obviously their demands weren't met. I guess

maybe they just got hungry. My friend Peter told me later that when the whole occupation happened he had been working in the cafeteria. And one day Dan called down to the kitchen and Peter answered. Dan said "The revolutionarys are hungry, could you bring us up some snacks?" I guessPeter didnt think the revolution was feuled on snacks and he refused.

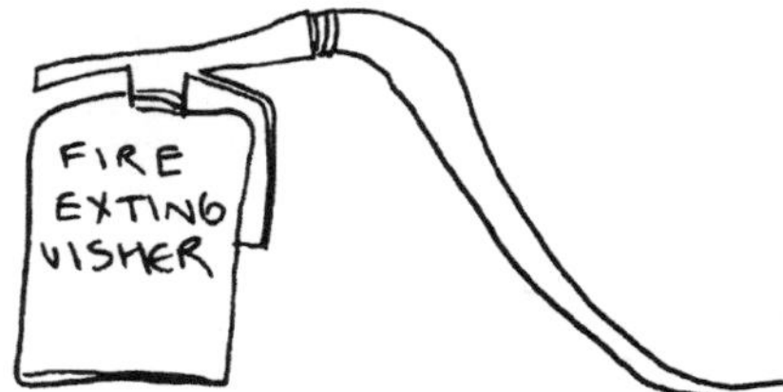

beds & doorframes

That first semester I spent all my time with Chuck and Mark and we were always trying to come up with new ways to destroy eachothers lives. Well, really, it was me and Chuck trying to destroy Mark and then him getting his meager retaliation. It started out pretty harmless. Kind of this weird bed obsession. See, you could take the beds apart a little, take the top part off and ballance it on the legs so when you get in bed the whole thing collapses. We all did that to eachother just about every night, it seemed.

When we didn't do that, we'd take Marks bed out of the room, put it in the common room or the front lawn or dining room. It was realy excessive and for that reason alone, it was funny. We made a pact to stop this taking apart bed business and then we took his door off the hinges. If he ever tried to make friends other tha n us, we thwarted it by comming into his room when he had them over, and sneeking by and removing every peice of furniture from the room while they tried to ignore us. When he was out of town for a few days I attempted to fill his entire room with crumpled newspaper.

Mark got back at us by throwing fireworks under the bathroom stalls when either of us were in there, setting our clock ahead so we'd wake up at 7am and think it was 11 and we were really late. He emptied our sugar box and filled it with salt. Ruined our afternoon coffee. That really took the cake and something serious had to be done. I came up with a new game. It was a sort of contest. A diving on the bed contest. So when Mark came home from class I was all "Hey! We're having a jumping on the bed contest! Check it out!" and I ran through my doorway and dove onto my bed. He got excited all according to plan. had a minute hesitation 'You didnt take apart my bed, did you?' 'of course not. we made a pact. remember?' right, he said. But what I didnt tell him was that while he was awayI had taken his mattress off and hidden it, so all that remained of his bed was blankets and a board. He didnt notice. He got a running start, half way down the hall he started at, and by the time he reached his doorway he was full speed flying and there was nothing I could do. He dove flat onto that board. clunk. shit. I almost felt bad about his bruises. Mark had always been a good sport, but I guess he decided this called for some real action. He consulted Bobby. Bobby was one of the older students and the toughest kid drunk on campus. Bobby said 'seal them in'. And when Chuck and me woke up the next morning we couldnt get out of our room. There was spray foam insulation filling the cracks of the door. No way out. But Mark, dang, the guy actully didnt have a bad bone in his body. He left the windows unsealed, against Bobbys instruction, and when we realized that, we just climbedout.

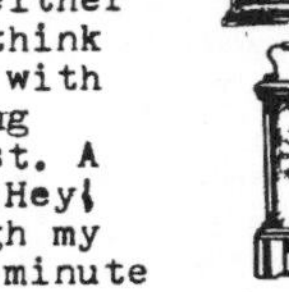

a couple semesters later, Chuck was gone and I was living with Bobby. Actully I was suppose to be living in this house in town, but the girl I lived with was really weird, she put dirty dishes in the cupbords and told me the most tragic stories of her childhood and I didnt even know her really. There was this giant dog that lived in that house with us, and it would chew up everything while we were gone and then cry the most loudest, most horrible noises as soon as it heard us at the door, cuz he was afraid he was gonna get beat. I guess its old owner was a total fuck. anyway, the place was miserable, so I mostly stayed at Bobbys. He lived in the fuckup dorm, a house full of boys, and we were all like one big fucked up family somehow. I'd wake them up every Saturday morning at some insane hour and make them watch cartoons on the TV that hardly got any reception and we made coffee, the kind that eats your guts right out, and made poptarts. There was this one kid, Shawn, and he was the worst of the bunch. I mean, not the worst fuck up, but just a pretty rotten person in general. He was one of those types that's just into being contraversial for no good reason, and he was always talking about how he was a young Republican. even had young republican convention stationary. He buged me. He was into snowboarding. And one morning he was up early to go hit the slopes, and on his way out he yelled something, some sexist shit. Well, that couldn't be allowed. And after he was long gone, me and bobby went into his room, turned everything upsidedown. the furniture, posters, everything we could find. We took all the lightbulbs out and opened the windows and locked his door. Then we split. The thing about Goddard is, no one locked their doors, and so no-one had keys. There were only two people on the entire campus who could let you into your room if for some reason you got locked out. Me and Bobby spent the night at my house, so we weren't even there when Shawn got home from the hospital at 3am with all the ligaments in both his legs ripped to shreds. He'd had a bit of a fall up on the hill, and he was totally screwed, just wanted to come home and go to bed. He inched his way up the stairs only to find his door locked, so he had to hobble all over campus looking for someone to let him in, and then there were no lights and the room was about 10 degrees below zero. Nobody thought it was funny at all except me and Bobby.

. end

bigcars smallwishes

lately i've been driving a car around. loud music with the windows rolled down. the same tape, one side and then the next. and the tape crackles when we come to a stop. i pick up my friends and take them around. stop here for a second chris says. and we wait. he comes out of some strange house, clean with his hair slicked back. that wasnt too long? he says, was it? i just wanted to take a shower quick.

i bring the car back to jason and he takes me cruising down to the lake. anna's head out the window. with the stearing wheel wide in his hands like that. ashing on the floor boards. singing along. i say lets go to castillito for a burrito. i wonder what it looks like tonight in el cerrito. one night me and my sister wanted icecream. 2am and jason climbs in the car. fast down to safeway he gets it for us. we leave town at midnight. cram everyone in the front seat cause the back shocks aren't so hot. drive to monterey and back. that car can take us anywhere. and then i try to leave the house to walk downtown for once, but the keys are handed to me and i drive. the roads are all one way and speed bumps i forget where i'm going. the turns come up too fast.

today i remembered my bike, and the hot sun and wind on my hands. i went to the places i'd been passing right by. houses my friends don't live in anymore, parks with drinking fountains and my favorite alley. i went to the sidewalk cafe. he was locking up the store for a minute to go getta case of soda, but he let me in. large coffee? yes. i hold the cup in one hand and ride fast up hill to the wet cement waiting there for me. i lost my sweatshirt but who cares. two post offices, the record store and the brick wall to sit on. the bricks in the shade are still hot from the sun and i could sit there forever watching the people walk by. the woman with her shoes that match her purse. the one with red sweatpants, limping her left leg. one guy stops next to me to fix his cassette tape that has come unwound. he winds it back up sitting in the doorway. his tape player is practically as big as my file cabinet and everyone in a ten block radius can hear his songs.

one time i did sit there forever. me and anna and nick and tom. i dont know how it started or why, but it was our duty. to sit there all day. we trapped who ever we could into our plan. sign this postcard. we said. get some coffee. no money, wait, we'll buy you some. 10 hours, and whoever crossed our paths wasn't allowed to leave. utreo tried and was bit by the dog. we had pizza delivered. drank coffee and then beer. center and shattuck. it was our wall alright.

today it was quiet: there was the girl who once stole me a big plastic C from the side of the Capri Motel, but she was sitting half a block away and i didnt see her until i was leaving. the other day that girl taught me dances. the shoppingcart and the lawnmower. i taught her the L.a. dance and a flailing one i forgot the name for. the other day was 8 years ago. my sister was here and we were doomed. looking for a new place to live and every phone call we made they said No Dogs Allowed.

. i even said anna was a retired seeing eye dog and still they said no. sorry but no. we were doomed, and my sister was leaving again. we were eating brownies down on sixteenth street. she said i don't know. maybe it could be fun. looking for a new place to live.   and you know what? all of a sudden it is. no explaining it, really. we are strange that way, my sister and me. and when we find a home i am going to get a desk lamp and she's getting a set of sheets.

but i know my desk will still be just milk crates and splintery wood and her bed will be still just a small piece of foam.

Don't Be Fulid!

This is what I have to tell you today. What ever you do don't be fulde You can be fulde by lots of things. Mostly Capidists and Goverment aficids. At school lots of people say theres freedom, but it may not seem like it, but your in an injust world.

First aball, capitalists fight over mony. Each store, school, factory, almost evreything you can think of is ownd. The schools want you to think that capitalisam is okay. They want you to think you should be ruld but it's not okay. This has been happining since god nose when. If it keeps up then evreyone will be without a home. Thats way I'm writing this flier because your parents probibly won't tell you. It's one of the resons why I'm telling you this. Thats why I'm an anarkist. Anarky means we will not be ruled.

CLASS WAR!

Title

Sometimes Portland was a warm kitchen & coffee & good friends & too much food & kids running past.

Watching Hanna dance & helping Abbey learn her letters. Skateboarding with Lelia through alleys.

I miss those kids and their mom. I don't even know how to explain it.

This here is a flyer Lelia made a few years ago to give to the other kids in her class. I sure hope she doesn't mind me reprinting it.

i use to hang out with these motorcycle boys. not the harly kind, but the kind that have old italian bikes and stuff that are always breaking down so they spend more time in some shitty garage than on the road, and motorcycle parts are always scattered everywhere. even in their beds. the kind who become heroin addicts and disapear. when i left minneapolis and left them behind, i was sorta bitter about it all and did my best not to think about them much. and i did a pretty good job at it too, cause when i did start thinking about them again i couldn't even remember anything we did except drink coffee and stare at their broken bikes. and i knew that couldnt be true. i couldnt have spent 2 years just drinking coffee and staring. but i couldnt really figure it out. and then one day i was sitting around with this new frined of mine. sitting around his warehouse not doing anything really. everyonce and awhile we'd hammer a few nails into some board. it was probably the slowest a loft has ever been built, but we were building it anyway. the place was full of junk and saw dust everywhere. and he was having a party there that night, kept talking about having to clean it up. and finally broke out a vacume, but instead of vacuming the sawdust off the floor he vacumed the walls. like it was perfectly normal. careful to get the dust out of the cracks in the guilded framed pictures, vacumed the seats off the chairs and the benches. and i just watched in amzement. yeah. cause that's how it was with those motorcycle boys. they had this storefront way out of the wayand it was gloomy and dark and tons of cockroaches. they had lots of big plans for it. like it had this huge basement andthey'd torn down the walls to make it just one big space. but then just piled the wall peices into the bathtub and left all the junk on the floors and no one ever went down there except to piss. we'd sit around and there was this one guy greg who'd sit over in the corner, cutting up paper and pulling on his beard. and he would come up with these amazing creations. like one time he took this kentucky fried chicken box and made this whole scene inside of it. you had to look through this tiny hole into the box and the hole was so small it was hard to focus on what was inside, but once you did, what was in there was a big butcher factory with slabs of meat against the walls and figures of workers with meat hooks and stuff standing around. and if you looked close enough you'd see bodies of naked women stuck in with the meat slabs on the walls. one time we were sitting around and it was like midnight or something and i said lets go to the airport, so we did. and we were standing around the airport watching the planes come in and the people come off the planes. shawns best friend in the world lived in newyork and the two of them were kind of obsessed with pop culture icons. so we're standing there watching a newyork plane come in and there, comming off the plane, was shawns best friends parents, holding a big lamp of elvis that was a gift from shawns friend to him. and it was crazy because you could tell the parents figured we knew they'd been in new york and were comming home on that plane and that we'd come to greet them. they just gave shawn a hug and handed him the lamp like it was no big deal. and we all just stood around andwatched like it was no big deal.

most days i'd walk down 31st. it was winter and there was snow everywhere and it almost made more sence to walk down lake street because at least that was a busy road and all the exhaust seemed to warm you up a little bit. but i walked down 31st, cold and wet and almost every day i'd run into the dog lady somewhere on that road. she was half bent over her two wheeled cart full of grocerys and blankets and stuff. if i was alone, on my way to work or something, she'd just pass by me without a word. but when Anna was with me she'd stop us both and try to pet anna's ears with her thin wrinkly hands and she'd ask me ten million questions. "what's her name?" "how old is she?" does she have any babys?" "where's her babys?" why won't you let her have babys?" "wheres her mother?" "do you go visit her mother?" see, at first i told her the truth. that my dog was fixed and would never have babies. and her mom lived ½ way across the country and we never went to visit. but she hated those answers and finally, after having to answer the same questions over and over every few days, my story started changing. i told her that Anna had 3 litters of puppys and they all lived with different familys in the neighborhood. they got together every night in the park. and my dogs mom? she lived just a few miles away and we went to visit her every weekend. the dog lady still asked the same questions every time i saw her, but now she walked away smiling instead of freting and sad disturbed. and there was something in me that toatally loved that woman. on days that i didnt see her, something seemed really amiss. It was the same way with Mumbles, the huge guy with a big beard who hung out in the little mall next door to the resturant i worked at. i would go to the mall after work and spend my tip money on photobooth pictures, and mumbles was always there, sitting at the deli with his cup of tea and staring a little too intently into space for a little too long, or lumbering over to the bookstore to look at the rows and rows of books, never once taking anything off the shelves. i didnt really have a name for him at that point, i'd never heard a word come through his lips, but i saw him all the time and was always trying to catch his eye, smile at him, give him some kind of acknowledgement because even though he was practically a giant, no one else seemed to notice he existed.

i dont know. the first time i saw him i thought he was this guy Bill Holm who stayed at my house when i was in 7th grade. Bill was a giant too, with a red beard. and when i met him i thought for sure he was some exfootball player, but it turned out he was just a poet, staying at our house to teach poetry in my stepdads school. he didn't seem to care that our house smelled like dirt and mold and catshit, and that the whole place was a mess except the kitchen. he sat himself down at the hopelessly out of tune piano that was sitting in the basement decaying, and hadn't been touched since christmas day when i was 9 and my parents told us they were getting divorced. me and my sister ran to the piano and played 'deck the halls" in duet, singing and yelling 'tis the season to be jolly' at the top of our lungs. i dont know why we still had that piano even, but Bill sat himself down at it and played the most amazing music I'd ever heard. And for the whole month he stayed with us I'd be woken up in the morning to that music.

Nothing had ever sounded so good to me. and every-thing was calm that month. Bill would cook us these crazy good dinners out of junk in our fridge and he read us stories with his voice booming and then quiet. he usually taught in this small highschool in southern minnesota, and one time, he told his class to write a poem about boxelderbugs and bring it back to class the next day. no one did it; they all wined and complained about how it was impossable to write about boxelder bugs. so to prove them wrong, Bill stayed up all night writting. came to school the next day with 100 poems and spent the hour reading every single one.

The winter of walking down 31st, when the dog lady and mumbles were around, I reread all of Bill's books, Prairie Days, Boxelder Bug Variations, and this book Coming Home Crazy that was about his year in China right before the Tienaman Squ Square stuff went down. I loved his books and I wanted to find him. Move down south to whatever small town he lived in, and somehow convince him to be my teacher. I needed a plan. Something concrete to get me out of that city I had moved back to. Because yeah, i had come home crazy too.

I had come home to a city after 3 years of country. I had come home to a city where there were people everywhere and I didn't recognize any of them. Thousands of strangers and I didn't know any more whether to smile or avirt my eyes. I had forgotten all the tricks of survival and all the tricks of numbing yourself enough to walk down the streets and stay sane. and really, sanity seemed rediculous. Kids were starving all over the place, women were locked up in their homes and beaten to submission. Soldiers back from the Gulf War were getting cancer like crazy and noone seemed to pay much attention. Barbie had come out with a new cearal, Ben and Jerry were giving 1% for peace, and thousands of black men were arrested and harrassed for the shooting of this one white cop. Yeah, and people were still walking around, sane. Like usual.

I've never understood crazy. What it is and who defines it. And why chatting at a coffee shop is fine and screaming on the street corner isn't. I had come home to Minneapolis after my Mom called me, crying and blurry and not making sence. I moved to the city and I'd go visit her. One day she'd be clear and calm and brilliant like usual, another she'd shake so hard she couldn't pick anything up without dropping it. And there were the days she spent crying in bed, not even able to get up. Her face swolen and hidden in her pillow. She didn't understand what was going on. Why, after all these years, all this stuff was coming up. Why she couldn't just keep putting it behind her. Maybe she was crazy, she said. She'd blur out half sentance that I had to peice together. She was sorry she hadn't protected me. Sorry we had to see my dad beat her. Sorry I had to see her like this. I should leave, she'd say, I should let her die.

i'd talked lots of people out of killing themselves. like this one guy who'd call me up and tell me one day that voices in his head were telling him to kill me, and the next day he'd call and say he had a gun to his head. there was my best friend who was always cutting herself, and the sad southern boy with wide eyes, and my mom, pleading with me. just let me do it, it would be alright. why are you making me stay alive? it's not worth it. -and yeah, what right did i have? i thought maybe I should stop trying to keep her alive

It was one of those days, with her face buried in the pillow, and I was tired of making sence of her words; Of her 'you wouldn't miss me. It wouldnt be bad, would it. Wouldn't it just be best if I didn't exist any more?' It took me 7 hours to get her out of bed and into some clothes. My plan was this; get her dressed up nice so she'll feel pretty, take her to the museum because she loves art; distract her, get her mind off it. But the skirt she picked out was too small and she could barly fit into it. Her shirt was buttoned all wrong and tucked in only part way. The mascara she put on the eyelashes of her swolen eyes was already starting to run. By the time we left the house she looked more insane than ever. I wished I'd just taken her out in her bathrobe.

i'll spare you the details of guiding her down the steps to the bench in the sculpture garden where she slumped into me and wouldnt even sit up. taking her to the shrink and the hospital we couldnt afford where they locked her up even though that wasn't what i wanted. I'll spare you those details cause this is what i was trying to get to. There, in the ward they hauled my mom away to, was Mumbles. and that's where i got to know him. mom was the only sane one there and mumbles was the quietest, in that room full of people screaming and lurking in the corners. Mumbles would stand, towering over us, and mumble his thick speech over and over about how he was getting out of there soon. in a week he'd be out in a week. and when he'd walk away my mom would look at me and laugh and say "somehow, i don't think he's right about that". mom grew to like him though, even though he was a little too intence and stood too close. she read him books to pass the time and tried to reasue him when he freeked out. i swear, she could have been mistaken for a staff member, not an inmate, if it wasnt for the way her hands shook. on the day they let my mom go, i was there, and mumbles came into her room, sad. "you look like my aunt lucy' he said, 'and my aunt jane and my aunt beth and my aunt lucy and my aunt jenie and my aunt beth and my aunt sarah and my aunt lucy and my mom" and with that he paused and let out a loud howl of a cry and yelled 'my mom is dead" and he started crying. my mom patted his shoulder and looked at me paniked and i led her away. 'he's not a bad guy8 she said, 'just a little loony" and she laughed. a few weeks after that, mumbles did get out, and i swear i saw him practically every time i left the house. he'd be at the mall when i went to work. if i went to kinkos he'd be lurching through the courtyard of the IDS. sometimes i didnt want to leave my apartment because i was afraid of running into him and having to think of that place where him and my mom had been. and sometimes i'd see him and want to befriend him. read him stories over tea like my mom had done. and i started to try and smile at him again. started to try and catch his eye. and one time i did. i caught his eye and waved. and i dont know if he just didnt notice me or if he was too distinguished to wave back.

escape

i had it all plannedout, my escape from portland. make some money quick. fix my car. pack everything up and drive down the coast til i found some small shack in some small town. just me and my dog and the wind and ocean and sand. i even had the perfect back up town in case i didnt find anything better. gibralter. this town where everything was plain and funny contradictions. big forests on a hill and clearcut. a giant G overlooking everything and this amazing donut shop with these painting on the wall that looked like bad normanrockwell paint by numbers, only they were selling for 50 bucks a peice. they had anual crab races there, and i'd been to one already. and they were pretty amazing. the whole town cramed into this one dirt parkinglot. on one end was this weird sectioned off ramp where people would stand and some guy would hand them crabs out of a big bucket and they'd shout out the names of their pet crabs and then race them down the ramp. on the other end was a crab fry. and everyone was eating crablegs at the picnic tables inbetween. there was this old deserted bar with a mural of casper the ghost fishing in a river and pulling up a beer mug full of frothy beer. i loved that town and thought maybe if i moved there i could get gerard to leave newyork and come live with me, cause his name started with a G.

so i had my escape planned out. the only problem was, i was in berkeley and i had to get back up to portland and i didnt want to go back. and then my sister called. 'i'm quitting shhool" she said. 'I'll be in portland in aweek." and i told her my plan and she said fine. some shitty ocean town where we would walk everywhere alone. yes. but everything went arye. my car had been totaled. smashed to bits while it was parked. but i didnt care. there was the plan. nothing to stop me. we'll hitch down thecoast. i said. we'll find a place to live. so we packed up our bags. with everything in them. campstove and food. sleepingbags and dogfood and clothes and paper and maps. and we walked with our packs and the dog, me and her, miles and miles to the first doomed on ramp where noone was going the fight way and it took forever just to get the shortest ride to some suburb on the outskirts of town. anywhere would be better than that ramp, i thought. and of course i was wrong. we stood forever with cars whooshing by with nowhere to stop even if they had wanted to. and it was doomed, caty knew it. we'd never find our new home this way. so we climbed ~~up the hill~~ to the dunkin donuts and i swear we were ther for 5 hours. making lists and new plans. trying to weigh everything and laughing at what was important:

one town had old friends. another this one really good dumpster. one town we'd never really been to so it had to be good. we were falling out ouf our seats from too many donuts and lives messed up and crazy. every hour i'd go to the payphone and call melissa to seeif she was home yet to see if she come get us and bring us back to the house we shared. the dunkin donuts regualrs eyed us suspiciously and the more we tried to talk quiet and sneeky about our new plans, the more our voices busted out loud at the most absurd sentances we could come up with. by the time melissa came and saved us, the list was gigantic and the dumpster town won.

remember cornfields

sometimes i think its weird, theway my friends move and move. never too long. trains and cars and bikes. on foot even. cover distance. newyork, chicago, canada, anywhere. and sometimes it seems crazy to me. how do they ever catch up to themselfes? all that weightlessness. all that distraction. i want to plant them and hold them in my room locked. and then it happenes to me. i start moving and its nearly impossable to stop.

i use to drive long and fast. i'd fly down the road for 24 hours. sleep a couple hours and drive more. i passed by all the towns. albany, syracuse, buffalo, cleveland, toledo, lacrose. i stayed right on the freeways. and on those trips, the only thing that was real was land. this huge sky and wide fields and so much emptiness that everything seemed possible. i dont know why, but with that much land it seemed like everything would be alright someday. i could stretch out my arms. sort everything out, calm and smooth in my head. drive for days down striaght roads. why stop? I'd get delirious and write long, complicated stories in my head and come up with amazing plans. and if my sister was with me i'd wake her up and make her write them down. like this one time i had been driving 20 hours and i was listening to the partridge family and i thought up themost amazing videos for a couple of thier songs. 'hey, wake up' i said, 'write this down'. one time, driving alone, i almost moved to cleveland. all my stuff was in my car and i had left vermont, couldnt go back, and i was going to minneapolis and wasnt sure i wanted to at all. i was driving and tired and comming up on cleveland. cleveland, i thought, sure. why not. and i meant to pull off. find myself a place to live there. but i passed right by the off ramp.

but this last time i drove i stopped. stopped everywhere it seemed. me and aaron passing by dusty shoe shops and wheelbarrow stores. in one town a blue haired old woman opened up her shop just for us. we were looking in the window and she unlocked the door from behind the closed sign and let us in. it was sheet music, and i wanted to buy some just to thank her and all, but i dont know how to read music. we stopped and walked for miles and miles looking for noone in particular and not finding them. drinking coffee and spliting up.

there are places i want to go to that i never do when i am at home. strange small museums. official looking buildings. movie theaters. they're all things i want to check out. i say i'm going to. i mean to. but i never do. so in ames thats what i tried to do. had coffee in the officialist looking building i could find.. went to the farm house museum. one of those places no one ever goes in. and when i walked in the door they looked at me confused. and when i walked out i felt guilty, like i'd stolen something.

maybe i had shoved the spinning wheel under my tank top, pocketed the hand sewn quilt. i went to this greenhouse. one of those ones with a big front room with a bench to sit on and a little waterfall surrounded by exotic plants. i sat there for a minute, but then shecked out the real greenhouse part. the part where they grow plants to sell or do something with. the rooms back there were weird. i mean, some of them were normal, full of spider plants and gereniums. but one room was just thousands of small pots of grass. one blade in each pot. and another room. it said 'no pesticides' on the door and when i walked in there were only a handfull of plants sitting on the tables. i left. there was no time for a movie. i found aaron again, on the path by the pond.

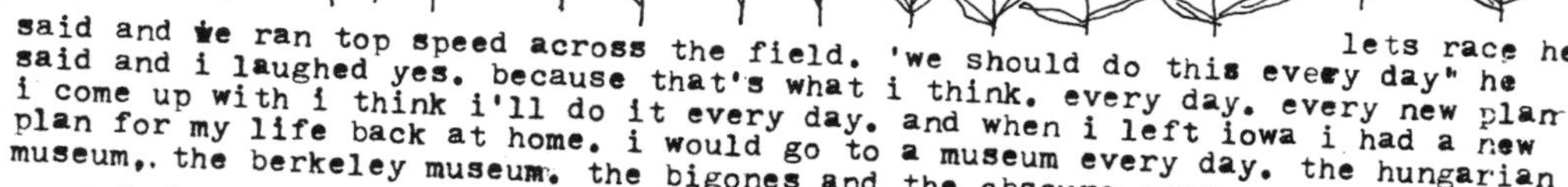

lets race he said and we ran top speed across the field. 'we should do this every day" he said and i laughed yes. because that's what i think. every day. every new plan i come up with i think i'll do it every day. and when i left iowa i had a new plan for my life back at home. i would go to a museum every day. the hungarian museum,. the berkeley museum. the bigones and the obscure ones. i would plan each day around getting to some weird part of town to go to some weird odd museum. and when i got home and told my sister this plan she laughed so hard she fell off the bed. and as it turned out, i never went to one museum. iwas restless. it was hard to stop moving. to stop long enough for everything i'd seen to catch up with me and make sence and settle in. i wanted to go again. i wanted to make casey move back to this continent and drag her down all the small highways of america, looking for rickety barn antique stores. her taking photographs, me doing interviews. i wanted to go back to lincoln because it seemed like the perfect place. when i was there and miserable, someone offered me a milkshake and then made it, while i sat on the kitchen counter. made it in the blender out of soymilk and crushed ice.

i wanted to go again, drive to southern states i've never even seen. red earth and deserts. but i stayed and waited for it all to catch up. and i'm still waiting. it's taking awhile.

vacation

i dont know how the fuck it happened but somehow i ended up in antigua. it was one of those family things, one of those vacation things and i knew way to much about antigua to be there as a tourist, but thats how it was. see, antigua is this little island in the west indies. it was conquored back in the days, by the british, and by the time the brits left, sometime in the 60's, they had taken everything. really. including the language. and they had instilled all those values of capitalism and greed and coruption. so things went on as usual. and so white tourists come, like we did. and most of them are oblivious to it all. to the crazy things, and the really simple things, like how it never hardly ever rains there, so even though its surrounded by the oeean and the sea, theres perpetual drought. i was there for a week. me and my sister and mom and stepdad and my two evil grandparents. we stayed in this little resort cottage. there was a sign above the door that said "freedom". the other cotteges had other names, like courage and sovereignty. and every morning these two black women would come in to dust and make our beds. me and caty made our own beds. we wanted to give them some sort of sign, some sort of secret code, some sort of glance that would tell them that we did not want to be tourists, exploiting them and their island. we wanted to tell them that we were on their side, but of course it is not that simple at all and there was nothing we could do.

we were tourists, no way around it.

we sat in the cottage and listened to my grandfather drunk telling my mom how gorgeous her legs were and then smacking his lips, i'm serious, in this way that made me want to punch him. we sat around while my grandma threatened to divorce him if he didnt stop sniffing at the dinner table. she got up and chucked a kleenex box at him and stormed off. in the morning, when we were leaving, sneeking out to try and wander off somewhere, my grandpa-racist as fuck- said listen to the natives on your way down to the beach. they have been thatching a roof all day long and singing Santa Clause is comming to Town. only they are so stupid they dont even know all the words. so we walked down toward the beach, listening. Antiguans have their own english. an english no tourist can understand. it's fast and rolling and sounds like another language entirely. but this song they were singing so we all could understand, crystal clear. there was only one line they were singing. "you better watch out. you better watch out. you better watch out'. and then they'd laugh.

you better watch out

me and my sister, we tried to make thebest of it. got lost in the woods. read books in the hot sun. we went and visited the tollbooth, see, there was this one road that was basically a tourist road, and there wasnt suppose to be a tollbooth there or anything. but some folks built one there, and charged all tourist cars a couple bucks to pass through. eventually the government shut it down, but it seemed like a great scam to me. and the building still stood there. rickety and beautiful.

do you know how it is, when you cant take anything anymore, and you would do anything just to get away? thats how it was christmas night. late night and i walked out of our cottege and down to the dock to listen to the waves splash against all the stupid boats. i was sick of everything. i wanted to dive in with my clothes on. these three antiguan guys rolled up in a car and i went with them. we drove the back roads fast me and junior and john and some guy whose name i didnt catch. that was the guy sitting next to me, feeling me up. sometimes i'd move his hand away, but he was pushy and i was tired. and to let him touch me was the less hard thing to do. it was dark, pitch dark, and we drove over hills and through villages and john would slow his english down to something i could understand, and he'd tell me the names of the places we were passing by. and whats his name's hand was down my pants, where i didn't want it, but fuck. it didnt seem to matter any more. you know. all my life my body had been fucked with. i'd fucked plenty of times when i didnt want to. boyfriends wanting it or whatever. and my body was so removed from me that it didnt seem to matter what went into it anymore. as long as i consented. so i always consented. like if i didnt consent then maybe they'd do it anyhow, and that would be bad. right. so there i was, a white girl in antigua in the middle of the night driving with three drunk guys i didnt know. and to be honest, if i'd been in that car with three white tourist boys i would have been scared. really scared. but as it was, i knew that they knew the power of a white girl charging a black man with rape on an island whose government relys on a good public image, a good tourist draw. i knew that they knew that if they raped me and i pressed charges that they would be fucked. they would be charged quick and put away. the law would come down on them.

i knew they knew this and the power that i had and i felt safe. safe and bitter. and i knew i could be wrong about it all, about my presumed safty. and i knew too that they werent necesarily rapists. but whatever, i was tired of thinking about it. and i was sick of having to defend my body. tired of having to ward people off. i was sick of my body, it wasnt mine any more. too much had been done to it already. so when we got to some place, some hill, and parked the car. i let him lean me against the back of the car. i stood there and let the tailpipe burn a big chunk out of my leg. i let him pull down my shorts so they rested at my knees. he was drunk. so drunk he couldnt even get it in me right, and i didn't want it, but i took his dick in my hand and i leaned back against the car. i put him inside of me. i figured we could get it done with because i was bored and wanted to go home and i was sick of it all, sick of dealing with it all. he fucked me, you know. and he whispered in my ear 'i want you to let my friends fuck you too'. i said no and he said why not and i said 'because you all hate me'. i pulled away so he was outside of me. i pulled my shorts back up and walked away. they drove me back to my cottage. i walked through the door with the sign above it that said freedom. i walked into my clean sheets.

this is the secret i never even told my sister. and the next day i walked around with her, through meadows and mud, past houses and ducks and a small horse and a forest. a hill with bones bleached quick by the sun.

chickens & picklers

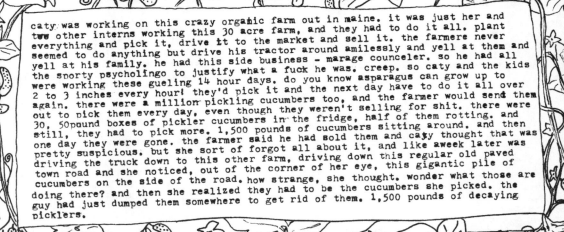

caty was working on this crazy organic farm out in maine. it was just her and two other interns working this 30 acre farm, and they had to do it all. plant everything and pick it, drive it to the market and sell it. the farmere never seemed to do anything but drive his tractor around amilessly and yell at them and yell at his family. he had this side business - marage counceler. so he had all the sporty psycholingo to justify what a fuck he was. creep. so caty and the kids were working these gueling 14 hour days. do you know asparagus can grow up to 2 to 3 inches every hour! they'd pick it and the next day have to do it all over again. there were a million pickling cucumbers too, and the farmer would send them out to pick them every day, even though they weren't selling for shit. there were 30, 50pound boxes of pickler cucumbers in the fridge, half of them rotting. and still, they had to pick more. 1,500 pounds of cucumbers sitting around. and then one day they were gone. the farmer said he had sold them and caty thought that was pretty suspicious. but she sort of forgot all about it, and like aweek later was driving the truck down to this other farm, driving down this regular old paved town road and she noticed, out of the corner of her eye, this gigantic pile of cucumbers on the side of the road. how strange, she thought. wonder what those are doing there? and then she realized they had to be the cucumbers she picked. the guy had just dumped them somewhere to get rid of them. 1,500 pounds of decaying picklers.

and then there were the chickens. see, these baby chicks were born in the basement of the shed, and they kept growing until they were full fledged chickens and they still lived down there, with no light or place to run around. the farmer guy told the interns to build a chicken coop in their spare time, but they never had any spare time. they barely had enough time to sleep. finally he pulled out some old fence thing and told them to just build a coop out of that. sothey built it, even though it was one of those white picket fence type things and it was obvious the chickens would be able to squeeze through the slats.

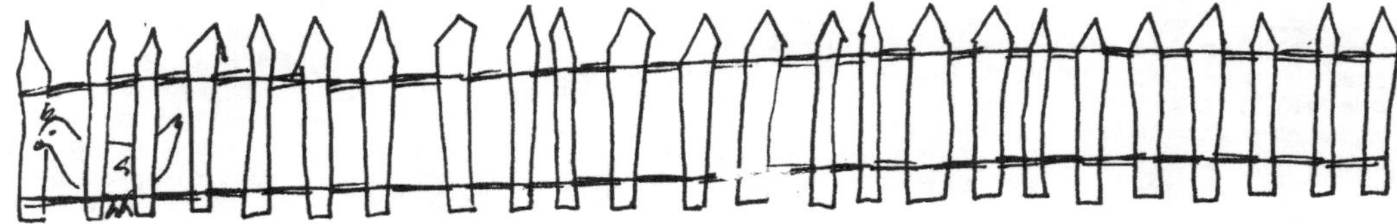

they had to go down in the basememt and catch the chickens. and chickens are probably the hardest thing in the workd to catch, they run around like mad and squak like crazy and somehow squirm out of your hads. so it was the three interns and a bunch af chickens racing around in this dark dingy basement, running into eachother and falling over and making the hugest ruckus ever. but somehow they would catch a couple, and then to carry them to the coop, they had to turn the chickens upside down and carry them by their feet, one chicken in each hand. but once in the coop, the chickens could get out easy, squeese through the slats or jump over the top. and they were so stupid they couldnt figure out how to get back into the coop to eat. so every morning the chickens would be standing around the coop, squaking to get let back in to eat. and caty would have to chase them around again, they'd run around and around the coop in circles, and sometimes she would get oneof the other interns to help her, comming at he chicken from another angle, trying to intercept it, but still, somehow they would allude her. and the farmer would gell that the chickens were eating the seadlings, and that the dog was eating the chickens.

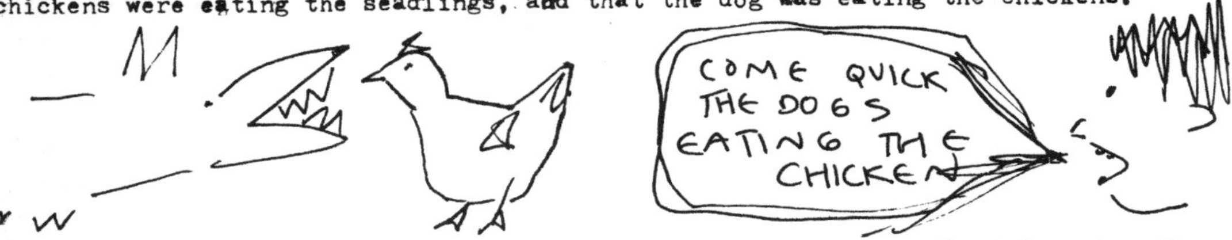

there were these two chickens who hid in the basement on that first day when they were trying to move them to the coop. they crawled back into this little spot that was impossible to get to. the next day one of the chickens got hungry and came out; but the other chicken didnt care. would rather fast for days than come out of its hold. it was a loner chicken, asortof meditation guru chicken. and sometimes other chickens would come visit it, one at a time. and if the door to the basememt was closed, they wuld just sit there, waiting to get let in to see their guru. very strange. it happened day after day, and the loner chicken never came out, but didnt seem to mind visitors. and as if that whole scene wasnt strange enough, i mean, who ever heard of a loner, guru chicken, as if that wasnt st range enough, a pidgeon showed up on the farm. and seemingly with the decided purpose to see this chicken. the pidgeon came all the way from NYC. they dont even have pidgeons in maine, and thisone had a band on its leg that said new york.

and it had come all on its own. and every day it would try to get into the basement to see the chicken. if the door was closed it would try and fly in through this hole in the wall, andit was very tricky, not easy at aal for the pidgeon to manuver its way through that hole. and if it couldnt make it in, it too would stand by the door, patiantly waiting for someone to open it. and then it would just sit around with the chicken. just hang out. i am not kidding, it was like that pidgeon had made afucking pilgramage. like it knew that the chicken was more than just some run of the mill loner chicken. more than just your average guru. that chicken was the god damn dalichicken.

riding around on my bike today, trying to ride off this bad mood. flatish tire, basket full of junk and my dog running beside me. up hill up to where the coffee is the strongest and no one ever goes up there. no one will find me.

that's all I want lately. for noone to find me, or for someone to find me if they've got something worthwhile to say. I am tired of small talk and fallen apart friendships. what's new. I ride my bike all day. to the hills and downtown. kensington, albany and west berkeley.

I want some old friend to be riding with me, all quiet and watching the road go by. I want to find some new in town stranger girl and pull her off the sidewalk and throw her on my bike and take her on a tour. a made up tour - random back street blocks and I'd make up weird lies about different buildings and empty lots. But, of course, I've never had old friends, and I can't find any stranger girl. not in this mood. Not when I pass by the Good Luck Chinese Resturant and there's newspaper over the windows and a big sign that says "Closed".

Riding around dizzy, hungry in the afternoon heat. And all I feel is contempt for almost everyone I've ever known. The way they all seem to let go easy, forget everything, no big deal. I hold on to friendships long after the other person has stoped trying. I have faith in plans that no one else even remembers.

Go to the ocean and make shellnecklases all winter, sell them to the spring break tourists. Move to spain and open a muffin and milkshake store there. start a junkyard, a rock and roll band. I had this one plan once, this serious plan. See, my group of friends in Minneapolis were all sort of spliting up.

But we had plans, you know. Not well thought out, but serious at least. We called it our 5 year plan, because we figured that's how long it would take for us all to get back together. Some of them were going to grad school and didnt want to get stuck in academia. Some of them were going to New York and didnt want to get stuck there. I was suppose to check out the West. Find a big warehouse or something for us and we'd start a school. We had some of it figured out, and other people from different places that wanted to join us. And I held on to that plan like water. I drank it down and it kept me alive. It took me 3½ years to give up on it. And now I'm not sure if anyone else even

It took me 3½ years to give up on that group, and today I'm thinking maybe they were never my friends at all. You know, how I settle for so little from a person and pretend that it something with potential, something real. One girl would wak around the lakes with me andask me about my life.

About all the hard things, family stuff, my mom. and she'd shake her head and yell"you have such a burden to carry". the next week she'd ask the same questions and I'd tell her the same stories and she didn't remember ever hearing them before. One boy I became friends with because he was depressed and no one else wanted to deal withit.

And the rest of them, well, they were my friends, you know, but we didn't really know eachother at all.

As a group we were fine. Spent lots of time together. Did great things. Put out

a magazine and had street protests that weren't boring. organized conferances and public forums. One time I was driving around withthem —John and Kate and Nancy and Bill. We had a car full of paint bombs and billboards to alter and we'd already gotten the difficult well lit one you could see from the freeway. the one that had to be dismantled, not just splattered with paint. We were driving to the next target with the raido blaring some english book critic and John imitating the dork. Kate was yelling "shut up john, Shut Up" and Billy passed me his paint bombs. "You have to do it," he said, "I throw like a girl". So me and John, we got up on the roof and the rest of them went to be lookouts. Except they ended up wandering around those empty streets all together, spray paint in their pockets, laughing loud. and the cops came and stoped them. Didn't see us or the bilboard half done on the roof. We layed down

flat and tried to hear what was going on. the usual Hands on the Hood stuff and What are You Doing, but we could hear the three of them still gigling. "coming home from aparty" said Kate, "Just goofing around" said Billy. And I was laying still and flat, couldn't believe they were laughing when there was wet paint on their hands, but it worked. the cops let them go.

And now, fuck it,

me too.

I'm letting them go.

moving...again

Sometimes it's hard to beleeve, the stuff my brain comes up with, Like last night standing around in my new room. no shelves, no dresser, just milk craaes and this thin board for a desk and tons of boxes full of stuff. And I couldnt figure out how to unpack. Where to put it all. So I alphabatized it. Little piles going all around my room starting at the door. A-amp, art shit. B- bracelets bus transfers, boxes, bartcards. C- catholic statuette, candles, computer, chalk, cigerettes, catys rafund check from the irs. D-desk, dog things, dictionary, disks, drinking fountain. E- envelopes, earplugs. and so on. Now I know where everything goes. It's just a matter of naming it.

There's something really good about naming things. Code names and nicknames and even remembering names in the firstplace. There was this cat that started hanging out on my old house's front porch. Just moved in like it lived there, like a lot of people seem to do. And this cat, orange and fluffy. I named it Leo because it looked like one of Paula's cats. And I'd yell LEO! at it like Paula did. And the cat would come running up to me. All it took was giving it a name for me to fall in love with it, and when I moved it followed me to my new house, walked after me without any coaxing. Well, okay, it took a little coaxing. It was 2am and it had followed me to the corner of Aileen and MLK and then it got distracted. I had my backpack and a backgammon set and was trying to get Leo to cross the road with me, yelling quiet "Leo, Leo. tsst. come on", and this guy walked up, eyeing me all suspicious, but I just kept going "Leo. psst. come on". And finally the guy saw the cat ad he gave me a little wink. "cat's dragging behind tonight, huh". "yeah", I said, "it's tough".

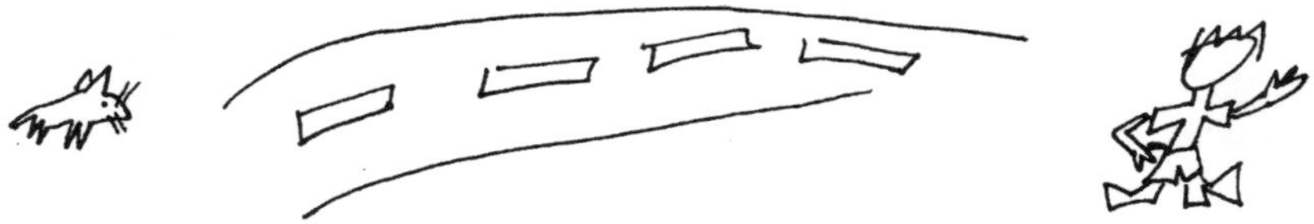

So now I've got this new place. green carpet and wallpaper that was glued to the walls upsidedown. It's amazing and almost uncanny how quiet it is. I get selfconcious doing dishes at midnight. And after the last place, sheesh, it's a hard adjustment. Seven months of noise and I always had earplugs on me. Me and Aaron were gonna make a tape. Sounds of Genoa. The phone ringing non-stop and footsteps walking right past it. The loudest techno music ever but not loud enought to drowned out the fucking. The doorbell ringing and dog barking and people swearing but not answering the door. A violin playingbaa baa black sheep at 7am and someone grinding keys on the key making machine in the background. It was a great place for awhile. I could scream loud for no reason and no one asked me what was wrong. I never had to explain myself. I could growl at my housemates and they still liked me, I think. one day i came home and the roof was gone. Some people had come and taken it right off. Didn't bother us none. What goods a roof anyway. really.

But me and my sister, it was time for us to move. pack everything again. load it up, unpack again. our long lists and big plans and piles and piles of books.

jonathan

Caty knew Jonathan's last name and Jason did and Isabel I think. But they were all out of town. The woman at the Ecology Center knew - she's the one who eventually found out he was dead - but I didnt knew her. I'm sure there were other people who knewhis last name, people who didnt know how to look forhim or didnt notice or didnt really care. But the thing was, I felt like it was all up to me. Like I was the only one who could find him. Cause me and Caty, we loved Jonathan strong and for real. He was the best most solid friend we had. And he fucking cared about us and had more to offer than anyone we knew out on this west coast. He noticed our moods even when we were hiding them from ourselves, he could tell by our shoulders, our voices, our eyes. And sometimes he'd just sit next to us quiet if that's what we needed and he always seemed to know.

I want him in my days again. I want to tell him stories and for him to hand me things. For me to lean into him and him to lean right back. I want to talk to him about the Weathermenand the SDS book I just finished reading. There's a new crop of punks in the park already and Jonathans not here to introduce them to me - and it seems crazy to me that they've never even met him.

born of fire

There was this one day, I couldnt believe Jonathan wasnt around anymore. His street urchin theater was full blown reality. It was this born of fire traveling festival, conference, melee - and first it was a week of Gilman in the daytime with puppet shows and colages and bookbinding and selfdefence and all laughing and consulting eachother and acting like it was the most normal thing in the world. And then came the parade. It was suppose to be an anticonsumerist protest down Telegraph and University, but it was really just one big punk parade with no discernable message at all. It was full of kids on stilts and masks and even the ones usually sullen and snarling were yelling and jumping around, laughing even. It was crazy and out ofanyone in this world, Jonathan should have been there. He should have been on the sidewalk cheering it on, running into the middle and passing off his basketball, catching it again. It was exactly what he d needed to see, I know it. And we would have argued about it later, me pointing out the bad tactics - like when the copssmoved in no one knew what to do or how to unarrest people or where to go. There was no plan. So they turned to the back streets and stood in the middle of an intersection arguing over which direction to take, south or east. They were trying to reach concensus about it with the cops moving in, and honestly, it wasnt that big of a deal, which way we went, as long as we kept moving. You know, when concensus fails, whoever makes the most noise wins, so we started hooping and hollering and running and South it was, yep. I would have complained to Jonathan about the whole scene and how rediculous it was, and he would have defended it, praising it for its randomness and play, and I would have conceded a little and he would have too.

i want i want i want. . .

I want these long talks with him again. To hear him whistle his bird trills and watch him play basketball with Ducky. I miss him so bad it strangle s me sometimes and I've got these things he gave me, all these things. But I cant seem to make them fit toghteher, you know, I dont know what to do.

Some days I love the rain. when it's all hard healed and coming down fast. I sit in the doorway of the post office off telegraph and watch people run and struggle with their umbrellas, broken by the wind. Big striped ones like canopies, keeping everything dry.

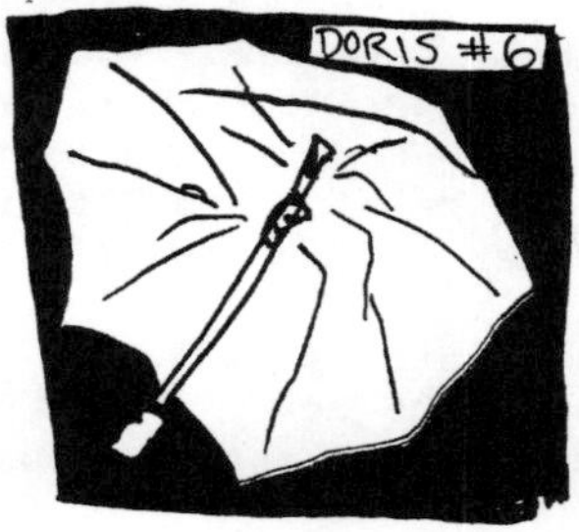

One time I went downtown and found Veronica there, huddled in the doorway, eating chips and cheese. She gave me her watch, still set on Montreal time. and a red umbrella, she was already soaked to the skin. Inside the folds she wrote a message. "I hope you keep that and think of me Veronica XX" And now, whenever it rains, I do.

One time I walked down University in the downpour. Me and Brian. He was skipping school. He was learning to lassoo instead of studying physics. He played the banjo and was giving himself a big tattoo. We got to the waterfront before the thunder and lightning. We hid under a bush. Made a tent out of my rainjacket. Nothing helped so we jumped into the bay.

Here I live close to the water. I can walk to the ocean, no problem at all. Past the shops, the old race track. the parking lot and the zoo. And the ocean is huge, like I always thought it would be. "You see the islands out there?" Nick asks, but I don't.

There was that one time when we went to Monterey. Two carloads, drunk driving and all that stuff. I snuck up on the sealions. Dove in when the sun was rising. We headed up to SantCruz to surprise visit my sister. I had to drive with my head sticking out the window because the fog was thick and the windshield wipers didn't work. Billy was eating straight sugar out of packets. By the time we got there, he was too delerious to getoout of the car.

My sister was living in a tent and working at an organic farm. Taking farming and gardening classess and learning all about the stuff. I wasn't sure exactly where to find her. We tromped up the hill, past the barn and the farm cats, through this archway of flowers that smelled almost too sweet. All the people we walked by were healthy and tan and bright eyed - the opposite of the 9 of us. We found Caty in the bean fields. I whistled our secret whistle and she looked up in shock. Yelled out half sentances "What the...how the...holyfuck!" She fed us green beans straight from the bushes. Marshal wanted to know where the 40 ouncers grew. Abe wanted to take off his shoes.

It's weird the way gardens and farms make me nervous. I get to feeling like there's some important part of life I'm missing out on. This importanat basic thing I know nothing about. We were all sort of that way. overwealmed in a good way and tired. We sat in the apple orchard, eating apples off the trees. Throwing the cores at eachother.

It was 50¢ day at the amusement part at the waterfront and some of us had never ridden a rollercoaster before. When we got there, the rides hadn't opened yet, but there was the ocean and beach. Me and Jason, we took off our shoes and went into the salty water just like that, all our clothes on. Chad stripped down to his boxers and joined us. We swam forever while everyone else sat on shore. We yelled about sharks and grabbed each others ankles. We tried to swim out to the dock, too far. And when we left the water, Tom shook himself like crazy. "This is how they dry off in the Army" he said, and he held out his arms and spun around and around. Chad, who I had never seen laugh so much before.

Lately I've been itching to stop harrassment. I walk the dark side streets, looking for Natasha's van to sleep in. Looking for Colby and his loud little dog. I stop in intersections and scratch at my ankles. If someone's walking up, I grimice and itch my head. If they think I have bugs, may be they won't bother me. I know it's a rediculous idea.

But truth is, I'm used to being bothered and take it pretty well these days. I used to carry around a switchblade, and in my head I dared anyone to come near. I was angry enough already. I wouldn't mind feeling someone else's blood.

And then with Anna, I owned the streets. People crossed to the other side when they wsaw my big dog. And now, I don't know, I'm not scared anymore. May be that's stupid, but it's true. The guy outside the hotel says 'How about it, baby?' and I look at him weary, simpathetic, and shake my head. It's that 'I know your situation, but I'm not your girl' look. More understanding than I actually feel, way more.

It comes from a life time of learning how to not agravate. How to keep tempers down to keep myself safe. I see both sides when there should be only one. With one look, one gesture, I prove myself their equal. I don't see them as agressor don't see myself as victim. And I know that it's bullshit, that my proof is all wrong. But that's what I'm doing, when itching doesn't deter them.

Truth is, I'm bitter. Bitter about a lot of things. Like my friends who live in a poverty fantasy. The ones who have access to money and always will. I can see them wanting to refuse it. Wanting to learn to make it on their own. I think that's important, I guess. And it would be fine if they didn't talk about being broke. Down to the last dollar. How are they gonna make it through the month. When I know all it would take for them is one phone call. One trip to the bank. Or something like that. And truth is, I don't understand it. I don't know how they couldn't see that their words are insulting to someone whose poverty isn't self imposed.

dry as wine

I'm bitter about my friends who have left me behind. I guess I let go easily or not at all. Once I learned about friendship. What I wanted and how it could be. Deep and strong and something that changed you, not just distraction, another face to help pass the time. Those days I wouldn't stand for shallowness. I wanted everything out on the table. No small talk. I pushed myself hard. I went over board, forgot to walk in the woods go swimming put my hands in the snow. But I learned what I wanted and now I have it. I know how to think into a person and push them for more. How to get them to grow. I know how to talk and how to be quiet. I can see them through their own experiences, not mine. And I'm pissed that no one I know seems to do that.

one – ten

I'm from neighborhoods where we hardly knew any of our neighbors. It seemed like everyone had an electric garage door opener except us. Houses with yards in front and back, but we couldn't cut across anyones lawn without getting yelled at. and they were always watching. We had gawdy green carpet upstairs and the basement flooded in the spring. everything was wrong. but sometimes I'd grab Jenny's hand and we could still find traces of things that were right.

There was the one old farmhouse with a greehouse attached. They sold plants there and we bought a venus fly trap with money pitched in together from our allowances, but we never could get the thing to eat. There was a path behind the Evansons house, and if we ran fast enough to get past Mrs Evanson, we could go back to the big meadow, land not divided up et, where there were still tall grasses and a mud or dirt pit, depending on the time of year. And past that, if we could get away for that long, was a dirt road with run down houses and everything perfect, like chickens running everywhere, broken down cars and a horse even.

It was amazing to us that some place so real could be that close, but still, we almost never went back there. We stuck to what we knew.

We stayed with everything wrong. Green carpet and was it stained with my mothers blood? broken nose, ripped out hair. hard to say. my memory's not that good. The way the faucet sounded. her asleep on the bed.

I remember the first time I saw her put on lipstick. She was driving the car while she did it. One time I stood in her room and she was naked. I was trying to ask her a question but I didn't know where to look. I guess I must have been staring at her breasts because she said angry "Look at my face when you talk to me!"

There were bloody knees and lost tempers. I learned to hold the silverwear right, put my napkin in my lap and don't let it fall. The kitchen had everything in i its right place. The toaster oven caught on fire. The blind dog next door was always sleeping in the road and two houses down they actually put up a white picket fence.

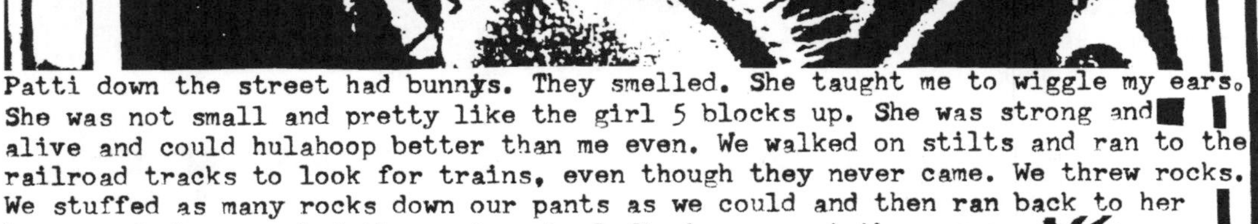

Patti down the street had bunnys. They smelled. She taught me to wiggle my ears. She was not small and pretty like the girl 5 blocks up. She was strong and alive and could hulahoop better than me even. We walked on stilts and ran to the railroad tracks to look for trains, even though they never came. We threw rocks. We stuffed as many rocks down our pants as we could and then ran back to her house and who ever had the most rocks left when we got there won.

I come from the usual secrets and problems, whitewashed by the usual portrait. Once with our new family we went to the mall. All of us girls got dressed up in Victorian costume and we sat there stony faced under bright hot lights. Suffocating for the photo. Caty was turning white. Her face falling. She passed out in the end. My family chose the first picture out of the bunch and it's hanging on the wall at my grandparents house. It's the one where Caty only looks like she's gonna puke, not die. Not the one where she's already out of the picture

eleven on

Where I lived, it smelled like liquor being sweat out of skin. Cat shit and suntan lotion. Garden dirt and good food. I rarely had anyone over because I knew their houses were different from mine in ways that didn't exactly seem right but I knew where.

Heather had microwave food for dinner and we watched DuranDuran videos on her big screen TV. She didn't mind my place. We'd go out in the yard and pull dandilions up by the roots. A penny per flower and she liked the work. And it seemed right to me. Better than her pretty mom who payed me sixty bucks to knit Heather a sweater for her birthday that I'm sure she never wore.

We stuck together all of the 7th grade and quick gave up trying to make other friends. Heather was Jewish. My pants were the wrong style. It was that kind of school. There was this one girl, Suzy, we especially hated. Everyone else wanted to be her friend and she had money like I couldn't imagine. She'd talk about how she went in to McDonalds for a double cheeseburger and they didn't have change for her $100. I think I overheard that story five times. She had it easy, she made me sick. her perfect world. Then one day her face was puffy from crying and I heard what had happened. She had found her mom convulsing on the floor from too much cocaine. And I knew then that she came from everything wrong. It was where I came from that was right. That much I knew for sure. on the good days.

downtown

what do you do when your best friend is dead and your sister is gone and your body is scraped out and bleeding from some medical procedure, and the boy you want near you shows up in town but he is lost too, more crazier than you, and you ride the tunnels together fast under the bay and him sitting next to you is the only comfort you have left, but he gets off the train at Powell St. station and says "I'll come find you before I leave," which isn't for a week, and you want to yell "Get back here and stay!" but you know you never wanted to need him, and you never wanted your love to be clutching, and you know that this individualist culture makes us think we can do it all on our own when we can't, no matter how much of a loner you are. and you have no community to fall back on and no family to run to and no history to ground you, and your comfort just left you at Powell street station.

ROMANCE 101
professor covemact

(an alternative to the abstimence only advice sheet)

I. tell the other person that you can't stand them. 2. kick them. 3. make the other person feel like shit. 4. spit. 5. have terrible times together. 6. tell the other person that you could care less. 7. crush them with your bare hands. 8. steal their bike. 9 give them a dead rat. IO, ditch them when they really need you. II. stand each-other up. I2. take them to Operation Dumbo Drop. I3. break both their arms and leave them to die in the woods. I4. make a special tape of hate songs. I5. talk openly about how annoying they are and how much you hate them. I6. become their neightmare. I7. steal their bed. I8. feed them to the ducks. I9. tell them to take a hike. 20. poison them. 2I. play with their emotions. 22. bring ants if they try to take you on a picnic. 23. insult them. 24. take them to a creepy health spa and ditch out. 25. try and drown them. 26.push them away. 27. cruise other people while you're grocery shopping. 28. burn their toast. 29. punch them. 30.spill coffee on all their importa nt papers. 3I. plan a road trip with them and then go with someone else instead. 32. kick them out of your party. 33. bake them worm cookies. 34. take them to the mortuary. 35. just leave them 36. take them to the mall 37. find out what the other person hates and then do it all the time. 38. push them down the stairs. 39.give eachother evil glares. 40.rip the radiator out of their car. 4I take them fishing and then push them overboard. 42. talk about them behind their back. 43. hurt them 44. get them fired from their job. 45. ruin their favorite song for them 46. destroy everything they ever ever loved 47. hold them at arms length 48. use eye contact to let them know how much they disgust you. 49. write eachother letters seathing with hate. 50. call them late at night and hang up 5I. lie to eachother 52. give them a black eye 53. make sure their family hates you. 54. trip them 55. make them sacrifice everything for you 56. send a letter bomb. 57. have no respect for them. 58. put them on a spaceship to the moon. 59. hide hate notes in all their clothes and everywhere, so that years later they will still be finding them. 60. give them dirty looks. 6I. publish their obituary 62. send thorns 63.burn their house down 64. take them to a Phish concert. 65. watch TV from sunrise to sunset 66.drive them up a wall 67. feed them to your pet snake 68. go sightseeing 69. make them watch all your family home videos 70. borrow their leather jacket without asking and lose it 7I propose marriage 72. cut off their ear 73. be worst enemys 74. get a horse and trample them to death 75. go out with all their friends

76. break their musical instruments 77. flirt with other people 78. scream 79. cheat 80. distress eachother 8I. make a list of things you hate about eachother 82. read their diary and discuss it with your friends 83. steal their friends 84. put a severed horse head in their bed 85. cook only things they hate 86. find out what makes them miserable 87. drive them insane 88. be uncaring 89. watch them leave 90. die 9I. dedicate the song 'fuck you' to them on the radio 92. send death threats 93. destroy their life 94. step on their feet 95. play mean jokes on them 96. think about how much you can't stand eachother 97. find out what makes the other person sad and then bring it up all the time. 98. steal their skateboard 99. trade insults I00, shove icecubes down their pants I0I. fuck

thanks to Coty, Megan, Carolyn, aaron and the Canadian for helping compile this list. ♡123

40 days

This time I went back to every home I ever had. Plainfield where the kids still jumped off the bridge into the river. Laura still talked about leaving and Denise about buying land. There was the graveyard and the church wall and Paula's livingroom where we sat and talked like I hadn't been away for three years. Michael drove by in a car and waved, like of course I was there, no point in stopping, it was perfectly normal to see me walking down route 2 up to Maple Valley cafe, where Dudley let me behind the counter to fix myself a sandwich and I felt like his daughtor figure again.

There was Portland where I stuck to the basements and back streets. Afraid to run in to the people I loved there. Lisa and her three kids, 5, 7 and 9. Hanna used to take me on roofs and we'd get stuck there. Lelia brought me to the alleys picking blackberries and apples. Abby drew me pictures and climbed under the covers in my closet room. I used to think I would live with them forever, but this time back in Portland, I hid out, afraid my heart would break to see them for just one day.

I went to Minneapolis for band practice. Me and Wade playing music until my fingers were too sore. We talked about all the important things.

One time when I lived there still, and it was November and cold and dreary, me and Wade decided to have a holiday. Haymarket Day, to commemorate the state sanctioned murder of 4 Anarchists back in I886.

See, back in those days the Anarchist movement was strong. Organized and articulate and getting things done. In Chicago alone there were 3,000 people who belonged to anarchist groups and five anarchist newspapers that came out in different languages. Socialists and labor unions were a lot stronger too. There was a lot of solidarity. The U.S. economy was doing really good, but still people had to work 12 hour days in lousy conditions. So there was this big general strike called to take place May 1. Everyone was supposed to quit working until the bosses gave them an 8 hour day. And the strike was going really good. There were meetings and demos and picnics. It was going so well that it seemed like it might not stop. There was so much solidarity it seemed revolution might be possible.

Then there was this one rainy day rally in Chicago and pretty much everyone had left already. The mayor had even been there checking it out and told the cops it was no big deal, it was all under control, and then he split. All of a sudden, 200 more cops show up, start ordering everyone to disperse and not really giving them a chance to do it. And out of nowhere this bomb explodes in the police ranks and cops start shooting like mad, mostly shooting eachother. No one knows who threw the bomb, whether it was a provocative government agent, an anarchist, or just some shmoo. But the whole thing started this huge campaign to associate anarchism with bomb throwing chaos.

They used the incident to begin a reign of terror against organizers throughout the country, breaking into offices and houses, destroying presses and whatnot. arresting tons of people for conspiracy. They arrested 8 of the most influential anarchist and socialists in Chicago andput them on trial for the deaths caused by the bomb. Seven of them were sentanced to death, even though there was no evidence against them. And on November 11, four of them were hanged.

That's what we were commemorating. The deaths of those guys and the way the idea of anarchism and our history have been practically erased in this country and replaced by the simplistic, stupid fucking image of anarchism as chaos.

But this spring back in Minneapolis, I felt kind of crazy. Most of my old friends had left. I still looked for them on street corners and empty lots - places they never even went when we all lived in that town together. They were always in their houses, at work, in meetings, busy. And that is something I miss. That serious commitment, that frantic, thought out politics.

a.w.o.l.

It's impossible to explain that group of friends I was doing political work with back then, and practically impossible to explain what we were doing. The words I would use to talk about the problems we were working on - sexism, racism, homophobia, ecological destruction, capitalism, domination and oppression - aren't taken seriously any more. These days, everything seems to be looked at in this PC, antiPC framework. Catagorized and easily dismissed. Nothing is taken seriously enough and all these words have been made trivial.

So now I don't know what to say - how to explain our politics and make it come out right. We were way more than just all the things we did added up. We went to protests and made them exciting with theater and energy and life. No slow marching, no boring old chants. We took over streets and passed out flyers that explained the complexities of the issues at hand. Some of us worked at a food co-op, kicked out the manager and made it worker owned. We published a bi-yearly journal of theory and action, held public forums, organized a midwest ecoanarchist conference and were trying to pull together some kind of national anarchist network. We did direct actions and coalition work. Tried to create a prefigurative politics as well as a responsive one. There was so much strength in our politics then. There was this sence of urgency that we've somehow lost. We didn't have to wonder whether there was hope. We had to be that hope. We had to change things fast. And there was actually a lot of potential. There was all kinds of activism and organizing going on across the country. And it's pretty amazing how quickly it disapeared. How completely watered down the ecology movement became.

When I went back to Minneapolis, most of what I'd had there was gone. It was just me and Wade, playing music and trying to make sense of things.

end

Playing With Guns

When I first met Casey she was in to Elvis Tom Jones and art made out of baby doll heads. and she told me a story of when she was a kid and her mom carted her off to Christian summer camp. They weren't religious or anything, it was just a way to get rid of her for awhile. So she came back from camp with a glow in the dark bust of Jesus. Got all her cousins together into this one small room. They all had these toy guns that shot huge foam bullets. Casey would hold Jesus up to the light, then flip the switch and throw him up into the air. And the room was so small that Jesus always hit someone on his way back down and that person got blasted. Everyone opened fire. They called the game Bazooka Jesus.

hands. feet.

I was walking home down Mission St. There's this one part of the road where it's all residential and late at night it's really quiet and nice. When I walk that way , I like to stop at the bridge that crosses over the freeway and smoke and think about the day.

So the other night I was standing there, smoking and watching the traffic, when this guy comes half running up to me, gesturing wildly and speaking Spanish. I was like - fuck, I am not in the mood for this. I didn't want to deal with some nut andI didn't want to deal with someone trying to shmooze on me, and I figured it was going to be one or the other. I just wanted to be left alone, but he came cruising up and asked me for a cigerette. I gave him what was left of mine and walked away. I was pretty sure it wouldn't be that easy to get rid of him, and I was right. After a second he comes tailing along after me. apologizing for bothering me and trying to catch up.

He didn't speak much English and I know almost no Spanish, but he talked to me with gestures and some words we both knew. He told me he played music and asked if I did too. I told him I tried to play the bass but was terrible at it, that I really couldn't play at all. He shook his head. All sounds are good, he said, and to make his point, he nodded to the apartment building we were passing by. Someone inside was slamming doors. "Slam, bam, ba dam dam slam", he said, "music". I laughed and agreed and we walked along listening to the night noises. The electri c bus lines, the rain in the gutter, the dryers of the laundrymat, the sound of someone moping.

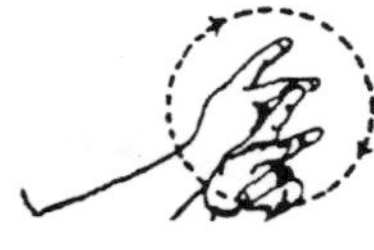

When my road split off from his, he didn't try to follow me, he pointed in his direction and said he was going to write. He scribbled in the air and kept walking.

mice

My second house in Portland had drop cealings in the kitchen, and one day I decided it would be good to remove all the panels and have a higher cealing So I climbed up on the sink and pried a couple of the panels out. It smelled really strong up there. Really good and familiar. And for the longest time I just stood there, trying to figure out what it smelled like. Finally it hit me. My Grandma's house. She usedto live in this little cabin on the Saint Croix river, and we'd go down there and visit her. Her house wascrammed with stuff, magazines and books on the stairs, hat boxes full of socks in the attic, She was always watching tennis matches on TV, cooking key lime pie and drinking whiskey sours. She was my step grandma, so she didn't come in to the picture until I was twelve, but she wasmore like a real grandma than either of my real ones.

I never really knew her that great, and I didn't think of her often, but it was so reasuring to be around that old familiar smell again. Not so much because of the memories, but it's just that there is so little consistancy in my life. Everything changes and disapears. I had almost forgotten what it's like to know something as well as I knew my grandma's house. Someplace where I didn't have to try and constantly figure out what was going on around me. I already knew. It already made perfect sence.

I've been thinking about that a lot lately. The comfort of being around stuff that's familiar and how it allows for a certain kind of clearheadedness, and how little of that I have. It's funny cuz I want new places. That way they make life all exciting. Different faces and streets and geography. New perspectives and people to wonder about. But it makes me feel all ungrounded, and I am. I don't know where my roots are. It's weird the places I find myself drawn to all of a sudden, like this one part of San Jose where the sidewalks are so thin you can hardly walk on it. Bushes on one side and cars rushing by. Just like this one road I used to walk down every day to escape from my mom's house when I lived with her. I could walk down that street half asleep and never stumble. If some candy wrapper that had been laying in the dirt for a week disapeared, I'd know. I hated that walk, the whole 3 miles of it. But now every chance I get, I walk up San Jose. And I've been going to strip malls. The small ones that have a Payless, a shoe store, discount clothes. Like 7-Hi by my old highschool. A place I'd only go toas a last ditch effort when I was incredably board. I'd try on clothes that I'd never think of wearing, pretend to steal from the drug store just to see how many security guards I could get to follow me around. I'd go to the mini arcade and play pacman so loud and violently that everyone in there would leave. I hated it there too.

I never thought I'd want to go back to those places. They were desolate and unworthy and I certainly didn't love them. And it's not reminiscing that draws me to their closed. It's some kind of stability, some simple kind of comfort I can't really explain.

TRUST → ← MISTRUST

I was on this huge anti flea campaign and I was vaccuming the house like mad. Standing on the couch and vaccuming the cushions. Singing Green Day songs at the top of my lungs, and I could picture all the fleas getting sucked up into that long lube, cartoon style, screeching and tumbling around. I guess I must have watched the right amount of TV as a kid or something.

It was storming out so hard, and Caty walked into the livingroom, head to toe in green rain gear. She was holding the mop with a big knife duct taped to the end of it. She looked at me quick and then walked out the door.

Ten minutes later she came running back in. "Buses keep driving by and cops and I'm still not tall enough!" she yelled, "Grab a milkcrate and come help!" So I did. I was the milk crate handler and look out. She cut down the signs.

They'd been creeping us out, these election signs. The TRUST signs had gone up first. All over SanFrancisco. High up on every lamp post on every block in the city. just TRUST big and bright, in red white and blue. It took us a week to figure out they were part of the mayor's re-election campaign. yeah, trust the guy. he's a fucking dick.

And we couldn't believe it when thenext round of signs went up. Long black signs with white letters and a picture of his opponent's face. MISTRUST it said. It was so fucking racist that we could hardly believe it was real, but it was. and the signs were driving us nuts. But what could we do? They were too high up to get to, and taped on to those lightpoles really good. We were all stumped except for Caty, wielding her makeshift harpoon.

atlas

Me and Caty, we've got a new plan. Fuck this house that we layed all our bets on. It seemed perfect for awhile, all big and out of the way, a kitchen with chairs that rolled from the breadbox to the toaster. a basement where I could fire up my circular saw. We've got a big back yard, so what that it's concrete. We'll garden in boxes - right? Maybe this place could have worked alright, but we've been trying to do the same thing for too long. Put down roots. Stay stable for awhile. Start projects that are based in our community - long term. and for one reason or another, it hasn't been working. Sometimes other people's fault, sometimes our own. And I know we'll figure it out someday. find the people and the projects we need. But in the meantime, we gotta get our lives back. We're getting a truck or a van, packing our tents, buying a cooler, finding some small place to put our loom. And for the next year it's gonna be small towns, new librarys, beaches, books and building pinatas. We'll come back to the city for a couple days to work. grab one of our friends, drag them out of their life, bring them along. Maybe I'll learn to take good snapshots and do interviews. Maybe we'll teach workshops at small highschools. It's funny how a new plan can make the possibilities seem endless. We've got a ton of ideas now. Maps spread out on the floor. Caty's already got a toaster that works on a camp stove. Without a house, Anna might get rid of her fleas. "What about the rainy season?" Caty asks. "We'll go to the desert" I say. The atlas has all the answers, when everything else has failed.

letter from sam

RAIN. AND FROM MY STEREO THE SOUND OF SOMEONE TRYING TO MURDER THEIR DRUM SET. IT'S SUNDAY, MOVING-DAY, WE'RE MOVING INTO MY NEW HOUSE TODAY, ALL MY STUFF'S BEEN TAKEN OFF THE WALLS, ALL THE JEWELERY I USUALLY DON'T WEAR IS ON MY FINGERS TO KEEP FROM GETTING PERMANENTLY LOST IN SOME BADLY PACKED CARDBOARD BOX, KRISTINA'S SPIKE BRACELET ON MY LEFT WRIST, MISMATCHED SOCKS ON MY FEET. THE GIRLS IN MY SIGN LANGUAGE CLASS GANGED UP TO ASK ME WHY MY SOCKS WERE DIFFERENT COLORS THOUGHT I WAS ON SOME PUNKY BREWSTER STYLE COUNCIL, THEY DON'T UNDERSTAND A WORLD WHERE THE DRYER COULD EAT EVERY SINGLE LAST MATCHING SOCK. IT'S WEIRD THERE, I DON'T FEEL THAT MY CLOTHES'VE BEEN SO STUDIED SINCE MIDDLE SCHOOL. THEY ALMOST GET TO THE POINT OF TELLING ME HOW TO DRESS SOME DAYS, I CAN SEE IT ALL, THE EXPLANATIONS OF IRONS, LIPLINER AND EYEBROW TWEEZERS.

AUGH! RUN RUN

COFFEE ONLY MAKES ME HYSTERICAL WHEN I'M SAD but maybe it does more for you.

Love,
Sam

letter to sam

Today I was totally insane. yesterday I was tired. all I wanted to do was sleep. But when I got home and got in bed it didn't work at all, so I started reading. Read an entire book. gave up, got up and did a bunch of stuff. I was moody. Crazy tired and hyperactive, the way kids get, you know, so I tried again. I layed down but I couldn't even seem to close my eyes, much less sleep. I layed there for an hour thinking about what an insomniac I used to be, and how I hadn't had insomnia for 9 (nine) years. I thought about how I had this one month, 4 years ago, where I had nightmares every night and I never could figure out why. Half the time they were weird dreams about getting stuck inside video games or getting chased by dolls that had come alive. and I didn't even play video games or watch horror movies, so it seemed pretty weird. But the mornings when I couldn't remember my dreams were even worse than the mornings I could 'cause I just had a sunk stomach and frantic mind and no dream story to place it on. I tried not to sleep that month 'cause it sucked so bad. Last night I was seriously hoping that wasn't gonna happen again. I wondered if I should take my bike down to the van my boy lives in except I was pretty sure he wasn't there and plus maybe I'd been seeing to much of him. I thought may be I should go curl up with the dog, but she always gets up and leaves when I try to do that. I thought maybe I hadn't been getting enough protein. Maybe I should go to the store and get some eggs and make scrambled eggs and toast. I even turned on the light and put on my pants for that idea, but then decided it was a stupid idea. and layed back down. I thought maybe I should go down to the basement and climb in bed with my best friend, but actually his bed is small and uncomfortable and I didn didn't want to bother him and I didn't really feel like going down there anyway. So I finally got out the one remaining novel in the house I hadn't read yet, andrread that. 5 hours later my roommates were getting up and getting ready for work, and the rooster across the street had crowed so much already that his voice was horse. I was still reading. All I wanted to do was sleep. I worried that maybe I would NEVER SLEEP AGAIN. I mean, I actually worried about that. A lot of times I wish I never had to sleep, but not last night. I hadn't even had any coffee (after 5pm). I was worried. I thought maybe I should just give up, get up, make coffee, eat, bike down to Kinkos, start the day. I knew if I did that I would have a nervous breakdown. I fell asleep.

I was out at Fishermans Wharf working at this weird garden show. I'd stand in the rhododendrons and point out the integrity of the handbuild Japanese tea house, the versatility of native California grasses. But mostly I just sat there, watching people walk up and down the stone paths. Handing out flyers or business cards. It was three days of work and I just sat there and thought. It was probably the first real thinking I'd done in months.

"I'm ready to move back to Vermont" I told Caty, "Our truck living plan sounds kind of grim".

"Vermont!" she said "Really?" It was where she had wanted to move all along.

Yeah, I don't need these cities anymore to inspire me, or all these people around me to keep my head reeling. I was ready for country. A small house. Dirt roads. Maybe I'd wash dishes again at the old cafe. I'd probably sleep at night and without my shoes on. I wanted some time to sort through my head. Figure out what's happened to this world these past two years, and figure out what's happened to me. It's hard to keep up with all the changes. I wanted to sit alone with my sister, cooking good food andwriting my novel and playing fetch with Anna until she was tired. And I wanted to see all the old people and places. See what was left of our friendships and projects. What could be salvaged and what could be built on. Caty wanted to plant a garden and stay somewhere for awhile. We were all packed up and ready to go. Taken apart our loom. Smashed all the dishes we didn't want anymore. Everything was in boxes, we'd said our goodbyes. We were driving across the bay one last time, stuck in traffic, and we realized we hadn't made a list. When we pulled out paper and plans, the weirdest thing happened. All our charts and graphs, all our pros and cons, all our arrows pointed in the wrong direction. It seemedfickle to stay, but stupid not to. "We can always go later" we said.

NO ONE EVER GETS TIRED OF PLAYING FETCH WITH ME

So here we are, still in the city, and I'm working on this solitude thing. Holed up in this garage with double doors opened out to the day. Typing and not going out much. I walk half a mile down to Caty's little shack. It's almost like country there. I bring her water and candles and food, and we lay in our lawn chairs in the sun.

Running Away

I don't know what my problem is. I always end up running away from home. Freaking out and packing up and leaving. When I lived in Minneapolis, I'd ride the bus and walk for hours and sleep in the cornfields. When I had my house alone in the woods I'd spend weeks sleeping on friends couches. In Vermont I ran away to Maine, in Berkeley I ran away to Eureka, and in Portland I just ran away. I couldn't figure out what else to do. I packed up some dog food and pens, a loaf of bread and three hats. Grabbed my dog and tried to sneek out of the house. There was a party going on and it was hard to be sly. Melissa grabbed my ankle and yelled at me "where the fuck do you think you're going?" I lied and said "nowhere" which in a way was the truth. By the time we got to the on ramp it was dark already.

evan + cloe

We'd been driving for a couple hours before we started talking much. He let me smoke his cigerettes and Anna sat between us. His dog Cloe was in the back of the van sleeping. Anna rested her head on the dashboard and watched the road like it was a movie. She'd bump her nose against the sterio and change the radio channels. We were headed south on I-5. I told him I was going to Sacramento. When we hit the mountains and we couldn't drive fast anymore, that's when he told me his story.

His best friend was dead and he was trying to make it back in time for the funeral. His dog was dieing and he was spending all his money on vet bills. And all he wanted was to be back in Alaska. To sit on his porch and watch the snow fall. He hadn't talked to anyone about anything real for weeks and he didn't think he should burden me, but like always, I listened. He told me stories about rattlesnakes and cattle farms and growing up in Texas. About his friend who had just committed suicide. And maybe he should have known + maybe he should never have left him. He talked about walking down roads in Alaska where the snow banks were so high it was like walking in a tunnel.

It's strange + kind of great and pretty worrisome all at once, when people I barely know pour their hearts out to me. And I try to figure out how much to give them and what to hold back, and where they stand. It seems to happen to me a lot. People telling me their stories. I worry because I know how easy it is for me to wrap myself up in other peoples lives.

When Evan's van broke down in Yreka, we walked the tracks to the river. I told him funny stories to distract him. About my fort in the bushes where I kept my typewriter and notebooks. Planting potatoes in empty lots. Stealing toasters and painting buildboards. We threw rocks + then bottles. Ate pizza + drank beer. Sat on the roof of the van + tried to figure out what to do next. I wasn't in a hurry to get to nowhere + I knew by then that Evan was harmless, so I stuck with him.

He slept in the front of the van with Cloe, and me + Anna slept in the back. "Listen to this" he said to me + he put in a tape. He'd been listening to it every night since his friend died + he said I'd probably hate it. But when the music came out over the speakers, I sang along so loud + out of tune it made him laugh. When it was over he asked me what I was doing out hitchiking anyway. I didn't know what to say.

Portland

I've never loved so many people and had such hope in so many projects + had it fall apart in so many ways that were out of my control. I even loved the city, waking up in my fort under the bushes + stumbling through the rain to the bar by the waterfront where I'd drink my coffee black and stare out at the warehouses + the ships + the shipyards. I would have been fine if I'd stuck to that. Slept outside. Stayed by the water. But I didn't. There was more than that I wanted to do. There were three houses full of people I was wrapped up in. My house was kind of fucked up but we mostly ignored our differences, heaped all our garbage into one big pile + called it compost. We sat on the front porch listening to loud music + watching the neighbors carry their pet pig down the stairs. Around the corner was the angry girl house. They read the SCUM manifesto and we'd sit around making collages + drinking coffee and talking for hours. They had strong ideas + strange rationality. Courtney sewed herself a bunny suit so she could walk around the streets without getting harassed. There was another house, I had lived there once, with a printing press, a music room, and three screaming kids. That was the house where the womens group started. Where I finally learned enough about my body to feel like it was a part of me + not something to be afraid of. We were talking about setting up a home school there. We were talking about finding a small house in the country + an apartment in the city so we could take turns living back + forth. and I wanted so much to live with those kids forever. watch them grow up and be a part of their lives.

all our houses were completely different, but we tried to work together. Each house had a women's night. Each house did stuff for Food Not Bombs. We were doing four lunch servings a week + a Monday morning serving of coffee + pastries + cigerettes out on the steps of the courthouse for the people getting out of jail after a long weekend.

We all rode our bikes in big groups around the city. We stole for eachother + laughed a lot + fought a lot too. Everything was highpowered. Everything was quick. and the faster it got, the less room there was for growth + forgiveness.

It was totally screwed. There were small political differences no one wanted to talk about. Things about class + sexism + the validity of creating radical culture. National organizing versus community work. and the more we tried to work together, the more fractured + reactionary everyone became.

ME + SOMA COULDN'T SEE WHAT THE BIG DEAL WAS.

I kept trying to pretend like things were still the way they had been, but whenever I'd go over to my old house I couldn't figure out how to fit back into their lives. and whenever I left, the kids would come running after me. abby would attach herself to my legs + scream at me "don't leave!" It was torture.

The angry girls started leaving death threats at my house for something someone had done years ago. They poured lacquer in our locks + I kept having to try + talk them out of murdering various mutual friends.

No matter what happened, I kept thinking that somehow I could single handedly pull us all back together, but it didn't work out that way. It didn't work out at all. That's why I was running away from Portland. I needed a break. I needed long roads + distance to clear my head. and once me + Evan got his van fixed + he dropped me off in San Francisco, I knew that this time I had run away for good. There was no reason for me to go back to Portland + I never did.

-the end

My dad used to take us on canoe trips. Me and my older sister, Arthur and his kid. My dad paddled in front and Arthur in back and they sung us songs, showed us maps, and pointed out things. The lake water was so clean you could drink it, and we could see fish and the rocks at the bottom, even when it was 20 feet down. One time, early in the morning, we saw a bear. One time I saw baby wolverines playing. One time me and dad climbed a cliff and at the top was a million blueberry bushes. And the way the sun came through the tree leaves, bright and light green, it felt like a fairy tale book.

My dad worked in an office on the 6th floor. Carpeted with a big desk and windows. On the bookshelf was a picture of our garden, the year mom planted tulips and they bloomed and then it snowed. I don't remember any pictures of us, but they could have been there too, who knows. He worked late and came home tired and we didn't see him much, but he taught me things I remember. How to set up wood to build the longest lasting fire. How to read and how to whittle without cutting yourself. How to bowl and how to pick the right bowling ball. And which bird call was a chickadee and which was an oriole. Or maybe mom taught me to read, I can't remember.

One time I couldn't sleep and he came into my room and instead of reading me a story, he taught me how to make one up myself. And I've been putting myself to sleep by making up stories ever since.
There was the time I was 10 and my parents got divorced and for some stupid reason we had to pick who we wanted to live with. I'd always wanted to be my dad's little girl. Wanted more of his time, wanted to be like him, but I didn't want to live with him, not at all. I had this strong sense of fairness andknewmy parents needed taking care of, so when my older sister decided to live with mom, I ended up at Dad's. I'd walk home from school and play records in the livingroom, and he taught me how to make macaroni and cheese. On weekends we'd go jogging together around this swamp by the freeway. I don't know how he jogged slow enough for me to keep up, but he did. I was funny even then, and thought I could be everything. I tried to act as adult as possible and asked him questions about work and listened closely even when I didn't understand at all.

THE HANDMADE KIND. NOT FROM A BOX.

Truth is, I've always loved my dad in this fierce and hopeful way. Even when he started fighting me, I tried to blame it on the fact that we were too much alike. And after I stopped talking to him and after he destroyed my self-confidence completely, I still had some sort of sympathy for him. And one time after not speaking to him for a year, I called him up on Father's Day and took him out to dinner. I was 17 then.

what's hard to explain is this:

What's hard to explain is this: that I could sit by his hospital bed when he was in for back surgery and going through his second divorce and fired from his job. And he was broken and guilty and lonely. And I could look him in the face and ask him what he wanted in life and try to get him to let go of his conventions and follow his dreams. That I could sit at the foot of his bed, giving him words and understanding. I wanted to see if he knew what went wrong in his life, because it seemed pretty clear to me. The way he was raised, he never saw any options. It was go to school, get a good job, get married and have kids. And so that's what he did, even though what he needed was wilderness. A small cabin. A pump for drinking water. A sailboat.

When my dad taught us to sail, mom stood on the dock smiling. She was not so skinny then and her hair was thick and full. And she had not started to keep a list yet, of what he had done to her. But she made that list eventually, and I found it crammed in a file between the cookbooks. I read it even though I knew most of it already.

mom's list

"spanked so hard I can't sit down"
"told I'm worthless every day. Bad mother. Stupid."
"dragged by hair around the house."

I remembered that one. It was because the plants weren't watered.
"raped" ...

So what's hard to explain is this: that I could look him in his face and try to get him to follow his dreams, when I know everything that he's done. And I've confronted him on all of it, and he only admits to some. And as much as I'd like to just hate him pure and clean, I'm left with this mixture of resentment and hatred, memories and pity and some kind of love. And I still want more from him than I'll ever get. And I still answer the phone when he calls. -The end

bitterness about old friends dead friends secrets doomed plans I miss crazy

ALL THE WORDS + THEMES SHE'S TRYING TO NOT WRITE ABOUT IN THIS ISSUE, ALL WRAPPED UP INTO ONE SHORT PAGE

It's one of those weeks where the liquor store guy is more worried about what happened to me and my old friends than my friends seem to be. We used to go in together, one big mess of a crowd, now I walk in the doors alone, buy myself a bottle of wine and Zack, behind the counter, smiles at me. "Where is everyone?" he says, "You've all split up?" I shrug my shoulders and tell him I don't know. I tell him we'll be together again someday, all of us. But I don't know. I'm not sure I believe it myself. And sometimes I'm not even sure I want them again.

dead friends

I keep looking down the street and thinking I see Johnathan standing there. Basketball in his hands, hat on his balding head. And what I wouldn't give to be able to see him once again. To rest myself on his shoulder and sigh. Listen to his theories and his life and mine.

doomed plans I miss

I think I've given away too many secrets and the ones I have left are too hard to explain. And I miss my doomed plans. The truck living and pinatas and blackberry pie. They all start dooming before I get to seriously plan them, and it's not quite right. Something's wrong.

crazy

I lay in bed with my sister and tell her I've gone crazy. She rests her hand on my forehead and laughs.

One Week

Caty always hated RV's and I don't blame her. In Plainfield she'd walk down route 2 and they'd woosh by so close they'd almost blow her over. She had to walk down that street every day, and she got this huge vandetta against them. When her and Zoe went on a road trip, Caty made a gun with her fingers and shot every RV they saw. It seemed a bit excessive, but then she got hit by one. It slamed into the side of her car. "I told you they were evil" she whispered to me over the phone.

evil

And I have to drive fast to her hospital bed. Only I miss the turn and end up driving 8 hours in the wrong direction. When I started seeing signs for Portland, I figured something had to be wrong. I end up driving through Yosemete at noon. Slapping my face to keep from falling asleep at the wheel. My boy sits beside me, picking out tapes and lighting me smokes. I stop the car at vista points and scream. Together we scare away the tourists. And end up in this strange small town, cooking tea for my sister over a camp stove in the parkinglot. I have to hold the pan so it doesn't tip over and I watch the water boil. I watch my sister and her broken ribs. I sneek Anna in the window to say hi. And I don't know what else to do.

I DIDN'T KNOW WHAT TO DO EITHER. LITTLE MISS LOOKED SO SAD THERE IN THE BED
AND SHE WOULDN'T PLAY FETCH WITH ME

hotchocolate at laundromats

I guess it probably seems like it's the little things that keep me going. The way roses grow from trees here and the wind flys through the subway tunnels. How one woman sits at the bus stop with her shoulders hunched, hair pulled down over her face. And the girl next to her is reading the same book as me. And I cant tell if they know eachother, if they'remother and daughter, or strangers.

Paint on the sidewalk and the way Mission street looks at 4am. The sign in the window of the clock store says "Sale. Buy one get one free kitchen", and in the shoe store there's a sign "no food, no drink, no icecream cones". I walk by the broken kid toys and old needle caps and an empty lot filled with garbage and protected by barbed wire with a realtor placard saying "no trespassing...welcome home".

The other day at northside, I ordered falafel. The woman standing behind me, she ordered falafel too. She had a pretty dress on and almost sensible shoes, and she turned to me and told me that when she walked in she didn't know what she wanted, but when she heard me order with such confidence she decided to get the same thing.

I do love this stuff - strange exchanges and contridictions. The way cold metal feels against my palms, the way my feet hurt from walking on concrete. Maybe it's true I give these things too much meaning, but I don't know what else I can count on. This fascination and curiosity, these little things I hold on to.

WHAT ABOUT ME? DON'T YOU LOVE ME?

One time me and Walter were in Mammoth Lakes where the mountains on all sides made me claustrophobic and the air was hot and dry. the buildings all looked the same - like ski lodges with heavy slanted roofs, an the people were all from somewhere else. Tourists with spandex or fancy clothes. And me and Walter were driving around and freaking out and getting lost. He said the only way he could deal with this aspect of American culture was to know that he could go back to Oakland, get an AK47, come back and blow it all away. I know that feeling well, but I was looking at all those people and thinking something else.

I was thinking about my cousin Jane and how she wants to be a veterinarian, live in a small town and be an animal doctor. But instead she works for a multination corporation, doing something, I don't know what. Because she wants these things, these perfectly reasonable things. She wants health insurance and enough money to grow old without too much worry. enough money to raise kids when she has them, ar enough money to put them through school. So she works withing the capitalist syst doesn't question it much, because nothing else seems viable, it's the only way sh knows. But I'm sure she would make other choices, if only she felt they were ther

I have this strong empathy for the way people struggle and the ways they get by in this fucked up world. I wonder all the time about what people would be doing if they were presented with options that they didn't normally see. How they would be living and relating to eachother and looking at the world and what they wanted, if there were alternatives that were real and strong.

It's strange because it used to be so clear to me what we needed to do. What kind of organization was most effective. For a few years I worked at the Institute For Social Ecology, an anarchist school in Vermont, where activists from all over the world (kind of) would come to study. We studied philosophy, community development feminism, alternative technology, agriculture and architecture and tied them all together. I went something like this -- the domination of nature stems from the domination of man over man and you can't solve the ecological crisis without changing the very basis of our society and creating a whole new ethics based on freedom --- It was more complex than just that. But it did seem then like this widespread enviornmental destruction would be the stumbling block of capitalism. That the world couldn't withstand the continual growth that capitalism demands, and the capitalists wouldn't be able to ada and the whole fucking system would implode. Well, that's what was counting on anyway.

I went to Minneapolis to be on the Youth Green Coordinating Committee (that was when the greens were still largely radical and lots of anarchists in the group, and they weren't even considering national electoral politics) The idea of the Youth Greens was to have all these political collectives all over the country doing different local work, and then coming together twice a year to discuss politics a plan strategy and coordinate national actions. It sort of worked for awhile, but the ecology movement got co-opted quick and defused. And now I'm not sure what to do.

The thing is, I don't have room for resignation. I don't see any point in giving up. It's more depressing to me to sit around hopeless, than it is to work hard and sometimes, maybe even usually, fail.

Maybe it seems ironic to be saying that, since I haven't done much of anything in the past two years, and I used to spend most of my time doing anarchist organizing, creating and strengthening our politics. When I stopped, at first it was just to take a break, to study and live and try and figure out where to go next. I wanted to start a serious West Coast anarchist school, and I was looking for the right place to put it, but that fell through. Then I was looking for the right people and the right projects to fall in my lap, because I coudn't seem to find them. But I'm sick of waiting, that I know for sure. I've got to put my mind to it an figure something out.

tour stories

I always loved Louise, even though I hardly knew her. The first time my sister brought her over, I was sleeping in my bed with my blanket wrapped around my head like always. Louise gasped and pointed and said to Caty "Does she always sleep with a turban?"

Louise was kind of quiet with the Midwestern style. Caty told me all Louise and her sister ate was cereal. They had 40 boxes of cereal in their basement. When one box was empty, they'd run downstairs for more. One time, their dad brought home 30 pounds of banannas just because they were on sale. And the other thing they ate were sunflower seeds, because sunflowers are a crop of beauty.

When Caty andLouise graduated from highschool, Caty would get letters from her and read them to me. Louise had befriended these two juvenile delinquent boys and she'd pile them and their friends into her car and take them on tours of Moorhead. To the grocery store - she was their tour guide through the isles. To buildings and parkinglots and alleys, where she'd make up historical lies and strange stories. She brought them cigars and made the boys smoke them. And she did it all matter of factly. Not trying to show off or come up with some wacky kind of fun. it was simple. this is what she liked to do.

I love that idea of tours. Leading people through your town, especially when they live there too. You get to see the city again through someone else's eyes.

I took Sascha through the streets the other day, telling him everything I knew about each neighborhood, history, current development plans. I made stuff up when we were in places I'd never been. We walked by one guy who gave us a whole box of donuts. We put some in our pockets and passed the rest out. On one quiet road, a comic guy was painting a mural. The fabric dumpster had strips of blue velvet and corduroy. by the time we got to the waterfront, the sun was low in the sky. A guy appeared out of nowhere and invited us to his fire. He had a little encampment set up there, and a boat he'd rowed over from where he usually stayed. We talked about the Bay and the docking regulations of SF. About Mexico and motorcycles andSSI. He offered us squash he cooked, and we ate it, walking back home along deserted streets, steep hills and the edgeof the freeway. I know I was supposed to be giving Sascha a tour, explaining the city and it's setup, showing him out of the way places to go. But the funny thing was, it made this city finally make sense to me. They layout and the people and how I can live here without going insane.

MAYBE NEXT TIME SHE'LL TAKE ME INSTEAD OF LEAVING ME AT HOME

3rd floor & passed out in doorways

SHE KEPT FORGETTING TO FEED ME

It was nice down at 7th and Howard for awhile. I'd push my dog through the small hole in the garage and then squeeze through myself, feet first, stumble down the dark hallway and up the back stairs. I hear the second floor was nice, carpeted and painted with clean rooms, but I never went there. I went to the third floor, and from the porch you could see a small part of the skyline. american flags on rooftops and neon signs saying "Hotel" I'd knock loud on the locked window and Pirate would let me in, show me his paintings quick. Six foot tall canvases with hinges and doors that opened to something else. In the back room there was alex "hey babe, come sit here by me" and Staples "Christ, not you again". Both of them glad to see me, which is sometimes enough of a reason to like a place these days.

Depending on the time of night, there were other people around, a few or a whole crowd. Jake passing out with her wild Irish Rose, blue paint covering her hair and hands and face, Tim yelling at her "stop fucking with me!" Drew screaming "shut up or we'll get kicked out!" There were kids shooting dope and me drinking beer, and for awhile I liked it, I don't know why. The graffiti on the wall said "667 the neighbor of the beast" and another one "undereducated, nondirectional, fucked up kids". We argued and joked until we passed out. We woke up again when the pidgeons started making too much noise.

But it wasn't the same as being downtown, outside, sitting on the corner and the alleys in the afternoon sun and the cold night air, passing the bottle when my friends were still in town. I was addicted to that corner more than the beer, sprawled out on the block reading books while my friends fought and made big plans they'd never follow through on, told stories and made fun of each-other. The city passed by while we sat there-suits and crackheads and tourists, neighborhood people, friends, and the motherfucker I tried to fight the night before. The neighborhood people smiled or glared, depending on how they felt. Limos would pull up and drop people off for the opera. Juan would yell over and make one of us help him home. It was the city allright, and one of the only places where San Francisco made sense to me.

I'd go down to the corner in the daytime to find Steven, check up on him and we'd commiserate together. "What's up kid?" I'd say to him. "Another day of hating it." He knew me the best out of everyone there, knew what questions to ask to make sure I was all right and cared enough and noticed enough to ask them.

Around the corner we'd find Holly, listening to a walkman, singing Roger Miller loud. She had the best voice and could sing more songs straight through. Her face lit up beautiful whenever you mentioned Michael Jackson. She showed me the best sandwich joint on the block and she could make me feel sane when I wasn't. I'd sit down next to Holly and she'd wrap her arm around me. "What's up lady?" she'd say. "Ah, same old, same old." She'd pass me the beer. I love that girl.

And Sascha and Fish, there was almost nothing better than seeing the two of them walk towards us up the street, walking close together like they anchored eachother. Both with crazy eyes and charming smiles. Both with missing teeth.

There was Johnny, who I recruited to be my big brother, and he played the role perfectly, protective to the hilt. and each of them, before they left, told me something of their life stories, drunk or sobar, subtle or explicit. They saw me through shit and they saw through me. I would have never guessed it, when I first met them, and we sat on that corner drinking away our despair, that these would be the kids who would teach me to want more again. Get back this part of me I had started to leave behind. To expect realness and commitment and true stories, sad or good. To want to hold on and learn more and let eachother go.

My sister's bike rides fast, and I was riding it for awhile. Eyes glued to the road in front of me. Aware of car doors and curbs. Shifting gears and going up hills. I can get from Oakland to Albany in 20 minutes instead of an hour, and I guess that should seem preferable, but really I like to ride slow. Time to wonder and sort things over between one place and the next.

I'm in love with my one speed, my yellow low rider. Even though it hurts my knees. Riding it is hardly any faster than walking, but I like it that way. I can watch the expressions and movements of people in passing, stores that have shut down, new construction, flyers and friends. And the pedals get my thoughts rolling.

Lately I've been thinking about first times. Simple first times. How things I'd never thought before were introduced to my life. Like how one day in Plainfield, Connor showed up in our town. He had walked all the way from Montpelier, found his way by following the river, climbed along the banks for 30 miles. "Why didn't you call?" we asked, "We would have come and gotten you." He shrugged his shoulders and looked at us like we were weird. Like it was the most normal thing in the world to walk from one town to the next. He probably didn't even consider hitchiking or taking the bus.

One time when I was young and still lived at home, me and David were sitting on a bench in the East Bank. He told me about walking through alleys and digging through people's trash. How down by the lakes, the trash after Christmas was amazing. He told me about all the stuff he'd found. Somehow I never knew you could do that.

I remember the first time I found out I could kiss a friend and still be friends, everything still clear and simple. And when I realized you could put problems away for awhile and think about them later, didn't have to be overwhelmed by everything all at once. There was the time I said that SandM in heterosexual relationships was always about oppressing women, and someone else said "not necessarily". They didn't even have to say more than that for me to change my mind. I'd just never questioned it before. Same with the assumption that we were all working toward complete insurrection. That'that's what we wanted in the end. I mentioned it to Paula one day and she said that she though that in this society, armed revolution wasn't even a desirable goal.

I remember the first time I looked at my friends life and realized I'd be alright even if I didn't find a place to settle down. And when another friend taught me how to scam public transportation. I'd never thought to try that.
I've been riding my bike around, going over these things. What I take for granted that I didn't used to. Single sentances andparticular days that changed me, and how I can use that experience to change things.

#8

i drempt we had a pet camel

IT WAS HARD TO WALK AROUND TOWN WITH IT.

EAST

THE MAIN PROBLEM WASN'T THAT THE CAMEL ONLY ATE BANANAS.
THE PROBLEM WAS, WE WERE MOVING.

OUR TRUCK WAS ALREADY FULL OF ALL OUR JUNK

CATY SAID I SHOULD JUST TAKE A PLANE + SHE'D DRIVE OUT + MEET ME W/ THE CAMEL

I WAS AFRAID SHE'D GET HIT BY AN R.V. AGAIN.

I SAID I'D JUST RIDE THE CAMEL ACROSS THE COUNTRY.

OUCH

d b

SHE SAID MY BUTT WOULD GET TOO SORE

WE ENDED UP ON 6TH + MARKET

PST. WANTA BUY A CAMEL?

dear sam.

the other day i gave my mechanic my magazine. basically because he's a young mechanic andhe was making a personal phone call when i walked into the garage andhe said 'i loveyou' into the phone when he was hanging up and the person on the other line had obviously already hung up. right. so i give him the magazine and later asked him to go drink a beer with me down at the tracks.maybe i was trying to pick him up, may be i just wanted to kick around town with someone i had no history with and so no mixed feeling about or expectations of. one or the other. same thing. anyway, he didnt go drink beer with me, but the coolest thing happened. when i went back to the garage because my truck broke again, the receptionist woman says to me "I was going to call you". and she is this lady, older than me and really friendly, loves my dog. she pulls out my magazine - the boy had lent it to her , and she starts talking to me all about how she was trying to get her kids to write her stories about their lives for christmas. anything, just a story. and she starts telling me abouthow she didn't care if they wrote one sentance or a big long thing and how hard it was to get them to do it. and how one of her kids wrote one real short story about how his dad (and she had this pause there like she was going to explain something but then didn't) had told him it was a bad idea to slide down the stairsin a cardboard box but didn't try to stop him from doing it. i don't know. it was so nice. she wasn't pouring out her life to me. just talking about something she wanted - some thing she was trying to do andget her kids to do. i felt all awkward because the boy was there and hadn't returned my phone call, and she was a mother and i didn't know what was appropriate to ask or say. and i wish i would think 'yeah. I'd liketo call that lady up and kick around town with her.' but thats not what i think. i think 'i'dlike her to adopt me'. she is going to give me her extra set of chains for my tires so i can get across the mountains when i leave.

♥Cindy

*apple of my eye

He had a wandering eye, that's why I fell for him, even though his name was Hank. We'd cruise around the alleys, me on my bike, him on my skateboard. I'd stand in the dirt and look up at him while he threw me apples and plums from the tops of trees. "another apple, another step closer to self-sufficiency" he'd say.

Hank believed wholeheartedly that when conditions were right, the masses would rise up out of nowhere and organize spontaneously along the precepts of mutual aid. Fighting the cops, feeding the hungry. The transit workers would take over the transportation, workers would sieze the means of production, students would take over the schools. all people needed was the faith that they could do it. He wanted to instill that faith in them.

We'd walk all over the city together. I was looking for a warehouse to move in to. He was devising escape routes and drawing up maps for when the army of the poor took to the streets again.

The army of the poor? He had to be joking.

Every kids tree fort was a potential safe house. Every large bush, a hidden communique center. all the telephone poles and lamp posts displayed our flyers. His, the Black Panther 10 point program; mine, poetry and collages. It was nice to be with someone who wasn't smarter than me for once, and who still had big dreams of revolution.

On good days, he'd take me out to eat at Sisters of the Road. $1.25 or a food stamp for a plate of watery pinto beans, soggy rice and a little salsa on the side. He taught me to look for dropped wallets in parking lots. We spent a lot of time doing that. And searching through dumpsters for stuff we didn't know we needed until we found it. He showed me the best blackberry bush in town. It had a big sign next to it that said "don't pick. Pesticides"
"They're lieing" he said "greedy bastards. We can wash them just in case. You can never be too sure."

If we got home early, the kids would grab us, screaming for attention as we tried to sneek by. Our room was the hallway linen closet. One little window. One small bed. We couldn't even stand up in there.

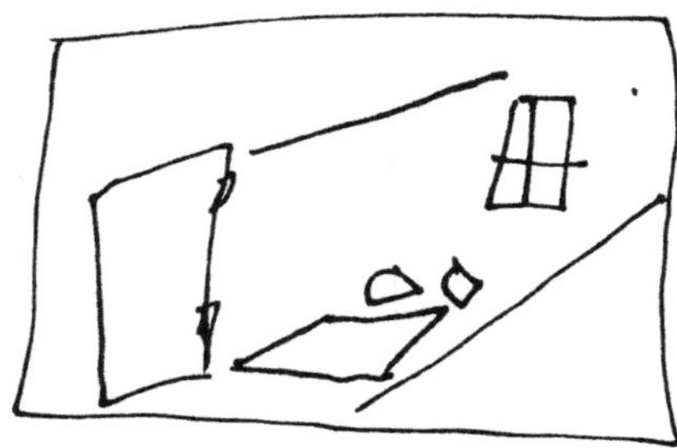

But wait a second. Hold on. You need some background information. See, two years before I moved to the West Coast and met Hank, I was living in Minneapolis. I ran the Youth Green Clearinghouse, was a member of the political collective AWOL, and helped edit "Free Society." Comrade Paul found out I wrote short stories and he lent me a fanzine. He handed it to me like it was contraband literature. We were suppose to be studying Heidegger, not punk. I carried the magazine with me in my pocket and read it three times before giving it back. Where did Paul get such a thing? And who wrote it? I'd never heard of a fanzine that wasn't dogmatic tirades or irrelevant garbage. I confided in Paul that I wanted to do one myself. One where I interviewed everyone I knew who was involved in politics. Ask them how they would be living and what projects they would be doing if they had the people and means to carry them out.
"What would you be doing?" Paul asked me. I wasn't completely sure. I wanted a house with music and lots of people around. A place to be inspired and sustained. A collective in a loose sence, where household problems wouldn't take precedence over our more serious work. But the main thing I wanted was a printing press. I had to laugh when I told Paul that. It seemed like an impossible dream.

So I was really surprised when I ended up on the West Coast and showed up at the Food Not Bombs house to volunteer. Laura gave me a tour of their house slash community center. "That's the library" she said, as we walked by a few rows of disheveled books. She brought me through the kitchen and down the stairs "The junked bike parts pile, the music room, the art supply closet that's actully just full of Hanks dumpsterd junk".

"What's in there?" I pointed to the one closed door.
"That's the printing press room."

"A printing press!"
"Yeah. But Arthur dismantled it so no one else can use it. A little bit of a power trip. He thinks the press is his".

Back upstairs and into the kitchen, Hank was chopping carrots and staring at me out of his one good eye. Laura handed me a knife and a bucket full of zucchini and left the room, leaving us alone. Hank made me nervous, I got sullen and quiet, trying to think of something interesting to say. He was looking me over, I was chopping zucchini, finally he broke the silence.

"Are you a cop?" he said.

I've always had this fear of people thinking I'm an agent. Probably because my Minneapolis friends had been so paranoid. We only talked to eachother from pay phones. They never let me take their pictures.

I spent three hours explaining to Hank my political background. Disclosing as much of myself as I could and feeling more suspicious the more I said. A week later we were going out and I moved into the closet with him.

It took awhile to get to know everyone else. The kids were outgoing but everyone else pretty much kept to themselves, or were wrapped up in their own relationships. We all got along fine, cooking soup and complaining about Arthur. We probably could have gone on like that forever if I hadn't stole an espresso machine and brought it home.

"Another soy latte?" Keith would yell from the kitchen. He stood vigil by the thing, cranking out one after the other until we were wired to the hilt. We stopped leaving the house. There was too much to do inside. Organize and reorganize the library. We'd bang on the drums, all of us together, while the kids played the guitars. We'd laugh at their nightly theater performances. Yell out our life stories. We couldn't sleep. We'd burn the soup. "Capuccino anyone?" we couldn't refuse.

Then the purges started. First it was Elroy. He was a non coffee drinker. He was a drunk. And one day Faith bumped into him in the hallway. "Fisherman's whore" he shouted in Spanish, unaware that Spanish was Faith's first language. That very night he got the boot.

Nick was too bourgeois. And he didn't help us cook. He wasn't vegan. Never stole toys for the kids. He didn't even attend house meetings. We held secret sessions and devised our plan. We'd just treat Nick like shit until he'd feel so ostracized he'd leave on his own accord. It worked.

Next came Arthur, but he picked his own fight. And he picked it with me, the stupid jerk. It started with some minor disagreement, but he took a strong offensive and stood inches from me, yelling and sticking his finger in my face. I yelled back twice as loud, stuck my finger in his face like a sword. I was ready to duel. But I had moved past our original dispute and was yelling about how oppressive his argumentative style was, how reeking of violence his posture was, how his whole attitude upheld sexist values of keeping women silent by the threat of force. Eventually the whole house stood behind me and eventually he was out on the street too.

Then came me.

We got the news that Love and Rage was sponsoring Lorenzo Irving on a speaking tour. Fuck yeah. Lorenzo Irving. I was excited. He wrote to us, since we were the Anarchist Community Center, asking if we could raise money for his travel expenses and set up a speaking hall and all of that. None of us had jobs, we were all on welfare, except Faith and Chako who had paper routes delivering the daily lie. But a couple hundred bucks, I was sure we could get it somehow. I posted the letter on the collective bulletin board. And right away notes started piling up. Crude remarks covering Lorenzo's letter.

"The new anarchist darling"
"Who is he to speak for anyone"
"Opportunist pig"
stuff like that. At the house meeting, it was decided that if he wanted to come and hang out in our kitchen and talk to us as equals we'd welcome him. Anything beyond face-to-face communication was authoritative and oppressive. Love and Rage was a bunch of white guilt bourgeois fucks. I kept quiet the whole meeting. I

abstained from the vote. I couldn't believe my comrades I knew so well were so completely different from me. I moved out of the house shortly after that. Nobody knew why.

Shortly after that, me and Hank were walking through the woods together. Holding hands and pretending to get along. He said "what I'd really like is to be a fruitarian. But to do it you have to eat the fruit at the precisely right moment. As it's falling off the tree but before it hits the ground."

I could picture our lives together. Broken printing presses, screaming kids, me eating candy bars and him running from tree to tree. His very existance depending on being under the tree when conditions were right. When the fruit would fall and he'd catch it.

"Fruitarian?" I said and I couldn't stop laughing. He looked at me with his one eye sad, his other eye wandering, and that was that. It was over. Maybe I was an agent provocature after all.

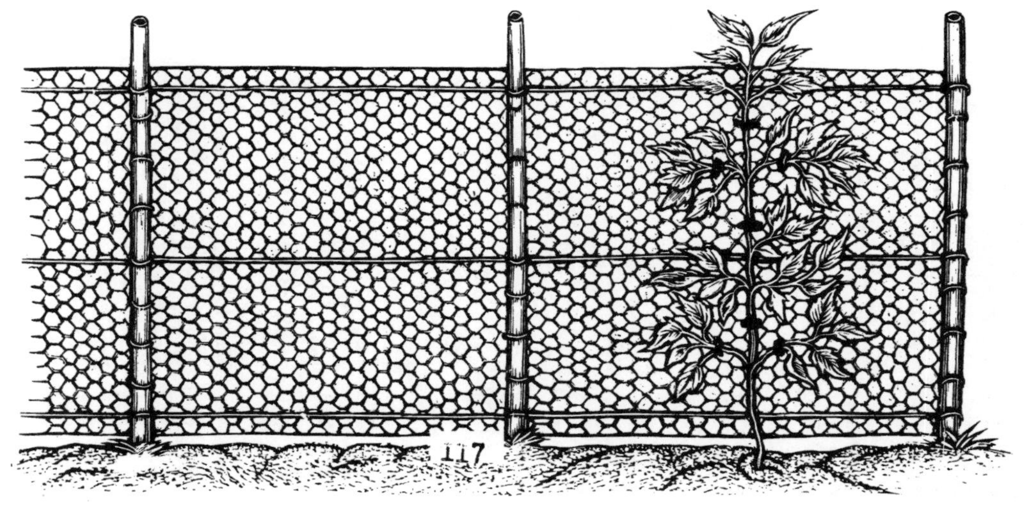

no one understands
a girl
and her dog
z
z
z
BED
OK OK
FANCY
RESTURANT
BUTCHER
POLUTION
STOP ROLLING
IN DEAD
THINGS.

SHIT, IT'S COLD OUT

WHERE ARE WE GOING TO SLEEP TONIGHT?

KNOCK KNOCK KNOCK

WHAT!

MY DOG DOESN'T SMELL BAD

NO

SHE'S NOT GONNA PISS ON YOUR FLOOR

WAIT A MINUTE!!!

girl age 15

being around the girls too much made me nervous. they talked about real personal things like family, relationships, sex, body image - all things i would have liked to forget

the boys talked about vague concepts. made jokes. discussed motorcycle repairs and new yonk city. neutral ground. they never asked me questions so i ended up with the boys.

it wasnt that i devalued womens friendship, but i was embarrased by the way Haley went hysterical when she saw her boy with another girl. i couldnt stand to see her reduced to that. i hated how they were always hounding jessica for details about sex. she was the only one of us who'd had it. i mean, i'd had it too, but i pretended i hadn't. what was i going to say? "Yeah, you lie there on the floor while he's all on top of you and it goes on forever and you end up with rug burns up and down your spine".

i didnt like the way they seemedto embrace drama and confusion. I couldnt figure out where i fit in or what the hell we were doing, or why Wren dressed all sexy style, slickedback hair andred lips. 15 year old tits stuffed into a bustier and that blank untouchable stare that made it so obvious what had been done to her. Our contradictions were so apparent. But if I didnt hang out with the girls, i didnt have to think about it as much.

It was easy with the boys. I had my place- I was Noah's girl. and his friends didn't expect me to talk much andI didn't expect them to understand me. i didnt expect much at all.

i thought i was growing up fast by hanging out with the older boys. i thought i'd get to skip past this awkward phase my friends were in. i thought i'd skip past the self doubt and self hate and get to something collected and in control and cool. but instead i just learned to stop thinking for myself.

i was a quick learner . i studied those boys good. and i learned to act how i thought they wanted me to. I was cynical and stood square shouldered and tall.

i pretended like i knew what they were talking about even when i didnt. i never showed curiosity about new things or ideas because i was afraid it would betray my youth. i stopped questioning just about everything.

it was really fucked up, because even though i came off as strong and mature, i wasnt. my diary reads like this:

Jan 4.
"wow. I haven't talked to Noah in 2 days :((it seems like much longer) I hope he wants to do something tomorrow. god. I hope he likes me as much as I like him."

Jan 8.
"Noah makes me so happy :) ! he called me today just to say hi. I'm worried because last time we hung out at Tims house, he shot up :(. He's not one now but I'm I'm scared he might become a drug addict. I'm worried."

I know i was too old to be making smily and frowny faces, but i was still too young to express my more complicated emotions. and i didnt know myself well enough to trust my own needs and goals and desires.

i still find myself doing the things i learned back then. instead of trying to figure out what i think about things, i try and figure out what i'm suppose to think. i act out what other people expect.

all the time, i find myself going along with other peoples plans and ideas - fulfilling their needs instead of my own. i've gotten so use to it, i don't even know what it is I want most of the time - don't even think about it. thats what being a young girl, hanging out with the older boys did to me. and thats how deeply ingrained it became.

i dont think it's across the board bad, young girls older boys, i just think that the boys are kind of clueless. they're easily tricked.

sometimes it's the gawky, awkward girls who can hold on to their self identity and sometimes the girls who seem the toughest are the ones getting swept away.

..., Oakland
FREE CARTOON CARNIVAL
Elmwood Theater from 10am to 1p
day, September 30 and Sunday, Oc
Just a part of the fun at the Elmwood
Crafts Faire at College and Ashby in
The Faire runs from 10am to 6pm both
FREE DEPRESSION SCREENING of
5435 College Avenue, Oakland, on N
Depression Screening Day, Thursday, C
5 between 8am and5 pm. No appoi
necessary. Call 652-4455 for infor
"COMMUNALISM, Ethnic C
temporary Politics in

it was national depression screening day and all we had to do was wake up andget to rockridge by 5 and take a short and easy test. later that same day, some professional would determin wheather we were depressed or not.

it was the only me and caty had been looking forward to it all week. thing we hadto look forward to.

allison spent the night so we could all go together. we didnt wake up in time.

"oh well" said caty, " i already know i m depressed. I'd throw myslef on the electric thiid rail if i didnt think it would upset you".

"I'm not depressed", i said, "I'm as happy as can be". caty got a good laugh out of that one.

What about Allison? neither of usknew her all that well. "yeah, hey allison. what about you?" she tilted her head down and lookedup at us. "that's why i wantedto go with you guys. I'm really not sure."

"not sure?! well, of course you're depressed. who isnt". andwith that we rode our bikes across town, shouting at eachother as we rode.

"the best cure istons and tons andtons of coffee"
"depression is fine as long as you're by the ocean"
"I've heard eating a banana every day helps"

caty found an intertube we got our supplysandheaded down tothe bay. and made a giant slingshot. Allison taught us to make a whistle out of grass. we hauled bricks up from the beach and rearranged slabs of concrete until we had something resembling a cave, then we climbedin. we needed a fire. we needed s'mores. i biked back up to the store while alison andcaty scavenged wood. by the time i got back the fire was blazing. they'd built a table out oftiles anda plank of wood. i dumped out the grahm crackers, chocolate andmarshmellows. "too bad we missed that depression day bullshit"

"well, there's always next year" caty said.

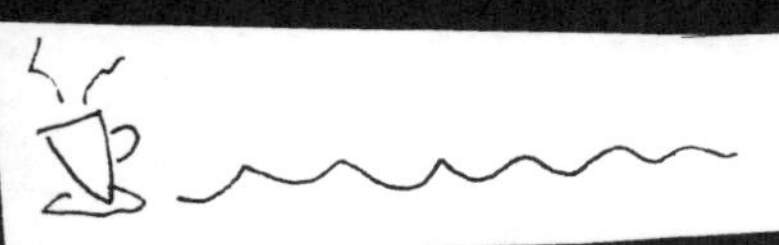

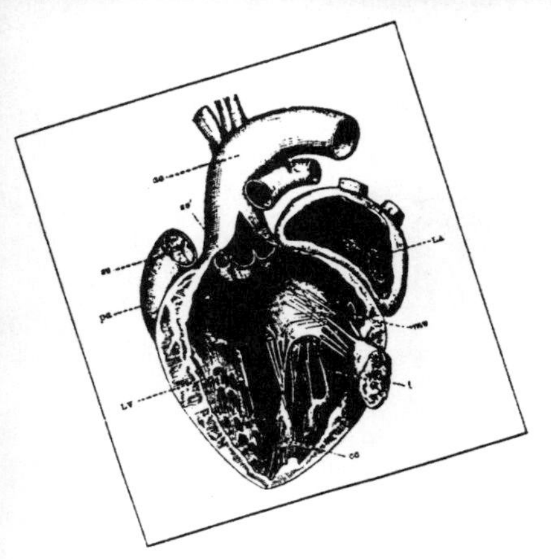

renville

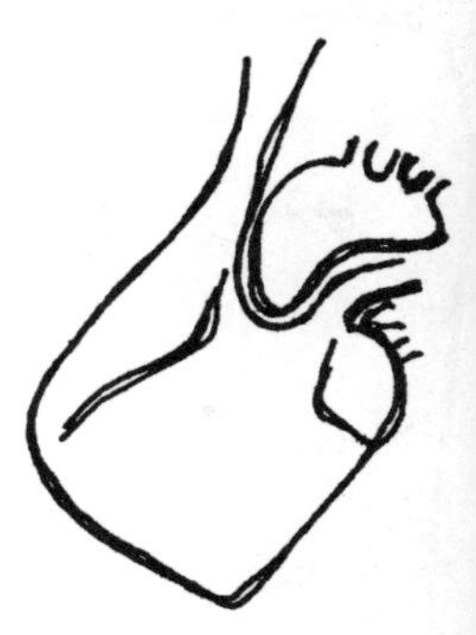

I go and look for my heart in the sugar beet town. Wait by the liquor store hoping he'll show up. Walk through the streets past every van, peering in the windows to try and see if it's his. Finally I see a redhaired girl and I follow her up to the front door. "Does Colby live here?"

His shoulders are wider and he looks older. He holds me tight to him like he always does, in that way thats comforting and draining and clears my head and fills it with new questions all at once. I look around nervous, wondering how I'll fit in to this life, this time, for this one day.

"my head broke", he says, and points to the engine sitting on the livingroom floor. He explains to me valves and combustion and sparks. I tell him I met my little sister for the first time. I tell him it was good to see my dad. I tell him I've been feeling less crazy because I decided to give up on almost everyone I know and now I don't have to worry about them anymore. Both of us know I'm half lieing, but he thinks that i think that i'm telling the truth

He's not my heart like he use to be, when I wanted too much and convinced myself that I wanted nothing at all. When I said love is a loose thing, but I was tied tight to him and couldn't fall for anyone else. This time it's different. He is farther away. I am holding more back. This time it's the same. We don't talk much. We drink until we pass out in eachothers arms and sleep without having to worry about whether or not we're suppose to fuck.

i lose track of things

It's finally winter, after 3 years of perpetual spring summer and fall. In Vermont I wake up and look out Paula's window. The ground is covered with snow, just like it should be. A white field with one big sunflower still standing, drooped over and dried into more shades of brown than I usually notice. And a jay bird lands there on the head of the flower.

This is what I keep forgetting. These colors, these things.

Walking down the railroad tracks with Kris, drinking Pepsi out of long neck bottles, snow comming in over the tops of my shoes. There's someone standing in the river with waist high waders, casting their fishing pole.

I know how to bait a hook and gut a fish. I know how to row a boat, paddles or oars. I know how to tell if the ice is thick enough to walk on. These are the things I know.

FIGURE #1

In California I've gotten use to the palm trees. I'm not startled by lizards sunning themselves on the rocks. I pick armfulls of flowers from peoples gardens who have so many roses they won't even notice a few gone. My friends there invent new instruments out of junk they find in dumpsters. They solder together wires and motors and needles and build entire sterio systems just to give away. They do things like walk from Santa Cruz to Oakland. Ride bikes from Berkeley to Chicago. They know about sticking together and living on the fringe, they don't worry it's abnormal.

In someways I can still pretend I live in a small town. I know where I can usually find Janelle in the afternoons. I keep running into Aaron at 2am. My housemates cook me breakfast and we don't have a telephone.

Sometimes I'm so glad to be in the city, like everything I need is right there and it's only a matter of finding. But still, I can't quite grasp it - Oakland B erkeley Albany SanFrancisco.

I stay up late with my friends, on rooftops, on bikes, in alleys, sitting at desks, driving around. And everyone's frame of reference is so different from mine. Sometimes that's refreshing. I've learned new ways of thinking and looking at problems. H ow to be close without suffocation. But lately I just keep wanting to go home. If only I knew where that was.

In Ithica I walk donw the railroad tracks and there's more Canadian Geese in the sky then I've ever seen in one place. They're flying this way and that, half in formation, half contradicting eachother. It looks like they're suppose to be migrating, but they're not sure which way t o go. Or maybe they're not sure wheather to leave at all since that water is still unfrozen.

Obviously, I'm wrong. That's not what the geese are doing.

They know exactly what they need.

in '85 i thought it was kind of weird that my friends were always beating up skinheads. they were all so skiny and nice.
"hey guys, what's up?"
"going to the club to beat up skinheads."
"come on guys, we're gonna be late."
"you comming cindy?"
= bad
= good
= can't remember
i couldn't figure out how they could tell the bad skinheads from the good ones.
"excuse me sir but can i get a closer look at your patches so i know weather to watch your back or stomp you?"
7 YEARS LATER
"i say it's fine to disrupt nazis from speeking."
what about free speech?
"what good is free speech when we don't have freedom? it's a farce"
ARA
me
imagine many more people in chairs
i was really shy and never talked. i just brought in articles and essays all the time.
everyone thought i was pretty weird.
but what was really weird was that the public library let us meet in their conference room.
LIBRARY
"i brought in copys of this article 'repressive tollerence' by Marcuse. there's copys for everyone, um, here"
"great cindy, now who's going to draw up the agenda"
one day we decide to try and stop the nazis from going on the collage radio.

everyone said there would probably be violence so i didn't go. i still got freeked out memories of violent shit.
SINK
make them stop
SISTER
smack!
slam
"i work all day and come home to this mess! where's dinner?!"
it turned out there was a big fight on the pedestrian bridge campus cops siding with the nazis, of course.
so the next day at the ARA meeting everyone was pretty worried the nazis would come attack us at the library
"all clear over here."
LIBRARY
"no nazis on this side either"
a couple guys had walkie talkies. they kept watch outside
INSIDE
we practiced defensive and offensive moves using chairs as weapons
chair barricade
IT WAS SO FUCKIN FUNNY. HA HA HA
PUNKS
6TH
WAIT. WHAT. SO DID YOU KICK SOME NAZI ASS?
NO. THEY DIDN'T EVEN SHOW UP.
SO WHERES THE FUCKIN STORY. WHATS SO FUNNY?
WE FUCKING BARRICADED OURSELVES INTO THE PUBLIC LIBRARY!
IT WAS GREAT! IT WAS FUNNY!

GRACELAND

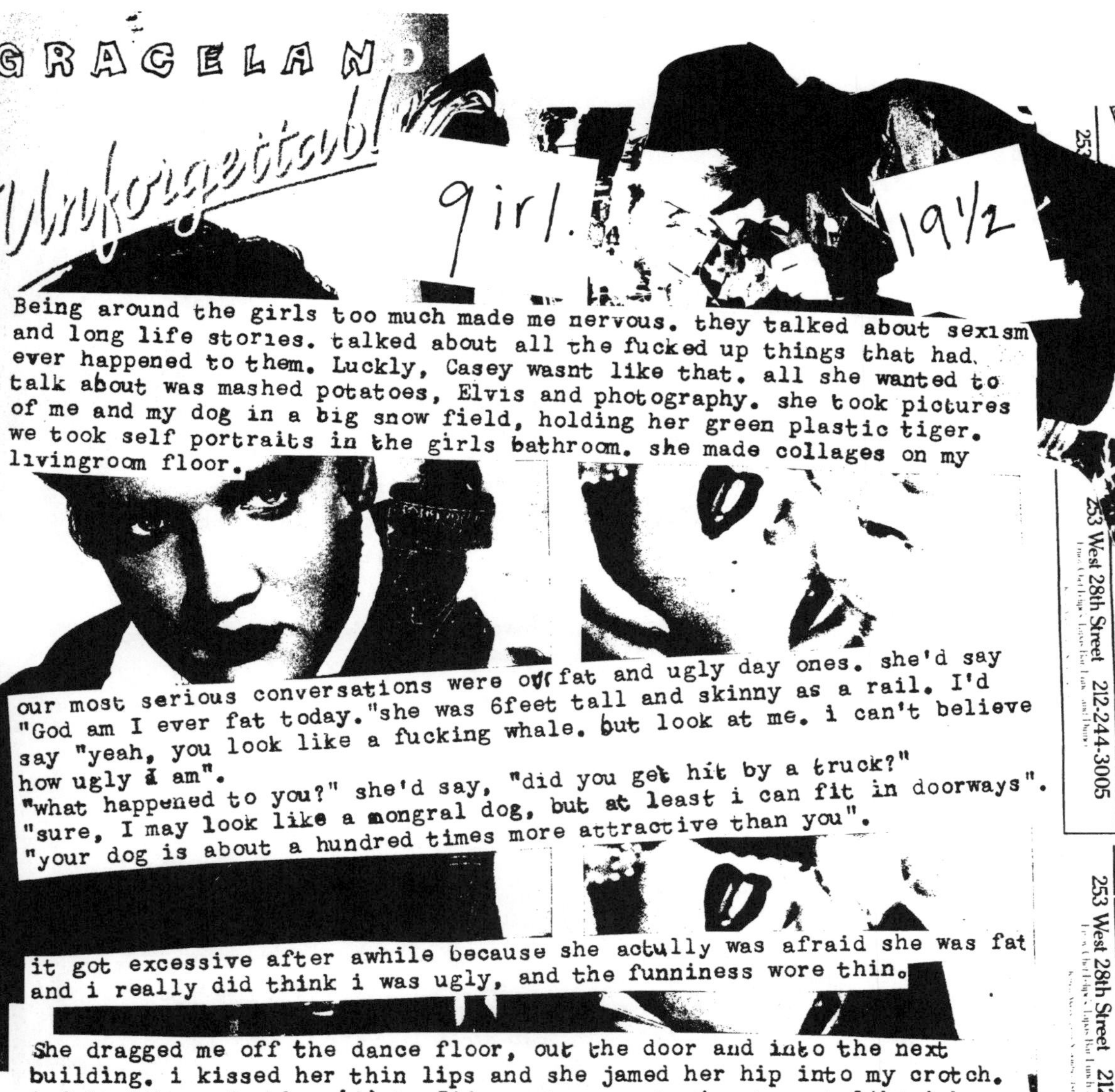

Being around the girls too much made me nervous. they talked about sexism and long life stories. talked about all the fucked up things that had ever happened to them. Luckly, Casey wasnt like that. all she wanted to talk about was mashed potatoes, Elvis and photography. she took pictures of me and my dog in a big snow field, holding her green plastic tiger. we took self portraits in the girls bathroom. she made collages on my livingroom floor.

our most serious conversations were our fat and ugly day ones. she'd say "God am I ever fat today."she was 6feet tall and skinny as a rail. I'd say "yeah, you look like a fucking whale. but look at me. i can't believe how ugly I am".
"what happened to you?" she'd say, "did you get hit by a truck?"
"sure, I may look like a mongral dog, but at least i can fit in doorways".
"your dog is about a hundred times more attractive than you".

it got excessive after awhile because she actully was afraid she was fat and i really did think i was ugly, and the funniness wore thin.

She dragged me off the dance floor, out the door and into the next building. i kissed her thin lips and she jamed her hip into my crotch. i felt like a fucking idiot. I'd spent years trying to act like i knew what i was doing when i was making out with guys andi finally understood it, but this girl thing was really different.

i wanted to be her girlfriend but didnt know how. she wanted to be my girlfriend the same way she use to want to go to Graceland. it was fun to talk about but kind of sucked once you were there.

san jose

you know how sometimes you get a town stuck in your head - some place you've never been. like albuquerque or lovelock, andyou know it's stupid, but the name sounds so good and you think may be you should just pack up and move there? that's how i was with san jose. I found this sign once - chipped plastic and blue faded letters. san jose it said, and it fit right in the palm of my hand. i brought it home andput it on my windowsill, up on the very top, almost out of sight. where i'd catch it out of the corner of my eye every day andit would sneek its way into my brain.

every day i'd be stuck on that song 'do you know the way to san jose', andit wasn't annoying either, like it usually is when you have the same song stuck in your headfor weeks and weeks. i'd walk down the avenue, humming the one line i knew, thinking about driving broken cars where the brakes are so lousy you have to use both feet on the pedal to get the thing to stop, and the oldies playing on the raido - the one channel that comes in, and your best friend beside you laughing loud.

san jose. everyone i asked said it was a shit hole, but what did they know anyway? i stopped asking. i got out a map and found out where it was.

we finally went there, me caty and aaron. woke up early and loaded ourselves into the truck. made it down in time for the free outside afternoon mtx show. danced on the sweltering concrete. we were the only ones dancing, probably the only ones accully there to see them. everyone else looked like they'd just happened by. they sat in the back rows of the ampatheater and snarled. they didn't come down to our lemonaide stand. 'cold lemonaide, 10¢' i would yell. i only had one taker. it didn't really matter though. it was san jose. it was great.

philadelphia

phili was all burnt buildings, cops and sandwiches from the corner store. me cutting glass and soldering it together to make new windows for all the ones that were broken. saul cutting wood and fixing the stairs. sanding down doors to fit in doorways, talking to the people whose squat it was. i just listened, didnt say much. i was shy.

i think everyone there thought we were crazy, and they were basically right. we were driving around the east coast, we had this plan. actully it was saul's plan, i just went along with it cuz it sounded good, and plus i had no ideas of my own. we were going to drive from city to city, boston, phili, ny, i cant remember where else - hook up with squaters and fix up the squats. be this traveling squat repair team. we were gonna learn solar power and different kinds of alternative technology and try and do a bunch of stuff like that and build some kind of mass squaters network. saul said it would be great, i didnt know. i'd never even heard of squats before i met him. there were a couple problems off the bat. all our tools got stolen, and we didnt know shit about solar power or wind power or anything because we were always too busy fighting to study.

we were trying to have the perfect anarchist relationship. that was his idea. i didnt even know what an anarchist was until i met him. he said the couple was the perfect place to start in the prefiguration of a new society. we had to learn to trust eachother completely, know eachother entirely, communicate on levels that seemed impossible. push eachother to overcome all our neuroses. break through all the barriers that we'd learned to put up around ourselves. then we would be free. then we could change the world. i believed him.

it didnt take long for him to get me to tell the truth for the first time about how i was sexually abused. and thenhe kept asking questions. how didit effect me? how didi feel? and i was bawling and he kept asking questions. he got me to admit that i felt like a slut. that i always thought i was bad. that sometimes i thought the only worth i had was sexual worth, and a lot of times that's what i used as my defence - it didnt matter what happened to me, nothing could affect me, no one could really hurt me if all i was was a body.

he dug up everything i was afraid to look at, put it in one big pile and pushed me into it. all my history and self hate and fears. he was trying to get me to look at my life within a social context. all i knew was if i didn't deal with it all fast, i wouldn't be good enough.

saul seemed to think that everything went in some kind of formula. some kind of rational order. like confession, confrontation, resolution. i had to write long letters to my family and my best friend, in distant, dogmatic language, telling them what i was dealing with and why it wasnot only important to me, but also a revolutionary imparative that they deal with all their own bullshit too. i was trying to get my mom to quit drinking, my older sister to stop hiding from her past, my stepdad to stop being distant, my best friend to stop being so dreamy. i was trying to sue the fucking psychiatrist i'd gone to. everyone failed me, but i wasnt alowed to accept defeat. saul said i had to keep fighting.

i started counting corners in the room, knobs on the stove. i had nothing to hold on to. it was all too much, too fast, too soon. all i had was saul - and then he said our relationship was screwed. it wasn't equal. i was too passive. didn't take initiative. didnt show enough interest in his problems. i was self absorbed. he couldn't trust me to be there for him.

i can't believe how screwed up it was, this ideal relationship. i was pushed to the point of collapse and then told to pull myself up, prove myself. i tape recorded our conversations to study later, see where i went wrong, why i couldn't reach him. i fixed his car to show that i was capable of at least something. i spent all my time with him.

somethings wrong with me. i said. all of a sudden i feel all terrified of sex. i said. i think i can't have sex for awhile. i've got to deal with this. he said if we werent haveing sex we weren't boyfriendgirlfriend. i didnt get the semantics. i said, but i can't he said, you're breaking up with me? i cant believe after all this you're just breaking up with me. i couldn't afford to lose him. we kept having sex. every night.

i thought the squat idea sounded good. we'd be away from our house our cramped bed, our normal lives. we'd be around other people. we'd be moving, we'd be doing something. and it did turn out to be a good distration sort of. the squat was kind of funny, full of stoves that didn't work and huge piles of junk for when they turned the first floor into a free store. Bill said he'd give us a tour of the city, andhe did. showing us all these abandon buildings, some of them so oldand cracked that trees grew right up through them. it was was really nice. i went with jenny to go put up flyers that said 'you can't rape a .38' big bold letters with a picture of a gun. the the next day, under each gun, someone had written 'but you can rape with one'.

i spent my time on the thrid floor, alone. piecing together glass, cutting my fingers, installing windows, trying to keep out the cold. there were twelve broken windows and i fixed eight before we left. but the wind still swept through that room.

it didnt work out with me and saul. i tried to kill myself, i tried to holdus together. i never did understand exactly what it was he needed from me. but by the time he finally left, there were a couple things i understood. that it's fucked up to expect one person to be everything for you, and that some things have to be dealt with slow. when he finally left and i didnt have to think about how i'd failed or how i'd failed him, it was almost funny how clear things became.

MOVE

a couple streets away from the squat was osage avenue, and you could walk by all the wreckage. the burnt up buildings, the lot wherethe MOVE house use to stand. it's pretty hard to believe what happened there - hew the cops came on may 13, 1985, and did their best to destroy MOVE. they shot over 10,000 rounds of ammunition into the house - uzis, m-16's, shot guns, automatics, a 20mm anti-tank gun. flooded the place with fire truck hoses, flooded the place with tear gas. tried to blast through the walls with military explosives, and when none of that worked, they went up in a helecopter and dropped a bomb on the house. stood by while the whole block burned to the ground. and when MOVE members did try to leave the house, they were shot at. 6 adults and 5 kids died. the medical examiners office helped cover it all up - leaving the bodys unrefridgerated. and all the tests were delayed so everything was inconclusive - no one knew the cause of death, no one could be blamed. years later when there was a reexamination, and i guess they must have dug the bodys up, there were bullet fragments found in the bodies that had never been reported. there were limbs that had been cut off and were missing. john africa, the leader of MOVE, had his head cut off - it wasn't burried with him.

i don't really understand exactly what MOVE's politics were or why the phili police force was so dead set on their obliteration. MOVE started in the '70's as a sort of revolutionary, urban, back to nature group, with a really strong focus on family and community, natural life styles and a reverance for all life. they were trying to wake people up - show how unjust and oppressive this society is - get people on the move, get people off their asses, get people fighting to be free.

they had an in your face, loud, direct style - and held protests at pet shops, political rallies and media offices. they didn't advocate violence, but believed in self defence. and the phili police force gave them plenty of reasons to need to defend themselves.

philadelphia cops had a national reputation for racism and brutality. and when MOVE started speaking out against the police force and the hypocracy of the judicial system - holding demos that

were so successful, other communtiy groups started asking MOVE for help in planning demos in their neighborhoods - when that happened the cops began making a real effort to arrest MOVE members as often as possible.

the cops brutality toward MOVE wasn't confined to breaking up demos. they'd harrass them randomly on the street, like in '74 they stopped 2 pregnant MOVE women who were walking to the store. stopped them and questioned them and beat them up, slamming one stomach first into the cop car. stuck them in jail overnight without water or food. both women miscarried.

in '75 they arrested another pregnant MOVE woman, dragged her from the holding cell, held her spread-eagle and kicked her in the stomach and crotch. she miscarried too.

in '76 the cops came to the MOVE house one time when people were being noisy or something. they dragged one guy off the poarch and beat him so bad they broke a night stick in half over his head. they pushed this one woman to the ground with her baby in her arms, and stomped on her until she was nearly unconcious and the baby was dead. later the cops said they had never been to the house that night. they said the broken night stick, which had been left there, was stolen property. and they refused to admit the baby even existed - since it had been born at home and had no birthcertificate no leagal documentation.

this was just some of the shit that happened. by '76 there were hundreds of MOVE cases in the philadelpia court system. MOVE defended themselves and fought a pretty successful battle. but the police harrassment kept getting worse and worse. and MOVE started worrying that the same kind of campaign that was waged against the Black Panthers would be waged against them. they put boards over their windows, stoodon their poarch holding guns, (which is legal by the way) and staged a major demonstration from their house, calling for the release of their political prisoners and an end to police harrassment.

police set up a 24 hour watch around the MOVE house, and eventually sealedoff a four block area around the house in an attempt to starve MOVE members out - the justification was that there were supposidly people inside who had warrents out and hadn't shown up for court.

after 2 months of this blocade, they negotiated, ended the barricade searchedthe house, and found nothing incriminating. MOVE was suppose to leave the house, and the city was suppose to help them find a new place to live within 90 days.

after 90 days, MOVE was still in the house and the cops came in full force and ordered them to surrender. the cops buldozed the porch off. MOVE barricaded themselves into the basement. the cops pried the basement windows off and turned on the water cannons.

i've seen the police movie footage of people crawling out the basement windows, soaked with children in their arms. there were gunshots fired, cops say it came from the MOVE house, but most other witnesses say it came from across the street. a cop was killed. police opened fire. tear gas was thrown into the house and more people poured out. there's footage of this one guy comming out of the house with his hands up over his head, and getting beat up so badly - kicked full force in the head. kicked so hard his body raises up off the sidewalk, dragged by his hair, hit with the butt of a gun.

the cop that was killed had been shot in the back of the neck, the bullet entering his body at a downward angle. it seems pretty unlikely that the bullet could have come from the MOVE house, since they were all in the basement - couldnt have shot from that angle at all. but 9 MOVE members were pronounced guilty for the thing. given 30 to 100 years in jail. no copsor officials were ever indited for any of this shit andeven the 1985 bombing wasn't considered excessive force. the federal grand jury declaired that civil rights hadn't been violated, and there are still 5 MOVE members in prison.

if you want more info you can write to move at: pob 19709, phili, pa. 19143. they've got a pamphlet, newsletter, movies

It had been more than a week since I'd hung out on 6th + Market. I was turning over
a new leaf
BED
BED
BED
OH FUCK. TODAY IS THE PARADE.
BED
GIRLZ GIRLZ
BOA
I'M NEVER GONNA MAKE IT IN TIME. FUCK. HOW CAN I GET PAST 6TH + MARKET UNNOTICED?
6
MARKET
HEY! CINDY! COME HERE!
WHERE HAVE YOU BEEN? THE BLOCKS NOT THE SAME W/O YOU, LADY.
SHIT. THERE THEY ARE.

HERE'S THE 12 BUCKS I OWE YOU. I'M FINALLY GETTING MY METHODONE FOR FREE
OH COOL
YOU SHOULD HAVE SEEN IT, THIS LITTLE DOG WAS GOING UP THE ESCALATOR + IT'S FUCKIN' FEET GOT STUCK IN THE STAIRS + IT WAS MAKIN' THE FUCKIN' LOUDEST YELPS + THE GUY CAME + TURNED THE WHOLE ESCALATOR OFF
HMM. INTERESTING
WE'RE GOING TO MY HOTEL ROOM TO WATCH PORNOS WANTA COME?
XXXX
NO.
HAS THE PARADE BEEN BY YET?
I DIDN'T SEE IT.
SURE YOU DID. ALL THOSE LOW AIRPLANES AND THOUSANDS OF PEOPLE. DIDN'T YOU NOTICE?
WERE THERE ANY SCANTILY CLAD CHEERLEADERS?
GOOD BYE
FUCK THOSE ASSHOLES
I'M GOING TO THE PARADE
WHERE IS EVERYONE?
ITS OVER
FUCK
6
MARKET
YEAH. COME ON. I GOT 12 BUCKS.
YEAH YEAH YEAH. I MISSED YOU GUYS TOO. HEY GET YOUR PASSED OUT ASS OFF THE SIDEWALK SAM. WERE GOING TO GET BEER.

I am jelous of them. The way they joke and are compfortable together. Their bookstore/coffeeshop. The way they argue . They've been together 15 years they tell me. They met in the service in Korea. Two dykes running the only queer place in aredneck town. I can tell they like it here and that they'll never leave. Grace is 64, Bea's 51.

She says I can have a neverending cup of coffee. Drink as much as I want. Drink it all, no problem, she'll make more. Customers come in. You can tell they're tight knit. One lady tells them that she's leaving reno because of a broken heart. One woman s ays she's trying to quit smoking because she's afraid of going blind. Grace gives advice and yells over to me, "Youre helping yourself to the coffee now, aren't you?" I've already had four cups.

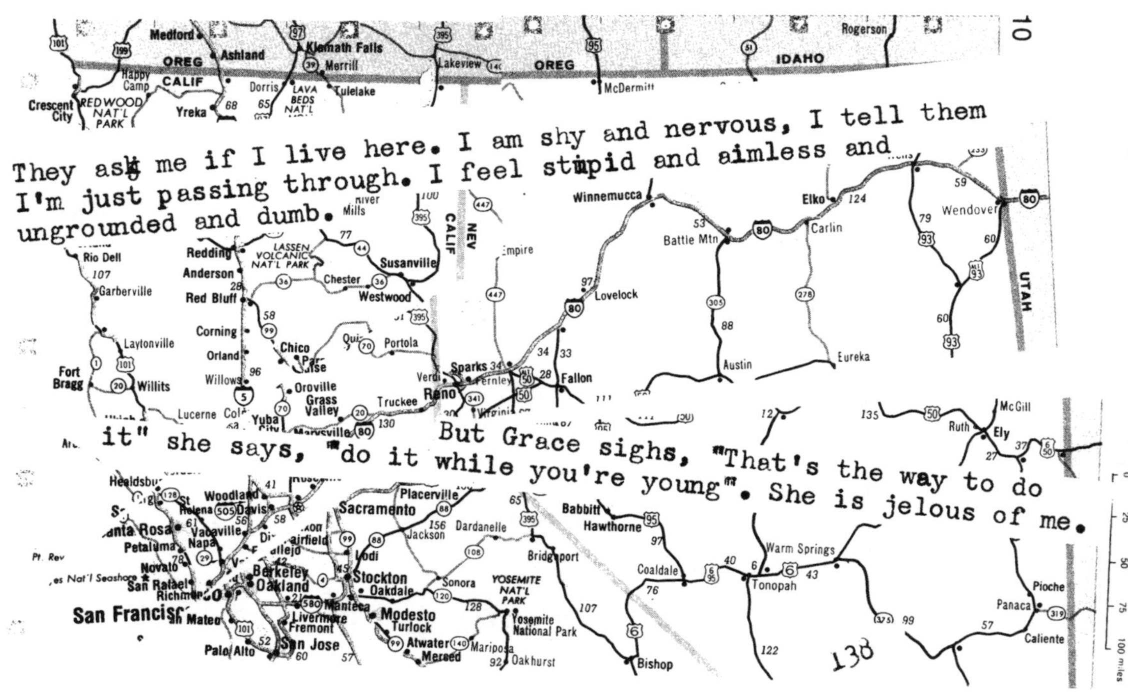

They ask me if I live here. I am shy and nervous, I tell them I'm just passing through. I feel stupid and aimless and ungrounded and dumb.

But Grace sighs, "That's the way to do it" she says, "do it while you're young". She is jelous of me.

atlantic

this town made meridith poetic. She wrote about the old people's wrinkled hands. Mrs Mackensey and the ladys at the soda fountain, the way they'd shake their heads at eachother when the kids and the queer boys would swear.

meridith volunteered at the library, read books outloud for the elderly and the blind. she knew how to become part of a town. she adapted easily. could make herself belong.

She walked around with her girlfriend on the beach. broken shells and bits of rope and tides. she hardly

ever wrote me letters anymore. when she did they were about seagulls high in the cold winter air, dropping clams onto the breakwater rocks. cracking the shells so they could get at the insides. I read the letters over and over looking for clues, trying to read between the language. if she had something to tell me she should have said it.

i started hating poetics.

I write to caty and tell her about my boat. the first time i took it out i'd forgotten you could take off your shoes and socks. that's what a city girl i'd become. i pushed the boat hard and ran into the ocean and jumped in. the waves washed me into shore. i had no oars. i sloshed around for two cold days in wet shoes. the lauddrymats are closed for the season and my toaster wasn't strong enough to dry them. i have a hard time figureing out this town. i eat sandwiched in the back of the library. i read books that tell me what to do. cookbooks and car repairs. how to build a tool shed, insulate a basement, draw comics the marvel way. i want solid instructions, step by step rules, something to make me feel less lost.

home sweet home  . . .

i wrote this postcard to caty. it went something like this. 'hey miss. Ithica! so much water. waterfalls you can jump off of. clean water. rivers. streams. lakes. woods. deer. punks. nerds. free coffee. 24 hour diners. smart people. huge houses. for rent signs everywhere. free icecream. good librarys. it's kind of a shit hole but lets move here. free movies. snow. railroad tracks.'

it wasn't so much that i was sold on ithaca, but i couldnt figure out where else to go. Lincoln seemed alright, thick crab grass and dried corn fields. wind and loud crickets you can hear all through the night. Chad, who would tilt his head back and look out the bottom of his eyeswhen he talked. happy proud and drunk, making me tea . and shane in a skirt, sitting on my tail gate, telling me about the time he found all this junk and glued it together with a satanistic doll head on the top. droppedit off at the governers mansion and they thought it was a bomb. theycalled the bomb squad,they hauled him in and sent his ass to jail. Lincoln? maybe, but chad

and shane were leaving. and even though i'd just met them, without those two Lincoln wouldnt be the same.

me and aaron drove from one coast to the other and back, and every town and every sity i looked at like i was moving there. we'd ride bikes and drove slow and every town we pulled up to i'd

hope would be my salvation, and and when it wasn't, i could hardly enjoy myself. couldn't take the town for what it was cuz i was so disapointed it wasnt going to be my new home. south bend, saint louis, columbia, wichita.

i thought may be lexington would be the place, i dont know why. i thouhgt it would be cheep and i could get a house in the country, live there with my sister, rent a warehouse in the town to keep my boyfriend and my loom. I'd get everyone i liked to move there. build myself a secret room and not let anyone in, ever. but leingt on was such wide empty streets and the coffee shop was in the mall.

so it was Ithaca. yeah, that's where we were going. but i ended up here insted. don't ask how. it had something to do with snow in texas. too much driving and no way to sleep. knowing my expectations were already to high. and the way the guy at the truck stop laughed when i said i was going to ithaca. "my brother lives there" he said. "he had to crawl out his second story window yesterday because the snow was so high."

I wouldn't have minded the snow really. shoveling rooftops and driveways. i know how to not crash on ice. but something about moving back north still feels like giving up. like I'd get stuck and not becausethe snow was covering my door.

i calledup Caty. "what about moving to Asheville?' i said. I'd never even been here before. she laughed and said sure.

so here we are. digging gardens and dancing at the punk alley shows. i sit in my room andget homesick about how no one will come kidnap me here - drag me out of my house at 2am. then the JC boyz call. it's midnight, they say they're comming down to Ashevills. comming to get me. we drive around through the tunnels yelling out windows trying to film a movie. they all stay over, 4 of us and a dog in one little bed. no pillows.

age 22

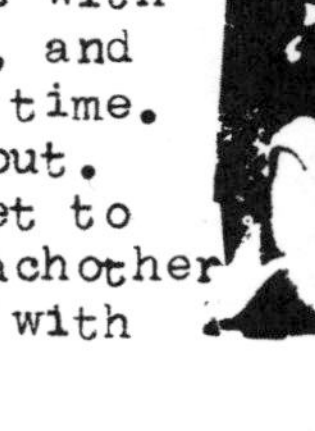

I'd pretty much given up on getting to be friends with girls. i mean, i knew i needed womens friendship, and that it had been missing from my life for a long time. but the thing was, it just never seemed to work out. maybe i was just too use to guys. the way we'd get to know eachother by joking around, making fun of eachother not taking things too seriously. it was awkward with girls. i expected more of them, and i was easily disapointed.

I'd decided not to worry about it for awhile, not to try to hard, not to beat myself over thehead when it didnt work. not to be too critical or too invested. I'd just moved into a house that was ¾ girls. I didnt know any of them very well.

but when they decidedwe needed a womens only space, every monday night for 3 hours in our house, i was right there fighting for it with them. i knew it was theorietically important for women to meet and organize and have their own space, even though i wasnt sure i really wanted it.

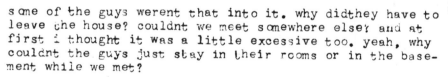

some of the guys werent that into it. why didthey have to leave the house? couldnt we meet somewhere else? and at first i thought it was a little excessive too. yeah, why couldnt the guys just stay in their rooms or in the basement while we met?

but i realized quickly it was really different with them gone. my head was clearer, i could focus better, and relax more. if guys had been in the house i would have felt the need to justify and explain what we were doing. i would have wantedsomething solid, something concrete to show them to prove that what we were doing was worthwhile. i never would have felt compfortable learning to do gynalogical exams. i never would have learned shit about my body.

mostly we didnt do a whole lot in that group. we'd sit around andread, cook some food, work on art. alot of times we didnt eventalk much, but we all became close anyhow. even Faith, who thougt womens groups were stupid and regressive, started comingout of her room and hanging out with us every week. i didnt always relate to them, and sometimes was frustrated that we didnt do more, but i learned how to have girls in my life again, and i connected with those women more than anyone before or since.

end

Down on the West Asheville riverlink bridge is this thing i noticed yesterday. every few feet, on the metal side rail, these dates and innitails are written. it's like "jr. er. hr. 2/18/91" and then er jr 5/27/90, and jr 8/6/92 alone. hr jr 10/3/91 in the rain. it's really nice, about thirty of these entrys, from every time they crossed the bridge.

biking down the riverside road and starting to feel pretty lost after an hour. i thought i was taking some long cut to downtown but i ended up in the next town over. right when i was about to start thinking i shoud turn around, i look up at the strip of grass between me and the freeway. it's only about 4 feet wide and a steep incline. and there were these two roosters just hanging out there. i don't know what they were doing. i told the IWW kids about it later and nathan says there's lots of wild roosters around here.

last year wasn't so easy. it was fucking hard. and i had to keep trying to feel a sence of purpose. do things i knew i'd do if i wasn't depressed, like get out of bed and walk around, dig through trash and look for secret new spots to bring people. stuff like that. i'd force myself to do it, and it wasn't sobad, but the excitement wasn't behind it.

and there was something about other people turning the things i actully did enjoy into these big deals. like for a long time i loved going down to sit in the falling apart factory by the tracks, but all of a sudden other people were like 'oh, fuck yeah, the factory. it's so cool. it's so crazy and rad'. it somehow blew it out of perportion. kind of ruined it for me. or like the basket ball games. it was so nice when everyone started showing up for them, and we moved them from the club down to the courts. andit seemed so normal. like exactly what we should be doing. i was so happy to see all my friends together. but there wasthis thing - like it was an event. like it was something outside our lives and amazing. i just wanted it to be common place, you see. it's hard to explain. but i stopped going.

and it's stupid, but the hard times went on for so long, that when they were over, i'd fallen into this habit. i'd gotten so use to just sort of getting by, that I'd forgotten that i could actully get out there and live. see what i mean, it sounds stupid, but its true.

so a couple days ago i told caty i was gonna be excited about life again. she thought that was a good idea and she's going to try it too.

I HOPE THIS MEANS THEY TAKE ME SWIMMING MORE.

DORiS # 9 was a comics issue

about how one day I was sitting in our shitty little basement apartment and an old friend of Caty's called up to invite her on a trip around the world. When she said no, I went insted. It is stories about hitchhiking through the Yukon and Alaska and living in Ancoridge while trying to get our papers. It was about the people we met and about being in love, and underneath it, so hidden no one saw, it is about denial. They are very surface level comics because if I started to talk about how it really was, talk about my insides, my realness, what was happening inside of me, I would have had to talk about and recognize that I was in a traditionally abusive relationship. Doris #9 makes me sick to look at. makes my stomach hurt and my body ache and my head hurt with self hate, disgust, self blame, and sad. I would like to explain the reasons for it, but you could look in any book about abusive relationships, and find the answers there. Anyway, I'm not reprinting it. I know I can't cut it out of my life but I can cut it out here.

2/1998

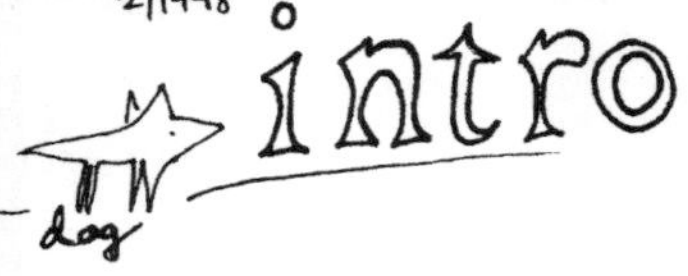

intro

I forgot to mention how blue the sky was there before it started raining, or the sound the ice breakup made washing into the shore. The mosaics and murals and the kids playing Red Rover. The store where you went to buy your bread. The man who trained dolphins, the way each city had its own small and faded amusement park, or the group of women all dressed in black, kneeling on the steps of the Kazan Cathedral in Red Square. I forgot to mention the mosquitoes or the missionaries. I guess there are a lot of stories that will come later, after I've made a little bit more sense of it all.

siberia

There were girls in bikinis, army boys eating icecream cones. It wasn't what I thought Siberia would look like. There were fancy new boats taking tourists out for joy rides, and rickety wooden boats bringing small town people into the city to stock up on supplies. It's the only way to get to some of the towns. No roads, just rivers. One old man got off the boat wearing a Canadian flag ski hat, it was all worn in. And I figured the Canadians probably sent over a whole shit load of those hats in some relief effort, but that's just one of those things I make up, who knows were that hat came from.

I had this idea that I knew about Russia just because I'd read a lot about Lenin and the Russian revolution. Really, though, I didn't have a clue. I didn't even have the most basic knowledge of where the country was at politically or what it looked like physically. Not even random facts you get from reading magazines like Time. I didn't know that the architecture was supposed to be drab and monotonous, or that people in the cities have little houses and plots of land in the outlaying countryside to grow their food at. I didn't really know how big Siberia was, and I thought it was all probably pretty cold, even though I'd seen the map and could tell it bordered Mongolia and I knew they had camels there. I didn't have many expectations of how Russia would be, that's for sure, but one thing I hadn't expected was for the teenage girls to be wearing flourescent orange miniskirts.

The markets in the cities were weird. One line to get your stuff weighed out and priced - potatoes, garlic, butter. They give you a slip of paper and you go to another line to pay. Then another line to pay. Then another line to pick up what you had priced and paid for. Only no one stands in lines any more now that communism has fallen. Everyone pushes to the front, and I let them, always.

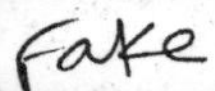

I'm into the pretend. Of making people think I'm super super sexy and strong and know what I want like that. like this. like skin and teeth and hours in bed. I'm a good fuck. Everyone knows it. And I like it that way, at first.

I like the rolling around and laughter, the showing off and looks. the strength and confidence and intensity. the falling asleep in someones bare arms. the held back excitement of new potential. And the closeness, the being right there and warm even when it's fake close. But even when it's something, when it's true love and so sweet, even when it's something, it ends up turning fake.

One time I learned that when you make noise it feels better, or at least it blocks out the stuff fighting to getiin your head. One time I learned that if you breathe like this and clench your stomach, you might start to feel something when otherwise you wouldn't. And it's important to keep looking sexy, keep breathing heavy, keep moving or they might catch on. Might notice.

dear girl

When I got to the middle of your magazine - pages 38-42 "The night I wouldn't call rape" - my heart just sunk. Partially because I don't want that to happen to you - and partially because I am fucked. I don't know, it's hard to say it. It's like I've had sex so much, so many times when I didn't want to - and now it's hard for me to know anymore what I really feel. The first few times I have sex with someone, I'm generally pretty into it. It's new and I've got something to prove. But as soon as sex becomes a habit - something assumed and expected - it gets all fucked up.

Half the time I don't even know whether I'm having sex out of obligation or because I want to. And if I stop and think about it, then I get sad and freaked out and get this flood of memories of all the boys and all the times before. I start to shut down, start to feel small and scared, so I just try not to think. It's easier just to go along with what's expected, and honestly, the guys can't tell the difference. That's when I start to hate them, and it's never really the same after that.

Do you feel different from other people? Do you feel there's something wrong with you deep down inside? That if people really knew you, they'd leave? Are you prone to depression? Night mares? Panic attacks? Have you ever worried about going crazy? Have you ever been violent or abusively angry? Do you feel confused much of the time? Do you find it difficult to trust anyone? Do you

THIS NIGHT WHICH I WOULDN'T CALL RAPE. WA INTO THE ROOM FEELING KIND OF HEADY AND SICK AIRPLANE RIDE TOMORROW, CRAWL INTO BED AND HE CRAWLS ON TOP OF ME KISSING. I COULD FEEL HIM CHANGING, THE ALTERED RHYTHM OF DESIRE. BUT I'M SICK AGAIN (SICK LIKE I ALWAYS AM). THE DAY BEFORE I BLEED AND MY UTERUS IS WRINGING AROUND LIKE A CLENCH IN MY BODY. I ALWAYS WANT TO LEAVE MY BODY I HATE THE THINGS IT DOES TO ME, IT'S ALWAYS WRONG. HE'S BEGINNING TO WRITHE AND I SAY "NO, CAN WE JUST CURL UP TONIGHT, I CAN'T DO IT."

OKAY HE SAYS AND ROLLS OFF BUT A MINUTE LATER KISSING, MORSE CODE MESSAGES BY TONGUE. OKAY, I CAN KISS YOU KNOW, KISSING IS NICE IN A MILLION WAYS AND I'M THINKING KISS LIKE A BACKRUB, LIKE WE'RE PLAYING ROUGHHOUSE KISS GAME MY BABY AND I. BUT I'M WRONG BECAUSE SOON ENOUGH HIS HANDS ARE AT MY CUNT RUBBING AND MY STOMACH SINKS. I LIE THERE AND HE MOVES AND

RUBS SAYS "YOU'RE REALLY DRY AND OUT OF IT." YEAH I SAY THAT'S CAUSE I DON'T WANT TO HAVE SEX. AND HE KEEPS RUBBING AND HE'S BREATHING HARDER. HE'S CLIMBING THE MOUNTAIN AND I FEEL SHIT, I'M A DEAD GIRL, NERVE-ENDING FREE. TOTAL BODY ANAESTHETIC. MY BODY I'M FLOATING ABOVE IT ALL. I'M ON THE CEILING LOOKING DOWN AND HE'S PULLING OUT A CONDOM. BETRAYAL AND I DON'T CARE ABOUT A CONDOM 'CAUSE THERE'S NOTHING TO CARE FOR IT'S ONLY MY BODY LEFT. IT COULD BE ANY BODY. AND HE SAYS "IS THIS OKAY?" AND I SAY "WHATEVER" CAUSE THE THING IS DONE AND I'M ONLY A BODY. IF THAT. "WHATEVER." AND THEN HE'S IN ME. I DON'T HELP AND I DON'T MOVE AND HE FUCKS ME. IT DOESN'T LAST TOO LONG 'CAUSE FUCKING A DEAD GIRL ISN'T WORTH MUCH UNLESS YOU'RE A FRAT BOY.

"THIS IS TOTALLY WRONG" HE SAYS AND I'M ALL PERVERSE: "WRONG HOW?" I SAY AND HE LOOKS AT ME SCARED AND I'M BLANK. A BODY DOESN'T CARE ABOUT YOUR FUNNY FEELINGS. FLESH, FLESH NERVE ENDING AND BONE

dear girl

ometimes I think I'm all over it. Like I'm strong and brave and got through i
all, and then sometimes I'm just the same as always. Like your story only i
ou take out the part about asking if we can just curl up tonight, because eve
hat is too dangerous for me. and change the laying like a dead girl to faking
so well. Sometimes I fake it because I think if I fake it I might get
urned on and get into it and start to want it, and it does work, sort of. But
ostly I just fake it because that's what I do (habit) and so I won't have to
alk about what's going on. Sometimes I fake it for so many days in a row, ov
nd over, that I start to think the fake is real. like maybe that is what org
eels like, quick breath and clenched stomach. like I don't even know the dif
rence between fake and real any more, because usually (not always) fake feel
kay. But I'm fighting with my head the whole time, and to be quite honest, i
eels pretty crazy - to not even know whether I'm feeling pleasure or not. Is
hat supposed to be pretty obvious? Tell me, is this what it's like for every

ately I've been thinking about the guys, ~~I mean the ones who weren't abused~~
o they get it? I mean, do they get it at all? Do they know that almost every
irl they sleep with has been raped/molested/abused? And that it's not just
lashbacks we have to contend with, not just the obvious shut down and tears
ut that it's every little dynamic, all these details and complicated things
don't think the guys know. Because if they did, wouldn't they stay attenti
ouldn't they be scared and want to ask questions? wouldn't they notice more
've been thinking about the guys and they seem so oblivious. Maybe they've
ead the statistics, but it sure doesn't seem like they know.

chechnya

We still had two days before we got to Abakan. It was a slow train on an off route and our car had been empty. We'd been playing tag in the aisles, reading outloud to eachother, smoking cigerettes with the train car attendent. Then we stopped in Tayshet and the Russian army got on. Our whole car filled up with teenage boys in khaki and tan clothes. Blue socks, tall boots. I have to admit I was pretty nervous. I imagined they'd be up all night, drinking and fighting, leering at me the way U.S. Army boys do. I dreaded having to walk down the thin hall past all of them to get to the bathroom.
But it turned out the boys were quiet and broken, polite and tired. No looks or jeers. They played cards a lot and went to bed early. I thought it was kind of weird.

The medic and sergeant sat across from us and the medic could read and write english some. He said "American? The only good music to come out of America was Motley Crew, 1985" He didn't use a complete sentance like that, but that's what he meant. I wrote, "Are you guys in charge?" He nodded and pointed back at the boys. "Youth Killers" he wrote.

I thought that was pretty funny. Those boys looked like their youth was being killed - getting turned into men. Like they'd been through a super hard basic training and now were heading out on their first assignment and they were nervous and didn't know what to expect, and they were scared. I thought the medic was pretty damn witty, so I laughed.. But he looked at me and could tell that I didn't understand. He wrote "each one has killed 10 - 12 in Cheehnya", I had to look at those boys again..

The war in Chechnya had been going on since 1994, and Moscow kept sending in all kinds of untrained, poorly armed conscripts, and everyone was getting massacred. These kids on the train, they were some of those conscripts, just coming out of the hospital they'd been shipped to. And they didn't know yet whether they were going back to war or not.

It freaked me out really, made me think all these things about war and nationalism, passivity and power, being sheltered or unsheltered, the way it's so easy to have a clear sense of right and wrong, when really it's all complicated and muddled. All kinds of things that seemed profound, but in the end turned out to be not much of anything.. Just how unscathed America is, and how war is mainly so abstract here..

On the day we pulled in to Abakan, the sergeant and medic were the first people off the train, and this boy came and sat down across from me. I had noticed him before.. He had this punk look to him, like I could have sworn that in a certain light, a patch of his hair was green, and I kept looking but it just wasn't.

He handed me two coins and said "they are very old". He handed me a little silver star. I fastened it to my shirt. I pulled out my backpack to find something to give him, but I didn't have anything really, just two pennies and a piece of blue seaglass I found at Lake Bikal. He held the glass up and made a motion like he would turn it into a necklace. Then he gave me another star. A bigger, gold one. The kind everyone in the army wears on the shoulders of their jackets and the more you have, the higher rank you are. He put it in the palm of my hand and I held it. He shook his head and said "Russian War" with sorrow and disgust. When he walked away, and we were all outside and they got in formation and started marching, I wanted to yell, run after him, get his address, give him something more. I waited for him to turn around and look back, but they just marched away.

- end

Chechnya is located in the N.Caucasus, a remote and mountainous region of Southern Russia, with a long tradition of struggles for independence, dating back to the days of the Tsar. After the Russian Revolution in 1917, many of the N.Caucausus natiions united and formed the Mountain Republic. They weren't able to hold on to independence, however, and became part of the Soviet Union in 1921.

In an attempt to dispose of potentially troublesome nationalities, Stalin had almost all Chechens deported to Central Asia and Siberia in 1944. In 1956, after Stalin's death, the surviving Chechens were allowed to return, but were not compensated or given their property back.

Not surprisingly, there was a lasting and wide spread anti-Russian sentiment in Chechnya. In the wake of the 1991 breakup of the Soviet Union, Chechnya declaired their independence. Yeltsin refused to accept it, and declaired a state of emergency. If Chechnya was allowed independence, other regions and republics might follow suit and the new Russian Federation would fall. Control of oil pipelines between the Black Sea and the Caspian Sea was alss at stake.

Yeltsin sent in a small force of occupying troops, but they were soon forced to withdraw. He had underestimated the militancy of the average Chechen, and the popular support for the successionist demands. For the next two years, Chechen rebels waged a campaign of terrorism aimed to force Russia to concede to their demands, and Russia attempted to oust the Chechen leader and isolate the region.

In Dec. of 94, Yeltsin and the parliment ordered invasion, despite opposition to the action within Russia. The war lasted 2½ years. Russia had full control of the Chechen capitol, Grozny, but it was clear they'd never be able to win the guerrilla war being waged in the mountains and countryside. Chechnya suffered heavy losses - tens of thousands of civilians had died and their infrastructure was demolished, but they would not give up. In may of '97, a peace treaty was signed. Russia withdrew troops, and is helping rebuild the oil pipeline. In a way, both sides lost. Chechnya is still officially part of the Russian Federation, but they proclaim their independence. Neither side is really talking about the issue, but there are groups within Chechnya who say they will continue to fight until true independence is won.

reflex

I walked around Abakan, looking for the army boy. I couldn't get him out of my head. I looked for him with that same kind of anxiousness of looking for a crush in the streets of Berkeley, all nervous and not sure what I'd do if I actually did see him. All full of hope and weird ideas about twists of fate and unexpected things that just might happen. You know, like what if I did run into him and he really was a punk and we fell in love somehow through all the language barrier, or maybe we'd just become really good friends and he'd come to America and we'd have to get married so he could stay. I had thought of something to give him. some studs from my belt and a little bouquet of flowers - bleeding hearts. It seemed fitting. I mean, what if he was the perfect one for me and I'd lost my chance. I hadn't thought quick enough. I'd just let him walk away. It wasn't very cool to be thinking that way since I was supposed to be married to or marrying Luke, but it was such a relief to be walking around like this, looking for my crush. Such a familiar, comfortable feeling. Plus, it was a good excuse to walk around alone. I wasn't used to love and long term committment, and making decisions with someone all the time, and being some place where you both needed eachother so badly. It was fine when we were on the train, or when we were in the country because I didn't know what to do with myself there. But when we got to cities, then I'd remember my former self and start to really worry. I was starting to lose it, actually. Overwealmed by all this strange terrain. I wanted something to save me.

I looked for the army boy down by the train yard, followed the path they'd marched away on, but it didn't lead to anything. I headed towards downtown, and that's when the short guy started following me. He was yelling after me, but of course I couldn't understand him, until he said "Australian?" and then I turned around. He got such a big grin on his face that I waited up. He was jabbering at me and trying to hold my hand. It was annoying. I'd let him hold my hand for a little while, just to be nice, and then I'd pull it away. He would grab it again. I'd sort of laugh and glare at him, I don't know. After a few blocks he started tugging on my arm, pointing to a building, making grinding fucking motions. I shook my head and pulled away from him and walked faster.

I thought he had given up, I didn't hear him creep up behind, but all of a sudden there he was, grabbing my ass. And there I was, spinning around and slapping him straight in the face. I just hit him. I'd never done that before, well, just once, but that was at a club and I had backup. Here I was in a foreign country on an empty street. It probably wasn't the smartest thing to do.

The short guy slapped me back, and I started yelling as loud as I could "Go Away. Leave me alone!" The exact words we had to practice yelling in my woman's self-defence class. I was pretty surprised. I had always hated that part of class. It always seemed so idiotic to stand in a circle, taking turns practicing screaming. learning to use the voice as a weapon of intimidation. It was obvious we needed it - unlearning that whole thing about women staying quiet, and it was actually pretty creepy how ingrained it is. It was really hard to yell loud - hard for me and at least half the women. We'd try to shout and our voices would just come out quiet and it was so humiliating. Such a weird self betrayal. But in those classes we had to practice and practice until we got it down, until it was a reflex.

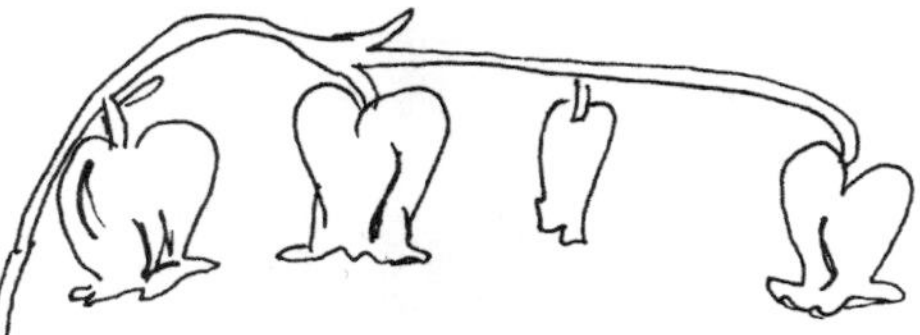

I never really thought I'd use my voice like that, but there I was, and the guy was pretty freaked out. He was making fun of me, but he didn't come any closer. Eventually we both got sick of it and we both walked away. I went to the post office. I was glad I had letters to mail. Just to do something normal, even though I wasn't sure which box to put them in. I went down to the Lenin statue and watched the teenagers walk around, arm in arm, dressed nice. I wasn't looking for the army boy any more. I didn't want to look at anyone too closely. I just wanted to blend in for awhile, which was rediculous because there was no way that I could. So I walked back to the hotel, through the tree lined streets and the little back alleys where the old ladies sat on their stoops and hung up laundry. I pretended I was in Brooklyn in the Polish neighborhood. I tried skipping and hopping and feeling the life in me. And things felt alright. I left the bleeding hearts by the water pump for someone else to find.

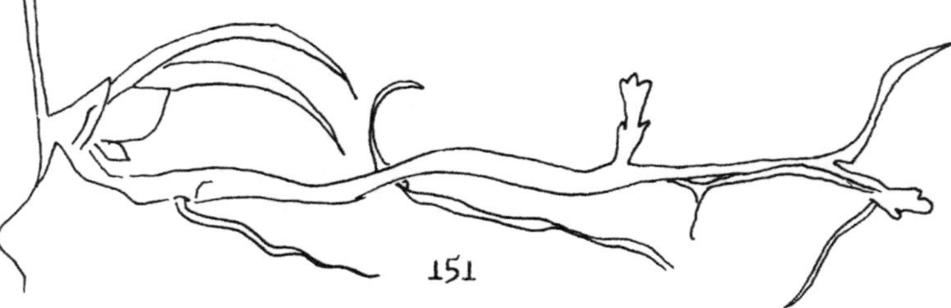

petra

Even the way she smoked was elegant. French inhale, lazy smoke rings. Her hair piled up on top of her head with a carved wooden hair pin through it. "They slaughtered the pigs last week" she said, "I liked those pigs, but the bacon's good too." She said "Every corner is a memory back in my old house. The smells and scratches in the walls. Cracks in the cealing. I remember every one. Here's where I stood for my birthday pictures. Here's the corner where Nana squeezed my hampster to death." She crosses her long legs, silk dress. Shakes her her wrist so her bracelet falls a little lower. "I guess Nana wasn't too fond of having to handle a rodent."

night

Caty and I stayed up late talking. We tried to think of what times in our pasts we would stitch together. I couldn't think of anything. Nothing I would want to have again until finally my face lit up - yes. I would take laying in the school nurses office. Caty put her hand to her heart. You're breaking my heart, she said.

isaac

I went back to get my cigerettes and he came out of the fish shack where they were drinking coffee, saying "You didn't even leave a note." He said "I woke up with all this room and thought - this is nice, but the girl is gone and that's bad." He said he didn't even get up to look for a note in case it said something mean that would make him not be able to get back to sleep. He walked me away, out of sight from the boys, to say goodbye and kiss my cheek. He said "Look at what good shadows we make", and it was true, me and him and my dog.

kelly

There was the time when we were I5, and she took off her shirt in front of me, we were just standing in her mother's kitchen, and she looked me in the eyes and took off her shirt. I was surprised her boobs were so big, such a small girl she was. and she said, "I finally know the difference between love and friendship", or maybe she said "I have finally accepted this body". I was stunned. I can't remember exactly. It used to be so clear.

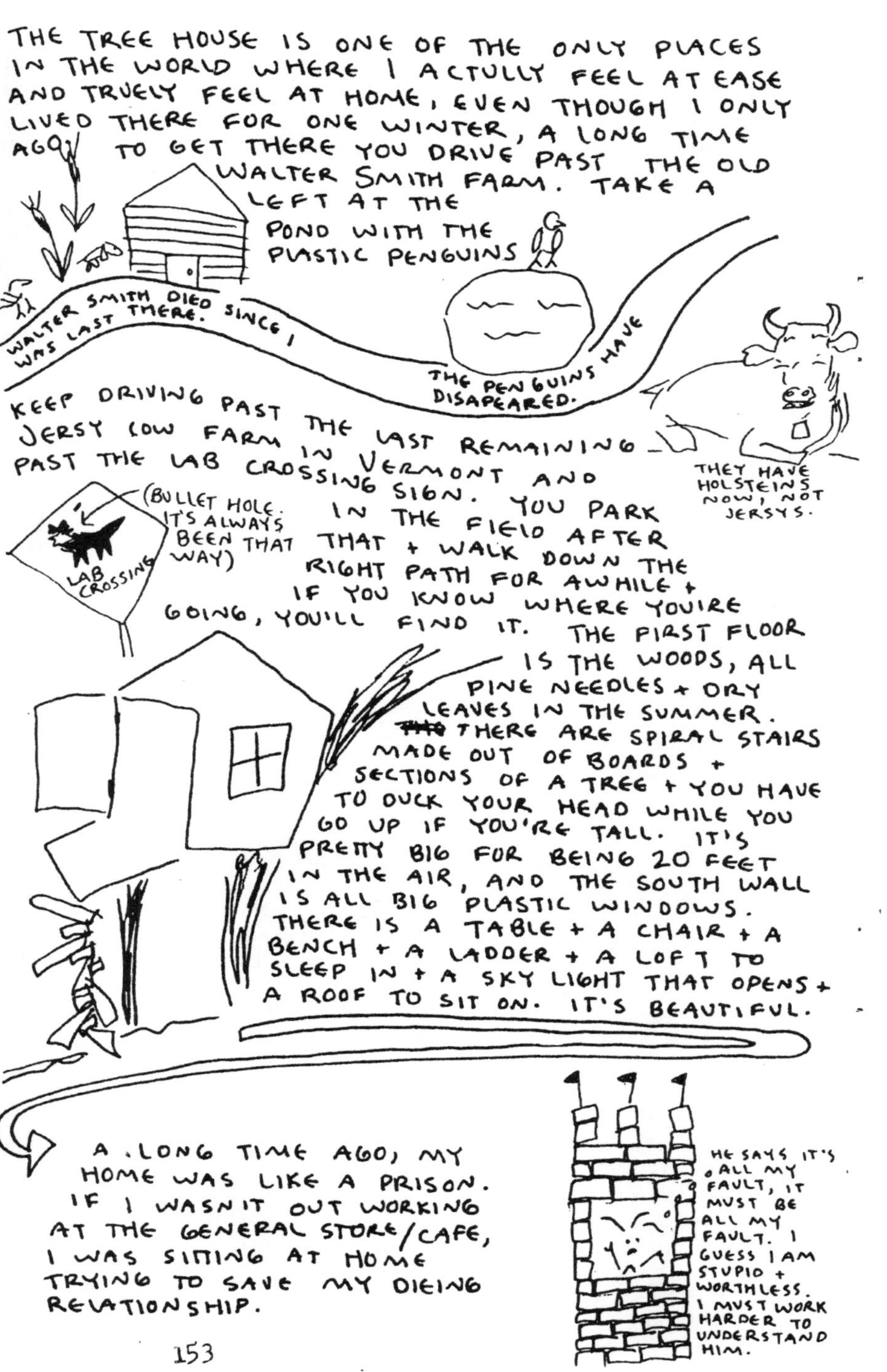
THE TREE HOUSE IS ONE OF THE ONLY PLACES IN THE WORLD WHERE I ACTULLY FEEL AT EASE AND TRUELY FEEL AT HOME, EVEN THOUGH I ONLY LIVED THERE FOR ONE WINTER, A LONG TIME AGO. TO GET THERE YOU DRIVE PAST THE OLD WALTER SMITH FARM. TAKE A LEFT AT THE POND WITH THE PLASTIC PENGUINS
WALTER SMITH DIED SINCE I WAS LAST THERE.
THE PENGUINS HAVE DISAPEARED.
KEEP DRIVING PAST THE LAST REMAINING JERSY COW FARM IN VERMONT AND PAST THE LAB CROSSING SIGN.
THEY HAVE HOLSTEINS NOW, NOT JERSYS.
(BULLET HOLE. IT'S ALWAYS BEEN THAT WAY)
LAB CROSSING
YOU PARK IN THE FIELD AFTER THAT + WALK DOWN THE RIGHT PATH FOR AWHILE + IF YOU KNOW WHERE YOU'RE GOING, YOU'LL FIND IT. THE FIRST FLOOR IS THE WOODS, ALL PINE NEEDLES + DRY LEAVES IN THE SUMMER. THERE ARE SPIRAL STAIRS MADE OUT OF BOARDS + SECTIONS OF A TREE + YOU HAVE TO DUCK YOUR HEAD WHILE YOU GO UP IF YOU'RE TALL. IT'S PRETTY BIG FOR BEING 20 FEET IN THE AIR, AND THE SOUTH WALL IS ALL BIG PLASTIC WINDOWS. THERE IS A TABLE + A CHAIR + A BENCH + A LADDER + A LOFT TO SLEEP IN + A SKY LIGHT THAT OPENS + A ROOF TO SIT ON. IT'S BEAUTIFUL.
A LONG TIME AGO, MY HOME WAS LIKE A PRISON. IF I WASN'T OUT WORKING AT THE GENERAL STORE/CAFE, I WAS SITTING AT HOME TRYING TO SAVE MY DIEING RELATIONSHIP.
HE SAYS IT'S ALL MY FAULT, IT MUST BE ALL MY FAULT. I GUESS I AM STUPID + WORTHLESS. I MUST WORK HARDER TO UNDERSTAND HIM.

I HAD NO TIME FOR FRIENDS. I DIDN'T TALK TO ANYONE EXCEPT MY INSANE BOYFRIEND. I HARDLY EVEN TALKED TO THE GIRL I WORKED WITH. I WAS VERY DEPRESSED. MY SELF CONFIDENCE WASN'T SO HOT.
UM, DEBBIE, I'VE NEVER MADE A PB+J SANDWICH BEFORE + SOMEONE JUST ORDERED ONE. DOES THIS LOOK RIGHT?
LOOKS FINE
OOOUH
HE WON'T TALK TO ME BECAUSE I DON'T ASK THE RIGHT QUESTIONS. HOW DO I KNOW THE RIGHT QUESTIONS IF HE DOESN'T TELL ME WHAT THEY ARE? GOD I WISH I WAS DEAD.
HOME = HELL
SOMETIMES WHEN I WAS HOME, STARING OUT MY WINDOW, THE HIPPIE GARBAGE MAN WOULD COME PICK UP OUR TRASH
BOY, IT SURE WOULD BE FUN TO RIDE ON THE BACK OF THAT TRUCK. WHAT'S A HIPPIE DOING DRIVING A GARBAGE TRUCK ANYWAY?
ONE DAY MY BOYFRIEND LEFT ME
HORRAY!
AND THE GARBAGE MAN GOT A JOB AT THE STORE
I DIDN'T HAVE A CRUSH ON HIM, WHICH
HI
HI
WAS GOOD BECAUSE WE GOT TO BE FRIENDS.

NOT THE KIND OF FRIENDS THAT ALWAYS HANG OUT TOGETHER, BUT THE KIND THAT ARE ALWAYS GLAD TO SEE EACHOTHER + ALWAYS MAKE EACHOTHER LAUGH. WHEN HE LEFT FOR THE WINTER TO GO WORK ON A CALIFORNIA FARM, I MOVED INTO THE TREEHOUSE. IT WAS QUIET AND COLD + I TALKED TO MY DOG A LOT. I HAD DROPPED OUT OF SCHOOL + LAYED IN BED READING ALL DAY. I WOULD BRING OUT BIG TANKS OF PROPANE FOR THE HEATER + STOVE + I WOULD SIT NEAR THE HEATER + DRINK HOT TEA + THINK + WRITE. IT WAS LONELY, BUT THERE WAS NO ONE TELLING ME WHAT TO DO OR NOT TO DO. NO ONE TO ORGINIZE MY LIFE AROUND. NO ONE TO WORRY ABOUT. NO DISTRACTIONS. THE LONELINESS WAS SCARY, BUT EVEN THAT WAS GOOD. I GO BACK + VISIT THE HOUSE EVERY FEW YEARS + AM ALWAYS SUPRISED TO FIND IT STILL STANDING SOLID. I'M SO PROUD OF THAT PLACE. IT IS EXACTLY HOW I THINK HOUSES SHOULD BE. GUTSY + SECRET + ALWAYS THERE FOR ME.

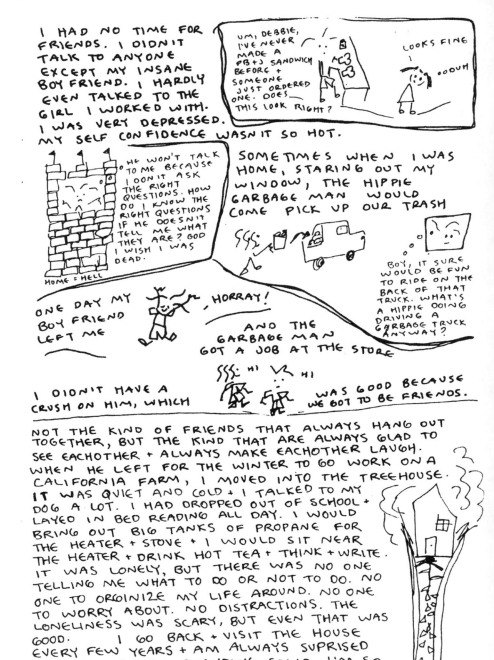

siberia again

The Hvarsk hotel was all chipped paint and yellow. A marble staircase and burnt out lightbulbs and beds that were skinny and short. There was a bright red plastic phone on top of the refridgerator and a bright red plastic radio mounted on the wall.. They looked like a child's play toys, but they worked. We walked down the sidewalks, close together, holding hands and touching shoulders. There were old women on the corners selling baked goods and beer. Mashed potatoes and cabbage covered in thick dough and deep fried. There were young kids on benches who spit and laughed at us, and flowers layed at the base of every Lenin statue that wasn't torn down.

The small towns had cows and goats and chickens walking in the street. Handcarved wooden windowsills on the houses and I wanted to look closely, but I didn't because I was a tourist.

There were buses. One we were lucky enough to catch just before the hail storm started. One took us to Tuva and another took us back after we were kicked out. I'd been thrown out of places before, clubs and restaurants and houses, but never an entire section of a country.

We met the arindeer herder at the boat building when we were waiting for a boat that never came. Him and his girlfriend were covered in hickys. They looked at our phrasebook and laughed at how useless it was. "I need a doctor" he said, "please give me some suntan cream", "Do you have any wooden spoons?"

I got shy there. Afraid to make the wrong move. Embarrassed at myself for not knowing the language.

We set up our tent at Lake Bikal, hitchiked north and climbed a mountain. Rode the train for days on end, birch forests and marshy fields, dirt roads and motorcycles with sidecars. We helped build a house. It was nice to do something useful after just traveling.

In Moscow we stayed with Janie and layed in bed watching Planet of the Apes, too overwealmed to really explore the city like we should have. We'd walk around in circles for hours, getting lost and always ending up back at the giant Cosmonaut statue.

It was hard leaving, just trying to figure out how to do it. Plane ticket? Scam bus rides through Eastern Europe? Hitchike through Scandanavia? We ended up riding local trains without paying, all the way from Moscow to St Petersburg and then to the town that borders Finland.

We thought the border was further away, We'd walk for awhile and then catch a bus, but it snuck up on us. We were there before we knew it, at the border, and they wouldn't let us cross. They couldn't figure out what we were doing, just walking up like that. The gate guard stared at us, smoking cigerettes. A Russian guy in a Hawaiian shirt said "It's your clothes". They held us there for two hours and then sent us back to town in some unwilling strangers car. They said we had to take a bus. The gate guard waved us goodbye.

An hour later we were at the border again, on a luxury bus from a luxury hotel. The same guard stopped the bus, got on and searched the faces until he found ours. Then he pointed - you and you - and made that 'come with me' motion. But when we started to stand, he busted out laughing, walked back down the stairs of the bus and waved. We waved back at him through the window as the bus pulled away. - the end

SOME TIES STAY

I've been growing up lately, I think that's what it is. I'm not searching so hard for something I don't have. I don't feel quite as wild-eyed, and that's strange. I don't worry so much about my friends forgetting me or leaving me behind. I see how it is, some ties stay, some don't. I still walk my dog. I miss my sister when she's gone. And sometimes I hunt down new people so I can show them a small part of my life - present myself at my best. Like when I invited the band boys over, and the way they were impressed with my tent made me proud. They stood at the fence staring at the neighbors cows. just staring like they'd never seen cows before. I was happy because I'm in awe of those animals too. They're so huge. Brian said "How do you get a cow over here so I can pet it?" I yelled, "Come here cows!" But they didn't pay me any mind. I taught the boys how to fix a radiator hose because they didn't know how to do it. I cooked them breakfest and then they drove away.

Everyone talks about leaving, getting the hell out of this town, even Caty and Kerb have gone to Miami, but all I want to do is stay. I've spent the whole last year being around people all the time, and I'm just not like that. I like to spend most of my time alone. I mean it. I know I said that last week, I just wanted everyone to leave me alone. And then I said "Let's start a kickball team" only we didn't have a kickball. "They've got a kickball in Chattanooga" Kerb said, and then the next thing you knew, there were two truckloads of us heading down the 140 to Tennessee. And everyone was so funny and sweet there, I almost didn't want to leave.

It snowed today, and I made it home on the slippery streets, and it just kept snowing. They don't have plows here. Don't salt or sand the roads. So I call up my friends and cancel our New Years Eve plans. "Yeah, I'm snowed in" I say. Truth is, I could probably walk to Asheville in 2 hours if I wanted to. But I'd be happy if it just kept snowing like this for a couple days. Just me and my dog out here. She loves the snow more than anything. She burys her nose in it, searching out old stuff left down there. sticks and bones. I tried to explain it to someone. I said I just want time to catch up on my writing, and to lay in bed and read, learn to bake bread, you know. But that's not really it. I mean, that's part of it, the part people understand. But really I just like solitude. Everything seems funnier when there aren't other people around. And I just get confused when I'm around people

too much, mixing up there needs with my own. At home I clear all the furniture out of one room so it's not so claustrophobic. I turn up the heat and wear my long-underwear and my sister's knee high golashes because it's wet by the door. I throw snowballs at my dog until my hands go numb. I lay in bed and read. I catch up on my writing. I learn to bake bread. You know.

pride

There was Nick leaning in the doorway downtown by the pay phone alone, swinging his pocket watch. Quannah in the kickball outfield with his straw hat, green hair, green shirt, gold tint glasses and shiny white pimp shoes. There's the way they all are when they're playing a new song, looking at eachother for the breaks and the cues. And Caty crouched down in the acres, harvesting beans. Carey in the kitchen with her new idea for life, hopping around explaining it with wild eyes that never once meet mine. Or when they all come back from spelunking, covered in mud from head to toe. Waking up in the morning with everyone passed out on the floor, Walking down the street in a big old group and I just fall behind and watch them. They way they look. I fill with pride.

One day in Chattanooga

This is what I missed about the city. Sitting out on the front porch, watching kids ride by on bicycles; the blind lady down the street; the man boarding up the windows. The vegetable truck rolls up, and this is something I've never had before anywhere I've lived. A vegetable truck - an old couple in a truck with crates in the back and their tailgate down, driving slowly down the street, just honking their horn until someone comes out and buys something. Mike gets bananas. I get strawberries and lemons + make lemon ginger tea + eat the strawberries in powdered sugar.

We walk to the store, the five of us, me on my bike. I hadn't been around the neighborhood much yet. There's an old military cemetary - a Civil War one. playgrounds + metal foundries + miscellaneous factories. we sit down by the one that looks most abandon, even though the light is on. There's big metal tables and piles of scraps. Kerb picks a flower up off the ground + smells it + tastes it. "This tastes like what it smells like," he says "Here, try it." I've lived in the same house with him every day for a year + I've never heard him talk like this - appreciating and being amazed by small, strange things. But it's spring now and a whole new time. or maybe I just didn't know him before at all.

We barbecue in the backyard + he tells me about the night he was walking past the neighbor's house at dusk and there was this young girl out there with long straight hair, standing in the yard + playing violin. "You can't believe how happy it made me", he said, and repeated the story again.

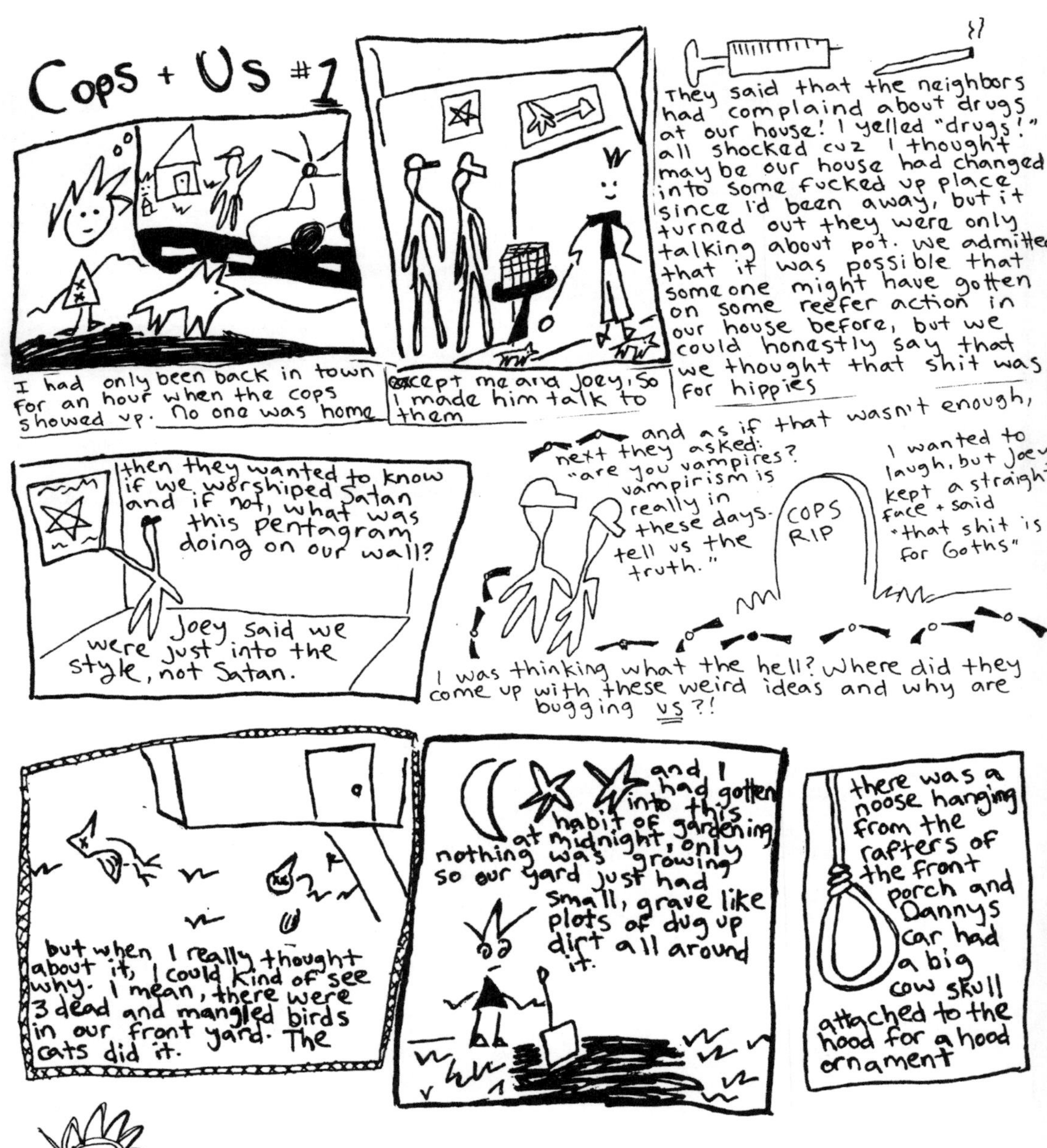

Cops + Us #1
I had only been back in town for an hour when the cops showed up. No one was home
except me and Joey, so I made him talk to them
They said that the neighbors had complaind about drugs at our house! I yelled "drugs!" all shocked cuz I thought maybe our house had changed into some fucked up place since I'd been away, but it turned out they were only talking about pot. We admitted that it was possible that someone might have gotten on some reefer action in our house before, but we could honestly say that we thought that shit was for hippies
then they wanted to know if we worshiped Satan and if not, what was this pentagram doing on our wall?
Joey said we were just into the style, not Satan.
and as if that wasn't enough, next they asked:
"are you vampires? vampirism is really in these days. tell us the truth."
COPS RIP
I wanted to laugh, but Joey kept a straight face + said "that shit is for Goths"
I was thinking what the hell? Where did they come up with these weird ideas and why are bugging US?!
but when I really thought about it, I could kind of see why. I mean, there were 3 dead and mangled birds in our front yard. The cats did it.
and I had gotten into this habit of gardening at midnight, only nothing was growing so our yard just had small, grave like plots of dug up dirt all around it.
there was a noose hanging from the rafters of the front porch and Dannys car had a big cow skull attached to the hood for a hood ornament

I'm not saying they had any right to come bug us, all I mean is, well, if I lived next door to us, I might think something weird was going on too, you know?

homesick

We met this dolphin trainer on the train somewhere between Lake Bikal and Omsk. These other Americans introduced him to us. They'd been talking to him for awhile and he seemed pretty glad to be out of their company. I didn't blame him. They were the kind of people who talked really loudly and empatically about the most boring stuff, like theweather and business deals. They'd come to Russia to adopt a Russian girl. She was about six years old and as far as I could tell, didn't speak English at all. They kept talking to her in these high baby talk voices, telling her they were going to take her to Disney Land so she could see Minnie Mouse. She didn't really look at them at all, just stared out the window, watching everything go by.

The dolphin trainer told us he used to be a fighter pilot, used to fly MIGs back in the 70's. The american woman butted in and siad "I was so scared, the second day I was here and saw one of those MIGs up in the sky, I though 'My God, they've finally come to nuke us!' Then I realized where I was and I knew the Russians weren't going to drop a bomb on their own land! Boy was I relieved!" She went away and he rolled his eyes and looked tired. He said he had always hated the military, but he loved flying so much and that's why he joined. They kicked him out eventually, back when Brezhnev was still in power, because he knew English and they thought he could be a spy. They didn't kick him out entirely, just didn't let him fly any more.

So he left and learned to train dolphins and fell in love with dolphins and another dolphin trainer. But there wasn't much work so he was on his way to Moscow to look for a job at an Embassy. We asked him what kind of dolphins he trained, like for the circus or what? And he shook his head bemused and said, "No, unfortunately, I train military dolphins."

It turned out the dolphin trainer's brother was as antifascist terrorist and had just blown up a Nazi headquarters the day before. I'm not sure he would have told us this right away, but when I was telling him my background, I mentioned this obscure eco-anarchist network that I helped start, that never really went anywhere, but somehow he knew about it.

This brother, Shurik, was trying to get a network of communal houses going all over different parts of Russia, where people could move from one to another whenever they wanted. The idea was to keep people from getting all insulated and neurotic in their own little scenes and to build ties and strengthen communication between regions. He was rebuilding a house outside of Omsk and asked if we wanted to come help. Of course, we said yes. What the fuck? What could be better?

We were staying in an abandon house next to the one they were rebuilding, and the front room made me really homesick. Every wall was covered with pictures. Old magazine pages and sewing patterns and newspapers. Every inch was covered, just like my room back home, only here it was for insulation.

In the daytime, we built the house. Plained the logs and notched them. Tied ropes around them and pulled them up. Built walls. Hammered in a floor. But the fucked up thing was, they didn't want me to be helping really. Even though they needed four people to pull up a log. And even though I was at least as strong as the terrorist. It wasn't women's work. They kept asking if I was tired. The punk girl brought us water and lunch. It was weird. At first I tried to prove myself to them, but eventually I got sick of it and left. Went and walked around the pastures for awhile and watched the crows and the guy with the horsedrawn cart, found the punk girl and fed the chickens and went and traded the neighbor some potatoes for some greens.

Solomon Yudovin

So we said goodbye to the dolphin trainer, went with his brother to his friend's house, and the four of us headed out to the country in a little car with no shocks. Neither of them spoke English, nor did the punk girl who was already out there. She was the first punk I'd seen, green mohawk, lock and chain around her neck. She smoked pot using rubles for rolling papers and took us to this murky pond with a big tire in it, to swim in. We drew pictures and comics for eachother to try to explain things, found some words in our dictionaries, but mostly didn't worry about communication too much.

At night, there were millions of mosquitoes, about eight hundred times more that I'd ever seen in Minnesota, and we'd have big fires and throw green pine boughs on it to make enough smoke to try to keep them away. She cooked us soup and we sat around listening to Russian radio. News mostly, but sometimes Russian rock, and once we heard the Spice Girls.

I was pretty glad I didn't speak the language, because I really didn't feel like talking about sexism or women's roles. Didn't want to debate cultural differences and the need to challenge or respect them. I tried to draw some pictures to talk to the girl about it some, but she just threw her hands up into the air, shook her head and took me swimming.

The next day, someone's uncle showed up, so there were four guys to do the work. The uncle guy was really terrible. He spoke some English, and they had thought it would be a good idea to ask him to come out so he could translate. The problem was, he had no idea that any of these kids were political at all, and we were warned before he got there, not to bring anything up about anything. So instead of

just sitting around, drawing pictures, being glad to be around eachother, we hac have these strange forced conversations around the fire every night. He was real into Nostradamus and wanted to know what our predictions were. I don't know how explain it, but it sucked. I didn't want to struggle that hard to communicate about a bunch of bullshit.

Shurik got frustrated one night, and started ranting in this crazy combination of Russian, Spanish, French, German and Italian that sounded so gread. Like if just spoke all the languages he knew, maybe he would get through to us. The un tried to cut him off, but Shurik raised his fist in the air and me and Luke an the girl all raised our fists too, and shouted "Anarchism, Antifascism" in uni The uncle looked confused.

I said "I'll sleep in your bed but I'm not going to fuck you." That's the way it was with us, I said "I love your girlfriend more than I love you." I said "You're sweet, no one ever does stuff like that for me." I said that when he stole some sugar packets for my coffee. I never left his house. I said "What are you doing after work? Coming home to me?" I said "You think you are my intellectual superior, what do you think makes me superior to you? He said alot of stuff, but not the right thing at all.

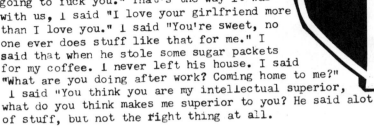

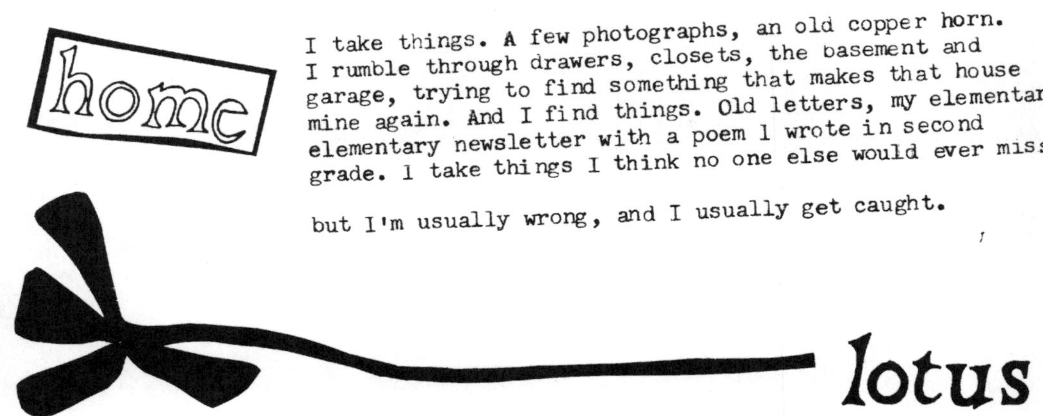

I take things. A few photographs, an old copper horn.
I rumble through drawers, closets, the basement and
garage, trying to find something that makes that house
mine again. And I find things. Old letters, my elementary
elementary newsletter with a poem I wrote in second
grade. I take things I think no one else would ever miss.

but I'm usually wrong, and I usually get caught.

You can tell by the way she pushes her bangs back that she's going to say
funny things. Spotty lightened hair, throaty voice. She's my favorite
waitress to work with. She says "Do you really think the earth is moving? Why
aren't we dizzy then?" She wants to be an airline stewdress, move to France and
never speak English again. She's almost done with her French class, and still
pretends she doesn't know what to do with sil vous plait. Or maybe she's not
pretending. I can never tell with her.

then & now

I used to think I trusted too easy. Cared about people too easily, and opened myself up too fast. I didn't think any other way wasworth it. I thought I'd rather be open and real and not playing stupid games and feel all those shitty let down feelings, than be closed off and never feel a goddamn thing. I didn't know there was some kind of more honest inbetween.

Chairs and Gardens

He spent all summer teaching the neighborhood kids to build chairs. When they had made enough, the kids all snuck out of their houses one night and took the chairs and put them in everyone's front yards. The next morning everyone was so happy and sitting in their yards talking. It changed the block for real.

After the chair project, Joel decided to make carousel horses. It was after I left so I never got to see them, but he sent me a bad photocopy of a blurry photograph and it was hard to make anything out. I think he took scraps; rebar, wood. Maybe old fish bones and dried kale stocks from the garden I planted before I left. I'd like to think that the sunflower bloomed and was held up in the horses mane, but those things are fragile.
It was a wild garden the year before. Kale and oregano running everywhere. Tomatoes that I didn't stake up right. The first time I picked one that was on the ground, I got a slug in my hand and I almost died. I didn't really know about slugs. I planted brussel sprouts in the front, and that one kid who had something wrong with his legs and fell down a lot, he came over for the leaves. Cooked them like greens. It was a wild garden, all city and untamed. Weeded, but messy. But it was that way - it looked like you could do it too.

There are garden stories I'm sure I've mentioned before. Planting potatoes in the empty lot. Laying down carpet in the back yard to kill the grass at Emerson. We had plans alright. Big plans for that yard. There was Oni and her gardening in the dark. I sung the Monkees theme song to her once and she looked kind of sad for maybe the first time I'd ever seen, and she said "It sure is that way", and I knew it must be hard walking through Oakland with that kind of color and style and life and always being confronted. I had settled for something inbetween. Something with some self protection. No more skirts except sometimes the petticoat and american flag riding my bike. But that was different. It's nicer when you have wheels like that.

But Joel, his story. I don't know what it was. Did he lose his mind? The carousel horse was so big, just kept growing there in the backyard by my new garden that I never saw, just the picture of it. Bok Choi, Nasturtum, Kale, of course. The carousel was so big it wouldn't fit through the door, couldn't bring it anywhere when he was done with it. Did he leave it there? I think he welded it apart and put it in the basement, and it'sprobably still down there, along with my two cases of printed, 2 color cover pamphlets of Toward an Ecological Society and some articles by Howie Hawkins or Brian Tokar, water damaged.

Joel wrote from Texas saying he'd fallen in love and was living in a bus and making smaller carousel horses to sell. I don't know if he sold any or not, but would like to think he did. He stopped by Berkeley for a day, but I don't remember what we talked about. We went to Edible Complex and I showed him the upper window across the street with the inside light and the piles and piles of chairs. the end.

boys again

I said "I'll sleep in your bed but I'm not going to fuck you." That was when I was younger and insecure and dramatic. When I was always testing him because he romanticized me and there's nothing, almost nothing I find more degrading than that. I hated it, but played into it, because I wanted his approval and it gave me some power, I was this magical thing.

Now it's almost funny that we played those games. We meet in the park and have the same conversation conversation we have ever few years - the one that goes "things are pretty bad. It's hard to figure out what to do. I know I've got to get it together soon." We talk about losing our sense of urgancy but not our hope. We listen to the drum player and laugh at eachother. It's reasuring and nice.

home again

When I'm away from home I get these weird ideas, about how when I get back I'm going to make a lot of changes. Like patch the walls, mop and sand and paint the floor, maybe get some food for the kitchen shelves. I think I'll get this new trend started and all my roommates will join along and soon our house will be a somewhat clean, artsy paradise. But then I get back and fall into the same habits, and it's all I can do to take ou the empty quarts, stomp on the floor to get the cockroaches out of the cat food, and plan another escape

new girl

I like the boys I know these days + I think it's kind of funny the way they poke fun at the way they're supposed to be. But sometimes it's hard to tell when it stops being a joke - when it crosses the line. Like when a new girl, cute girl, shows up in town. And at first they're going out of their way to make her comfortable, playing this game of who can get more of her attention, who can make her laugh - maybe they don't even really want to fuck her, but it starts to feel creepy that way after awhile.

"there's 10 thousand girls in this town + I'm gonna get every single one."
"I just want a honey in a tennis skirt."
"you guys are pigs".

I remember when it used to happen to me when I'd feel like prey in a new house, new scene, the boys vying for attention + I know that more than once I thought to myself "who am I going to have to fuck to get myself accepted + get the rest of them to leave me alone. It wasn't about how I was going to get ahead in the social game - it was about surviving this shit. I knew it was a stupid and sick way to think and I knew it wasn't my only option, but sometimes I was so worn down from all the years of being seen as part human, part object, and I'd just resign myself to the way things are. Sometimes the other choices were too difficult.

recap

There was Quannah at the bar with his mental patient haircut, falling over the drumset and clinging on to me. Carey in Landsing with an antibiotic IV. Raul breaking a bottle over his head, and I had to wash the blood off his face. There's everyone with their teeth rotting out and no money to fix them, and the way they all look when they're screaming at their bandmates. Caty laying in bed, overwealmed and confused. And the way I walk around, pink dress, rollerskates and scraped knees, through the grass on the campus. These days I don't even try to stop myself from crying in public.

what we talk about

It feels like siberia this morning, overcast and damp. Green mountains, wooden house, dogwood trees. I guess there probably weren't dogwood trees in Siberia. I don't remember. I didn't have a name for them then. Waking up and drinking coffee that's boil the water then put the grounds in. let it soak then hit the side of the pot until the water ripples and the grounds sink to the bottom. It's good coffee. That's what we had in Siberia, that's what I've got here at Colby's house.

In Russia I learned to make a small hot fire with little twigs under a pot ballanced on two or three rocks with a small space between them. Keep shoving twigs in and blowing on it and thewater will boil quickly with almost no wood needed. This is great when you're in places with not much wood. You can cook rice add dried black beans near the end, and maybe garlic.

The best way to blow on a fire like this is to put your face right low, close to it, and blow and then turn your face away and breathe in out of the side of your mouth, over and over. You've got to get close and you've got to do it fast. To purify water all you need is iodine. About II drops to a 2 liter bottle. shake it up and let it sit for two hours and it's good. I know it says iodine is poison on the label, but it's fine in that small of a quantity. I learned to make stick-bread pizza. Just flour and water mixed together and stretched out on a V shaped stick. Cook it over the fire like a marshmellow, spread on tomato paste, basil, garlic and cheese if you've got it. It's a little bit weird, but it's cheep and compact.

I try to tell Colby these things and he looks at me like I make no sense. But that's how it usually is with us. We have to be around eachother a little bit before we start right in talking. And it's awkward with other people around. This time there's a woman and a little kid. The kid is four years old and screaming "Mommy, hold me. Mommy, you don't take care of me right", and she keeps repeating herself just like that, top volume. I know this kid has it good probably, about love and life and independence and family, but jesus. Her mom says "baby, you are getting to my head", and soon they are playing like nothing happened.

I couldn't take it, the being a mother trip. Colby hands the kid a 2headed, 3legged doll and looks at me and says "Do you know about Hemlock?" And he takes me outside and tells me everything he's learned about trees and wood in the past year. What wood you can make fence posts out of that will never rot. How things burn and grow.

We used to give up on language alot. Just speak nonsense or the only foreign words we knew, sitting around the kitchen table, laying in bed. 'Je jou au tenis?' what the hell else was I supposed to ask him? Where have you been? We didn't talk about that any more. Where are you going? How long are you staying? They were more or less off limits too. He'd say 'You have a beautiful nose' in Spanish, I'd say 'My kittycat' in Hungarian. It wasn't enough really, but neither was anything we could say.

navicella bassa

May 31

When we moved away from the trailer at the end of April, we sold half our books and broke all our dishes. That was after Caty had already left to go be a farmer, and Bryan had come back South early because El-Nino had fucked up his fishing. We took the dishes down to our old spot under the bridge by the river where we used to have bonfires and drink, even in the summer when it was so hot, we'd still build a fire and sit around it.

We went there, me and Bryan andKerb. Covered over all the bad graffiti and drank wine. When we'd finish a glass, we'd smash it against the concrete pillar and grab ourselves a new one. In between we'd break the plates and bowls.

They took up yo yoing while I tried to hurry and finish all my work on the loom. They had wooden yo yos, Scorpians, Phantoms, Duncan Imperials. They started out pretty lousy but got good quick. It's the stance, the flick of the wrist. They broke strings, tried to break bottles on the outswing and still have the yo yo come back. Walk the dog while walking down the street with Anna.

One day in Chattanooga, I was sitting in the passanger seat of my parked car with the door open. Bryan and Quannah were yo yoing on the sidewalk. Bryan did a round the world but it snapped back and hit him in the eye so hard it knocked him down. He was laying on the sidewalk and had his hands over his face, screaming. At first I just laughed, but then I got scared and I hopped over to him with my cane. I'd sprained my ankle a few days before, dancing to Greese Lightning.

We were sprauled out on the ground, can and yo yo mixed inbetween us, him hollering and me saying "baby, are you ok?" and Q, he says "You two could make a lot of money like that". Mike Pack came back and drove us all away. Bryan in the back seat said he couldn't believe I'd laughed at his pain. I told him "baby, I was afraid your eye had fallen out. I was ready to call the ambulance <u>and</u> poke your eye back in!" Bryan tried to tell me that you can't <u>poke</u> people's eyes back in, but Mike stood up for me, saying that he knew you could because it had happened to his Granny. Then he told us the story of how his Granny had been in a bar fight and someone hit her in the back of the neck and just by chance, hit this pressure point back there that makes your eye fly out, which is what happened. But when they took her to the hospital, the doctor didn't do hardly anything, just poked the eye right back in. Mike has those kinds of stories.

Bryan told me stories about fish and lines and flys and boats. About how they used to get hungry walking around Dalton, GA and wherever they were, they'd just build a fire on the sidewalk and cook something up. He talked about drinking antifreeze with the natives in Alaska, and about this group of kids who were all in town now. How they'd stuck together and followed eachother around from Michigan to Miami andChattanooga.

Quannah told me about how his dad spoke Russian and joined the airforce to get out of his economic situation. He was supposed to be spying on Russian plane's radio transmissions, but it was boring. All they ever talked about was stuff like "Hey, are you going to take Olga to the dance?" So Q's dad gave himself a mohawk and told his commanding officer to fuck off. Got kicked out of the airforce, bought a motorcycle, and drove it all the way to Africa.

At night Kerb sat next to me on the couch, and said "I've always thought you were ugly as hell and stupid too. The only reason anyone hangs out with you is because we feel sorry for you." I said "I've always thought you were the most selfish, selfabsorbed, loudmouth bitch. I'm glad you're leaving. I wish you were going sooner". We leaned into eachother and shared our beer.

When they were getting ready to leave they tried to rent a Cadillac, bought blue block sunglasses and a bottle of whiskey. I was out gardening after walking around the block. Those three had become so wrapped up in my days, I wasn't sure what it would be like without them. I thought I'd just walk away so I wouldn't have to say goodbye, but I hate that kind of stupid shit, so I came back but was trying to sort of ignore them. Bryan yelled "Hey Cindy!" and when I looked up, he threw a crushed beer can at my head. I said "why don't you all get the hell out of here already" and they did.

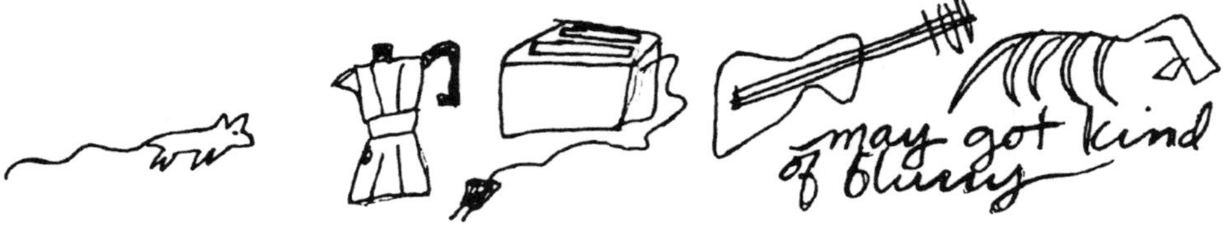

May got kind of blurry. we had cases of malt liquor, and cheep or stolen whiskey. Ten of us living in a two bedroom house. Carey made a list one day of all that we had in there: 5 coffee makers, 3 toasters, 8 amps, 16 guitars, a carcass, a broken penis pump, 11 cats, 1 rat, 1 dog (really big), fire extinguisher. By the next week we realized we'd forgotten to mention the leather jackets, plus by then we had to modify the list anyway, we'd acquired another rat and another dog.

I've never been anywhere so condusive to just sitting around and drinking. All these people coming and leaving and telling stories and playing music and going wild. Mike and I decided that even though alot of things in our lives were really fucked up and not so great and even kind of terrible, that there was no use being in a bad mood because everything around us was so ridiculous. Jeremy free style rapping for an hour straight, crackheads coming over and asking us for car rides and buying us beer. Mike and I decided that sure, you could be in a bad mood, but only for three forths of a minute. Then you had to laugh at the whole absurdity of our situations. One night I was drunk as hell and decided this was bullshit. I needed to sobar up, at least for three days. I had a lot of things to do. I was wasting my time, and this drinking shit wasn't really my style. So I tried to rehydrate myself by drinking lots of water. 3 quarts in an hour. I really thought it would work - wash it all out of my system - but I just ended up puking and then spent the next three days getting blacked out.

Then somehow I ended up in Miami and I was seeing how long I could float for, and I was drifting out to sea. I was on the beach listening to Dany tell me the story of how he had to flee from Peru, and Jason was walking down Ocean drive naked all the way to the store. One day we went with Raul, driving down the turnpike. He is the craziest driver I've ever seen. Cuts in front of people, switches lanes and speeds, drinking and getting stoned, he hardly looks at the road at all and everyone's always yelling at him and you sort of fear for you life, but also, for some reason, feel kind of safe. He was looking for this canal, so every bridge, he'd pull over onto the turnpike median, jump out of the van, and look over it. Then one time the cops pulled up and he said to us "hold on, I'm gonna go talk to these cops" and he ran over to them. I thought we were in for it, but instead they just gave him directions and told him not to park on the median. Next thing you know, we're down at the canal, walking up to the interstate bridge and jumping off. Jason naked again, cars honking at him.

Things got kind of blurry. I kissed Joey, rested my head on Sarah, thanked Eric and slept in my car. Every night me and Buddha talked until the sun came up. SteveO taught us to catch crawdads in plastic bags and then we cooked them over a fire, using a broken bottle for a pot. We had a pinata that I tore apart with machettes.

We lost our hearts, our minds, lost rings, lost jobs and felt kind of better for it. May was kind of blurry I guess, some of the details and hours are gone, but it's almost clearer than anything ever - the way these people so quickly became part of my life, and I learned to be straight forward and give up on guilt and some of my sorrow and distractions.

Saunaa

SAUNAS

My step dad said it was hard work, but you had to do it. sweat until you skin was new. He didn't say it like that. He'd say, what are you? a wimp? you have to stick it out and learn to sweat like a man. sit down. you had to learn to sweat. There were laugh lines around his eyes. He meant it the same way as when he said eat your beets, they make you grow hair on your chest. They make you pee red.

I'm a girl, I'd say, I don't want hair on my chest.

Not on your chest, he'd say, on the palms of your hands.

And my mom would roll her eyes and say his name in mock disgust. That's enough now Johnny, enough.

We'd sit in the sauna, the whole bunch of us. The two families com combined. My old siblings and my new ones. All of us in our awkward adolescence, except one. Embarrassed or shyly proud of our new bodies. I'd try to hide mine, scrunched up, knees to chest, until it was too hot to care, too hot to worry.

It was a real Finnish sauna. My stepdad's dad had built it, tiny to hold the heat close, wood benches. You had to build a fire. It wasn't electric. It was a dry expansive heat, well past the danger zone, and if we ever brought friends there, they just couldn't see how we could do it. They would sit down by the small air holes at the bottom of the door, breathing cold into their lungs. They would leave and come back in, leave and come back in, until Johnny said, what do you think you are? a cat? no more in and out. What kind of Finn are you?! They would give us that your dad is crazy look, and go into grandma's house and watch TV.

My stepdad would throw water on the rocks, which would send us all running, through grandma's yard, down the thin path to the Saint Croix river, snow falling around us maybe if it was the right time of year, and we'd jump in the water, lose our breath and come up gaping, wide eyes, new skin, stumbling to the shore.

Our friends stood on the porch. Aren't you afraid of pneumonia? our friends would say, but we looked at them like they were strangers.

Not at all, we'd say, This is what we do. It was the only thing we had, maybe, that was that simple.

abortion #1

It's raining hard, big rain where you can't do anything but watch. The kind that flooded Minneapolis and made cars float away into Lake Calhoun. That flooded my basement and Padrick came over to help me pick my wet records up from the floor and wait for my pregnancy tests to come back.

I didn't know they had do it yourself home kits then. Padrick was my friend, not the boy. My records were ruined, but the phone rang, negative she said, and I jumped up and down and we walked down Highway 7 to the Willhopin to celebrate with a game of pool.

Those were the days of being 16-18, and worrying forever about pregnancy. When I was on the pill, but still scared every month that my period wouldn't come and my life would be ruined. No matter what I did, there was always the chance that my body would betray me, I hated it and distrusted it for that. Abortion was one of those "it's ok. I'm not against it, but I couldn't do it myself" kind of things, and my friends mostly felt the same way.

I got my pills and exams at the teen clinic, where they made you feel guilty for even coming in the door. The old man doctor would put that cold metal speculum in, poke around without telling you a thing about what he was doing. That shit was more tramatic than the first time I got pregnant, 5 years later. I'd learned some things by then and knew that what happened in my body was my own decision. I didn't have any moral problems or guilt. but my emotional state was pretty fragile. I went back and forth between being fascinated and scared. Fascinated by what was going on and my reactions to it; scared because it felt all out of my control.

I started reading about the reproductive system. I had never been able to look at the pictures before. Just the diagrams repeled me in a strong, inexplicable way. Like one time, a few years before, in a class I was taking on sex and self-image, the teacher had us all draw a vagina. After about half a minute, I got indignant and stormed out of class, saying I didn't pay all that tuition for classes full of this kind of irrelevant garbage, which was true. I was used to really tough, intellectual women's studies classes, but what I didn't say was that I couldn't draw a vagina because I had no idea what it actually looked like. What I didn't say was that I didn't know because to think of my body tangibly - I just couldn't do it. It was an irrational fear, or maybe it was perfectly rational. If I tried to think about anything real about that part of my body, I got angry and protective and my mind shut down and my heart and lungs clenched up - like shock. That, I didn't explain.

when I was pregnant, I forced myself to look at the diagrams. Memorize the text instead of blocking it out. The eggs are formed in the overies, they go down the fallopian tubes... I only read it when no one was around. I locked the door and was jumpy and nervous, scared someone would catch me. I hid it like pornography.

It seemed almost cliche, but learning about my body and the changes going on in it, and knowing that it wasn't out of control, it made me feel like my body was strong and mine. It was a way I'd never felt before.

The abortion itself wasn't too bad. I had it done at a feminist health clinic and the women there took care of me the way it should be done. They held up a mirror, and that was the first time I'd seen those parts of me. They explained every touch and every second of the procedure. Now you'll feel the speculum, this is the local anesthetic, you'll feel some cramping now as she dialates the os, breathe deep.

One woman held my hand, talked to me and tried to help me relax. It was the first time I'd had a woman gynacologist and the first time anyone had bothered to explain what was going on. It was the first time I didn't feel alienated and violated by what was being done. They demystified my body and gave it back to me.

kirby house

Our room was the storage hallway to the backdoor and it was the hottest summer I'd ever been in, so I slept with the door open, the fan on, andmy dog at the foot of the bed to scare away anyone who might try to walk in, or to intimidate the film crews that would drive through the back alleys, reporting on the bad neighborhoods. We'd seen our house on TV once, our back porch was one big mountain of quart bottles, the yard was overgrown except for a fire pit, and we had a little graveyard for our kitties that were killed by the neighbor's Great Dane. That Great Dane was the worst thing in the neighborhood. I slept there all summer, half naked, with the door wide open and no one ever bothered me until Mr. Minneapolis came to town. Anna didn't even bark at him. He just walked right up in his Carhart coveralls and said he was a friend of a friend. I said, Come in, Aren't you hot in all that? and he said he was but he liked to keep his tatoos coverd up when he was on the road.

I felt kind of sorry for him at first, poor awkward modern primitive creep, poor idiot who though he was worldly because he'd been to Europe and couldn't wait to go back there.

It was sad to hear them talking in the room, my friend and him, in our house with the thin, thin walls, and she was agreeing with him, saying "yeah, punk is stupid. I mean, what are you going to do? be a punk and spend the rest of your life working at the Pickle Barrel and living at Kirby Street?"

That was our lives they were talking about! I don't know why I didn't start yelling. Fuck Yeah! That's exactly what we're going to do! Maybe the house sucked, but what if we were all still there in 10 years, same job, same house, closer than ever and true to ourselves. wouldn't that be a testament? Something to be proud of? I almost went down and got a job at the fucking bar myself, just to prove something, but I wasn't sure exactly what it would prove.

What am I talking about? who cares about Mr. Mple? I barely even talked to the guy at all. I just didn't see how he could sit around our house with a superior, bemused, condescending grin, watching us like we were some kind of anthropological study, when there was so much love and angst and confusion and drive; life that couldn't be pent up, and didn't try to shut itself off, but didn't know exactly where to go.

How could he come to our shows, where everyone was screaming the same songs, lifting eachother up and rolling around, and he just sat in a booth, and when I said "Come on! Dance with us! he just smiled and said "I don't like American punk rock".

Kirby sucked, what house didn't? we had roaches, some houses have video games. We yelled at eachother and the place was usually a dump, some houses are clean and full of uptight rules and resentment. It could get depressing sometimes that we were all such alcoholics, but them something would happen. Like Tom would put on his tap shoes. Carey would come up with an idea like Free Jaw Action, and then we'd all be down at the park, serving up beans and rice and coffee one day, hot dogs and shots of whiskey the next, with the punks playing guitars, drinking tall cans like it wasn't illegal, running around practicing flipping eachother, playing hacksac of all things.

I loved our house

I loved our house. I loved how Mike would wake up yelling about being broke and every day he'd go out and get a job, and then somehow get up some money for some booze and he'd come home to celebrate with us. We'd stay up all night, drinking to him and his new job that he was really going to go to this time. Of course, he'd pass out and not wake up until it was too late, and then he'd go out and do the whole thing again.

I loved the days when we'd go down to the pedestrian bridge and play music for money, Michelle belting out songs, Joey walking smoothly up and down the walkway, seranading the ladies. I even loved the days when we'd just walk around, when it was too hot to even be alive, and we'd just walk around all day, looking for everyone else.

Our kitchen broke so Joey just started cooking on the grill outside. One time he couldn't find the lighter fluid so he poured WD40 everywhere and tried to start it like that. It was the week that Joe and Mike didn't talk to eachother, they just yelled and insulted eachother, which was annoying, but not too bad. I was sleeping and Mike was yelling that Joey was going to poison us all. Dany ran though the room to save the chicken from the grill and I got up to start my daily routine of cleaning the roaches out of the coffee maker. Joey was screaming and Mike was screaming and Dany was cooking and blocking Joey who was trying to grab the chicken and start all over with new charcole and a cleaned off grill.

Dany was saying "No, I'm trying to remember how my mom cooked it". When he was done, he offered me a peice and we sat on the couch eating, with Buddha and Mike and Joey. Everyone was quiet and focused on the food. Dany looked surprised, like our lives had been levitated and put down somewhere new. He said "this is the best food I've ever eaten. I didn't know I could cook like this. I never cared about cooking but now that I taste this, I see how it is. I should go home and see my mom. I have a lot to learn from her."

Of course, we all had some things to learn, and one of the things I needed was to learn moderation, so I moved back to Asheville, where there was less love and less beer, but more of other things which are also important. I got on the up all night, sleep all day schedule so I could be alone and get some loneliness and start seeing the world again, instead of just my friend's stories. It was kind of depressing

No, see, this is not a depressing end of the story.

It's not a "we had this great house and I had these great friends, but now it's over" ending, because it's far from over. It's nowhere near over. It's just that I got so used to being around my friends all the time that I forgot how to be alone, and I got so used to listening to their stories that I forgot how to tell my own, unless I was drunk, of course, then you couldn't get me to shut up. And I'd have this nagging feeling that if I had so much to say when I was drunk, didn't that mean I had a lot to say? and why couldn't I think of any of it when I was sober? I lost perspective on the world. Couldn't think of anything really worth doing that didn't involve the whole bunch of us, and I kind of think you need to have something going on outside your group to bring back to it so everyone keeps being pushed and interested and it doesn't just go in circles and implode. So what's the end of the story? There is no end to it. I'm just getting my life back a little bit, before they come and sweep it away again.

the end

Angie said that if I waited 6 months, I'd be an honorary virgin

since I'd only had sex twice it hardly counted. I appreciated her offer, but it didn't seem to matter much, I proceded to fuck my way through life. I wanted true love and forever and complete understanding. Someone to care about me and tell me who I was. And of course, if they did, I thought they were tricked, they were stupid, I wasn't worthy, I didn't deserve them, I was bad, deep inside, I was evil, everything I touched would be ruined, I was guilty, I wasn't normal. Or maybe I was just bored with the guy and couldn't admit it.
I had great sex, good sex, ok sex, indifferent sex. Sex to waste time, sex because I wasn't supposed to and that made it exciting and rediculous and funny. sex because I wanted it like crazy, sex because I had nowhere else to stay. I had bad sex, terrible sex, sex to prove to myself that I was worthless, sex to prove that sex was all anyone wanted of me. sex to remove myself from my feelings. sex to prove that just because I was 15 didn't mean I couldn't fuck good. sex because we started kissing and I thought that's just what you did from there. sex I never wanted. sex where I just layed there and waited for it to be over. sex that made me feel like nothing else mattered, where I couldn't stop looking into the other person's eyes. sex to prove that everything was alright. sex that tangled my hair. sex instead of sleep. sex that made me cry.

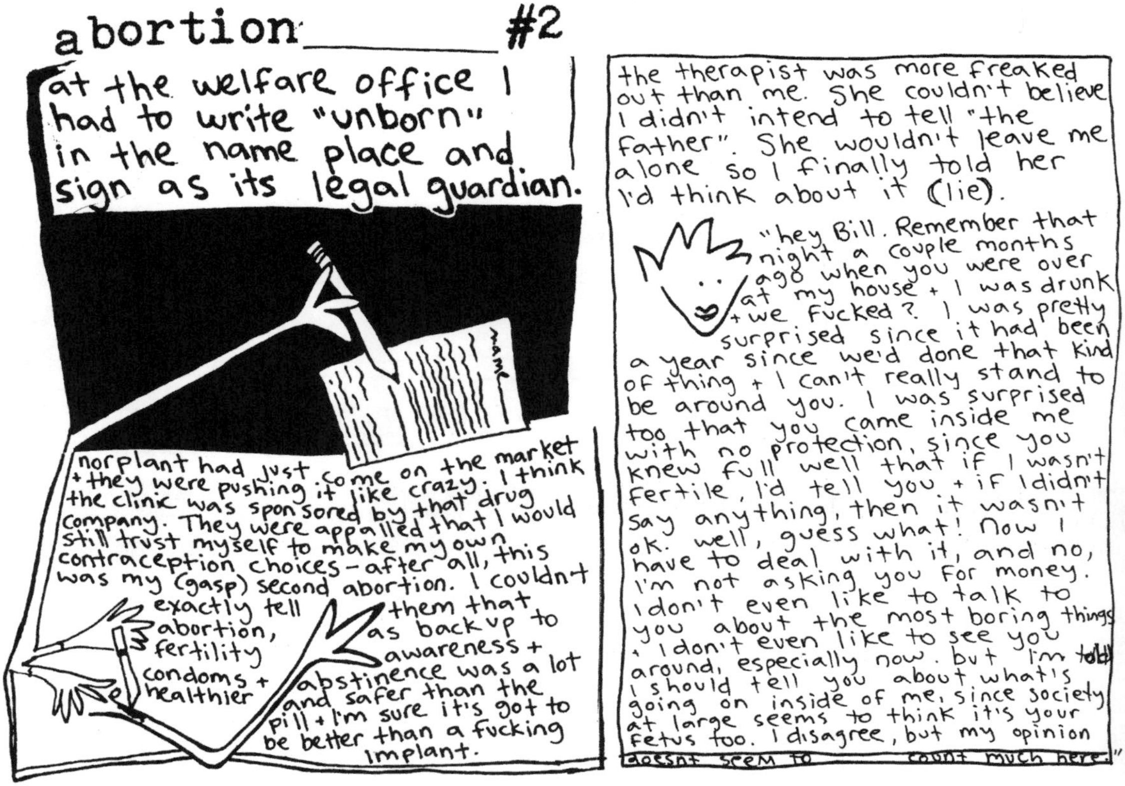

abortion #2

at the welfare office I had to write "unborn" in the name place and sign as its legal guardian.

name

norplant had just come on the market + they were pushing it like crazy. I think the clinic was sponsored by that drug company. They were appalled that I would still trust myself to make my own contraception choices - after all, this was my (gasp) second abortion. I couldn't exactly tell them that abortion, as back up to fertility awareness + condoms + abstinence was a lot healthier and safer than the pill + I'm sure it's got to be better than a fucking implant.

the therapist was more freaked out than me. She couldn't believe I didn't intend to tell "the father". She wouldn't leave me alone so I finally told her I'd think about it (lie).

"hey Bill. Remember that night a couple months ago when you were over at my house + I was drunk + we fucked? I was pretty surprised since it had been a year since we'd done that kind of thing + I can't really stand to be around you. I was surprised too that you came inside me with no protection, since you knew full well that if I wasn't fertile, I'd tell you + if I didn't say anything, then it wasn't ok. well, guess what! now I have to deal with it, and no, I'm not asking you for money. I don't even like to talk to you about the most boring things + I don't even like to see you around, especially now. but I'm told I should tell you about what's going on inside of me, since society at large seems to think it's your fetus too. I disagree, but my opinion doesn't seem to count much here."

resources:

A Woman's Book of Choices: Abortion, Menstrual Extraction, RU-486 by Rebecca Chalker and Carol Downer

Experiencing Abortion: A Weaving of Women's Words, by Eve Kushner

Talking Charge of Your Fertility, by Toni Weschler

New View of a Women's Body, by federation of feminist women's health centers

Seizing Our Bodies: the Politics of Women's Health, ed Claudia Dreifus

Witches, Midwives and Healers, or maybe it's Witches Nurses and Healers, I can't remember, but it's great and by Barbar Ehrenreich and someone else

a lot of times, society just gets me down.
ice cream
how much!
ooo baby baby
the people at the ice cream shop stare out + check the weather + assholes
at me when I'm just trying to walk
hoot + hollar when I'm trying to put up
flyers
this is part of the reason I stay up all night. You get less society + more sweet alone time.
it feels like it's just me + my friends against the world...
DONUTS
give me somedonuts!
knock knock
CLOSED
I have had friends who could interact with the world at large and it always amazes me.
because I live with this impression that if you ask anyone for anything they will be mean, suspicious and evil and it's just not worth even trying. Better just to keep to yourself.
today I woke up early to go to the leaf compost place to get leaves to put on the garlic beds of my sisters new farm,
but when I got there I didn't know what to do. There was a city worker guy
city only
and a city vehicles only sign + I wavered around, thinking I could come
back at night or steal leaves from people's yards. Well, hell, I got up the courage to ask the guy.
I tried to explain very thoroughly because I knew he would think I was lieing. What would a punk want with leaves anyway.
but he just smiled + said . . .

of course, honey, that's what they're here for.

society is pretty amazing. And it's not just the little things in life, like feet sinking into a leaf pile taller than my house, the sun on my arms for the first time in months, the sound of the brook and the traffic. Those things are good, but they are only small things. What amazes me is organization, how satisfying useful work is, art, literature, the desire to create, CURIOSITY, the ability to use logic, the complexity of our emotions, introspection, the need for challange and change. I have friends who want to cut themselves off from society completely, which I can understand, but it sounds so boring to me, and I have friends who can only see injustice. Me, I hide ½ the time + then I go out + am either appalled or amazed. I either want to lock myself in my room again and only go out when no one else is awake so I can appreciate the world without having to really see it. Or I want to start a whole cheerleading squad for humanity, my eyes shining at everyone, my head spinning with possibilities and the unrealized potential of this whole confusing system I'm a part of. Society! Yeah! Go!

abortion #3

I think it's the waiting that's the worst. That's why #3 wasn't so bad. I pretty much just convinced myself I wasn't pregnant until I was two months along. I had one day of swearing and cursing and worry, got a test the next day and an abortion the next, and it was over.

I guess it wasn't really as easy as all that. There were things - like I wasn't sure if I should tell anyone because I wasn't sure I wanted to deal with their reactions. I figured I'd just go it alone - walk up to the clinic, past the protesters. Spit in the protester's faces. Then I rememberd that I'm kind of anemic, and it's kind of nerve wracking, and I'm not always that strong. Abortions hurt, there's no doubt about it, but it only takes a few minutes - the pain part. Some women get sedated and don't really remember it, but I like to know what's going on. It's scarier for me to not know. In the end, I went alone, but I had told my best friend, and he made me hot chocolate and soup.

At the clinic, in the recovery room, a couple women seem freaked out, but most of them had this glow of relief.

What am I talking about this for? Because it seems like no one ever talks about it. I read horror stories about abortion from the right wing, and horror stories about back alley abortions from before Roe vs Wade. I read pro-choice articles in fanzines, but never about the actual experience. And I think women should talk about it and write about it. It's a common experience and a part of our lives, and I think it would be less loaded and scary if it was out in the open more.

a single beginning

I remeber what it was like when it was so hard to start. when every word was supposed to be something and endings were supposed to exist and be dramatic.

I pictured myself someday, with a house like other people's houses. A school teacher maybe, living with someone who had kids. This was before I knew what it was like having kids around. when I thought they were just something cute and stumbling around your feet, maybe climbing up into your lap for a minute and then you could shoo them away. I thought kids were something that made life wholesome and cheery

I remember thinking I'd make tea. drink tea in the morning. I read an interview with theBeans of Egypt woman who told the story of going to a writers conference even though she couldn't afford to get in. She and her friends tailed the famous writers around to the resturants on break, trying to overhear and find out some tricks. What they found out was black tea. Rose Red. It's supposed to keep you steadier than coffee.

who knows if it's a true story. I can picture her in the resturants, leaning back in her chair, straining to hear some secret, and finding it - tea! yeah tea! and then going home and writing up a novel, on her typewriter that was missing all the vowels.

There's something powerful about creating a life that looks like a writers life. Warming hands on homemade mugs in the morning and writing for hours and hours. It sounds good, but it is not the life for me. Not now and probably not ever.

I'm not saying I don't somedays sit around writing for hours, that's not what I'm talking about. It's the lifestyle, this mythical thing, where you stare at a blank page until genius spurts forth. where it's so hard to start because every word is supposed to be something, and endings are supposed to be clear and dramatic.

I can't think of anything worth writing about, so I write about the stupidest of all things.

I have a green dress that was my sister's dress and a green dress that was my mother's dress and before that was my Grandmother's. I still have Tom's yellow Cuban shirt and the brown pants Raul gave me. The plaid sweater I bought at the thrift store in Vermont that was $7 and I wasn't sure it was worth it until Casey said she'd buy it if I didn't. That was 10 years ago, almost.
Plaid shirt of Bryans, plaid skirt Nathan gave me, plaid skirt I bought to impress a boy. I got underwear out of the dumpster.

There is a black dress I wore to prom, which I thought would be funny. We went to Jimmy's Italian Kitchen andBuffet, up on Cedar, or what was that street name? Where MayDay books used to be before they moved to the West Bank? I didn't know about MayDay books then, and thought it must be some kind of flowery thing with May baskets, pastel and spring renual.

Jimmy asked why me and Dylan were so dressed up, we told him prom and he got a broad smile and led us to a back table, like every other table, with a red plastic checked tablecloth. He brought us coffee and plates. At Jimmy's, you served yourself. Lasagna, garlic bread, salad, and Jimmy comes around with a big low stainless steel bowl full of fresh rigatoni, heaping it on plates, telling everyone to eat more.

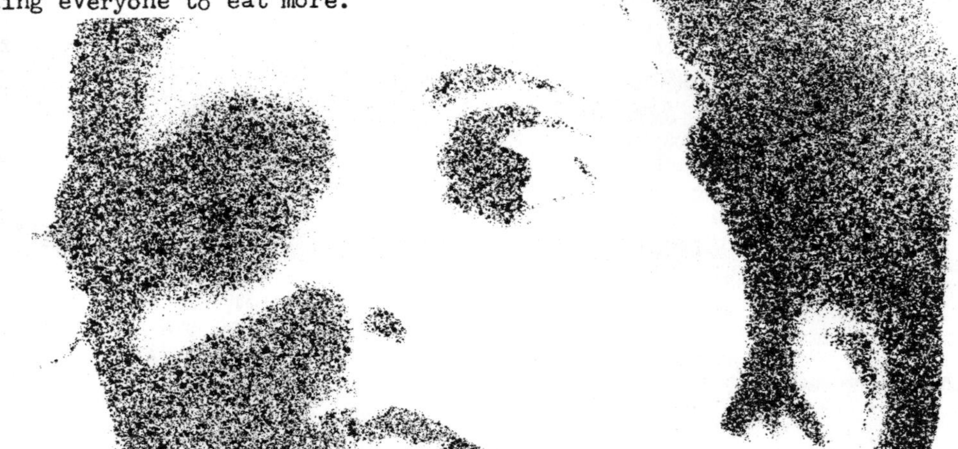

Prom was boring. No one was shocked and amazed to see me, even though I hadn't been in school all year. They didn't care about my 57 Rambler, or me in my black prom dress, or me with a date. The band didn't remember that I was the girl who brought them grapes when they played Loring Park, they just played their accordian rock and roll with accordian poka stint. I got mad at my date for no reason and stood on the deck watching the parkinglot.

I have an orange sock that I got I don't know where, a red sweater I thought was Brandon's when he was walking around with the punk Mr. Rogers look. The camel shirt Kerb made, green tights thatmake my leg hairs itch. Brown shoes Anthony gave me when I left my shoes in Atlanta. How could I drive all the way home from Atlanta without realizing I left my shoes there? I always drive barefoot. You can grip the pedals better. Everything I have I think was someone else's first, even the rat and the dog, but not my rope ladder.

One Must Show Good Nature

I've been trying to make things small to fit on these little pages. and my life started getting small like this too. closing in around me in simple and familiar ways, until I wake up one morning, sick and not enough sleep, and I feel it break down inside me. can't stop crying. feel like my arms are stick thin and my body is shrinking and I can't stop crying and I want someone to come find me and I really hope no one does. It's a familiar feeling, it's been a long time since I've felt it just like this, and I think it's curious, between sobs. I think, wow, where the hell did this come from? I think, damn, I'm glad I'm not a suburban housewife, I can see how easy this can happen - trapped, can't escape life except when cooking, no fulfilment or reason to live except to take care of things.

I think maybe I've been reading too much '70's feminist novels. Maybe I've been thinking about mom too much. Maybe I'm scared of life being good, of things being stable and feeling sort of content. I'm used to things being hopelessly doomed and somwhat romanticized to take the edge off of caring too much or trying too hard.

I try to think about what the hell my problem is, and my head starts swimming until I'm thinking of nothing, just trying to cry quiet enough to be ignored, maybe loud enough to be found, because I don't know what I want anymore, or what I need. I think, fuck, I wonder how long this is going to last.

What if it goes on all day, what if it lasts for a week, what if this is it, I'm actually crazy this time, I know really I'm not. At least I know that much by now. I wonder if this is a panic attack. I sure don't feel like I can leave the house, even in my disguise.

I swear to pull myself together, this is stupid, what am I doing. I crawl out from under the table and just start crying again. At least I made it to the bed this time. And it starts to slow down. I test my head, go through a list of possible feelings to see which ones trigger it off, and it ends up to be pretty much just writing and sex. I wish it was something more abstract, or at least just one of those two things, because it's been a long time sinse I've shrunk into corners and wanted to lock myself in bathrooms, and I'm not sure I can take it, I'm too old for this, I'm glad it doesn't happen more, but between sobs, it's kind of interesting, almost reassuring that I can still feel this intense, because I was worried that a part of me was becoming too numb.

Doris #13

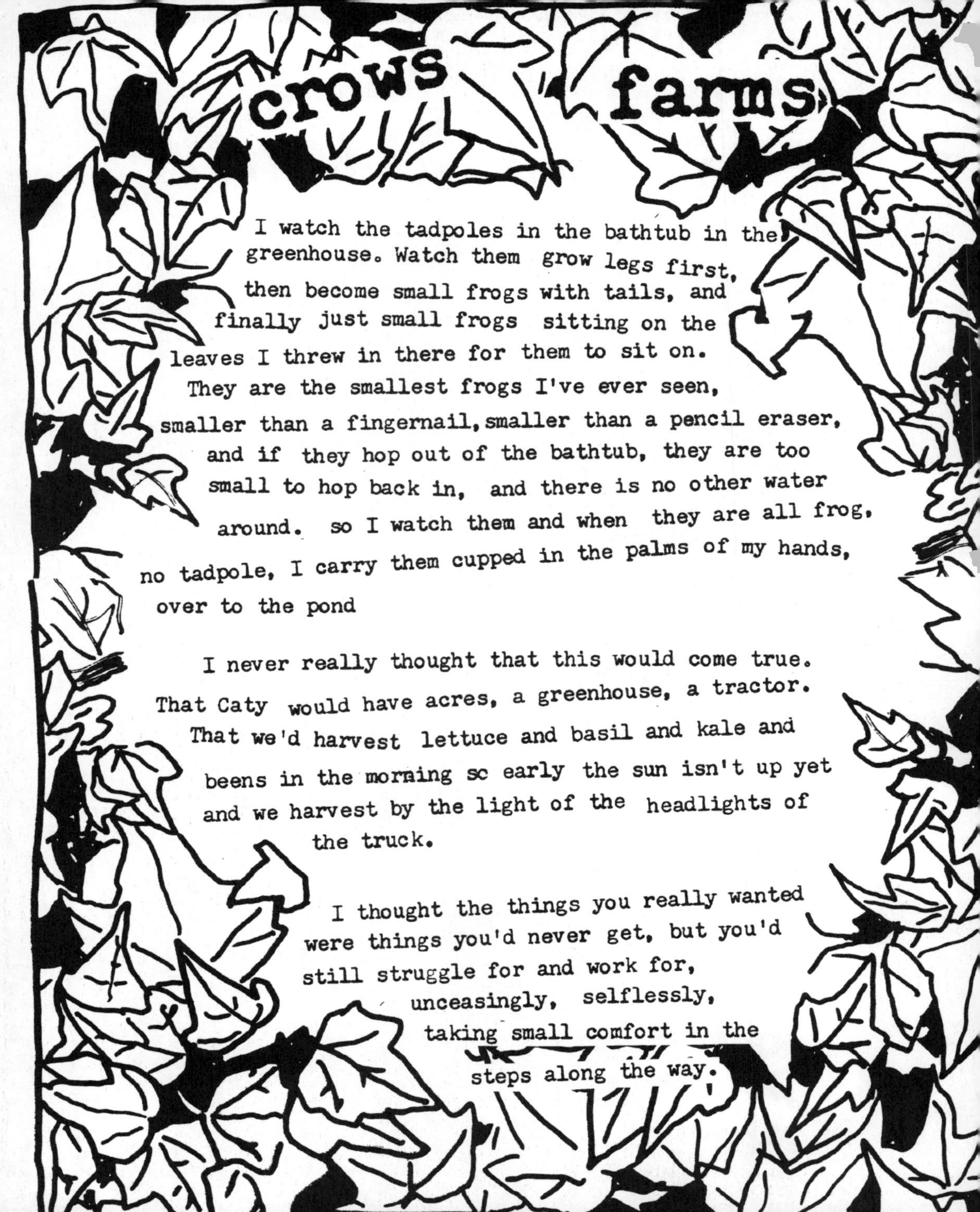

crows farms

I watch the tadpoles in the bathtub in the greenhouse. Watch them grow legs first, then become small frogs with tails, and finally just small frogs sitting on the leaves I threw in there for them to sit on. They are the smallest frogs I've ever seen, smaller than a fingernail, smaller than a pencil eraser, and if they hop out of the bathtub, they are too small to hop back in, and there is no other water around. so I watch them and when they are all frog, no tadpole, I carry them cupped in the palms of my hands, over to the pond

I never really thought that this would come true. That Caty would have acres, a greenhouse, a tractor. That we'd harvest lettuce and basil and kale and beens in the morning sc early the sun isn't up yet and we harvest by the light of the headlights of the truck.

I thought the things you really wanted were things you'd never get, but you'd still struggle for and work for, unceasingly, selflessly, taking small comfort in the steps along the way.

Once I was on the greyhound with Issac and while he was sleeping, head against the window, restless sleep, I pulled out my camera and took a picture of his arm. The flash woke him up. He said What was that? I said, My camera went off by accident.

The way I saw it, he had everything already, home community music and friends. He had places to go and places to come back to, and was perceptive and articulate and challenging.

The way I saw it, I had tricked my way into his life, he was important to me, and I had so little, and to him I figured I was only a distraction.

I took the picture because I wanted something to hold onto when he passed me out of his life.

Caty bought her tractor in Michigan. I forgot it's brand name, but for short it's called a G. It's a small tractor, orange and small enough to fit in the back of a regular pickup truck, but not small enough to fit in the back of a shortbed, which is what we have. So she bought a trailer and hauled it behind, all the way down I-75. At every gas station someone would yell out to her, "Where did you get that G?" They stopped making them a few decades ago. Moved on to bigger tractors for bigger farms. But at every gas station there would be som e old farmer who would come stand close to it, and talk to her, so pleased.

I pitched my tent by the woodchuck hole and try to teach Anna to chase the rabbits. I made a scarecrow to keep the crows out of the corn, with a skirt from the freebox, converse hightops, the shirt I'd been sweating in for days and days, and for the hair, Issac's dirty socks. It kept the crows away.

bombs

In the suburb where I grew up, all history was ancient, and I don't mean there was a strong sence of history: there was none. There was nothing to hang onto.

I went to one of the best public schools in the country, and I still didn't see how past events had any relevance to my life.

UNFAIR
STAY AWAY
CREAMETTE MFG. CO.
Wages are in dispute here and we ask your support
Food and Candy Workers Fed. Union Nº 20120
A. F. of L.

All facts were memorized and immediatly forgotten or dismissed.

There was no public life. Nowhere to go to even be in public. It was an older suburb, not the Suburbia or Over the Edge style where the houses look the same and kids roam the streets in packs.

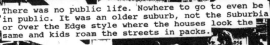

Everyone I knew lived in different parts of town. Life was incredibly private.

There weren't any punks in my school, just a handful of weirdos who didn't even get to feel like part of some larger social movement, community, or collective protest. I listened to the Ramones, the Replacements, watched Repo Man and Liquid Sky, read I Don't Want to Live This Life, and knew Dead Kennedys lyrics but had never heard their songs.

We were cut off. We didn't even know how to get information about the rest of the world and so our imaginations were left with what we could piece together and create on our own. And so our protest, for the most part, was individual. Pajamas in public, and ugly, unmatching clothes; not hiding our moods; writing on walls and occasionally calling in a bomb threat or skipping school.

I was filling out an application at KMart when I heard on the radio that the U.S. was bombing Granada and I walked home down the highway thinking "My God, we are at war." But the whole thing blew right over and I never knew what the bombs were for.

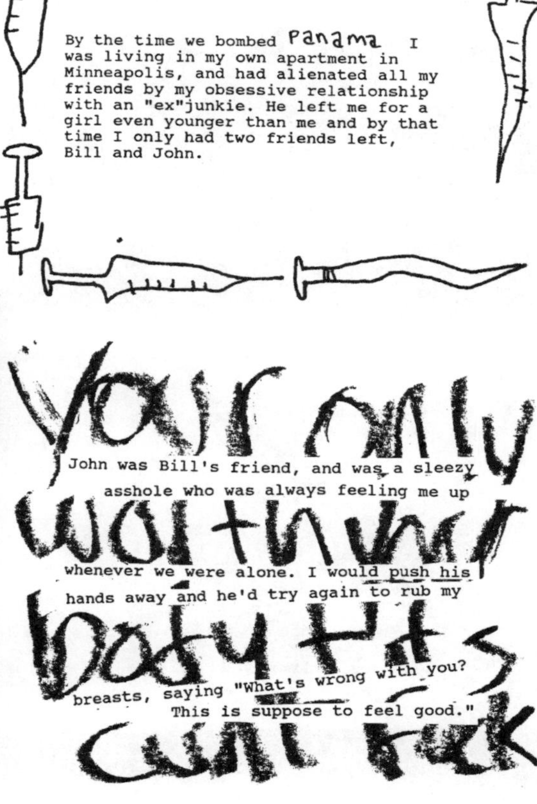

By the time we bombed Panama I was living in my own apartment in Minneapolis, and had alienated all my friends by my obsessive relationship with an "ex"junkie. He left me for a girl even younger than me and by that time I only had two friends left, Bill and John.
John was Bill's friend, and was a sleezy asshole who was always feeling me up whenever we were alone. I would push his hands away and he'd try again to rub my breasts, saying "What's wrong with you? This is suppose to feel good."

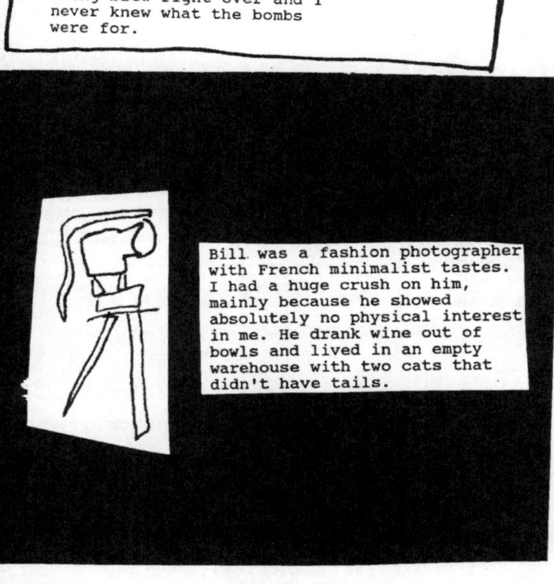

Bill was a fashion photographer with French minimalist tastes. I had a huge crush on him, mainly because he showed absolutely no physical interest in me. He drank wine out of bowls and lived in an empty warehouse with two cats that didn't have tails.

John lived right Uptown in a ratty apartment above a chinese resturant that was full of roaches and has since burned down. It was right on the corner of Lake and Hennepin, and so one night, while I was at home cooking them dinner, they walked out of his apartment and into a mob scene. Not a mob scene, but the whole intersection was taken over, thousands of people; with barrels and dumpsters burning in the streets. They saw Greg trying to make molatov cocktails behind the Uptown Bar, and when Bill tried to film the police moving in to disperse the crowd, the cops chased him down, hit him, and stole his film. They were late to dinner because they were protesting and fighting back the cops,trying to keep control of the street, for hours.

I was mad because it sounded exciting and I missed it and nothing exciting ever happened to me. And I was mad because I would have been there too, if it hadn't been for these boys, the junkies and ex-junkies who I'd given up my younger friends for.

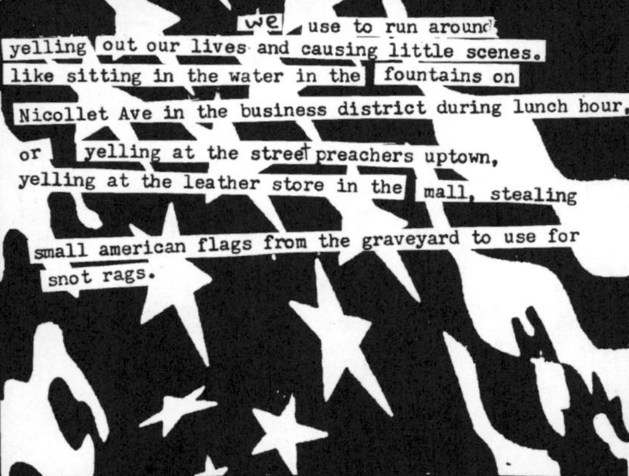

we use to run around
yelling out our lives and causing little scenes.
like sitting in the water in the fountains on
Nicollet Ave in the business district during lunch hour,
or yelling at the street preachers uptown,
yelling at the leather store in the mall, stealing
small american flags from the graveyard to use for
snot rags.

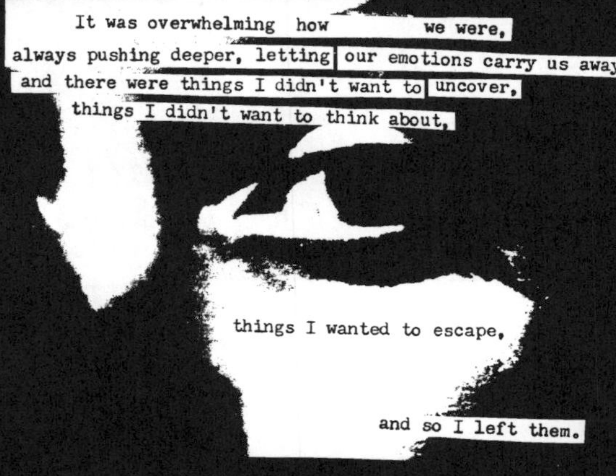

It was overwhelming how we were,
always pushing deeper, letting our emotions carry us away,
and there were things I didn't want to uncover,
things I didn't want to think about,
things I wanted to escape,
and so I left them.

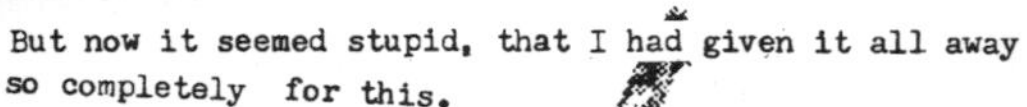

But now it seemed stupid, that I had given it all away so completely for this.

For Bill and John and purple glass antique dish sets, dentist chair funiture, rotary phones. Thick coats with big buttons, avant-garde films and nice hair cuts,

and acting like nothing mattered except calm and beauty, hiding always that anything touched me, hiding curiosity and excitement.

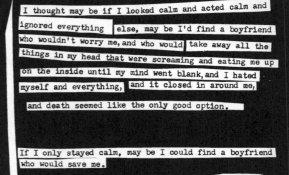

I thought may be if I looked calm and acted calm and ignored everything else, may be I'd find a boyfriend who wouldn't worry me, and who would take away all the things in my head that were screaming and eating me up on the inside until my mind went blank, and I hated myself and everything, and it closed in around me,

and death seemed like the only good option.

If I only stayed calm, may be I could find a boyfriend who would save me.

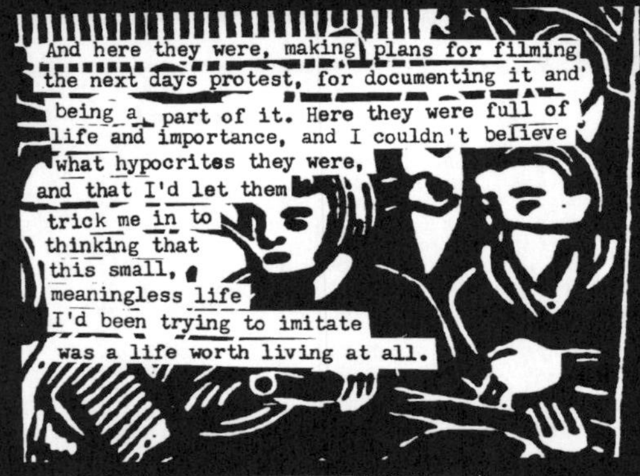

I wanted them to leave. I wanted my old friends back.

3 out of 3
she said "I can tell you how to get rid of hiccups.
Lay down and breathe deep. Now picture your solar plexus.
Breathe deep,, picture your solar plexus and a warmth
around it closing in slowly, not a suffocating warmth,
but a calm one, warming your center.
I thought - hell, this is embarrassing - but I didn't
want to offend her, so I did exactly what she told me
and it ended up it worked.
she said "I learned that at the mental ward I just got
out of", and then she talked about incest. about memories
and wanting to die and not wanting to be locked up any
more, and hoping she could make it-finish her dissertation.
Not dissertation, whatever it is you write to graduate
from college.
We shared a room for five days, and this was the first day, the first
time I'd met her.

I can't remember which of my friends I went to visit in the mental ward. Was it Rachael? Did she try to kill herself? Did I even get in to see her? Was it a friend of a friend and I just waited outside? Was it my best and only real friend and I blocked it out? There was a mental ward. I remember the sidewalk and lawn outside. It was right there, right on the bus route, benign looking. Any of us could have been in there. Jenny, Rachael, Corry, Lisa, Beth, or the girl who hung herself on fathers day. How could I have forgotten her name already? It was 15 years ago. I use to see her at the bonfires. She hung herself on fathers day and we all must have wondered the same thing. - fathers day. Do you think... - but none of us talked, not that I heard anyway, maybe hints, but not like this woman, my roomate, who says "One out of three. What bullshit. It's got to be more like 3 out of 3. So. Tell me. What did they do to you?"

Ten minutes after meeting me and she cures my hiccups and then wants to know. Me? What happened to me?

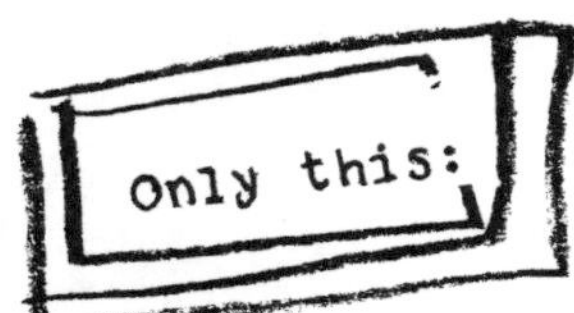

I tell her.

"It wasn't much of anything. Not like what's happened to some people. I mean, I don't even know, just this. I wasn't raped exactly, you know, just this and that and other things along the same lines." I told her the trut

She said "Never compare it. Everyone I've ever met tries to invalidate what happened to them by saying it was worse for someone else. I met one woman in the mental ward who had been tied up to a chair by her father in front of her brothers and he put a gun up her cunt, and this woman, she said 'it wasn't as bad as it could have been. I wasn't raped'"

Me and Angie went to the Take Back the Night march. They had premade, handmade signs we could carry. I grabbed one that had two women symbols on it.
"Do you know what that means?" Angie said.
"Yeah, sure. I mean, not really."
"It means you're a lesbian."
I put it down and got a new one.

That was 1986, I was 16. Me and Angie would always walk down hockey hall, holding hands. We did it in defiance. We did it to piss them off. The jocks and cheerleaders would taunt us. They'd yell Dyke and we'd just laugh. In school we held hands and they didn't dare to touch us, but at the march I put the sign down. I didn't really want to be mistaken as one of them. Not one of them, really, it was just a joke. I was joking.

We made fun of the Take Back the Night women. "Take back <u>these</u> streets? This is nothing to be afraid of. We should take them down to Chicago Ave. We don't need this huge group to walk around here." But regardless, we marched. We liked parades and jumping around.

I was pretty positive I would become a statistic. I carried a switchblade that I knew would be used against me, but it made me feel more dangerous, and I thought this attitude might help prevent, or at least delay, an attack. I always checked the back seat of my car before getting in. I didn't consider myself already a statistic.

No one I knew talked. Of course we learned the statistics, One out of three, but the images were always the lone maniac waiting in the bushes or the back seat of your car, in alleys and parks late at night where you shouldn't be anyway, Date rape wasn't even a word yet, at least not a word I'd heard, and no one really talked about incest.

Laura brought it up once when we were in a parkinglot. She told her story and I listened, horrified, and in responce, I told lies. Her stories were big hands and her small body, flashes she couldn't place, every week

she'd remember more. Her father, Grandfather, someone she couldn't place, these flashes that didn't make any sence to her. She talked in monotone and didn't ever cry. I lied because my story wasn't so interesting, and quite possibly didn't merit any attention at all.

One out of three? In 1988, I was 18, No one I knew talked. For awhile they talked about this acquaintance of ours who was attacked in Loring Park. She fought and got away, but she'd see him standing across the street from her house.
"do you think she's just paranoid?"
"I heard she calls the cops and they never come"
"fucking cops"
"chauvinist pigs"
god, that poor friend of ours.

Sing To Me

I carried things on my head better than anyone I knew. Three encyclopedias, all the way from one side of the classroom to the other, no hands. My stepdad said it was my flat head, but I knew it was something else. It was my talent. My undiscovered talent. Different than my singing talent which I showed to the empty world, walking home to my dad's town house from school.

I cut back behind the playground and down around the old swamp that had been rerouted and designed to make it a series of ponds and dry land with a bike path and jogging path and exercise stations. Usually I went that way, because I wasn't in a hurry to get home.

I'd get home and clean closets and try to find things to organize. There wasn't much to do, but I was the woman of the house and tried to be useful. I thought it was important. I felt a little burdened. I would steal change from the gallon icecream bucket in the middle drawer above the sock drawer and

I'd take the change and walk to the bowling alley, call dad at work and tell him to pick me up there on his way home. I was eleven. It didn't strike me as strange that I'd be there, bowling alone. I felt kind of proud, worthy of admiration.

TALENT SCOUT
NICE LADY
HELLO LITTLE GIRL. DID I JUST HEAR YOU SINGING?

There were days when I walked along the highway instead of the swamp, and I'd sing songs from Little Orphan Annie as loud as I could. I was waiting for a talent scout to drive by with her window rolled down. She'd hear me and discover me and take me places. I only sung in private because I wasn't really sure that I was any good and I'd heard what bad singers sounded like. It was a talent that counted. It mattered what other people thought. Not like carrying things on your head.

I knew no one would ever appreciate that, and no one did until Marta came to our school. Our school was white, as far as I can remember. A middle class, public school, alternative program, when Carter was still in office and there was a little bit of funding for those kinds of things.

we learned about racism and gentrification and city planning when we were in fourth grade. Nelson Mandela, Lech Walesa, struggles for freedom.

Marta came to our school when I was eleven. She must have been older than us, big boned and showing her adolescence. She was from El Salvador, an orphan. She had lived by selling fruit that she would steal, carrying it on her head and selling it door to door. That's what my stepdad told me when he introduced us. Marta, Cindy. We made friends immediately. She could carry things - whole tote trays full of different sized objects, things that shifted around.

We would race, me with my books, her with her complicated jumble. She tried to show me how to shift my body with the different weights and laughed that I could never master it.

We walked together, heads held high and straight ahead, arms out slightly. I stopped doing school work. We walked up stairs, the ladder of the slide, but not even Marta could go down the slide with things on her head, no handed. We walked over the blacktop and down the hill where we weren't allowed. Through the halls while everyone else was in classes.

Marta was happy to be with me, and I wanted to imitate her. It was near the end of the school year, and I knew summer would come, full of long days of sitting on the rocks and watching the egrets, checking huge stacks of library books out of the library and spreading my blanket out in the meadow and reading the books, one after the next. Days of dreaming I was the only person left on earth, which made everything a lot easier. Walking through the woods and looking for deer trails and hoping maybe they would take me in as one of their own. Summer went on forever.

It was near the end of the school year, at our end of the year talent show, where we always repeated the same bad skits, like the one about puppies and lemonade stands. The repetition and knowing we were boring the parents to death made it all the more funny. The talent show itself was one big joke. None of us had talent, nothing worthwhile, except Ashley, who was a violin prodigy, and always gave us a recital that we'd squirm through. And this year there was Marta. Her name on the program and I watched her emerge from backstage. And the music started.

It was a song we all knew. A song from the movie Greese, but dubbed over in Spanish, and Marta was singing along with it too, and dancing with everything she had in her, covering the stage, belting out the song, and smiling like she couldn't be happier. I crept along the wall, trying to get closer. Thinking may be I could stop her. I was embarrassed for her, you just didn't do what she was doing. I was creeping along the wall, and I saw Mr. Denning in one of the aisle chairs. Mr. Denning, who came into class sometimes, but never seemed happy or friendly at all. And there he was, at the edge of his seat, singing along in Spanish too, tapping his shoes and nodding his head and smiling, this man who I'd never seen smile.

He was proud of her, and I crept back to my chair, ashamed, and wishing I had the guts to sing like that too.

end.

I don't know the details of how the core group of my old political collective started, but I guess it went something like this...

"We, the youth of this large, leftist organization, realize the special role of youth in revolutionary movements. We understand that as one grows older, one often acquires responsponsibilities, such as the raising of children, that cause one to become more hesitant, rightfully so, to put oneself on the front lines.

"As youth, we wish to learn from the experiences and knowledge of those older than us, yet not be bogged down in the disillutionment and responsibilities many of you face.

"We want the freedom to organize, as youth, to attempt to rekindle the spark in the smoldering ashes of the revolutionary movement of today!"

CANADA
MAINE
VT
NH
NY
MA
CT
PEN
NJ

They had regional conferences

and biyearly national conferences

one was even in the small town I lived in. I was too busy and self absorbed to attend, but I walked by once when they were taking a break.

"hi, I'm Cindy and this is my dog Anna".

she's her own dog".

she's mine I paid 50bucks for her.

(this guy probably didn't last too long)

At the time, I didn't know hardly a thing about the old left or the new left or the way people had organized and what had torn groups apart, but in retrospect, I think they must have known a lot of history, and been trying really hard not to repeat the mistakes of the past.

They were committed to forming really coherent political principles.

mocratic Decent

Different subjects were given to different groups of members, who wrote drafts and brought them to the biannual meeting where it would be debated, edited, revamped, and eventually adopted.

nti-Racism

volutionary Du

Opposi

This, and the fact that you had to be an active member of a local group to have voting privileges, were seen as elitist and centralist by some anarchists, but when you looked at the complainers' groups, these practices made a lot of sense.

The first conference I went to was in Knoxville. Me and Petra drove down. It was my first time south of the Mason Dixon line. I'd never seen red soil before, or these broad thick leaves. I kept wanting to look at everything. She would only drink coffee at Dunkin Donuts and so we'd pull off the freeway and drive through all kinds of small towns, looking for the Dunkin Donuts, and me, looking at the porches and sky. When we'd pull over to nap for just a couple hours, we ended up sleeping for eight.

We were days late, but when we finally got there, I was blown away. Everyone was good looking. Everything they said was interesting. The whole thing seemed really important. I was tagging along. There were informal discussions long into the night and some kid showed me the tape a dollar, trick a soda machine into giving free soda and change back, trick. I started to feel like I was part of something great.

Actually, the first day I just felt stupid, until mid day the conference split up by gender and one woman said that she had been noticing how eyecontact is really important, and people have a habit, when talking to a group, of looking at the person whose opinion they think matters the most. And how rare it is that people address the women in the group. And even in this group, even the women, when they talk, they look at the men.

It was an observation - all very rational - and when it was brought up, when the two groups had reconvened, everyone was surprised to realize it was true, and things really changed after that.

for the better...

Like I said, we were all about rationality. Even our local collective was careful about a lot of things - like not letting our meetings turn into bitch sessions or personal therapy. We didn't see ourselves as a vanguard movement, merely a small part of a multifaceted struggle. None the less, we made fun of other groups.

"I was at this ---- meeting, and it was pathetic. All the women there spoke question speak. You know, where it's too much of a threat to actually make a statement and so the end of each sentance ends with this raised voice and turns it into a question. I hate that. It's so weak. And I tried to bring it up as a bit of constructive criticism And Julie of all people, in dead earnestness, goes 'You are making me feel like my boundries are being crossed, and I'm feeling unsafe, and I'm going to put on this helmet, until you go away.

(we had our own helmet, but we used it to initiate new members. It was a mexican riot helmet and the one to be initiated had to put it on, and then the last new member got to hit them over the head with a baseball bat.)

There were the glorious days of the Commie Parties, where we'd go en mass to debate them (and drink their beer)

How can you call yourselves communists when you don't even know what happened in Kronstadt? Jesus. Where's Curly? Get Curly in here. Curly! I'm yelling for you! What are you teaching these kids? You should be ashamed. They don't know their history! Tell them about Kronstadt Curly, go ahead.
KEG

We had to quit that strategy of sharpening our debating skills, when Curly, the head communist threatened to slit our throats when the revolution came.

fuck the commies, you can drink with them but you can't work with them. They're irrelevant anyway, see, who does Bellacort * call for coalition, us or them?
Mr. Bellacort? Of course. We'll do everything we can.
* A.I.M. American Indian Movement

to be continued

what I meant to say

"You can't count on conditions becoming ripe. The situation doesn't always get worse and worse no matter how much it seems like it will when you're wrapped up in it. Radical social change is never inevitable. You have to plan your strategy and how you're going to keep your sanity for a long term struggle. What's wrong with us anyway? When things were a million times more repressive and hopeless, there were people who would organize and educate and fight all their lives knowing they would die before they saw any kind of wide spread effect. They were thinking of future generations, or maybe just doing what they needed to do to hold on to their own humanity.

Lately it seems like people want immediate gratification. If they don't see results, they get cynical and pissed off and think it's all pointless. Like the 60's, the whole "Revolution Now" thing. It was inspiring, but when the revolution didn't happen, there was mass disillusionment.

Capitalism has an amazing ability to co-opt movements and stifle dissent. They know they have to make concessions, some real, some false. They have fucked up ethics, but they're not stupid.

In the 80's we thought the end of capitalism was near. It was a bit of a Marx ripoff theory. Marx thought that the contradictions in capitalism would necessitate it's collapse. Since capitalism depends on continual growth and competition, and in order for companies to stay competitive, they must become more and more exploitative, there would come a time when the workers conditions would become unbearable and the workers-the proletariat-would have no choice but to rise up an seize the means of production and create a Socialist state.

Sadly, it didn't happen that way.

In the 80's we thought the environment was like Marx's idea of the proletariat, only it couldn't be bought with token gestures or divided against itself or repressed into silence. It didn't have a psychology to be manipulated, and it had real, concrete, limits. If they kept exploiting nature at the rate capitalism seemed to require, there would be total ecological collapse. It couldn't be ignored. Capitalism was destined to fall. it was inevitable and we were working to form groups of logical, ethical anarchists, building a new society in the wake of the old.

What happened? I don't know. It went so quickly, I was leveled. The Greens, which had been founded by anarchists and was committed to local, grassroots organizing and confederation, was overtaken by newagers and electoralism. The market was flooded with products that made you feel like you were doing your part, new technologies claimed to solve many of the problems, and the other issues got boring and dropped out of sight. The movement died and capitalism remained firmly intact. No one I knew really knew what to do."

That was more or less what I meant to say - a warning against putting faith in the idea of catastrophe or a catalyst - something big that would force an exciting kind of change.

But what I said was

"Oh god, no, inevitability?! Not that. Like Marx, you know what we thought in the 80's? Forget it. I mean, you just can't count on that stuff. You know, cooptation. I mean, the welfare stuff is going to go on forever. Shit. Do you think it's 6am yet? Want to go get beer?"

dear Shari

...sitting down by the railroad tracks, a few blocks from Gilman, drinking warm beer alone. I walked around Berkeley today, excited to be back here. Excited and sort of lonely, sort of cocky and proud - wondering what it would have been like to be a cocky and proud teen - because lord knows I wasn't.

Even here, three years ago, I felt like I had something to prove. Had to act crazy to cover up what I felt, which was crazy, so may be I wasn't covering up anything really at all.

These tracks have memories of anxiety and not knowing how to take life any way except by the horns. Always on these loading docks instead of inside the shows.

This is where I met Kelly, who was too wild for me to really get to know. She wore a ripped up yellow prom dress, made movies and danced in the pit. I caught her once when she was too drunk to stand. She sang the song "I'll get a fucking abortion if I want to". I always wanted to get near her, but not too near.

t's funny, not funny but predictable. I've never been around girls that much. I use to worry about it a lot - my internalized sexism. I dealt with it for a year in Portland, and then here it was all boys again. But the tracks, they hold memories.

Ulla, my Ulla, not the one the punks talk about. Ulla I met at the Infoshop. This self-contained, serene woman with a bihawk, not put up, fine thin hair, calm voice. I said 'do you want to hang out?' I got her number. I called, I said we could color pictures with color crayons on my roof. I didn't know what girls did. She said 'I'm not really into that kind of stuff'. I said we could drink 40's in my garage. It was before I was a drunk and I was practicing. Trying to build up tollerance so I could drink with the boys and not have to run off somewhere all sneeky like to puke.

Me and Ulla drank in my garage. She was always so calm it made me ten times more crazy talking, nervous. It was nice. It clicked somehow. She was the first girl I ever saw piss in public. Just

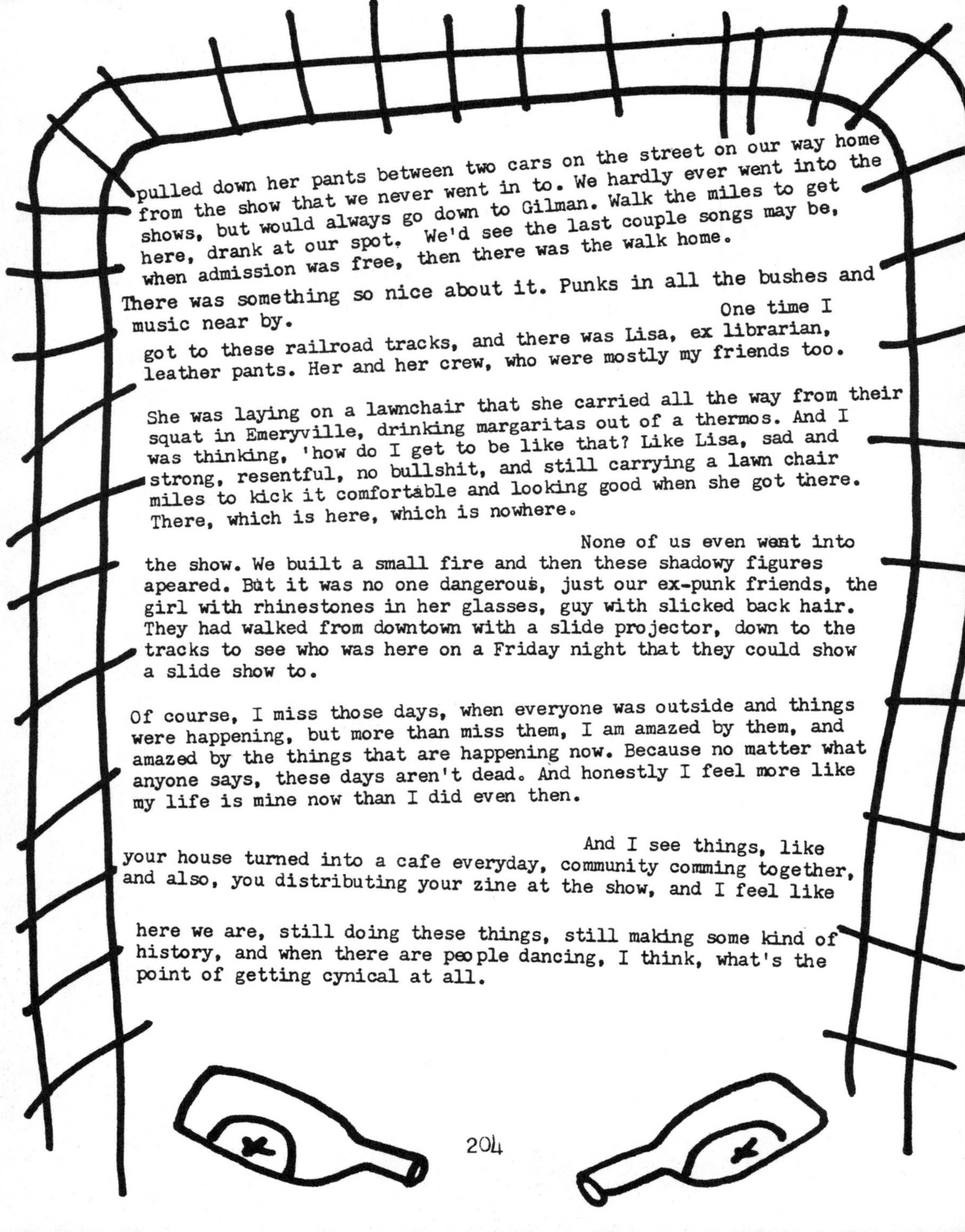

pulled down her pants between two cars on the street on our way home from the show that we never went in to. We hardly ever went into the shows, but would always go down to Gilman. Walk the miles to get here, drank at our spot. We'd see the last couple songs may be, when admission was free, then there was the walk home.

There was something so nice about it. Punks in all the bushes and music near by. One time I got to these railroad tracks, and there was Lisa, ex librarian, leather pants. Her and her crew, who were mostly my friends too.

She was laying on a lawnchair that she carried all the way from their squat in Emeryville, drinking margaritas out of a thermos. And I was thinking, 'how do I get to be like that? Like Lisa, sad and strong, resentful, no bullshit, and still carrying a lawn chair miles to kick it comfortable and looking good when she got there. There, which is here, which is nowhere.

None of us even went into the show. We built a small fire and then these shadowy figures apeared. But it was no one dangerous, just our ex-punk friends, the girl with rhinestones in her glasses, guy with slicked back hair. They had walked from downtown with a slide projector, down to the tracks to see who was here on a Friday night that they could show a slide show to.

Of course, I miss those days, when everyone was outside and things were happening, but more than miss them, I am amazed by them, and amazed by the things that are happening now. Because no matter what anyone says, these days aren't dead. And honestly I feel more like my life is mine now than I did even then.

And I see things, like your house turned into a cafe everyday, community comming together, and also, you distributing your zine at the show, and I feel like

here we are, still doing these things, still making some kind of history, and when there are people dancing, I think, what's the point of getting cynical at all.

I can see how it sneeks in. Things were different when I was younger and there were a million possibilites not dismissed yet. personal ads, theme bands, a million bad art projects, chasing boys over state lines, trying to figure out how to kiss a girl, building huge art gardens, creating a secret bourgeois life, learn to bake bread, act mute for a week, documant every single thing. every street, every conversation. hop trains.

Punk opened the world up, but created so many possibilities, that the possibilities started closing in on me. I would go over the list. How many times would it happen? That I would move to a new house with my plan. lush yard. statues and bowling balls. And then never even plant a single flower. The possibilities became weights. Things I should do but never would, never get around to it. And I got bitter that way. Blamed it on the same things everybody does. On the times, on our celebrating our confusion, our irresponsibility, the friends that didn't care or didn't want our community, just wanted to hang around and fuck it up and leave.

But the bitterness past by quickly, even though it seemed like forever. And now here I am.

I ran into Jimmy who I use to bring spaghetti to and cigerettes when he wasn't doing too well, and he says - I've been thinking about you. How nice you always were, bringing over pineapples, and whatever you were always doing, and none of us cared. It sucks. I never really knew anything about you.

Jimmy has a Beatles haircut and a scooter now, but we sit around talking all night, about music, highschool and family and relationships. The past, the future, the neighborhood, the grocery store, how late it's become. And he looks me in the eyes now when we talk.

I hear Laura's become a boxer, Colby's learned to cook, Francine become an archeologist, and everyone has more skills, and it doesn't seem as stupid to ask what they want and why and how are they going to get it.

So I'm sad they're not still down here on the tracks, outside the show, drinking with me. Sad that they're not living in big fucked up houses where I'd be welcome to stay for as long as I want. But I'm curious where they're at and what they're doing and how they're changing, and I'm glad I had different lives and different goals and different ways of living before this one.

but I love

The big loud house I live in full of things going on and personalities, where i feel like now more than ever my life is mine and I have something to offer. That I can give some and hold some back for myself, where as before, back then, I would give everything I had and then go crazy

In my new town, that is not so new, but still feels new when I'm away. In that town I learned to sing loud. learned to sleep through entire band rehersals, entire shows, with only carpet for walls to seperate me and the music and the crowd. I've bought a van like I always meant to and the possibilities are opening up again in a way that they wouldn't have if I'd closed myself in, cut myself off from the comunity that I love and hate and love.

I'm going to drive down to the ocean, to your town Shari, and collect seaweed for my sisters farm. Does she need seaweed? I'm not really sure. I read something about it in a book one time. I'm going to figure out newyork, figure out world history and figure out mine. Learn to write articles, learn to write fiction, learn to make gravy and a big art garden in this back yard. hop trains. I don't know. You see how it is? Now that I'm older and more settled in my head, and less chasing things that I don't know how to find. Now that I'm more solid, less scared, less needy, I feel less like settling down.

caty & me

We read outloud to eachother those days. It wasn't out of depression and the need to hear someone elses voice. That kind of loneliness that craves the rhythm of words, tones and cadence, tv or radio turned on low in the background, where you can't quite hear it but you feel less

alone. When it seems like there's no more stories to tell, like you've exhausted all subjects except the ones you don't want to talk about, so you read stories out loud because it's close to talking and in a way even more intimate because you don't need defenses, don't have to

listen too closely, don't have to worry about response. and it's calming, that voice, the words, language.

There are things I know because sometimes any words are better than none. Me and Kyle and Zeb ended up at Chris' mom's house in the rain. It was before I knew Chris, and

he was in bed on his knee machine. I sat in the livingroom, waiting.

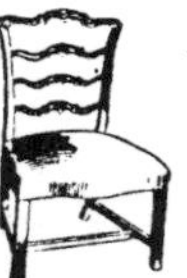

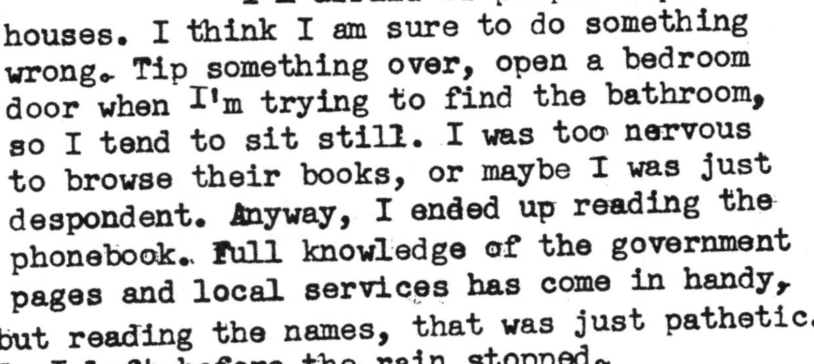
I'm afraid of people's parents houses. I think I am sure to do something wrong. Tip something over, open a bedroom door when I'm trying to find the bathroom, so I tend to sit still. I was too nervous to browse their books, or maybe I was just despondent. Anyway, I ended up reading the phonebook. Full knowledge of the government pages and local services has come in handy, but reading the names, that was just pathetic. So I left before the rain stopped.

Those days, me and Caty read to eachother out of books that articulated our unadmitted feelings and beliefs, or the ones we admitted but didn't have the voice for, or the ones we had the voice for, but couldn't say that beautifully, couldn't say in writing, couldn't present to the world. Like Marge Piercy's For Strong Women, and A Woman is Not a Pear Tree; Audre Lorde's Uses of the Erotic: The Erotic as Power; Sharon Olds' I Wanted to be There When My Father Died. It's hard to say exactly what it was. We must have felt more alone and alienated and crazy than we thought we did, because we'd read these women, and sometimes just the simplest line would legitimize our most basic truths. "Listen", she'd say, "let me read you this", and it was a weight lifted, our lives finally recognized.

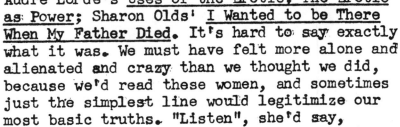

I was making a cave behind the closed down bank on Telegraph, half way between my uncle's house and People's Park. There was a space five feet wide between the back of the building and a property dividing wall. It was a thin corridor of tall pricker bushes and a canopy of vines. I was cutting out the undergrowth to make a hide out. I wanted a secret place to sit around and read, that was so close to being in public and almost like being in nature and a lot like a post apocalyptic bedroom, and definitely a place to call my own. I brought Nina there the first time we hung out, aside from in a large group of friends at the café. Me and her and Caty went there, and it's true I hadn't cleared it out completely yet, it was still a tangle and there was only one chair, and it wasn't quite large enough for three people to be comfortable. I'd brought stolen juice and the books. We took turns reading poems, me andCaty, but it sounded melodramatic, like the words had lost theirmeaning, and I couldn't tell if it was because I had turned it into an event and the audience looked at us strange, or if we had finally incorporated those particular words into our lives and didn't need the reassurance and validation anymore.

breathe it out

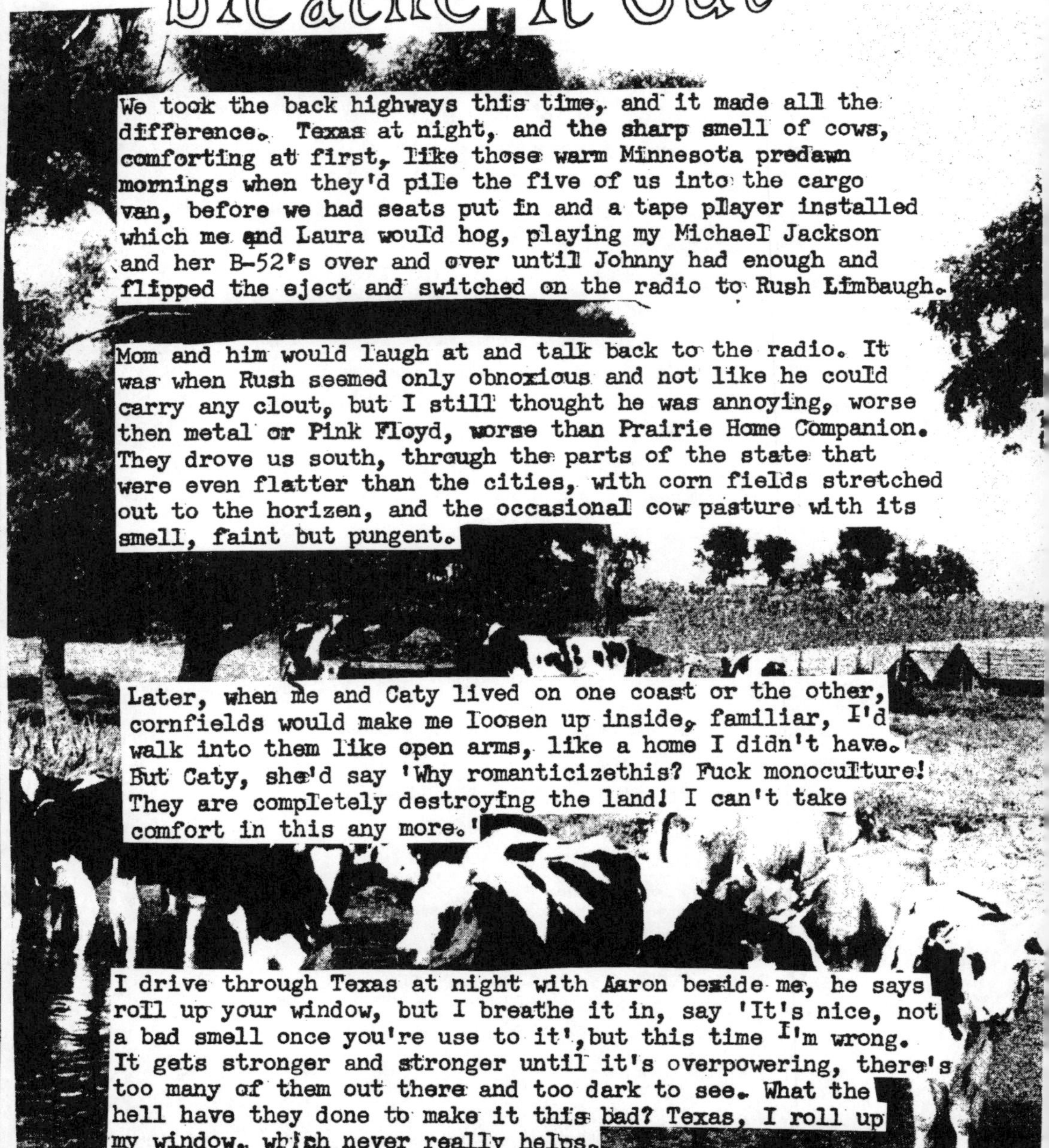

We took the back highways this time, and it made all the difference. Texas at night, and the sharp smell of cows, comforting at first, like those warm Minnesota predawn mornings when they'd pile the five of us into the cargo van, before we had seats put in and a tape player installed which me and Laura would hog, playing my Michael Jackson and her B-52's over and over until Johnny had enough and flipped the eject and switched on the radio to Rush Limbaugh.

Mom and him would laugh at and talk back to the radio. It was when Rush seemed only obnoxious and not like he could carry any clout, but I still thought he was annoying, worse then metal or Pink Floyd, worse than Prairie Home Companion. They drove us south, through the parts of the state that were even flatter than the cities, with corn fields stretched out to the horizen, and the occasional cow pasture with its smell, faint but pungent.

Later, when me and Caty lived on one coast or the other, cornfields would make me loosen up inside, familiar, I'd walk into them like open arms, like a home I didn't have. But Caty, she'd say 'Why romanticizethis? Fuck monoculture! They are completely destroying the land! I can't take comfort in this any more.'

I drive through Texas at night with Aaron beside me, he says roll up your window, but I breathe it in, say 'It's nice, not a bad smell once you're use to it',but this time I'm wrong. It gets stronger and stronger until it's overpowering, there's too many of them out there and too dark to see. What the hell have they done to make it this bad? Texas, I roll up my window, which never really helps.

There was a time when everybody was traveling, talking about nomadic tribes and how much freer their lives had been, but I didn't think movement and subsistence was freedom, thought it was mainly escapist and irresponsible. I'd say 'traveling is overrated, what do you do? You go somewhere and you never really get to know it enough or stay long enough to make a real difference. You meet people, and it's hard to communicate except for small talk or vague but grand scale themes. You form bonds that you think are real, but there's actually almost nothing there, you just need to feel something to keep you going, you make it up just to feel less alone'.

But there were times when my mind would get stuck in circles, repeating the same problems until life felt lifeless, and neither writing, nor my community, nor political projects seemed worth the time, and I'd have to get out to get a perspective on things, break out of my habits and see where I'd gone wrong, there were new people and places and they could bring new meaning, and besides, what was so bad about trying to feel less alone.

We drive through Oklahoma with the map between us, and on the back highways, it's a landscape I've never seen before. I don't know whether it was the dustbowl or desertifacation, or if it always just looked this way, empty, small hills, fields and cactus, more beautiful than I could have imagined. It's the world in front of me, and I grow curious again, instead of withdrawn and nervous, which is what I had become at home. But I'm still too shy to embrace this humanity the way Aaron does, joking with the old men at the diner, sharing his newspaper with them, and asking question to the people in Roger Miller's home town.

It is a town just like the songs describe it. Even at the rest stop, the mockingbirds sing to us, in the trees by the picnic table where we're wrapped in blankets, drinking beer, waiting for the storm to hit us and drive us back into the car where I've knocked out the back seat to make a bed that stretches all the way into the trunk. We lay there, sealed up with the windows rolled tight. Not freedom, but I start to come out of my shell.

My Grandma doesn't reminisce much. She's almost always busy, taking care of things.
casserole
but once, with a little prodding, she told me that she had once been minneapolis' greatest Charleston dancer.
hey Grandma! will you teach me to dance the Charleston? Please?
I'm too busy dear
Please?
well, ok.
Late at night, after Great Grandma Bessie Bell had gone to bed, Grandma would sneek out of the house and tip toe down the block to meet her ride to the dance hall.
She said it was such fun. The lights and the people, and the music, oh the music. All the fellows wanted to dance with her and would try to sweep her off her feet. But you had to be careful, she said, because they always wanted to buy you drinks.
"Just swing your leg up and around, then...
(laughter)
I am really too old for all this"
!
?
but, she said, it is very unbecoming to a lady to drink too much, but rude to refuse a drink, so the thing to do was to pour it in a plant when they weren't looking, or take tiny sips and then "forget" it on a table when you went out on to the dancefloor.
put a little more swing and hop into it
Like this?
that's great, now try it on your own
I could see that she was passing down advice for my future when I would be in a similar situation and since I never did get much of this kind of advice, I took it to heart. but it made me sad because I knew that no boy would ever try to buy me anything. No boy had ever even looked at me twice.

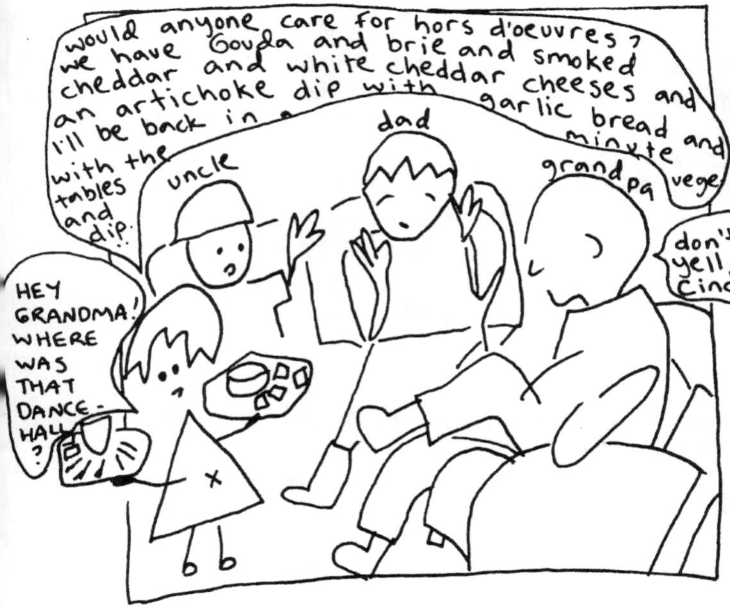

would anyone care for hors d'oeuvres?
we have Gouda and brie and smoked
cheddar and white cheddar cheeses and
an artichoke dip with garlic bread and
I'll be back in a minute
with the vege-tables and dip.

uncle

dad

grandpa

HEY GRANDMA! WHERE WAS THAT DANCE-HALL?

don't yell Cindy

lake st. & Lagoon

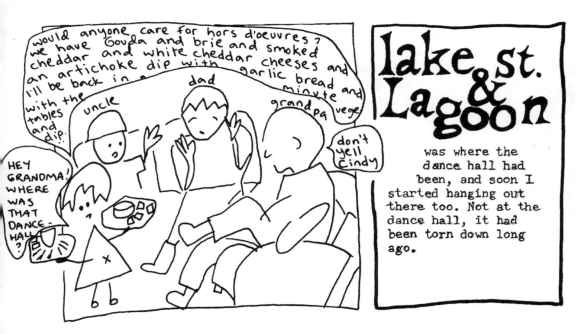

was where the dance hall had been, and soon I started hanging out there too. Not at the dance hall, it had been torn down long ago.

There was a McDonalds in its place, and the punks hung out there, yelling at the Christians, the yuppies and pretty much anyone who walked by. They yelled at me the first few times, walking past, hand in hand with Angie, with our matching housewife dresses, singing in our loudest voices to our favorite Melanie song.

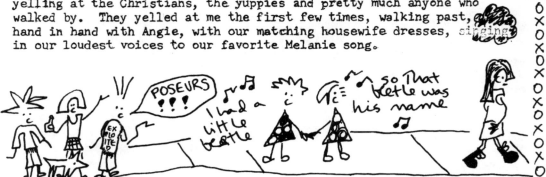

Shannon walked half a block in front of us, muttering under her breath and cursing us for embarrassing her so. She was older than us, had records and phone sex and had once burnt off half her hair trying to light a cigarette while applying hairspray. She walked ahead of us and muttered - did we always have to make a scene? She was just trying to take us to the movies! - We saw the Harvey Milk documentary, and she took us to the one about Joy Division too, and that was it. She couldn't take any more. We were cut off. We'd have to make it on our own.

I get confused as to what the story is. Is it the story of riding the bus to go on my first date with a surfpunk keyboard player Shannon had introduced me to? He said, meet him downtown. First bus ride alone, glued to the window, front seat by the bus driver who I'd asked to let me know when we got to 7th Street, afraid to miss my stop, I'd never been downtown. I was afraid to look obvious, no wide eyed gaping, I acted like I knew where I was going and passed right by the record store and past the Gay 90's and the guys standing in the doorway, whistling and calling out "girlfriend, why don't you put on some shoes", and me flipping them off, not realizing.

I use to think of those days the same way I thought about childhood, all bad memories with none of the glory. But I see it now in my guitarists voice when we round the corner of I-75 and see the sprawl of Chattanooga lights in the nighttime and the way he says, with a sigh, with wonder "man, this is what it's all about" - fascination, like he explains the protest to me, for Mumia, outside the Federal building, holding up signs and he said people, just regular people, stopped their cars and rolled down their windows and asked what they could do to help - he said "it made me feel so good".

When the world was all new, we took it on like a high speed chase, walking three miles in chinadoll slippers through the snow to catch the 12D to take us away from our families that we were too wrapped up in; take us somewhere where we could begin to create ourselves.

I learned to flirt and would walk all over town to do it - way up Lake street to look for the sign painter who had been engaged to Mary and then she left him and now he admitted need and depression, which were things I thought you had to hide. Then down pastthe graveyard and over to the WestBank to drink weak coffee at the collective cafe with the boy who worked there and wait for Dan to get out of class. He was in his last quarter, even though he'd just started. They were cutting off his financial aid because he wouldn't register for the draft. From there I'd take the secret railroad path, and walk through the roads of old boarded up buildings and empty store fronts down to Ragstock to visit Paul, who was actually a friend, so I couldn't flirt with him. When I met him he looked like one of the Beatles, when I left he was an anarchist organizer.

It was a stupid reason to be walking all over town, and usually I think of it like that - this desperation that I'm glad to be rid of. But I hear my guitarist's voice, the way he explains each new thing, and I've been thinking about punk or whatever it was that drove us to live these public lives. How hard it is to feel like the world is yours and how it's hard to fight to change it if you don't, and how I don't think I would have gotten much of anywhere if I hadn't had some excuse to walk around.

When I turned I7, I got my own apartment and worked a cubical job in the day and took night classes at night and never hung out Uptown anymore with the weird little community that use to be there of the punks on one side of the street, junkies, intellectuals and artfilm kids on the other, antiracist skins and anarchists passing through and the hippie street musicians down the block. When I stopped hanging out, that's when the US bombed Panama, and the whole divergent crew took over the street for hours, and of course I didn't know about it holed up in my apartment, trying to learn all the basterdized eastern religions and new age crap all at once, gettingin to pop-psychology and whatever was the new cure all.

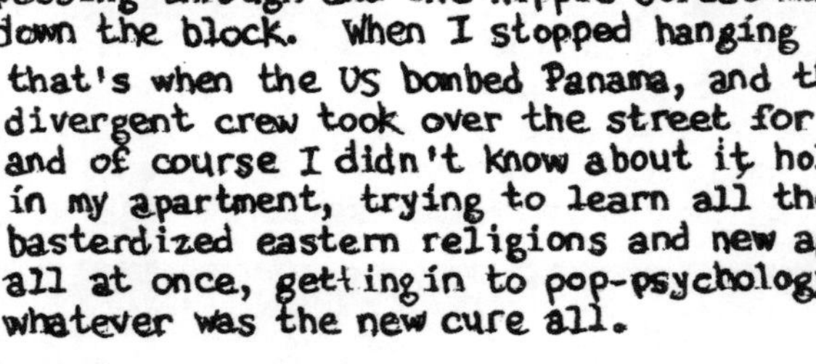

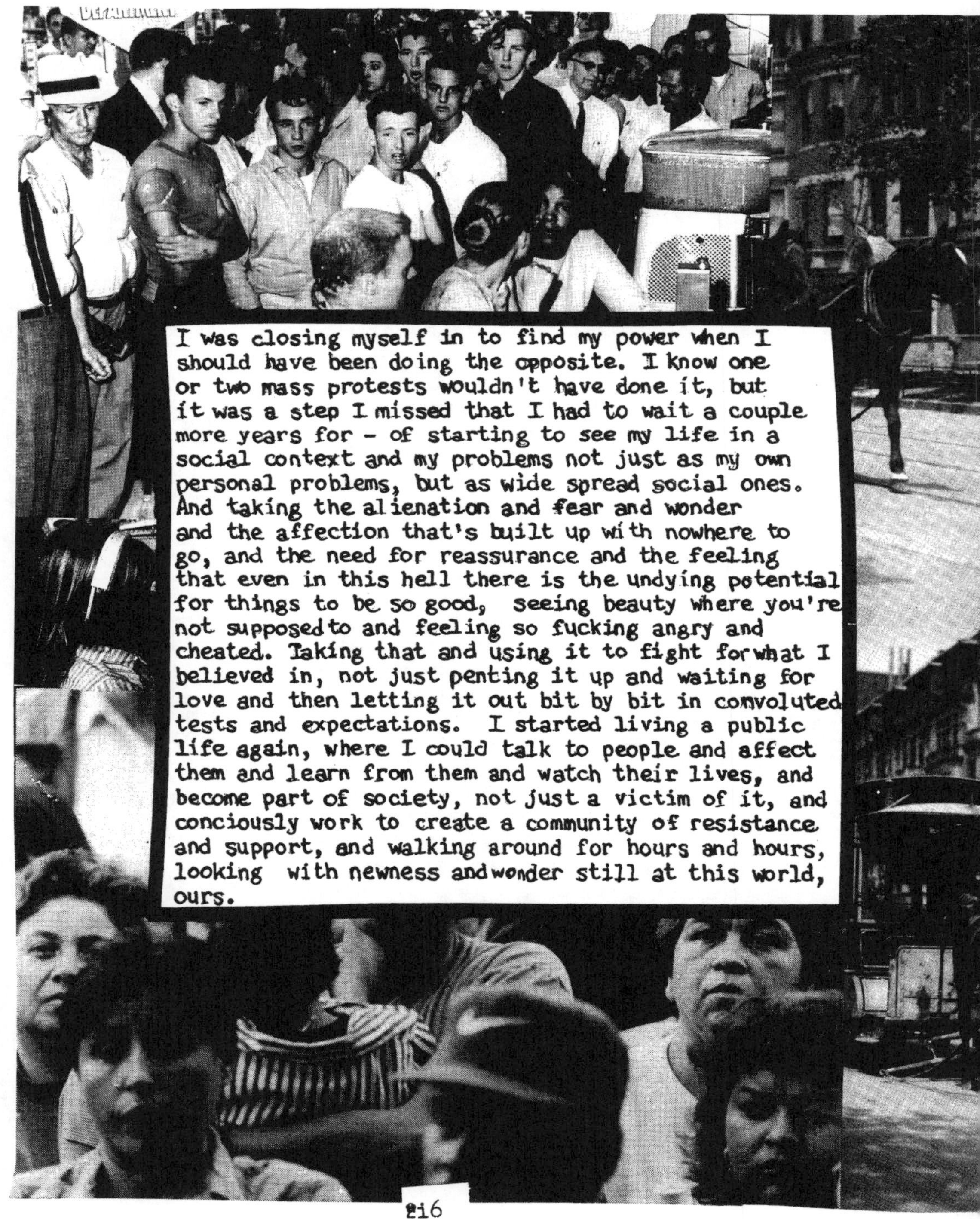

I was closing myself in to find my power when I should have been doing the opposite. I know one or two mass protests wouldn't have done it, but it was a step I missed that I had to wait a couple more years for - of starting to see my life in a social context and my problems not just as my own personal problems, but as wide spread social ones. And taking the alienation and fear and wonder and the affection that's built up with nowhere to go, and the need for reassurance and the feeling that even in this hell there is the undying potential for things to be so good, seeing beauty where you're not supposed to and feeling so fucking angry and cheated. Taking that and using it to fight for what I believed in, not just penting it up and waiting for love and then letting it out bit by bit in convoluted tests and expectations. I started living a public life again, where I could talk to people and affect them and learn from them and watch their lives, and become part of society, not just a victim of it, and conciously work to create a community of resistance and support, and walking around for hours and hours, looking with newness and wonder still at this world, ours.

Minneapolis Tribune

NRA MORNING EDITION

Three Cents in Minneapolis

In 1934, Floyd Olson was elected governor of Minnesota under the Farmer-Labor party. He was an old IWW guy, and his plan was to form a cooperative commonwealth, where the basic and monopolist industries, like steel, oil, textiles, grain elevators, mills, railroads and big banks, would all be taken over by the government; small businessmen would be guaranteed the right to private property and the right to a reasonable profit; co-ops would be expanded and production would be geared toward use rather than export. The problem was, he couldn't actually do much. The legislature that got elected along side him was conservative, and they vetoed every single bill he tried to pass.

I would like you to know that I am behind you 100% and I hope that the current system of government goes straight to hell!

STOP FARM FORECLOSURES

capitol building

olson

farmers

snow

cow

1932

Olson's main opponents were a group of powerful and well organized businessmen and bankers in Minneapolis called the Citizens Alliance. There were 800 active members in the group, and they had a paid staff and undercover informants. Their original purpose was to keep unions out of their city. They were successful in fighting off every major strike. Minneapolis was the worst scab town in the whole Northwest ~ (I know you probably consider it midwest, but they considered it northwest) - There was no union recognition in Minneapolis at all.

National Guard troops march on Minneapolis, July 27, 1934.

Teamster local 574 changed all that. They were the biggest, and I think one of the only industrial unions around - comprised of truckers, packers, shippers, and people of various trades that didn't have the numbers to start their own locals. There was even a section of unemployed.

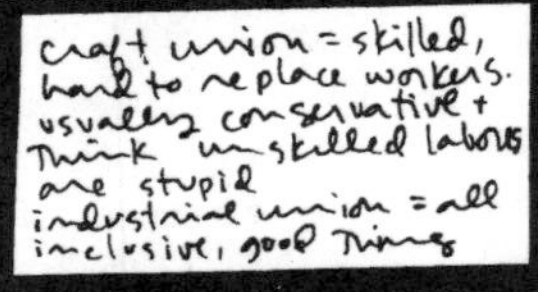

craft union = skilled,
hard to replace workers.
usually conservative +
think unskilled labors
are stupid
industrial union = all
inclusive, good things

The leaders of local 574 were Trotskyists who believed in painstakingly preparing for any action. They rented out a building before the strike to serve as the strike headquarters, a repair garage, a dining hall, and a small hospital. They gave permits to trucks delivering hospital goods, and to ice, milk, bakery, brewery trucks, and to city owned trucks with union drivers. They also made arrangements to allow local farm trucks into the city to set up a public market in an empty lot, it was so successful that they kept up this farmers market long after the strike was over. No other trucks would be allowed to move.

Any businessman will tolerate a revolutionary if he is impractical and utopian. Efficiency is intollerable!

Their demands were simple, but had far reaching implications- They demanded recognition as a union and that was it. Once they had recognition they would have bargaining power and could fight for larger things. It was the first important step in breaking the power employers had over their workers. The employers knew this and wouldn't give in. So, with their demands presented and rejected, the 3,000 members of local 574 went on strike.

One of the problems with many strikes is that the workers get bored with the single picket line and waiting at home for the employers to capitulate - and so this strike was planned as a 100% active one, with strikers and their families involved - cooking for and serving 4-5,000 people a day, taking turns patrolling every road leading into the city.

There was a fleet of motorcycles and cars that people would take and drive around the outskirts of Minneapolis, 24 hours a day, and if anyone saw a truck trying to sneek in, they'd call headquarters and there would be immediate mobilization of pickets sent to block it's entrance. Every trucking center had picket lines, and I guess some public officials houses too, because that's what my Grandma says.

Her Grandfather was the Sheriff of Hennipin county at the time, and she said it was scary as a little girl to have to have police escort in and out of the house, past the strikers who were always yelling at her.

It's strange how history gets distorted and passed down. My Grandma said Minneapolis had turned into a mad house, and then Great Grandpa called out the national guard. "He was the first person to call out the national guard on civilian population" she said

But I checked and he wasn't the one, and it wasn't the first time the national guard, had been called out either, unless in her vocabulary, strikers aren't civilians, which I guess must be the case. Because Minneapolis, 1934, was the first time, and probably the only time, the national guard was called out to protect strikers from the cops.

I'd like to simplify history myself, the strikers were out there striking and basically winning, until the bosses and cops got so fed up with it all that the police chief went down to the Citizens Alliance office and deputized 2,000 people they'd gathered together and then they went down with police escort and tried to move a truck with scab workers. The strikers blocked it of course, and the cops opened fire on the unarmed strikers. Shot 48 people, and out of those 48, 46 of them were shot in the back.

So Olson called out the national guard to stop the cops and bosses from killing the strikers and he said that if the employers didn't start negotiating, he would have the military take over the distribution of commodities, seize all the factories and warehouses and equipment and basically turn it over to the workers - So they didn't have much choice, the bosses gave in and the strikers won!

That's my simplification, and it's almost true. I just cut out the confusion like how the strikers killed one of the businessmen first, and how Olson didn't really have control over the national guard and the martial law Olson declaired outlawed pickets and even open air meetings; and the national guard had mixed loyalties, and kept letting all kinds of trucks run, pretty much breaking the strike; and they even raided the union headquarters and arrested the leaders! I always thought Trotskyists were for centralized power and anything led by them wouldn't change the fundamental way people organized themselves, but when the leaders were arrested, the union decentralized, and resumed pickets in defiance of martial law, with 50 picket captains on street corners, coordination and communication by pay phones across the city. And this is how they won!

When I look at it this way, I want to say "fuck you Olson! You liberal sellout asshole backstabber! What were you thinking? Right, good idea, national guard! How dumb can you get?"

But the truth is, my Grandma wasn't totally wrong.

Minneapolis was starting to look like civil war. After Bloody Friday, people went wild, arming themselves and both sides walking in military formation through the streets. 34,000 workers and unions called in support for the teamsters, and the metal workers all came down en mass with short metal poles, ready to beat ass. But the cops were on the bosses side, and they had more guns. So really, it was tricky. It looked bad. It would have been a mess.

So I start to feel like a liberal apologist

Olson was basically a hero, he was just a little delusional about what he was capable of

and a Trotskyist apologist:

If they hadn't limited the scope of the strike from the beginning, to just union recognition, they could have taken over the whole city with a huge general strike, like the one that was going on in S.F. at the same time! I use to would have been so mad at the Trotskyists: why did they aim so low? People could have seen, city wide, that they have the ability to live freely + as active citizens + that there are more interesting ways to go about it than free market capitalism. But, I don't know, Now I can kind of see where the Trotskyists were coming from. Maybe its good sometimes for people to aim low and for realistic goals so they can fight + win instead of always getting crushed, like in SF

I don't know, Cindy, I think they pretty much won in SF.
oh. I just assumed. yeah I've actully never read anything about it.

collectives part 2

"Hey guys! Remember when we had that meeting with the chief of the Mdwankin reservation when we were trying to do coalition work with the fucking liberals about that nuclear waste dump, I mean "'temporary storage facility' and we were trying to figure out what the Indians were doing and what was up with their negotiations with the power company and see if they wanted us to mediate between themn and EF! who was trying to sabotage NSP's shit and we brought a can of tobacco to give him. God, that was so awkward. Who told us to do that? Clide Bellacort or Vernon?"

neither

What? you mean we just decided that was the right thing to do? Tobacco offering? Hell, was it?

Cindy, He never showed up. And the only time Clide called us was to invite us to the Anti mascot rally.

blah blah blah blah blah blah blah

500 years of resistance

NO MASCOT

RESPECT

SELF DETERMINA

So maybe I don't remember every single part of it all that clearly, but there were a lot of parts to remember.

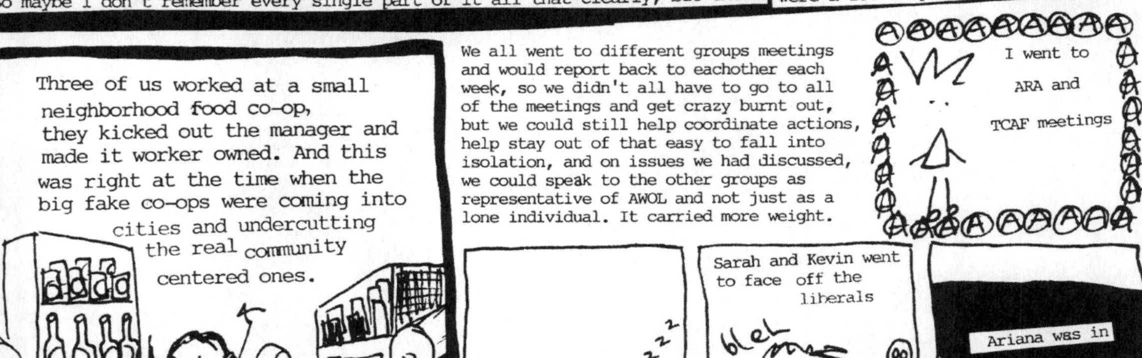

Three of us worked at a small neighborhood food co-op, they kicked out the manager and made it worker owned. And this was right at the time when the big fake co-ops were coming into cities and undercutting the real community centered ones.
We all went to different groups meetings and would report back to eachother each week, so we didn't all have to go to all of the meetings and get crazy burnt out, but we could still help coordinate actions, help stay out of that easy to fall into isolation, and on issues we had discussed, we could speak to the other groups as representative of AWOL and not just as a lone individual. It carried more weight.
I went to ARA and TCAF meetings
Sarah and Kevin went to face off the liberals
blah
arg!
Ariana was in ACT UP

Greg went to PSO

A couple of us were in touch with the international anarchist scene and would keep everyone up to date on their stuff.

it looked like we were chasing the cops

We put flyers up everywhere - all parts of the city, and passed them out on street corners for days before the demos, and people we talked to on the street actually showed up sometimes and marched along with us.

PROTEST

THE ISSUE

Prairie Island and the fight for an ecological and free society

Jorthern States Power (NSP) operates three uclear reactors in Minnesota. In a classic case of nvironmental racism, two of them are located vithin a stones' throw of the Mdewakanton Dakota eservation on Prairie Island. To add to it, NSP ow wants to build outdoor on-site storage casks o dump radioactive waste which will soon verflow their indoor storage pools. NSP has hosen on-site storage to avoid slowing down nergy production or shutting down the nukes. Because the federal government has not yet oerced any community into accepting all U.S.' uclear waste, power companies around the ountry are looking to Minnesota to see if NSP can jet away with their dastardly plan.

Vithout a place to put their waste, reactors like hose at Prairie Island will have to shut down. The ight against NSP comes at an important time because the federal government is looking to evive the nuclear power industry through fast-rack licensing for a new generation of 100 nukes. Clearly a renewed anti-nuclear power movement vhich, like the movement in the 1970s, makes connections to other issues is urgently needed.

The struggle against NSP's plan will be continued hrough state courts and possibly the legislature. This is important, but in order to stop the racism, ierarchic domination, ecological destruction and capitalist drive for profit which is at the very heart of NSP's plan, we'll need to participate in creating a social movement to fundamentally transform society. This is not a single issue. Only in creating a society in which the majority of humanity

controls the decisions which affects our lives can we ever hope to put an end to the genocidal behavior of the likes of NSP.

WHY DIRECT ACTION

Direct action movements represent the potential for a directly democratic future. They express our desires for a new way of life, embodied in the communities, counter-institutions, organizations and protests we create. Direct action has a decentralized participatory emphasis and is in fundamental opposition to anti-democratic control by formal and informal elites. From the barricades of 1848 to the factory and university occupations of 1968, direct action has expressed the best elements of what it means to be free and alive. All major advances in human history have been the result of intense struggle. Confrontation is inevitable as we get closer to actualizing our dreams of an ecological and free society.

The politics of opposition are difficult to actualize in the 1990s US. Yet if we dare to make our actions militant and creative, non-violent and confrontational, spontaneous and coordinated, a fundamental alternative would be powerfully voiced and our commitment to such an alternative clearly conveyed. Direct action draws attention to our ideas, making people aware that a new political alternative is emerging, while building the new society in the shell of the old. Direct actions also provide a clear indication of the urgency of the present crisis, integrating fragmented single-issue energies while facilitating dialogue between otherwise isolated activists. When anarchists call actions, it gives us the ability to explain the sweeping nature of our positions while fully participating in the struggles of the day.

Contrary to U.S. ideology, elections are not all there is to politics and running in them is not the only way to change things. Direct action – from democratic community assemblies to militant street protest – is making a major contribution to developing a revolutionary dual-power to (hetero)patriarchy, the state, and capitalism. Only when we pull out the ecological crisis by these roots can we ever hope to enjoy a healthy, ecological and free life.

COALITION UNTIY PRICIPLES

1) We work in solidarity with the Prairie Island Dakota peoples and affirm their right of autonomy and self-determination.

2) We oppose NSP's attempt to store radioactive waste on the banks of the Mississippi near the Prairie Island reservation and further advocate shutting down all of NSP's nuclear reactors. We believe the solution to the problem of nuclear waste is not to produce it.

3) We oppose the nuclear power industry and the elites who profit from it. Instead we advocate ecological, renewable energy (e.g. wind, solar), controlled by people at the local level.

4) We are committed to democracy and egalitarianism and thus oppose all forms of domination, including racism, sexism, heterosexism, ageism, and ablism. We organize in the way we hope society will someday be, free of elite control, ecological, and democratic.

5) We recognize that the problem of radioactive waste storage at Prairie Island is the result of environmental racism and an anti-ecological mode of thought, but also of the "grow-or-die" profit motive at the heart of capitalism and the policies of its defender, the modern nation-state. We therefore believe that an ecological and democratic future society cannot be either capitalist or statist.

6) Finally, we do not see this action as a singular "event" but rather as a moment in a larger process of collective action, carried out through a variety of means, to bring about an ecological and free society. By bringing together diverse groups and individuals for this action we hope to further develop community, raise our own and the public's consciousness, further pressure decision-makers to decide against the storage plan, and to advance to the next phase of social struggle. The possible defeat of NSP's plan will be but one victory which in no way signals the end of our movement.

ENDORSING GROUPS: Anarchist Youth Federation-Twin Cities, Anti-Racist Action, AWOL, Greens Gathering '92, Library Workers for Peace and Justice, Minnesota Green Confederation, Prairie Island Coalition Against Nuclear Storage, R.A.G.E. for Choice, Twin Cities Anarchist Federation.

A lot of the shit was pretty frustrating. We always had to be on the ball to make sure outside forces didn't turn someone into the "leader" - we had to keep demos fresh and interesting, short and potent or else people would get bored and cynical and not show up to the next one; and we tried to struggle with internal dynamics without becoming absorbed in them. We encouraged eachother and tried to teach eachother skills.

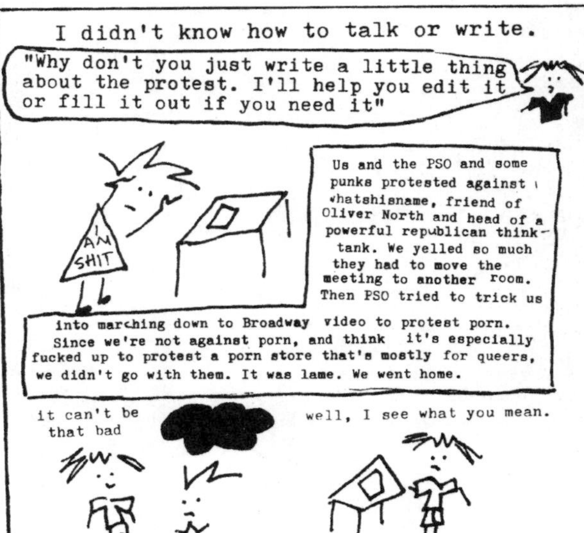

We put out a magazine of anarchist theory and practice which was criticized for being too intellectual, but what can you expect? It was challenging, but accessible. and I'm glad we didn't give in to the pressure to assume the masses are idiots who can't think deeply and need to be spoken down to.

But I will admit, the AWOL study groups were way over my head.
I wonder if I masturbate while reading Gramsci will it become more interesting?

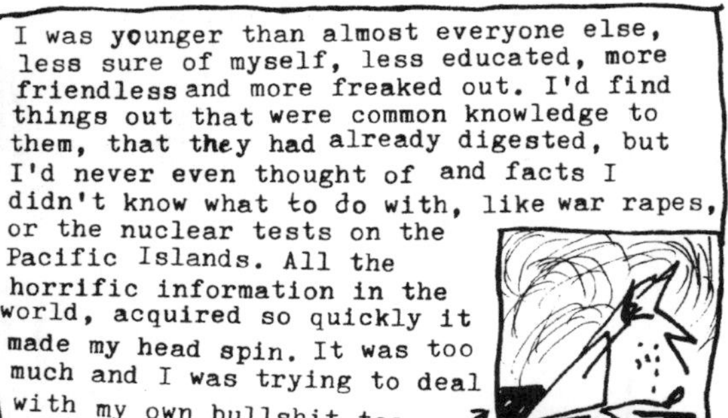

I was younger than almost everyone else, less sure of myself, less educated, more friendless and more freaked out. I'd find things out that were common knowledge to them, that they had already digested, but I'd never even thought of and facts I didn't know what to do with, like war rapes, or the nuclear tests on the Pacific Islands. All the horrific information in the world, acquired so quickly it made my head spin. It was too much and I was trying to deal with my own bullshit too.

Unfortunately, my political collective weren't always that supportive. We were suppose to have other friends, but I didn't really. It's strange to think of how important and consuming some things were back then, and I don't really blame them for wanting me to shut up.

I think I like girls, but I'm scared and I just don't know and the one girl I really loved fucked me over and maybe I just want to like girls cuz it's cool

God Cindy, what's your problem. Why wouldn't you be a dyke?!

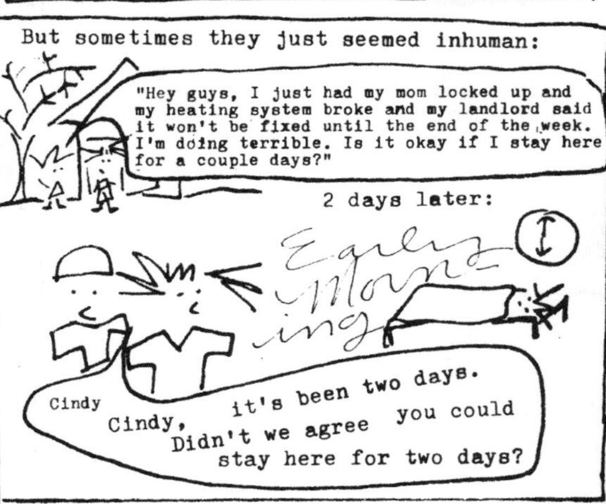

But sometimes they just seemed inhuman:
"Hey guys, I just had my mom locked up and my heating system broke and my landlord said it won't be fixed until the end of the week. I'm doing terrible. Is it okay if I stay here for a couple days?"
2 days later:

Cindy, it's been two days. Didn't we agree you could stay here for two days?

Like any friendship or relationship, a political collective shouldn't meet all your needs, but there was just something really different about them and me.

I decided I should have fun every day. I think I had been on a fun boycott or something. I don't know what my problem was.
What do you do for fun?

Anything. Walk to Loring Park and lay on the ice and look at the stars and throw sticks for my dog.
Walk through the alleys and look for stuff in the trash.
Put on music and dance.
You know, just a little over all world appreciation

Oh. That doesn't sound like fun.
?!
to be continued.
next issue: "should I become a hit man for the revolution?!"

three songs

Outside the show at the fire pit, with the older punks who are in a band that makes you move, makes me look with pride at this thing we've created, smiling and standing over the sad excuse for a PA, making sure it doesn't get knocked down and broken more than it already is,

amidst this crashing of bodies like a tide against rocks and me.

Caty shouts as loud as possible, right into my ear, hand on my arm for ballance. She shouts "You look like a mother whose kid just took its first steps!" I nod, I'm bursting that way, it's exactly how I feel. She screams "You look like that at every fucking show we do! Now get in front and dance!" She pulls me in.

Some people said the cealing was too short in this basement, we'd hit our heads and plus, there was too much junk down there. It would be too much work to clear it out and there was too much water, the equipment would rot, we'd all get electrocuted, the neighbors would complain, there was no way to turn it into a club. Our club, Oh My, named after the War Torn Babies song. We've got a small river running along the side, inside.

Our landlord was an "artist" and he filled the basement with "sculpture supplies" that rusted and molded into an undistinguishable heap. We filled a whole construction dumpster and more. Then the leak, city water, Janet tested it and it's chlorinated. So they built a mini retaining wall out of concrete, 2 inches high, running from the leak to the low end of the house. Then knocked a hole in the foundation to let it drain, and dug a ditch, 3 feet deep, all the way from the house to the river, put a pipe in, and covered it back up. Hard working boys. I was out of town.

We called the city. "Come fix your damn pipes!" But the city never comes. Actually, two guys came once to the side door. Came right in the house and started snooping around. They sai "we hear you've got water problems" Only Sweetmeat was awake, not a roommate, but around all the time. He demanded ID. They didn't have any. He said they'd have to come back when the person on the lease was home. "When is that?" they asked "She's usually here around 3am," he said, and then made signs "Fuck Off Developers!" and "No realestate agents allowed!" with a drawing of punks marching with a bloody yuppie head on a staff, which he posted on the outside of our doors.

I was trying to draw daily comics because journals get boring but I wanted to keep ahold of this place, this house, this project, and how every day is kind of ridiculous, or somethin ridiculous or beautiful or terrible or noteworthy happens here in this house that is half house, half public space.

Daily comics started with B. this night at midnight when Aaro broke the rule and called from our floor up to the upstairs and said "Charles! We're making the flyer. Is it Red Monkey or Red Monkeys?" and Charles said "Holy shit! look outside! What's on fire?! The cops are coming!" We didn't hurry, but we made our way out. In our parking lot there were 2 cop cars, 4 cops, and B and Zoe and the woman with the red hair doing a fire show, twirling fire and breathing it and I thought, there goes trying to keep some kind of low profile. These people don't even live here and they're putting it in jeoprady. They kept it up for awhile, and then put out the flames and walked over to the cops and talked to them for awhile, and a cop

handed B something and then they drove away.
I said "what the hell was that all about?" B said "we were just standing here in the parkinglot when the cops pulled up and asked if we were prostitutes and I said 'yeah, totally' but they didn't believe me so I asked if they wanted to see us breathe fire instead."
"But what did the cop give you?"
"Money. when we were done I said "now you have to give us money.""
"And they did?"
"We got 3.50"

Then there was the day I was trying to weave and at the same time, cook a 4 course meal timed to be ready when Panty Raid arrived. I kept running up and down the ladder. 5 inches waffle weave, stir the marinade, 10 inches plain weave, turn the oven down. And out of the blue, the J.C. boys showed up in town. I said "Boys! It's been so long! what have you been doing?" One of them said "we were just trying to walk around, but there was this chicken that had flown up on to this high fence and we were trying to get it down, and then it fell. We were trying to save it."
"You were chasing the wild chickens around?" (there is a guy who raises chickens somewhere nearby and whenever one of them is too unruly, he just sets it free and these bad girl chickens pack together and roam the streets of Asheville.)
"It's hard to catch those wild chickens" I said.
"No" Andrew said, "it was Perry's chicken"
"Perry's chicken" I said, "how sad". (Perry is the guy with the flower shop downtown, who has a chicken that lives inside).

There were other comics; about rats and jobs and unwanted guests - but the last one was about this day, when the sun was low in the sky, turning autumn. Luke had just left his mom in Texas and come back to us on the grayhound, so all the young punks were in the back yard, hanging out with him again on the stairs of the fire escape. Kerb had gotten a saw and took the top off our unreturned keg, and had gotten a huge propane outside cooker and was brewing up a whole keg worth of beer. The girls in knee-highs were on the back landing, talking about something, and i was in the garden, trying to distinguish plants from weeds.

Athena came up, I'd never met her, didn't know who she was, but someone had described her and said she'd been looking for me. She came up, full of nerves, couldn't make eye contact, trying to explain something, smelling like wine coming out of pores. I touched her arm, she started crying, I took her in my arms, she ran away, I didn't follow, didn't know if I should. I tried to go back to gardening to hide my hands that were shaking, but I caught Kerb out of the corner of my eye, looking with tenderness, shock and awe, which is how I felt, except I also felt validated and scared. Knee highs laughed down with condescension in her voice, "What did you do Cindy? write something that touched that girl?"
I was still open, plain faced, said "yeah, I guess so".

Yes, that's what happened. That's what I work so fucking hard for - like pulling teeth sometimes, like poking holes in arteries, doubled over, don't want to move or see.

I could just leave it; listen to new wave, carry a purse, fix my hair, hang out at the bar - but I feel a responsibility to look hard and deep and get it down as best as I can, even if most of the time, some of the time, I'd rather be doing something, almost anything else.

I tried daily comics, but I couldn't draw these things. The twisted angle of the fence around the new section of garden which is right in the middle of the yard, in the way, held up with rebar and lit with blue lights to keep people from falling in. The fence is falling over and the plants so small I think they're too small to make it through the winter, even if it is just kale and chard and Caty says they will keep growing. She says greens and cilantro and spinich last just fine.

I can't draw my bag full of plants that I stole out of people's yards in the hills at the crack of dawn. Pansies and Chrysanthemums, I stole them partially because I wanted to and petty crime is a good excuse for late night walking, exhilarating even if it is low impact - rich people's plants or the ones left out in the front of the grocery stores, change from the pop machine and garbage that is garbage to someone else, but not to me. Bag full of plants I stole, half because I wanted to walk around in the night with the light rain falling after a month of drought. Half that and half just me feeling like I needed to fill up the space, the part of the yard I dug up and fenced off and didn't get around to planting anything in.

Days later, after Athena had left, and me still wondering about what I didn't ask and what I didn't say, when is comforting someone an easier thing to do than trying to get to the heart - when is it better to hold her, say 'fuck these people watching, put your head down, I've got you, you can go ahead and cry' - when is that better? When is it exactly right and more than most people are willing to give, and when is it an excuse for not giving more, for not bringing her inside, making her coffee, saying 'tell me the facts not the feeling, tell me the root and we'll try to find a way to have it take you somewhere other than here, somewhere easier on your mind than this spiral where your eyes glaze over, Cisco or no, panic or immobilized, these familiar things, these well worn paths - get me to the root and maybe we can break out of it in a different direction this time.'

Days later, I'm standing by the garden, outside the show at the fire pit with the older punks, before the show. And I'm trying to welcome people in my awkward way, make them feel at home. Glad that we have a place and an excuse to come together, and like Deanna said at the last show, so stressed out and betrayed and sad she was, and then 3 songs into it with the heat and the music and our community with bodies moving like one big creature, all together, banged around, lifted up over heads, raised fists 3 songs and her worn down expression melted away, and she dives over to me, yells "It makes it all better, you know?!" This release, what we've created together.

The older punks who've been playing forever, 100 shitty bar shows, 100 shitty clubs, where the people think they're there to watch the band, think it's performance and observation, reenforce seperation and alienation instead of using it to break those things down - I'm glad we're broken and peiced back together and have life to give them, here in our shitty wet basement, low ceilings, embracing this love and anger and frustration and mixed feelings, politics and cynicism and rising above.

At the fire pit, burning pallets with these new people, I say "It's nice to be living in this back shack I moved in to. It's quieter than the house and I can get some peice of mind. I've only got the rats to contend with, and they're bad enough. One ran across my pillow while I was laying on it and not even asleep! And they eat right out of the dog food bowl and the dog is too deaf to notice. But still, it's easier to write back there, than it was in the house, where I had a room people walked through to get to other rooms, and Nathan was learning to scratch above me". They nod their heads, and say where they live it's easier, rent is so cheap you don't have to live with a lot of people, you can get a two bedroom house and split it with one other person, and if you're lucky they won't even be around much. I nod my head, but that's not what I meant, I wasn't complaining, just making small talk, and I think it's important to live this way - big houses, kind of public, with all the frustration and noise that goes with it. But I nod my head, because I don't want to be rude and I think it will take too much energy to explain. But if not this, this chance to talk about what and why I'm doing what I'm doing or what we're all doing and put it up for debate and challenge myself and everyone else who I assume common ground with, but am afraid to get down to it in case the assumption proves false. If not this articulation, it could become only burnt pallets and noise, so what do I think I'm saving my energy for?

I WANTED TO BE ON A STRETCHER, SPRAWLED OUT AND SCREAMING,
CARRIED DOWN THE SIDEWALKS OF MONT-PELIER, WITH BLOOD DRIPPING DOWN MY LEGS (FAKE BLOOD)
COAT-HANGER IN HAND, WHEN THE ANTIABORTION PARADE CAME TO TOWN
But Casey thought it would gross people out, and besides, who else would we get to carry the stretcher? So instead I just made flyers for the two of us to pass out...

I wanted our action to be as dramatic as I felt about it – to shock people out of their comfort and make them look twice and make them think about how we confine our expression, and what would they do if they broke out of the limits that had been set and accepted. But I was also trying to learn to use logic, and that was pretty liberating too – concrete knowledge and connection to history instead of only responding to the world emotionally.

I thought there would be a lot of protesters, but it was just the two of us. The first protest we'd ever been to. Just me and Casey, marching along in step with the right to lifers – them on the street, us on the sidewalk, everyone else inside. It was a Vermont town, and everyone was embarrassed by the spectacle and didn't want to see it – Ignore the really stupid people and maybe they'll just go away.

We were confused and disheartened, but with a kind of excitement too – stepping into stores where the customers waited for it to be over. We passed out flyers and I'd see them start to read ~~them~~ – it made me nervous – my words. . .

but not as nervous as I was back outside, walking along with the right to lifers. The teen girls with the gold crosses around their necks, they looked at us shyly, and I imagined they were embarrassed too, to be where they were, with their parents, signs, and babies. We gave them glares of contempt and scorn and then looks of warmth and pleading; tried to make where we were look more fun than where they were -- tried to think of some thing to get them over by our side.

Abortion Without Apology (6.00)
Women Under Attack: victories and backlash and the fight for reproductive freedom (5.00)
(these are small but good books from the late80's available through South End Press, 7 Brookline St. #1 Cambridge, MA. 02139. add3.50shipping for one book. plus .50for each additional one)

also everyone should have Our Bodies Ourselves

and also the pamphlet Hot Pants. (2.00 from me)

New York

I woke up in the van to the small sounds of the city, the church bells and garbage trucks and people's voices passing by. I'm hidden in there and getting one over on the world, that's what it feels like, stupidly, like it's me who's winning.

I dress under the covers, pour the piss jar onto the street, and step out, disheveled and looking up at the sun to tell the time. I walk down to the Polish grocery for coffee.

New York, "Coffee regular" means "put so much sugar and cream in there than anyone but me, and apparently NewYorkers, would think it was sick".

In Asheville, if you've got a skirt on, you can't walk from our house to downtown without some car trying to slow down for you or pull over for you, no matter what time of day or night, and our house is only two blocks from downtown.

I try different tricks, like wearing a backpack, whores don't wear backpacks, but it doesn't deter those 'heybaby cars'. Once I even got propositioned when I was just crossing the street, barefoot, with an armload full of eggplants to deliver.

We joke about it, but it's actually pretty sad, and I don't even realize how much I brace myself against it when I think I am taking it all in stride. -muscles tightened, ready to fight or run or throw back an insult or toss it aside.

So it's funny to by in NY, where I've always been afraid I'd get lost and end up in the wrong neighborhood, always been on edge, and trying to pass as native, always been kind of scared. But this time Issac drew me a map and said everywhere is safe, except probably parts of Harlem. I can't quite believe it, but I go almost everywhere and it's true.

I went to Blackout, the anarchist bookstore, where half my old collective use to volunteer when they first moved to NY, I had never been there. Couldn't ever remember if it was on 3rd St and Ave B, 7th St and Ave C, 2nd St and Ave D. That was the excuse, but actually I was just afraid to see them.

I'd like to see them now, enough time has passed and I don't expect things that I shouldn't, or things that I should but they're not going to give me. I don't expect anything from them, and not in a bitter way either. Time really does change things. I'd like to see them now, but they don't work there anymore. Instead I walk in and there's a bike with a bouquet of lambsear tied to it - a different aesthetic than theirs, someone I know from a different time.

"Stephan!" I say "Holy shit! I thought you were locked up".

He says "They let me out on weekends. What are you doing here?"

"I'm here for a boat wedding I guess, do you think I look okay? How do I get to the pier? I need to be there in a couple hours, I need some more coffee."

We go outside and sit on the stoop with Okra, who had stayed at my house back before I had my welcoming attitude on, back when I use to snarl at anyone sleeping on the couches or extra beds, and give them suspicious glances like everyone else, then wonder why they didn't integrate themselves into our community more. Okra stayed with us for awhile and straightened up our infoshop that had gone to peices. But I had never talked to him except to borrow his saw.

NY. Isn't it suppose to be alienating? We sit there and everyone that walks by knows them. Everyone's in a hurry, there's a sence of urgency, but they stop for a second and say "remind me later that I want to ask you about seed saving." or they stop and say "Community gardens bike ride, one hour" or they don't stop, just wave.

This couple walks up to us and when the woman talks, her hands move. She curls her fingers in towards her palms and then out with a fluid turn of the wrist and her arm moves along with it, as if guided and it makes me think she must have been in theater, or a dancer.

And his eyes behind his glasses are shining, calm, observant and direct -writer or intellectual or both. They push up to us with a stroller, unbuckle their kid who toddles out and flops to the ground, screaming something about the park.

The man points at him and says, "You wouldn't believe how hard it is to pick him up when he's like that. He's in his 'go limp' phase. It's an inherent trait, you see, not learned".

And she says, bending down, conspiritorial, "We are all monsters. This has turned everything on its head. We don't have patience or forgiveness or compassion. The Christians have all the books and sermons about how to raise your child under God because if you don't it will go straight to the devil. It's true! If we grew up without someone to guide us and love us and teach us, we would be complete monsters. We would be hell on earth. Murderous, spiteful, selfish, hateful monsters."

I meet Issac at the pier and the sun sets while we're out on the wedding boat, going around and around Manhattan. My dress is too short, and this boat ride is for three hours, with no way off except to jump overboard. And I can't drink, cuz if I drink I'll get drunk and be obnoxious and I'm among well dressed, well adjusted strangers, and I don't know how to talk to any of them.

Out on deck, the bridesmaid's cowboy hat blows off into the Hudson, and I try to catch it for her on it's way down. She starts talking to me about Reclaim the Streets.

Dear Reader, do you know what Reclaim the Streets is? I know a little bit about it, but not as much as I should.

I think it started in England, these huge street protests against the European Economic Community and the WTO. They get thousands of people out, uniting ravers and punks, in this direct action - taking over the streets with bodies and music and huge puppets with people hidden under the skirts, tearing up the pavement with jackhammers.

The bridesmaid was telling me how she helped organize the ones in New York. The first one was really successful. They held the street for a couple hours and got a lot of information out and had a lot of fun, but the second time, the cops were prepared, and they moved right in and confiscated the generator and PA so there was no music to draw people in, and then they started making arrests. So for the third one, she called up the police station and told them the time and date the protest was planned for, and said they were expecting about 5 thousand people, just thought she'd let them know. Then she called back a few days later and said they had over estimated the amount of people who were likely to show. Then the day of the protest, it was just her and 3 other people, they brought a little boombox and a table and tea pot and cups and peach cobbler and played Pavarotti, quietly. But the cops were out in full force, waiting, in full riot gear. They had the intersection surrounded, and people would pass by, and the bridesmaid would invite them to come through the police line and have some tea and cobbler she'd talk to them about the WTO, and the people would ask the cops what the hell they were doing, and the cops would say, "protecting the peace". Protecting the peace against a tea party?

I don't want to take this time for granted, or assume things without giving people a chance. I should have looked more closely at the lights on the water reflected from the city, without having to be reminded that it might be the only time we ever see it from out there. I should have gotten up to catch the bridal boquet instead of mumbling in the corner about how I hate those kinds of things. I don't want to revel in every minute, but I also don't want to take it for granted, don't want to forget it or think of only bits and peices, or the parts that failed and the frustration of it all when we're wrapped up in it. When I take a step back, I can see the accomplishments, and how this is the life I have always wanted. Drawn out I see not a lost wandering and getting nowhere, but nearly a straight, concrete path.

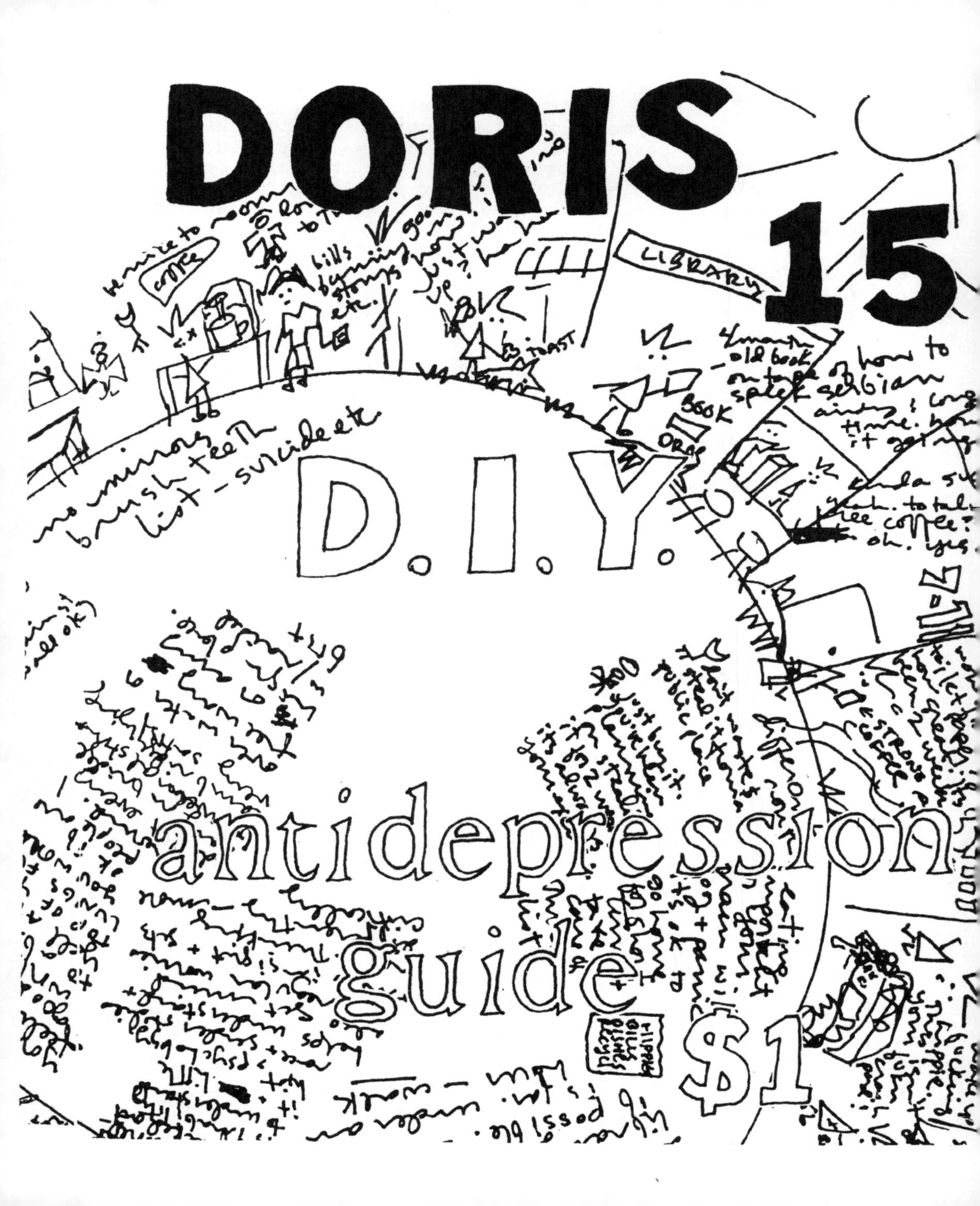

DORIS 15

D.I.Y. antidepression guide

$1

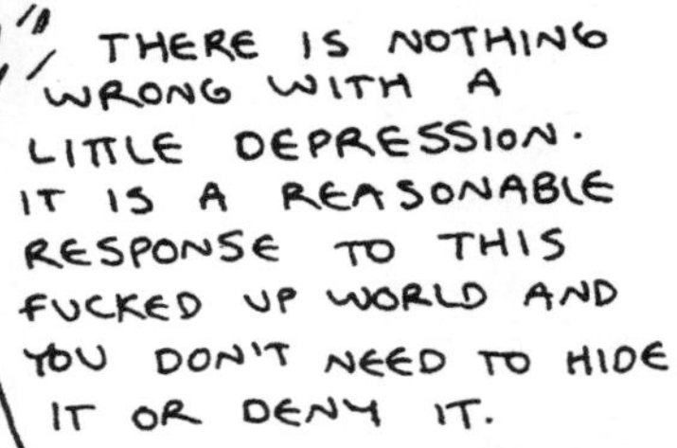

"THERE IS NOTHING WRONG WITH A LITTLE DEPRESSION. IT IS A REASONABLE RESPONSE TO THIS FUCKED UP WORLD AND YOU DON'T NEED TO HIDE IT OR DENY IT.

BUT TOO MUCH

DEPRESSION CAN BE A REAL DRAG

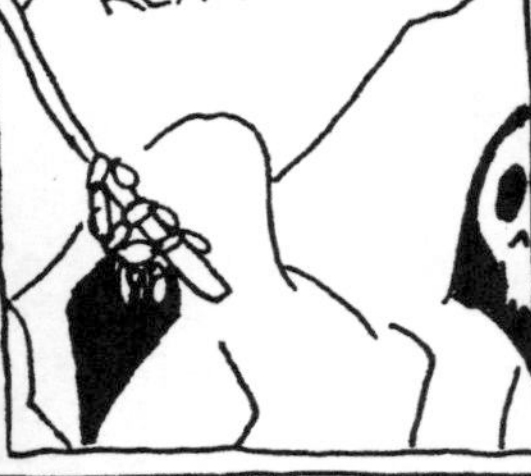

AND WHILE EVERYTHING IN HERE MIGHT NOT APPLY TO EVERYONE, MOST OF IT HAS BEEN TESTED AND PROVEN, IF NOT SAFE AT LEAST MODERATELY EFFECTIVE

THERE ARE A FEW BASIC TIPS TO START OUT WITH. YOU CAN PROBABLY SKIP AHEAD TO NUMBER 5, BUT SADLY, A RECENT FIELD STUDY HAS SHOWN THAT EVEN SOME OF THESE BASIC THINGS ARE SLIPPING BY THE WAYSIDE

one

SERIOUSLY, THE MORE T.V. YOU WATCH, THE MORE APATHETIC, DEPRESSED AND BORING YOU BECOME.

two

GET RID OF YOUR MIRRORS. NO MATTER HOW YOU LOOK, THEY FUCK WITH YOUR HEAD *and*

YOU ARE GUARANTEED TO LOOK BETTER WITH OUT THEM

here, have some coffee!

ok, but I usually drink tea.

NOT ONLY IS COFFEE A STRONG ANTI DEPRESSANT, IT ALSO MAKES IT NEARLY IMPOSSIBLE TO SIT STILL. IT FORCES YOU TO DO STUFF. IT IS ESPECIALLY GOOD FOR ANYONE WHO IS TRYING TO RETAIN SOME KIND OF FEMININITY OR COOL

three

ENOUGH COFFEE AND YOU WILL BE SCRATCHING AT YOUR FACE, TYING KNOTS IN YOUR HAIR AND TALKING LIKE A MAD THING. YOU WILL LOSE ALL REMNANTS OF NORMALCY AND THIS ALONE WILL MAKE YOUR LIFE ABOUT ONE HUNDRED TIMES BETTER!

My god! This shit is killer! did I ever tell you about... hell, I'm gonna quit my job! Just drink coffee all the time! How did you find out about this coffee drinking in excess anyway?!!

the story of
MY FIRST COFFEE FREAK-OUT
1985
BY MY LAST YEAR OF JR. HIGH I WAS SORT OF STARTING TO ADJUST
I HAD MADE SOME FRIENDS BUT WE WERE ALL PRETTY BORING AND MY PATIENCE WAS WEARING THIN. I WAS NEVER GOING TO BE A MODEL OR GET TO MEET EDDIE VAN HALEN, SO WHAT WAS THE POINT OF ALL THIS?
BYE LISA! I'M LEAVING!
LISA!
oh my god! He is so hot! Totally. No way?! He said uh...
TEEN BEAT
VH 1
ONE DAY IN THE CAFETERIA THERE WAS A DJ PLAYING OLDIES AND DANCE HITS WITH A JUKEBOX BACK DROP AND LOTS OF FLASHING LIGHTS.
IT WAS A PROMO FOR THE SCHOOL DANCE. I WAS HORRIFIED. WHY DID THE SCHOOL WASTE MONEY ON THIS CRAP?
EAGLES HITS
THAT DAY WAS STRANGELY TENSE AT THE LUNCH TABLE. KAREN WAS ASKING EVERYONE IF THEY "WERE GOING"
I HOPE SO
YES
GOD WILLING
I HAD NO IDEA WHAT THEY WERE TALKING ABOUT + SO TO BREAK THE ICE I SAID...
NOT ME! NO WAY!
THEY ALL STARED AT ME. KAREN TURNED SLOWLY TO FACE ME + INFORM ME, VERY CALMLY, THAT I WAS GOING TO GO TO HELL. IT WAS SAD CUZ I HAD SORT OF LIKED HER, DESPITE HER CHRISTIANITY
I LEFT TO GO STAND IN THE LUNCH LINE EVEN THOUGH I ONLY HAD 45¢ I HAD NEVER DRANK COFFEE BEFORE
LIBERTY
QUARTER
ONE DIME
ICE CREAM $1
PIZZA $2
SICK CRAP $1.50
COFFEE .15
FOUR COFFEES PLEASE!
I SAT DOWN AND DRANK MY COFFEES IN THE UNCOMFORTABLE SILENCE KAREN HAD LEFT BEHIND. CUP AFTER CUP
UNTIL IT ALL SEEMED VERY FUNNY
HEY, KNOW WHAT? I'M NOT EVEN BAPTIZED! HELL, HERE I COME!
+ THEN IT HAPPENED!
THE DJ PLAYED THAT SONG AND I COULD NOT HOLD MYSELF BACK ANY LONGER!
ROCK ROCK ROCK ROCK ROCK N ROLL HIGH SCHOOL ROCK
ITS THE FUCKING RAMONES! GET UP + DANCE! DON'T LEAVE LISA! GET UP HERE!
YOU BETTER GET DOWN CINDY. THE LUNCH LADY IS COMING!
LET THEM TRY + STOP ME! I'LL BURN THIS PLACE DOWN!

NOW BACK TO...
anti depression tip #4
on
Work, Security and standard of living
g
ONCE YOU HAVE A CERTAIN STANDARD OF LIVING, IT'S HARD TO IMAGINE BEING HAPPY WITH A LOWER ONE, BUT IT REALLY IS WORTH A TRY
HERE SIR
WHATS THIS?
MY RESIGNATION
MY OLD FULL TIME JOB
I'M NOT TRYING TO ROMANTICIZE POVERTY. I'M NOT EVEN SAYING THAT SIMPLE LIVING IS POLITICALLY OR MORALLY SUPERIOR. IT'S JUST THAT I'VE SEEN SO MANY FRIENDS MIRED DOWN IN DEBT, ALWAYS WORKING TO PAY IT OFF, AND PRETTY STIFLED AND UNHAPPY, WITH NEVER ENOUGH TIME TO DO THE THINGS THEY WANT. AND THE THING I'VE FOUND IS IT FEELS SURPRISINGLY GOOD AND DIGNIFIED TO LIVE WITHIN YOUR MEANS
WEAVE
WARP+WEFT
YARNS
MY JOB NOW
AND IT FEELS GREAT TO QUIT YOUR JOB AND HAVE THE TIME TO REALLY PURSUE THE THINGS YOU FEEL PASSIONATE ABOUT
DONT JUMP!
YOU ARE NOT TRAPPED! TRUST ME!
I KNOW THERE ARE A LOT OF THINGS HOLDING PEOPLE BACK, AND ONE BIG THING IS WORRY ABOUT THE FUTURE AND THE NEED FOR SECURITY, AND IT SEEMS ALMOST REASONABLE TO SACRIFICE THE PRESENT BY WORKING A LOT TO ENSURE A SECURE FUTURE, BUT HONESTLY, MOST JOBS, EVEN HIGH PAYING ONES JUST AREN'T THAT SECURE.
BIG COMPANY NOW NEW MANAGEMENT
OUT WITH THE OLD, IN WITH THE NEW!
OR TIME TO FIND OUT WHERE YOUR PASSION LAYS
ME GUSTA COCINAR
ME GUSTA COCINAR
I'M PRETTY SURE THAT IF YOU PUT ALL YOUR ENERGY INTO THE THINGS YOU BELIEVE IN, IT WILL PAY OFF IN THE LONG RUN. YOU WILL BECOME REALLY GOOD AT WHAT YOU LOVE, GAIN A STRONG SENSE OF SELF, HAVE A COMMUNITY TO FALL BACK ON. UNSEEN AVENUES WILL OPEN AND YOU WILL HAVE REAL, SOLID, LONG TERM SECURITY...

the PINK HAUS WELCOMES the "NEW" MILLENNIUM
GOD DAMN FEDS! JUST TRY IT
COME ON OUR LAND + I'LL SHOOT!
BUT DAVE, IT'S ONLY 2070!
WHAT DO YOU KNOW SO-CALLED BLUE BIRD OF HAPPINESS? THE TIME IS NOW!
DINNER!
ACUPUNCTURE! ACUPUNCTURE! WHO WANTS ACUPUNCTURE? CINDY? HOW ABOUT YOU?
JON, I'M BUSY AND PLUS YOU'RE HALF BLIND.
VAL! COME LEARN TO MAKE TINCTURES!
LET'S START A NEW PUNK BAND
DEFINITELY
FISCHER PRICE
ON OFF
... and people to help you out when you all grow old.

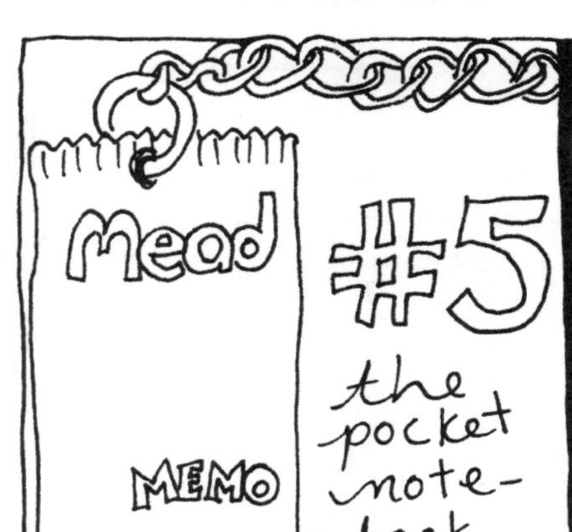

EVEN IF YOU ARE NOT A LIST KIND OF PERSON, IT'S GOOD TO WRITE THINGS DOWN SO YOU DON'T JUST REPEAT IT ALL IN YOUR HEAD OVER AND OVER UNTIL YOU FEEL CRAZY + THERE IS NO ROOM FOR ANYTHING ELSE...

... AND YOU GET DEPRESSED ABOUT HOW YOU NEVER DO THE THINGS YOU MEAN TO OR NEED TO DO. WRITING THEM DOWN AND GETTING TO CROSS THEM OFF PROVIDES A STRANGE MOTIVATION AND ALSO PROOF THAT YOU REALLY ARE GETTING SOMEWHERE

BUT MORE IMPORTANT IS THE LIST OF THINGS NOT TO THINK ABOUT . . .

JUST WRITE DOWN THE THINGS THAT PLAGUE YOU AND THEN THE NEXT TIME THEY COME UP, YOU CAN SAY TO YOURSELF "OH. I ALREADY HAVE THAT WRITTEN DOWN" AND YOU DON'T HAVE TO THINK ABOUT IT ANYMORE.

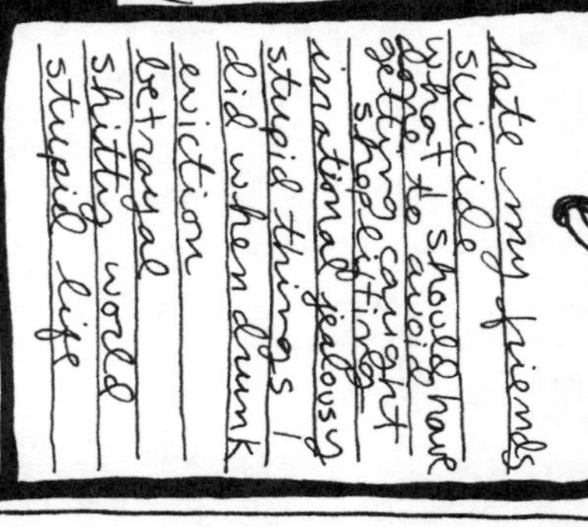

THERE IS A COMMONLY HELD BELIEF THAT IF YOU SPEND LOTS OF TIME AROUND OTHER PEOPLE, YOU WON'T BE LONELY. THIS JUST ISN'T TRUE. OFTEN TIMES, THE MORE YOU ARE AROUND OTHER PEOPLE, THE MORE LONELY, MISUNDERSTOOD, FRUSTRATED AND LOST FEELING YOU GET. ALSO IT IS EASY TO GET STUCK IN A RUT OF HANGING AROUND THE PEOPLE YOU KNOW, TRYING TO FIGURE OUT WHAT TO DO NEXT, WHICH IS USUALLY PRETTY DEPRESSING. MOST PEOPLE WOULD BE MUCH BETTER OFF IF THEY SPENT A LOT MORE TIME ALONE. THIS IS WHY YOU NEED A TRAVEL MUG, AS YOU WILL SEE.

I HATE TO DO THIS, BUT I KNOW SOME OF YOU WILL DENY MY COFFEE ADVICE, AND SO I CONSULTED CATY FOR SOME

helpful herbs

SUN IS ALSO VERY NECES-SARY

GUARANA – very high in caffeine, but doesn't irritate liver as much and it's not as hard on your nerves. it gives you a giddy, happy quality

TINCTURE – DROPPERFUL TIMES A DAY FOR SHORT TERM DEPRESSION. 1 TO 2 DROPS TWICE A DAY FOR GENERAL SLUGGISHNESS.

DAMIANA — MOOD BRIGHTNER, STIMULATES SENSES, CALMS MIND, RELAXES. – safe with antidepressants. – makes people hornier (which you may or may not want) →

TINCTURE – 15 DROPS TO SHOTGLASS FULL, 3 TIMES A DAY. – often good for people who are creatively stuck

caty's favorite

PEPPERMINT – tea, tincture or oil gives your brain clarity and also good for nausea.

TEA – AS MUCH AS YOU WANT, TINCTURE – 15 DROPS AS NEEDED, OIL – 3 DROPS AS NEEDED

ROSEMARY – good for the brain. good with peppermint tea. add 1-3 teaspoons per one cup water for tea.

GOTU KOLA – GOOD FOR MEMORY, IF YOUR MIND IS SLOW + FOGGY, ALSO GOOD IF YOU FEEL COLD AND HAVE LOW APPETITE

TINCTURE – 2-5 DROPS 3 TIMES A DAY.

YOU PAY FOR IT, YOU HARDLY USE IT, AND THEN IF YOU GET A SERIOUS OR CHRONIC ILLNESS, THE HEALTH CARE COMPANY WILL DROP YOU LIKE HOT COALS AND NO ONE ELSE WILL COVER YOU FOR A PREEXISTING CONDITION. AND BESIDES, WHAT'S THE POINT? HOSPITALS ARE FREE! ALL YOU HAVE TO DO IS GO TO THE EMERGENCY ROOM AND USE A FAKE NAME AND FAKE SOCIAL SECURITY NUMBER (JUST CHANGE THE LAST FOUR DIGITS BECAUSE THE FIRST FIVE DESIGNATE CITY + STATE OF BIRTH) OR YOU CAN USE YOUR OWN NAME + JUST NOT PAY. THE EMERGENCY ROOM WILL NOT DENY YOU, EVEN FOR MINOR THINGS. (I'VE HEARD THAT SOME HOSPITALS DO REFUSE PEOPLE, BUT MY FIELD RESEARCHERS HAVE GONE TO MANY HOSPITALS IN MANY CITIES AND STATES — BROKEN RIBS, CAR ACCIDENTS, BLOODY HEADS FROM SELF-INFLICTED BOTTLE SMASHING INJURIES, PUKING UP BLOOD, STREP THROAT, PNEUMONIA, SORE BACKS, HEART ATTACK, SPRAINED FINGERS, VENEREAL DISEASE, POISON IVY, FROSTBITE, KIDNEY INFECTIONS, AND VARIOUS OTHER THINGS, AND NO ONE HAS EVER BEEN REFUSED.)

THERE'S STILL A FEW SUBJECTS THAT I WANTED TO ADDRESS, BUT CAN'T REALLY FIGURE OUT HOW.
like →
HAVING PROBLEMS WITH AUTHORITY FIGURES TRYING TO BREAK YOUR SPIRIT? TRYING TO RUN YOUR LIFE?
YOU ARE A FAILURE!
HOW COULD YOU DO THIS TO YOUR OWN PARENTS!
CAN'T GET THE RESPECT YOU DESERVE? TRY THIS FOR A CHANGE
FUCK OFF!
yeah
EVENTUALLY, THEY WILL PROBABLY COME AROUND, OR THEY'LL GET SICK OF HATING YOU
RING RING
HI DAD!
HEY CINDY! WHAT ARE YOU UP TO? HARD AT WORK?
OH GOD. YES. ALL I DO ALL DAY IS WORK ON THIS ANTI-DEPRESSION MAGAZINE I'M WRITING
ANTI-DEPRESSION MAGAZINE! THAT'S A GREAT IDEA! PEOPLE COULD REALLY USE THAT.
ah dad, that's sweet.
well honey, I mean it
next
HOW TO LIVE WITH A BUNCH OF PEOPLE SO YOU CAN HAVE CHEAP RENT
BUILD WALLS
we need 3 more pallets!
GET EAR-PLUGS
HOW TO TALK TO PEOPLE
totally, totally I know what you mean, that's cool, with smash you a bat, that band kind of sucked. I mean they were cool. if it's...
IF YOU TALK A LOT, SHUT UP SOMETIMES AND TRY THINKING A LITTLE BIT ABOUT WHAT YOU'RE GOING TO SAY
it's good to give the conversation some space, and not feel pressure to have an immediate response. Try to see what the person is saying through their own eyes.
ask questions and resist the temptation to bring the subject back to yourself.

THE CURE FOR BURNING HOT PISS

—by Caty

This is the best way i know of to cure a urinary tract infection (UTI) or bladder infection.

• BASIC RECIPE •

½ oz. marshmallow root simmer in a covered pot with a quart of water for ½–1 hr. Take off heat. Then add 6 Tbs. Uva Ursi (or Manzanita) + 6 Tbs. dandalion leaf + a handful of horsetail plus a slice of ginger root. Let it sit for ½ hr. Drink it throughout the day and for 2 days after all symptoms are gone, if you don't want it to come right back.

simmering an herb in water is called a DECOCTION. Pouring hot water over a herb + letting it sit (steep) is called an INFUSION

recipe from Adam Sellers

UTI's are caused from bacteria (usually ecoli from intestines) getting to your urethra. Girls are especially prone to them because of the shortness in length of our urethras + the very close proximity of the opening to the ass, where lots of ecoli hang out. Sex is the most frequent infecting reason. It can be pretty awkward to talk about, but basically you have to make sure that anything that has touched the region around your ass, intentionally or unintentionally, does not get anywhere near your vaginal region. Unless it has been thoroughly washed inbetween. This means fingers, cocks, sex toys, anything. Sex isn't the only thing though. I got them a lot when i lived in a place with no water + couldn't wash myself or my clothes very often. Sometimes even just excessive amounts of caffeine can give you one if you've had one before. Some people just seem to get them for no reason. Being really dehydrated will do it too.

OTHER TIPS

- try to piss both before + after having sex
- wipe from front to back
- if you shit your pants, or a fart leaks out more than you expected, CHANGE
- drink lots of fluid (beer + coffee don't count)
- actually, beer + coffee are worse than not counting. Very much of either are bad when you have a UTI.
- don't hold your piss in—piss as often as you can. Don't give those bacteria any chance to adhere to the lining of your urethra. It's annoying, but you gotta flush them out.

It's important to start treating the infection as soon as you can. When you feel the first twinges + aren't even sure yet, start treating it. Drink tons of water. Drink cranberry juice. It does not need to be unsweetened. If the healthfood store where you can get herbs at is already closed, go get cranberry juice + drink a lot. It changes the pH of your urine which makes it inhospitable to the bacteria plus it makes the walls of your urethra more slippery so it's harder for the bacteria to stick to it. If you catch it soon enough, you can get rid of the infection with just cranberry juice.

* IF YOUR LOWER BACK (= KIDNEYS) STARTS TO HURT A LOT OR IF YOU GET A BAD FEVER, GO TO THE EMERGENCY ROOM. IT PROBABLY MEANS YOU HAVE A KIDNEY INFECTION, WHICH CAN KILL YOU OR FUCK YOU UP FOR LIFE. *

THIS IS WHAT THE HERBS DO:

*if you can't find all the herbs in the recipe, use the ones you can find, or replace them with others that do the same thing.

UVA URSI [arctostaphylos] - disinfects bladder + urethra. Can be irritating to stomach, so take with marshmallow. Don't use in pregnancy.

MARSHMALLOW [althea] - disinfectant + antinflammatory to urinary tract. soothing to stomach lining

HORSETAIL [equisetum] - antinflammatory + astringent to bladder + urethra - it takes tissue + shrinks it down.

DANDELION LEAF [taraxacum] - a strong, simple diuretic. That means it makes you piss a lot. Also replaces electrolytes.

- other herbs -

PIPSISSEWA • good UT disinfectant (tincture 1-2 dropperfuls every 2 hr) (can use instead of uva ursi)

JUNIPER • (berries for tea) tsp. crushed in cup of water. No in pregnancy or if kidney problems or history of kidney problems. It's a simple urinary tract disinfectant + it stimulates the kidneys.

CORN SILK • yes, the silk of an ear of corn. You can just eat it, or take a dropperful 4x day of the fresh tincture. Diuretic + anti-inflammatory to urinary tract.

other diuretics ... things to make you piss...

NETTLES, CHICKWEED, CLEAVERS and there are many others.

ONCE UPON A TIME I DECIDED IT WAS UNHEALTHY TO ALWAYS BE IN RELATIONSHIPS BUT IT WAS HARD TO STAY SINGLE WITH BOTH MY HORMONES AND MY SUBCONSCIOUS WORKING AGAINST ME
dog
we are trained, from the moment of birth, to accept individualism, to ignore our true desires, to embrace alienation in order to perpetuate the status quo and the capitalist system
we can use the intensity of sexual relations to break out of our ingrained repression . . .
and begin to actualize the full potential of human kind.
PANT SLOBBER PANT FUCK SEX PEGGED PANTS GOTTA GET LAID FUCK BED FLOOR BED SEX
SPARE CHANGE?

I figured if I could satisfy my hormones I'd stand a better chance of crushing my subconscious. The problem was I had never learned to masturbate
in the expor on of
another person's body
we begin to exp e
the possibilities for
a pleasurable e istence
and feel deep inside
of us the need for social
real change
OH, SHUT UP ALREADY! YOU COULD RATIONALIZE ANYTHING. CAN'T YOU SEE, THE DEVIL DOESN'T EVEN CARE!
db
PURR
I had tried it once in '88, when I was dealing full time with incest stuff and I was trying to get over my fear of my body. But it didn't work. It just felt creepy to me and made me feel worse than ever.
1988 ME
INCEST SURVIVOR
COOM
81,82, 83,84
ASPRIN
This time I was not going to let alienation hold me back!
THIS TIME I WAS GOING TO TRY A MORE SCIENTIFIC APPROACH. I READ SUSIE SEXPERT'S GUIDE TO LESBIAN SEX AND STUDIED UP ON FEMALE ANATOMY and THEN MUSTERED UP THE COURAGE TO GO TO A SEXTOY WORKSHOP...

I know it's weird, but I had this hangup and I just could not get myself to go into a sex store, not even a feminist one.

When I was 15 Angie use to drag me to all the porn stores to browse and make fun of the weird shit, but I was very shy and those places creeped me out.

I figured if I signed up for a class, it would get me in the door. It was very embarrass-ing. I just wanted to buy the thing most likely to work.

ANY QUESTIONS?
I HOPE I DON'T SOUND LIKE SOME SUPER KNOW-IT-ALL PERVERT
SUSIE BRIGHT RECOMENDS A PLUG-IN CLITORAL STIMULATOR. DO YOU HAVE THOSE?
sorry, no. you can get battery operated ones at drug stores sold as "body massagers", but plug in ones you have to go to San Francisco
CRAP.
In retrospect, I shouldn't have been so picky. I have a friend now who has a battery one + she says she likes it even better. But at the time I did not want to take chances
give up. fuck someone. anyone. who cares about consequences
ha ha ha ha
we got you now
give up you are not strong enough to resist. go and get laid. do it do it do it.
SO FOR FOUR MONTHS, MY HORMONES AND SUB-CONSCIOUS FUCKED WITH MY HEAD UNTIL...
GOOD VIBRATIONS
I FINALLY HITCHIKED TO CALIFORNIA and BOUGHT MY VERY OWN HITACHI
it took a little getting used to, but in the end it proved to be everything I had hoped for, and more.
HEY WANNA FUCK?
NO THANKS
If you don't have a good local sex shop call 1-800-BUY-VIBE for Good Vibrations catalogue.

WHATEVER YOU DO, DON'T SLEEP TOO MUCH. THE LONGER YOU STAY IN BED, THE HARDER IT IS TO GET OUT AND DEPRESSION WILL QUICKLY CREEP IN.

SET YOUR ALARM. JUMP OUT OF BED AND PLAY ONE, JUST ONE ANGRY SONG TO GET YOUR BLOOD PUMPING AND TO SCARE AWAY THE ALIENATION.

MAKE COFFEE AND TOAST AND RUN OUT OF THE HOUSE. YOU MUST GET OUTSIDE AS FAST AS POSSIBLE TO AVOID DESPAIR

... NOW WALK AROUND. SOMETIMES IT'S GOOD TO RUN A COUPLE ERRANDS FIRST THING – GET A SENSE OF ACCOMPLISHMENT EARLY ON. EVEN IF YOU DON'T HAVE ANY ERRANDS, YOU SHOULD WALK. WALK AT LEAST UNTIL YOU STOP WORRYING ABOUT HOW STUPID IT IS TO BE OUT WALKING WITH NO WHERE TO GO. STRETCH + BREATHE REALLY DEEPLY AND LOOK AROUND A LOT. EVEN IF YOU HATE THE RICH OR INDUSTRIALIZATION DOESN'T MEAN YOU CAN'T ENJOY WALKING AROUND THOSE NEIGHBORHOODS SOMETIMES.

BANK OF AMERICA $
LOT 4 SALE
MR DOW CHEMICALS?
YIKES!
I AM WALKING DOWN THE STREET, ROBBING ALL THE BANKS. I'VE BOUGHT ALL THE EMPTY LOTS IN TOWN AND CATY'S HELPING TO COORDINATE THEM INTO COMMUNITY GARDENS. I AM A TRAINED ASSASSIN.
LYNDA BARRY! WHAT A SURPRISE!
bark
GRR
WE LOVE CINDY ONLY
JUST TRY AND FUCK WITH ME NOW, WORLD, I DARE YOU!
H.Q. DO YOU READ ME? I AM APPROACHING SECTOR 4!
REPORTING SUSPICIOUS GRANDFATHER TYPE AT BAMBOO HOUSE
GRANDMA?! GRANDPA?!
CINDY?
IS IT YOU?
WE KEPT THIS DESK FOR YOU IN CASE WE EVER FOUND YOU! NO ONE WILL DISTURB YOUR WORK HERE. WHAT KIND OF COOKIES DO YOU LIKE BEST?
?!
I AM AN ASSASSIN WITH A BOMB THAT'S ABOUT TO GO OFF. I AM A LITTLE BIRD LOOKING FOR A HOME. I AM MARY MAGDELINE. I AM DON QUIXOTE. I AM TINKERBELL, NO WAIT, I HATE TINKERBELL. I AM A GREAT PAINTER. I CAN PAINT ANYTHING.
WTO CENTER
I AM A TRAINED ASSASSIN
HELLO MISTER PRESIDENT
I CAN BREATHE UNDERWATER
I am a trained assassin
WAIT, WHY DOES THAT FEEL SO FAMILIAR?

collectives part 3

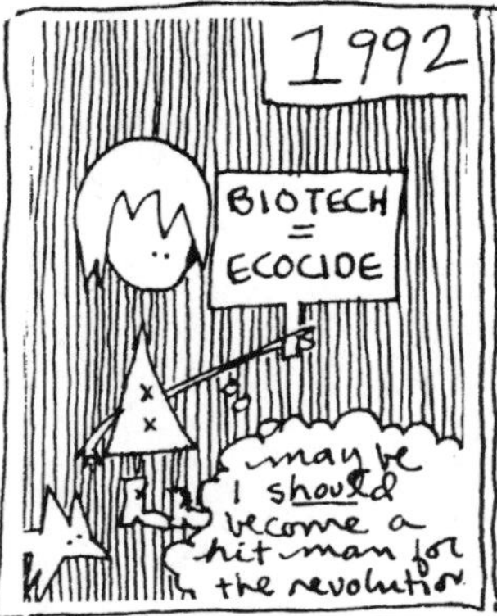

1992
BIOTECH = ECOCIDE
maybe I should become a hit-man for the revolution

AFTER YEARS OF HARD WORK, OUR NATIONAL ORGANIZATION DISINTEGRATED, AND EVEN ALL THE DIFFERENT LOCAL GROUPS WHO HAD COME TOGETHER TO FIGHT GULF WAR #1, WERE SPLITTING APART AND SPLINTERING AND INFIGHTING AND FIGHTING EACHOTHER IN SOME PRETTY SAD WAYS.

I HAD ALWAYS ASSUMED THAT THE MOMENTUM WOULD GROW AND GROW, BUT IT WAS DISSIPATING FAST AND I WAS STARTING TO THINK THAT THE REVOLUTION WAS NOT GOING TO HAPPEN AFTER ALL.

I STILL BELIEVED IN THE HUMAN CAPACITY FOR COLLETIVISM, AND I COULD SEE THE HUMAN IMPULSE TOWARD FREEDOM. I COULD ANSWER MOST OF THE BASIC QUESTIONS, LIKE "HOW WOULD THE POSTAL SERVICE BE RUN IN AN ANARCHIST SOCIETY?", BUT I JUST DIDN'T SEE THE REVOLUTION COMMING RIGHT AROUND THE CORNER LIKE I USED TO.

SO I ASKED GREG, BECAUSE HE WAS SMARTER THAN ME, BUT WAS ALWAYS HAPPY TO ANSWER MY QUESTIONS + DIDN'T THINK I WAS STUPID TO ASK

DO YOU THINK THE REVOLUTION WILL HAPPEN IN OUR LIFE-TIME?

he said

NOT A TRADITIONAL, VIOLENT REVOLUTION. OUR MILITARY ARE JUST TOO BIG, BUT ONCE THE PEOPLE REALIZE THAT THE GOVERNMENT HAS NO WAY TO REALLY DEAL WITH THE GROWING ECOLOGICAL CRISIS, THERE WILL BE SUCH WIDESPREAD DISCONTENT THAT NO ONE WILL BE ABLE TO STOP US, ALTHOUGH THERE MAY BE SOME CRITICAL JUNCTURE WHEN WE WILL NEED HIT MEN TO KNOCK OFF A FEW KEY PEOPLE.

I COULD SEE MYSELF DOING IT! MAY BE THIS WAS MY CALLING! NO ONE ELSE IN THE COLLECTIVE HAD THE STRENGTH OR MORAL STAMINA FOR THE JOB...

THERE IS A PLACE FOR ME
I'M NOT USELESS AFTER ALL. THERE'S A ROLE FOR ME, FINALLY

I GOT A SECOND JOB TO MAKE THE EXTRA MONEY I WOULD NEED TO TAKE SHOOTING LESSONS AT THE SHOOTING RANGE

AGENTS OF REPRESSION

AND I STARTED READING THIS BOOK THAT WE CARRIED AT THE OLD Y.G. CLEARINGHOUSE/MAILORDER (MY DESK + LIVINGROOM).

ABOUT TWO CHAPTERS INTO IT, I COULD SEE THAT IT WAS NEVER GONNA HAPPEN THE WAY I HAD BEEN THINKING IT WOULD.

THERE SHE IS, BOYS! ARREST HER!

BUT SARAH!?!

THIS WAS MUCH MORE LIKELY

WELL, HELL, I'M ALL FOR DELUDING YOURSELF TO BUILD UP SOME HOPE, CUZ HOPE IS PRETTY USEFUL IN HOLDING DOWN THE DEPRESSION THAT KEEPS US FROM BEING ABLE TO ACT UPON OUR CONVICTIONS, BUT YOU GOTTA HAVE SOME SLIGHT GRASP ON REALITY AND SOMETIMES YOU NEED TO DO WHAT'S RIGHT, EVEN IF IT SEEMS LIKE IT'S NOT GOING TO GET YOU ANYWHERE. WHAT I MEAN IS, I THINK IT WAS PRETTY IRRESPONSIBLE OF MY MORE EDUCATED FRIENDS TO PUSH THIS IDEA OF REVOLUTION IN OUR LIFETIMES – WHEN THEY KNEW EXACTLY WHAT HAD HAPPENED TO A.I.M. AND THE BLACK PANTHERS AND THE FEMINISTS AND EVERY FUCKING SOCIAL MOVEMENT IN THE 60'S AND 70'S, INFILTRATED, FUCKED WITH, SUBVERTED, DISCREDITED AND DESTROYED. WE WERE TOO FULL OF HOPE; WE COULD HAVE USED MORE OF THAT OLD RUSSIAN ATTITUDE, BEFORE THE REVOLUTION, WHEN THEY WERE STILL UNDER THE CZAR, WHEN THEY FOUGHT, NOT BECAUSE THEY HAD HOPE OF SEEING ANY CHANGE IN THEIR LIFETIMES, BUT BECAUSE THEY SAW THEMSELVES AS PART OF A BIGGER STRUGGLE, AND THEY FOUGHT TO MAINTAIN THEIR HUMANITY AND TO PRESERVE HUMANITY IN GENERAL. WE COULD HAVE USED MORE OF THAT – KEPT OUR RADICALISM BUT BEEN MORE REALISTIC ABOUT IT, BECAUSE THE WAY WE WERE GOING, WE WERE BOUND TO BECOME DISILLUSIONED WHEN WE WEREN'T ABLE TO FULFILL OUR ROMANTICIZED IDEAL. WE WERE TOO SHORT SIGHTED WITH TOO MUCH SELF IMPORTANCE, TOO MANY UNREALISTIC DEMANDS PLACED ON EACHOTHER, AND AN UNSUSTAINABLE URGENCY THAT WOULD TEAR US APART IN THE END.

and now back to...
PST. CINDY! AREN'T YOU SUPPOSE TO BE DOING A COMIC ON HOW TO WALK AROUND?!
OH, GOD. THAT'S RIGHT!
THAT'S RIGHT, WHAT DID I SAY ALREADY? WALK A BUNCH. PRETEND YOU'RE A BUNCH OF DIFFERENT STUFF. RIGHT. I FORGOT TO MENTION MAPS!
IT'S GOOD TO HAVE A MAP, EVEN IF YOU KNOW YOUR WAY AROUND. IT HELPS TO GET YOU ON THOSE BACK STREETS, TAKING SHORT-CUTS THAT TAKE TWICE AS LONG. I USE TO HAVE A RED PENCIL, AND I'D MARK THE STREETS AS I WALKED, TRYING TO EVENTUALLY HAVE WALKED ON EVERY STREET. MAPS HELP GIVE YOU A DIFFERENT SENSE OF PERSPECTIVE ON YOUR TOWN + YOUR PLACE IN IT. MAKES YOU LOOK AT IT + IT'S POSSIBILITIES IN NEW WAYS.
NOW, THE TRICKY PART IS TO KEEP YOUR MIND OFF THE
"LIST OF THINGS NOT TO THINK ABOUT"
I'VE FOUND IT USEFUL TO HAVE A FEW TOPICS OF THE DAY TO PULL MY MIND BACK TO, SUCH AS...
THE PROS + CONS OF BEING EXCESSIVELY DISMISSIVE OF THE PEOPLE I HAVE PROBLEMS WITH...
OR, HOW DO I ARTICULATE WHAT I THINK OF TECHNOLOGY AND HOW PEOPLE ARE EMPOWERED OR DISEMPOWERED BY IT'S SPECIFIC FORMS
John deer
HEY JESS? WHAT DO YOU THINK ABOUT WHEN YOU'RE WALKING AROUND?
ACTUALLY, YOU'RE NOT GONNA BELIEVE IT, BUT I HAVE A LIST!
I TRIED MAKING A LIST OF THINGS TO THINK ABOUT BUT IT MADE ME FEEL NEUROTIC.
ME? WELL, LATELY I'VE BEEN THINKING ABOUT THE PAST. NOT THE PAST IN GENERAL BUT SPECIFIC TIMES AND PEOPLE THAT WERE TOO DIFFICULT OR WENT BY SO FAST THAT I NEVER GOT A CHANCE TO REALLY SAVOR WHAT MADE THOSE TIMES AND PEOPLE GREAT. SO I'VE BEEN DRUMMING THEM UP AND APPRECIATING THEM. IT'S BEEN NICE. IT'S AMAZING HOW MUCH THERE IS THAT I WOULD HAVE JUST FORGOTTEN OR PUSHED AWAY.
?
IF YOUR TRAVEL MUG IS NOT BIG ENOUGH, YOU SHOULD GET MORE COFFEE WHILE YOU'RE WALKING AROUND. SOMETIMES CHEAP GAS STATION COFFEE IS GOOD. SOME TIMES YOU NEED FANCY ESPRESSO

BY THE TIME YOU GET HOME, YOUR MIND SHOULD BE MOVING SO FAST THAT YOU WON'T BE ABLE TO THINK OF ANYTHING BUT SOME "GREAT" PLAN.
HOMEMADE HOT AIR BALLOON
TELESCOPE
SHARK
BLAZE THROUGH THE HOUSE AND DO JUST A COUPLE THINGS REAL QUICK, TO GET THEM OFF YOUR MIND
WAKE UP YOU FUCKING HIPPIE! GET OUT OF OUR HOUSE! HOW MANY TIMES DO WE HAVE TO KICK YOU OUT?! DIE! DIE! DIE! DIE!
hey Janet! heres bill money
COOK UP SOME FOOD TO TAKE WITH YOU TO THE LIBRARY
COUNTRY CROOK DEEP FRYER
I'M ALL FOR THE IDEA OF PUBLIC LIBRARIES, BUT THEY ARE USUALLY TOO LOUD + DON'T HAVE SUCH GREAT BOOKS OR GOOD PLACES TO SIT WITH NO DISTRACTION
WHY DO YOU HAVE A MUSTACHE?
WE'RE GONNA GET POKEMON
ARE YOU A LADY OR A MAN?
WAAH!
WE'RE GONNA TELL MOMMY ON YOU
COLLEGE LIBRARIES ARE REALLY GOOD + THEY ARE ALMOST ALWAYS OPEN UNTIL NEARLY MIDNIGHT. EVEN IF COLLEGES ALIENATE YOU, JUST ACT LIKE THE LIBRARY IS YOURS
PART OF THE POINT OF GOING TO THE LIBRARY IS TO REALLY FOCUS YOUR MIND ON SOMETHING. BECOME REALLY INVOLVED IN SOMETHING THAT IS NOT YOUR LIFE. I RECOMMEND SPENDING AT LEAST TWO HOURS THERE, AND I DON'T MEAN TWO HOURS ON THE INTERNET. IT JUST ISN'T THE SAME.
I WOULD SUGGEST READING SOMETHING YOU'VE ALWAYS WONDERED ABOUT BUT NEVER THOUGHT YOU'D ACTUALLY EVER LEARN. LIKE THE HISTORY OF IRAQ, BRA BURNING, HOME BREW, BIKE REPAIR, BONNIE AND CLYDE.
if I have the time, I try to read a couple hours non fiction, and then an hour of fiction or biography.
It's amazing what having some new things to think about can do for your mental stability

ON YOUR WAY HOME CHECK THE DUMPSTERS
annes floral shop
SOMETIMES I WILL NEGLECT DUMPSTERING. LIKE I WILL LOOK JUST ONE PLACE AND GIVE UP IF IT SEEMS LIKE IT'S GARBAGE
CLOSED 9-6
BUT FINDING GOOD STUFF IN THE TRASH REALLY IS AN EXCEPTIONALLY GREAT THING
BON PAIN
HEY NICK! WHAT ARE YOU DOING OUT TONIGHT?
I'M OUT LOOKING FOR A SHITTY JOB THAT I'LL HATE + I'LL WORK MY ASS OFF MAKING THE BOSS RICH AND WITH THE PITTANCE I GET, I'M GONNA GO TO THE BAR AND WASTE IT ON FANCY BEER, OR MAYBE BUY SOME VINTAGE CLOTHES SO I CAN FEEL LIKE A DECENT HUMAN AND EKE SOME JOY OUT OF WHAT'S LEFT OF LIFE
BOOKS + NEWS
PHOTOS
HA HA HA HAHAHA HA HA HAHAHA
NO, REALLY?
I HEARD THEY THREW OUT A BUNCH OF CLOWN SUITS AT THE UNIFORM STORE TODAY AND I WAS GONNA SEE WHAT THEY'VE GOT DOWN AT TRADER JOES AND AT THE BAKERY
THRIFT TOWN
BAGEL O'RAMA
PIZZA GALORE
ARTS + CRAFTS STORE
PUT ON YOUR CLOWN SUIT!
LETS SIT + HAVE A BEER
POUR BEER INTO TRAVEL MUGS TO TRICK THE COPS
WANT PART OF YESTERDAY'S NEW YORK TIMES?
SURE
DAMN, WE HAVE ENOUGH PORTABELLA MUSHROOMS AND RED PEPPERS AND ASPARAGUS AND BREAD + JUICE BOXES TO HAVE A WILD FEAST!
WITH EXTRAS FOR THE KIDS ACROSS THE STREET AND FOOD NOT BOMBS
WHY DON'T THEY EVER CHECK THE FISH PLACE FOR ME?
THIS MAY SEEM CRAZY, BUT IT FEELS REALLY GOOD - EVEN IF YOU ARE IN A GOOD MOOD AND HAPPY ABOUT SOCIETY, YOU SHOULD STAND ON A BRIDGE, OR ON SOME HIGH PLACE, RAISE YOUR FIST + YELL
FUCK YOU WORLD!
AT THE TOP OF YOUR LUNGS.
IT'S FINE IF PEOPLE ARE AROUND. SOMETIMES IT'S EVEN BETTER

WHEN YOU GET HOME, COOK UP A BIG MEAL (AND MORE COFFEE!)
YOU DON'T KNOW HOW TO COOK! IT'S TOO HARD. DON'T MAKE TOO MUCH, YOUR ROOMMATES MIGHT EAT IT AND WHAT HAVE THEY EVER DONE FOR YOU?
COOKING IS EASY! IF YOU FUCK IT UP, JUST TRY AGAIN. OR ASK ADVICE. EXPERIMENT. COOK EXTRA. IT'S SAD WHEN EVERYONE ONLY COOKS FOR THEMSELVES. MAYBE YOU CAN START A HOUSE TREND
EAT AND MAYBE READ SOME OF THE NEWSPAPER, BUT DON'T LOITER TOO MUCH, BECAUSE NOW IT IS TIME TO SETTLE IN AND DO SOME WORK!
THIS IS REALLY GOOD! THANKS GUYS!
WORK?! I THOUGHT YOU SAID I SHOULD QUIT MY JOB!
TO GET SOME FULFILLMENT OUT OF LIFE, IT'S PRETTY IMPORTANT TO WORK HARD AT SOMETHING YOU REALLY CARE ABOUT — WHICH IS DIFFICULT SINCE IN OUR SOCIETY, THE ONLY WORK THAT IS REALLY VALUED IS A REGULAR JOB. AND MOST OF US HAVE INTERNALIZED THESE VALUE JUDGEMENTS, EVEN IF WE REBEL AGAINST THEM, AND IT'S HARD TO REALLY COMMIT THE TIME + ENERGY TO MAKE OUR DREAMS INTO GOALS AND THEN TO TAKE REAL STEPS TOWARD REACHING THOSE GOALS
YOU'VE GOT TO BREAK THROUGH THE SELF-DOUBT + FRUSTRATION AGAIN + AGAIN
AAARGH!
CRACK
POP
BASS FIXING KIT
AND IT IS HARD WORK. EVEN IF IT'S SOMETHING YOU LOVE — WRITING, ART, THEATER, RESEARCH STUDY, POLITICAL PROJECTS, LEARNING A TRADE.
IF YOU STOP DOING IT WHEN IT STOPS BEING FUN, YOU ARE DOING YOURSELF + THE WORLD A DISSERVICE
WHATEVER DUDE. I SAY IF IT'S NOT FUN, WHY DO IT?
I SUGGEST WORKING, UNINTERRUPTED, FOR AT LEAST FOUR HOURS
IF IT STARTS TO GET TO YOU TOO MUCH, PACE OR DANCE AROUND, DO A LITTLE YOGA OR STAND ON YOUR HEAD TO GET YOUR MENTAL JUICES FLOWING
OW
NOW... IF YOU'VE BEEN FOLLOWING THIS GUIDE DIRECTLY, YOU SHOULD HAVE 3-4 MORE HOURS LEFT TO YOUR DAY, AND NOW IT IS TIME TO...
relax

now it's time to...
drink
carlo rossi
fuck
masturbate
HITACHI MAGIC WAND
socialize
eat cake
WHOS BIRTHDAY?
YOURS
rock out
YA YA
raise hell
spray paint
burn down the town
swim in the lake
walk around
did I ever tell you...
steal a canoe
have a little romantic rendezvous
CINDY?
PSST. OVER HERE
ROCK OUT, RAISE HELL
DOG
H2O
HEY BABY, WHY DON'T YOU COME BACK TO BED?
I WILL, I WILL, BUT FIRST I GOTTA MAKE SUSHI! I JUST REALIZED THAT IF I MAKE IT NOW AND PACK IT UP, I CAN GO STRAIGHT FROM MY WALK TO THE LIBRARY WITHOUT EVEN COMMING HOME FOR LUNCH! AND PLUS, IT'S SO FUNNY. SUSHI IN THE LIBRARY. YOU KNOW. HAHAHA
...the end

it is easier to focus and more relaxing to be up in the night when everyone is sleeping and all the stores are closed.
making sushi every-day is help-full too
if you need a hide out, build a shack on squatted land
the end!
keep out
knock knock
WHAT?! WHAT DO YOU WANT?
HEY CINDY! I DON'T MEAN TO BUG YOU, BUT YOU HAVENT LEFT YOUR ROOM IN TWO MONTHS! WANNA GO WALK AROUND?
I DONT HAVE TIME!!! ALL I DO NIGHT + DAY IS WORK ON THE FUCKING DEPRESSION MAGAZINE! IF I DON'T GET IT DONE SOON I'M GONNA SHOOT MYSELF IN THE HEAD!
see
oh. right

Snarla wrote about pissing on her fingers. She wrote about costume and camouflage - about the power she got from acting crazy and giving people visible reasons to think that she was. It was an act put up to distract people from the real crazy thoughts that were in her head.

She called this disinformation, which was a good word for it, but I knew she was lieing. It was my lie too.

Snarla was the first girl fanzine I ever saw, and it was so important. so explosive, so secret, something I could do. It was a way to explore these things we tried to hide or hide behind, a forum for public discourse that we could control and define.

I acted crazy on purpose, but at the same time, I was scared that I really was crazy. I didn't know how to judge my emotions. I had no idea how normal people felt or survived. It's hard to explain in words the terror of this, but it was very real.

And the books and movies were no help at all. Crazy women were either just totally out of their minds, or else they were this symbol of innocence - they embraced life too strongly, or were too effected by injustice; and these women either killed themselves, went real crazy, or in some other way died or disapeared. The message was you couldn't be truely good and live in this world. You couldn't lift your face to the rain and say it tasted like wine. You couldn't love purely or live fully. You had to grow numb, but I didn't want to, and so I was afraid.

Snarla had a new conclusing, and I carried it with me in my pocket like a weapon. Maybe she did piss on her fingers, and we both wore fucked up wigs, and I walked around twitching and talking to myself when no one was looking. Maybe we did these things, but neither of us were crazy, not any more than anyone else was.

I read this book called Beyond Capitalism and Schizophrenia. not the whole book actually, just one small part that was pointed out. It was about how a lot of psychological and social problems are caused and reinforced by habit and the strict social rules that classify any response outside the norm as crazy. It said it was a political necessity to break out of these habits. If we were going to be able to imagine and create a new society, we had to create new responses and new ways of perceiving our world and its potentials.

I started with smoking. I knew it was stupid and not really what he was talking about, but what the hell. I'd leave work to go on a smoke break, but instead of smoking, I'd jump up and down and scream.

I tried different ways of walking, like looking up at the tops of buildings instead of in front of me, where I was going. People had to get out of my way I walked with low, long strides, trying to imitate HotHeadPaison. Life seemed more full and better. I could see the beauty and vibrancy. I could laugh outloud alone in the street, and grasp a world worth living and fighting for with selfish desire, instead of a sort of martyism. And if I cried in inappropriate places, refusing to hold it all in. If I didn't quiet down when my boyfriend said 'hush'. If I could not stand to be touched in some places, but happy as hell other places, other ways. If I could not leave the house after reading the newspaper. If I was scared shitless by the whole fucking world some days and felt like I could never trust anyone. And then other days was just bowled over by the fragile beauty of humanity. If I wanted it all, wanted to feel it all and grab it all and push everyone else to want it all too. No compromise, even though it obviously wasn't attainable. If this was crazy, if I was crazy, then fuck it, maybe crazy was the appropriate response to our situation.

Gulf War #I

Me and Casey baked a giant cake and wrote "Fuck You George Bush" on it, and brought it down to the rally at the state house. A cake to keep the spirits up and an excuse to interact. But one woman said "that language is violent and this is a non-violent protest".

In Minneapolis, the Youth Greens were staging puke-ins. You get 3 people to eat instant mashed potatoes, one person's dyed red with food coloring, one person's left plain, anothers dyed blue. They were attacking police and avoiding arrest, and once

help

stormed the TV station with a bunch of other groups, swarmed it, disrupted the news broadcast, almost tore the walls down, and then beat it out of there, cops everywhere in pursuit. My friends linked arms and started singing "We Shall Overcome", and ran into Nicollet Mall. The cops were stumped, what could they do with all these liberal shoppers around, cooing at the sweet 'nonviolent' kids. It would have been bad press to arrest them.

I wanted to be there, in Minneapolis, with them. So I moved back for that, but also (mainly) because Mom kept calling, drunk as always (was she drunk or did she just sound that way because she'd gone crazy).

I thought it was my fault that she had finally lost it. I had pushed her too hard, I had called too much into question. I had said "why didn't you protect me", and I had made her tell me her past. She had cried and held herself tightly, away from me, scared, saying "I put it behind me. Don't make me do this". I told her I needed to know.

That was the trend at the time; full disclosure was the only way to become a healthy person. I thought she owed it to me. I made her tell me.
I thought that was what broke her, the last straw, me making her speak it outloud. I thought it was all my fault, but that's what I thought about most bad things then. Out of self importance, or guilt, or a combination of it all, I usually felt like most things were my fault.

World War Two

During WWII, there were not enough men left around to fill all the traditionally male jobs, so they had to get the middle class white women to do them. The images of women in the popular media changed; partially because women were now actively involved in the media, and partially because the change of image was a social necessity.

Movies, advertisments and women's magazines started showing women with options and dreams. The heroines in the stories were independent and strong-willed, adventurers, carrerists, or at least more or less holding their own. They were out of the house and active, vital participants in the running of society. When the war was ending and the boys were coming back, these women were pushed out of their jobs and into the prefab houses and suburbs created, ready and waiting for the post war baby boom.

Businesses had to hike consumer sales to make up for their lost war contracts. I am not assuming this or making it up - it was a financial decision and talked about outright in research studies and magazine articles.

Women were considered the best market, and it was in the country's financial interest to help women find their identity and sense of self worth in ever more

effective housekeeping - to educate women through advertising and encourage them to be modern housewives.

Women with financial resources needed to getback to the home, and the social fabric needed to be rewritten again. With lightning speed, the images changed, glorifying traditional feminine qualities; subservient and smiling with a house, a husband and kids. If you didn't have these things, or if you weren't fulfilled completely by this role, there must be something wrong with you.

By the late 50's, women were marrying at a much younger age and having twice as many kids. Women were dropping out of college to get married in record numbers. Having too much education was seen as a liability, too smart was not desirable in a wife, and what would you do with a degree anyway?

Life in the suburbs was supposed to be the perfect American life, but it had it's downside which for a long time went unspoken.

The women felt crazy. They cried for no reason, felt like they didn't exist, empty, incomplete. The therapists, when they'd finally seen enough cases to admit that it was a wide spread phenomenon, called it "Housewife Syndrome" and the accompanying physical symptoms that sometimes came with it - blisters and hives and excessive sleeping - "housewife blight".

Soon schools took on a new sex-directed education plan to help deal with this problem. They decided to teach girls and women to adjust to their roles, protecting them from the desire to use critical or creative skills.

Many schools, both highschools and colleges, had compulsary "functional courses in Marriage and theFamily. Classes like "Mate Selection", "Adjustment to Marriage", "The Slick Chic"(a jr. high class that taught the importarce of wearing slips and bras).

Ivy League colleges and women's colleges even bought into it, taking on incredable slogans like Mills College's "We are not educating women to be scholars, we are educating them to be wives and mothers".

It was all pretty unbelievable and sadly effective. One study showed that IQ levels were dropping in adolescent girls. When these girls were interviewed, they talked about not wanting to be too smart. They had consciously arrested their mental development to conform to the feminine ideal.

My mom didn't go to college in the 50's. I think she entered in '64. Smith college, an Ivy League girls school. Everyone there had to have their photograph taken, it was judged for posture and if it wasn't good enough, you had to take a class. You could not graduate without passing your posture picture.
It is hard for me to imagine that world, and I'm afraid that we are losing ground and that the gains we'vemade are being taken for granted. I'm surprised that so many women I know don't consider themselves feminists. I think it is so important still.

Studying feminism helped me understand my mother's life and mine. It gave me such a stronger and less reactionary, less hopeless view of the world and how we could change it.

laquer and spring

When we left Asheville this spring, I felt like we had failed. Like I had nothing left to give to my community, and most of the people around seemed to be in a similar boat - working on things they cared about that no one else really took much interest in. I had forgotten how to talk or interact with anyone but Caty and Issac, and I felt crazy, didn't know if it wasme or the town.

So I drove to New York, to the skyline and into it, into the tangles of traffic, under blimps and planes with banners, and I wondered how people kept their eyes on the road when there was so much to look at.

I parked the van. I had to find a bathroom and a phone and get some change and make a call. Simple things I know, but I'm not so good at them. I used to be better when I was young and bold and still creating myself. I felt all the time like I was on stage, and I acted to amuse myself or to fulfill what I thought other people might want to see. Most often, I acted out something that had the potential of being saved. I slipped in and out of this fantasy, walking to the back of a bar to make a phone call, I would look nervously around, pretending I was a runaway being followed, or a junky, or an escapee from a psych ward, talking under my breath to my other personalities. I stood with good posture and slipped inaand out of fantasy, which wasn't hard because the world was still untested and I had very little comprehension of what the possibilities were.

Now my alienation is more sunk in and I feel uncomfortable in most inside public places, like there's a code word and it's not my world, not even my world to consume in.

For awhile this was alright, because I didn't want to be a part of this world anyway. But now I'm trying to use logic and stop being so neurotic. So down on 8th street and the west side highway, I slide into an old diner. I order whatever I can think of first. I make a phone call and wait, writing postcards in the corner, almost at ease, waiting for Roo.

He walks in and I know him even though I've never met him. He has crooked glasses, crooked teeth, lock and chain and he bounces with each step, welcoming and overexcited and keeping eye contact the way he is in his stories, which is the most of what I know of him, written over the years, photocopied and sent.

I thought maybe I had forgotten empathy, or had finally grown up and lost interest. Or that friendship took up too much time, or that I'd forgotten how to be part of people's lives without being enveloped. But right away, Roo's manner and his words spilling over, and his genuine interest in things; and then Amy on the back porch, frustratedly sawing a fish out of wood to laquer her resume to, and Jon in his room, busy working despite the noise. Like a dream I'd given up on, a group of people I could grow and flourish with, they made sense and they had a place for me.

We sat around the table, talking about things I never get to talk about - how much to fictionalize, lay out problems, punk, city planning, whether to paint the shadows first or last, ethical issues, future goals, growing older and developing a stronger sense of self. Jon came out of his room holding up a chart and shouting "I've figured out how the brain processes music! Look!"

We made coffee, more coffee, and smoked cigerettes on the back porch, and then drank to e achother when the sun went down. Drank for Darby in Israel, and took a shot every time the stock market decline was announced on NPR.

The next morning, I decided to leave. I figured they must have been just being polite when they told me their house was mine and I should stay for as long as I liked. I told them I was going to Cape Cod to get out of their hair, but they just climed in the van and came along.

It was spring, and I thought it would still be too early for tourists, and that it would look like it had the winter me and Issac squatted there. I told them they could come with me, but when we got there, I'd have to walk it alone.

I'm not surewhat I wanted exactly, but it felt like I wanted to unbury something there. Trace the worn path through the woods to the unexposed side of the house, and then back again, past the Senior Center, down to thebeach with the seagulls, and to the library to the How To books, where I sat trying to figure out how to turn our water on. I wanted to unbury the glory of it, because I know it was a good life, and I know I wasn't miserable there. But when I thought about it, I mostly felt just the loneliness and fear.

I thought it would be a ghost town, exactly like how I'd left it, but it wasn't, it was packed, it was unrecognizable. I lost my bearings immediately, we tried to walk on the beach and kids divebombed us with kites. I said "This is terrible, this is not what I meant. I don't know what to do. I'm so sorry, don't leave me alone with this mess!" They laughed and said "Do you want to just get the fuck out of here?"

We drove to the ocean side of the peninsula, tall hills of sand between the road and the ocean. We climbed up one to see how far it was. It looked far, but not too far, a dark band in the distance. We walked and walked, sometimes together and sometimes apart, pointing out flowers in the briars and paths through the twisted sand dune trees. Walked and walked and finally got to the thing that we hadmistaken for the ocean, a small airport runway. We watched the small planes land and decided to cross it and keep going. There was a plane in the distance and I ran down the runway, acting out that movie, like the plane was after me, and when I looked over my shoulder, it was. It was right there behind me! Planes come in a lot faster than I thought. I tell you, they are probably better not to mess around with.

We walked further and finally we got to the ocean, walked right up to it and crouched down, hands out on the wet sand, waiting for the next wave to come in. I almost forgot to tast it. I took my glasses off, put them in my pocket, splashed the water on my face, trying to get it in my eyes. I stuck my tongue out and tasted the salt dripping down my face.

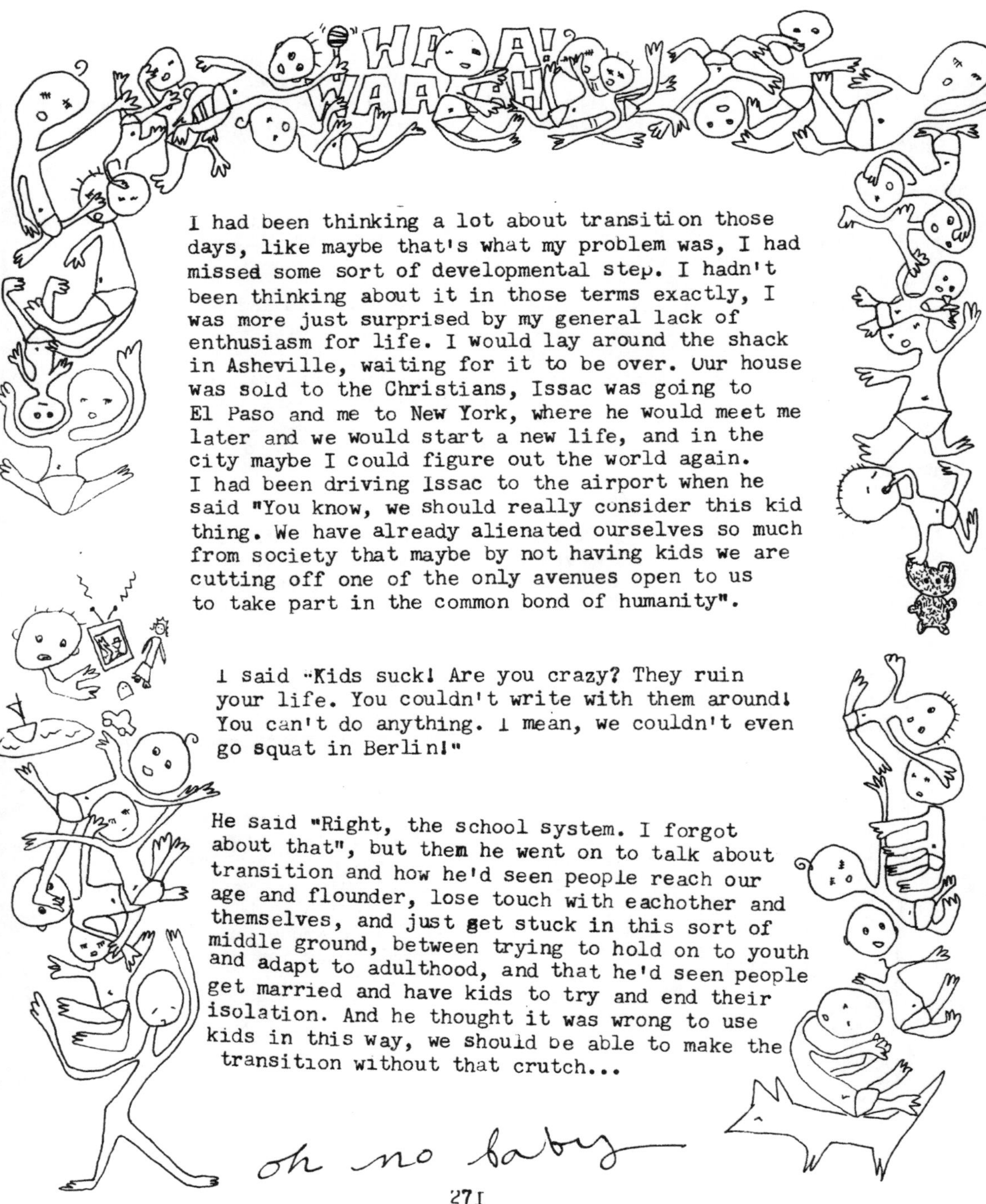

I had been thinking a lot about transition those days, like maybe that's what my problem was, I had missed some sort of developmental step. I hadn't been thinking about it in those terms exactly, I was more just surprised by my general lack of enthusiasm for life. I would lay around the shack in Asheville, waiting for it to be over. Our house was sold to the Christians, Issac was going to El Paso and me to New York, where he would meet me later and we would start a new life, and in the city maybe I could figure out the world again. I had been driving Issac to the airport when he said "You know, we should really consider this kid thing. We have already alienated ourselves so much from society that maybe by not having kids we are cutting off one of the only avenues open to us to take part in the common bond of humanity".

I said "Kids suck! Are you crazy? They ruin your life. You couldn't write with them around! You can't do anything. I mean, we couldn't even go squat in Berlin!"

He said "Right, the school system. I forgot about that", but them he went on to talk about transition and how he'd seen people reach our age and flounder, lose touch with eachother and themselves, and just get stuck in this sort of middle ground, between trying to hold on to youth and adapt to adulthood, and that he'd seen people get married and have kids to try and end their isolation. And he thought it was wrong to use kids in this way, we should be able to make the transition without that crutch...

oh no baby

But I did know why. It was because here we were, the punks, anarchists, etc. We'd created a world and broken the barriers for who and how to love and the role it plays in our larger lives; for what and how to feel - intensely, everything, disgust and hate and beauty and curiosity. We picked up garbage and made art and houses, left messages for strangers, and what now? right? what now? because it wasn't new or challenging, it wasn't enough to repeat it all. ride bikes looking for something or someone or nothing, up all night because there was so much to see and feel and do, no time for sleep, all music and plans and disclosure and testimony and kissing, sleeping any old place. So what now? Because I didn't want to keep being so sad this way, going through the motions to try to get the feeling back, and wondering why, if I was so glad to get older, every year less self hate, less drams. If I was so glad, why did half my insides feel like I had given up and grown bitter? I thought we just needed new challenges, and I did really want to study. I wanted the kind of contentment I could see coming, where I would be able to focus and sit at my desk every day for hours, practicing dialogue, description, metaphor, learning control of this language, which I have always wanted but always been too distracted, too full of living. I could see it, and see it in a context of a larger community, but I didn't have it, didn't feel it yet, not so completely.

I got lost in his sentances. Couldn't figure out why he was talking about this, or what his problem was. I thought adulthood sounded great. I felt myself growing into it, getting calmer, less defensive, more self assured. But something was missing, that was for sure. I'd get drunk and talk about how suicidal I was, and how strange to feel that again after all these years. Out at the bonfire, I brought it up like casual conversation, andRyan pulled me to him, took my hands between his two and asked me why, but I didn't know why, that was the sucky thing.

I had gotten this weird idea in my head that the rest of the world was doing just fine and it was only us, left to stagnate, confused. We had wanted too much and jackhammered up the traditional roads. I had been talking about this to my sister before I went to New York. I said "Maybe Issac was right, you know, not like you have to have kids, but he did have a point, and what are we doing anyway? I mean, fuck, what if we blew it, and it'll be too late after the vasectomy." Caty said "Wait, are you trying to say you're wondering if you need to have kids to get that wonder in life back? To be happy?"
"I guess that's what normal people do", I said.
"Normal people are on Prozac!"

We both just laughed. What had I been thinking? It's a shitty world, we aren't doing so bad.

I ran into my old political collective at the all day punk street fair, where there were ancient punks doing skateboard tricks and I didn't see how they did them without breaking bones. All day, bands playing and drinking in the street, and I sat on the curb, first time in NY that I'd ever sat still. Akward, shy, happy, and bored.

The cops came at sundown, and we went to the bar, and my old collective, they got me drunk, as usual, and I turned into the crosseyed, leaning and yelling over the music, maladjusted freaked out girl, repeating more or less the same refrain as I do every year.

"Are you happy? Do you feel well adjusted? Like people understand you?" They said "Yes, no problem, we're satisfied".

I didn't like or trust the answer, I never did, it seemed wrong to me. I yelled "Well, what do you do with your anger?"
They said "Play baseball", and then they asked me what I did.

I was sick of it all. They wanted to know what I did with my anger? I yelled "Fight!" and started wswinging with a seriousness that surprised me, and then left the bar to try and make it home before blacking out. But it was Brooklyn and I had no idea where I was going. So I curled up by the dumpster, layed my head down on my bag and tried to fall asleep and forget about it all. I was thinking that if I had the energy to pull the dumpster a few inches from the wall, I could slither in behind it and sleep there just fine. No one would dare fuck with me. I had slept in worse places, but I had always had my dog.

I was thinking I had lived a better life than those people in the bar, and then I was thinking about how my life had been one big waste of time. And then that I was being stupid and melodramatic, and why did I always think they had better answers than mine

when I knew they didn't. I crept back into the bar, and they laughed with their tender concern, and walked me to the subway, arm in arm.

On the street, there was a man sitting on the stoop of a store with the metal gate closed over the door. He was feeding the pigeons as I walked by. Another man came up. "Hey Hal! You still living here on 4th?" "Yep, still here. Give me another year I'd say", and their conversation fades behind me. There are little flower gardens under all the trees, purple flowers I don't know the name of yet, and a nursery right on Houston.

There was a man and another man, one with rollerblades, on with a bike and a boxer puppy. They were trying to teach the puppy to sit. and then said "Now we teach you to run with the bike", there was exhasperation and love in his voice, and I knew it wouldn't be easy.

It is the weekend of forth of July, and everyone's on the corners looking at their maps. We go to the free sundown movies at the park behind the library. It is raining and I thought it would be canceled, and so did Issac, but he met me at the steps anyway and I showed up too, with a huge umbrella that I found in the garbage because the handle had broken off.
They didn't let therain stop the movie. And the cops in trench coats joked around with the people, ignoring the wine cups with the picnics here and there.
It was a small homey crowd. A plane flew overhead and dropped little pieces of tissue paper, red white and blue, that moved jerkily with every catch of the wind. People reached out their arms to catch them. Everyone staring up at the sky, murmering "it is so beautiful", or once "what is this? state sponsored littering?" People were catching different colors and trading. Issac said "Some people really know how to make a city", and I'm not sure if he means the planes and papers and having an excuse to look up with wonder, and the people moving in circles, arms out, bumping into eachother; or if he means the young punk who was sitting in front of us, eating strawberries with his date, umbrella cast aside, who were right then walking by us, girl on his arm and she was saying, very skeptically, "Are you sure you know where to get coffee around here?"

reprints
doris
#17
these are all stories That were written for other people's zines + The short story from before I'd discovered That such a Thing existed

It was kind of amazing, the amount of crap my uncle had stored up there in his attic. Crates of wild rice, hundreds of computer disks, old tools and cords and switches. clothes he would never wear again, posters he made in the 60s. There was a small piece of foam crammed between it all, and for a month and a half, that was mine and my sisters home. It was our own little purgatory where we'd sit for hours, drenched in sweat, reading and grumbing and trying to figure out what the hell to do. We'd escaped one city where there were death threats on our answering machine, laquer poured in our locks, and we ended up in the attic of the only family member we could stand.

Attic living was a blur of heat and sleep. In the day I'd ride around on my bike looking for one of my crushes, I'd find my sister in the park warding off creeps, and we'd sulk back through the house, trying to avoid friendly concerned questions. We'd crawl up into our hovel. It was my sister and me, living together at last, but our plans were thwarted, our dreams doomed. Steal a car and go to North Carolina, find some small town, somehow, somewhere on the ocean and move there where everything would be salty and quiet. But she was sick, the dog was too big, and secretly I wanted to stay.

At night we'd make soup out of half rotten vegetables, we'd sneak our 2 friends up into the attic and read them bedtime stories, trying to give them some hope even though we didn't really have any to spare. I hauled out my typewriter and started writing my secrets, laughing and pretending that I could draw. We played music and danced on our bed, talked confused politics and read to eachother, we'd collect dirty dishes on top of the unplugged tv. It was our crazy desolate sanctuary, and if we could make it out of there, we said, we could make it out of anywhere.

for attic zine

ice cream · short story

Dear Neigre,

It snowed yesterday, two feet of soft bitter cold, and it looked like the day after the apocalypse. I walked to my job, and had to borrow a shovel from the corner market to clear the sidewalk in front of our shop. I call it our shop already, as if it were mine. I've worked here two months now, and Joe lets me open and work most of the day by myself. He comes in at six and drops off the caramel rolls and muffins. I make the coffee and ice cream. Joe's working on building a kitchen in the side room. He asked me which tile to get, white or red. I didn't know. He'll hire a baker once the kitchen is done, and I'm not looking forward to it. I like working alone. The sound of the ice cream mixer turning and turning is much softer than someone's voice. Joe bakes everything now. He stays up all night kneading dough and boiling sugar into caramel. The kitchen in his house is huge, with two black ovens. I've never seen it and he's never told me about it, but I'm sure it is this way.

Paul stopped by the shop today. I gave him ice cream for free. What else could I do? He rode his bike all the way across town in the snow to see me. I wish he hadn't. It's been two months since I moved out of his one room apartment and he still tries to talk me into coming back. He tells me how dangerous my neighborhood is. I'm not afraid and I don't love him. He doesn't understand the first thing about not having money, nor does he know how to cook or kiss or ask me what I want with my life. He doesn't know how to run through the sand or make angels in the snow. I wish he would leave me alone. I wish he had left me or hit me or cheated or lied. Then I wouldn't have to feel so bad and he would understand why I left and wouldn't ride his bike through the snow to order mocha ice cream.

I went out last night with a boy I met at work. He's a regular and has muffins and coffee every morning. We went to a cafe down the block and played cards. He was not like how I thought he would be. I thought he was a sculptor who made huge people out of metal scraps from the junkyard. I thought he was from Ireland and wrote notes to himself on small pieces of paper. I thought he lived with two dogs and a parakeet that talked, but I was wrong.

I'm sending along some photo booth pictures. I colored them in, but my hair really is that shade of red. Do they have photo booths in New Zealand?

I don't have any photo booth pictures but I'll go uptown after work and get some taken with the change I've made in tips. Every time I write Neigre she writes me back. I think it's strange. Her letters talk about plays she's seen, dances she's gone to, her friends, her boy friend. They're full of advice that I ignore.

The baker Emma starts today, and I don't want to meet her. Every time the door opens, I think it will be her, tracking in slush and whistling. She isn't due 'til nine but I'm afraid she'll be early.

I go into the side room and start up a batch of butterscotch. It's a kitchen now, with two big black ovens, green tiles, fluorescent lights, a long white counter, and pots and pans hanging from a thing on the ceiling. When Emma's here she'll stand at the counter, look to her left and watch me sitting on my stool.

I make a new pot of coffee, pour myself a cup and drink it with a spoonful of cinnamon ice cream. From my stool behind the ice cream counter, I look over Joe's accounting. Business is slow. I'm good with numbers, though if anyone knew me, they wouldn't guess it.

A woman in jeans and black galoshes walks in, stands in the doorway, and taps her heals together to knock off the slush. She doesn't wear makeup and has thick black hair. She's not whistling.

"Hi," she says as she bends down to take off her boots. "I'm Emma".

I say, "Yeah, Joe told me you'd be in today but he said you were coming at nine."

"I thought I'd come in early and have some coffee and meet you and all that. Did he finish the kitchen last night?"

"Almost," I tell her, and she walks behind the counter like the place is hers. I pour her a cup of coffee, hoping she'll go back and sit at one of the seven white tables. She walks into the kitchen and looks around.

I hand her a list Joe left with me of things she's supposed to make. She smiles but when her eyes meet mine, her smile wavers a bit. I wish I could apologize, but I can't. In the first five minutes of meeting her, I can tell she's glad to be coming here and she's wishing I'd become her friend. I don't want her to like me and don't care to think stories about her.

A young girl comes in with her very young sister. They ask for tastes of three different flavors then order chocolate on cones. They've been ice-skating on the pond nearby with their Irish Setter. They tied her to a tree to keep watch over their skates. They live in the basement apartment of a young couple's house with their mom and dad. Their dad is young and sings songs in the morning with them so loud the neighbors sometimes complain. He's saving money to buy the girls a banjo and a fiddle. The apartment has only three rooms, two bedrooms and a living room with a kitchen right in it. They don't always have money to eat ice cream but they found a five-dollar bill frozen in the pond and picked at the ice with their skates until it was free. I know this because the money was wet. When they eat their ice cream, they get chocolate all over. If I were their older sister I would wipe their faces with a napkin.

Emma knows I don't like her. We've worked together four days now and we barely talk, which makes me dislike her less. This morning a girl my age came in and ordered coffee and a raspberry croissant. She ate slowly while she studied calculus. She doesn't hate her classes, which are all too big, so she sits in the first row. When the professor isn't looking, she draws pictures of him with larger than life features. She has friends and likes to sit on the top of city parking ramps late at night and watch the cars and people below. I go into the kitchen to check on the chocolate fudge brownies Emma's making, they are not quite done. I watch Emma knead dough, her hands covered with flour and water. I don't hate her. "Emma?" I say, wishing I hadn't said her name, and she turns around.

"Yeah?"

"Do you like ice cream?" She hasn't had any the whole four days. Not even a taste.

"I love it," she says, "but I didn't really feel right just taking it."

"Well, do you want some?"

"I'd take vanilla."

I get it for her and leave the kitchen quickly. I hope she doesn't start talking to me.

I got a letter back from Neigre. Her sister got married and the whole family got together and celebrated for a week. Neigre still has a father and mother. Paul has a father and a mother too, and grandparents. I guess this isn't so strange. I have a mother and no sisters. My grandparents are dead. If I get married, there will be a very small wedding. I can't imagine wearing a white gown.

I give Emma ice cream most every day and she's brought in a stool. She asked if I'd mind if she sat behind the ice cream counter with me. I could only say I didn't. It's not so bad. She brings out her big, floured cutting board and kneads dough on the counter. When the ice cream mixer is going, it plays harmony to her hands. Her first day sitting next to me, she poured me a cup of coffee, put in a spoonful of cinnamon ice cream and said, "You don't like talking much, do you?"

"No."

"That's fine," she said, "I understand. I don't blame you. But if you ever want to," and her voice trailed off. I'm not sure what she understands, but she doesn't talk to me any more and I watch the customers.

We've worked together a month and a half now. I know nothing about Emma but I feel like she knows too much about me. I don't tell her anything so I don't understand how she knows. I never think about her when I'm at home. I tried once, but couldn't remember her face, or even the way her hands move when she kneads bread. When I'm at home I make collages out of the garbage I find on the street. I cook Indian food and draw pictures of the neighborhood children plying. They play hopscotch now that the snow's gone from the sidewalk.

Emma is learning to speak Spanish and sometimes she talks to me in that language I don't understand. It's pretty so I don't mind. Yesterday she wrote something down on a napkin and gave it to me. I put it in one of my collages, wanting to ask her what it means.

She is making apple bread. The door opens and Jonas comes in. He's a dancer and drinks black coffee. I pour him a cup and he leaves the change on the counter. He doesn't say hello, never does. When he shuts the door, I look over at Emma and she's not there. She's taking croissants out of the oven and putting in cinnamon rolls. I get up and start a batch of coconut ice cream, pour myself a coffee and offer Emma a cup. She's taken to drinking her coffee with a spoonful of cinnamon ice cream too, and sits on her stool next to mine.

"Hey Polly?" she says.

"Yeah"

"What do you think about, sitting there?"

I think it's strange that she wants to know. I tell her "Just now, when that boy was here, I was thinking of his grandmother who used to take him for long walks. When he was a kid she taught him to find wild blueberries, track deer, catch fish. They'd take picnics to the meadow, eat oranges and watch the caterpillars, inchworms, grasshoppers, ants, and those big black beetles with long antenna and hard shells. I was thinking about how he hasn't left the city since she died."

Emma stares at me and I think I shouldn't have told her. She says, "It didn't seem like you knew him. I mean, you didn't talk to him or anything."

I sort of laugh.

I don't mind Emma. It's strange now. Whenever she's not busy, I tell her about the people who come in, about this man who has had six tanks of goldfish since he was five, the boy who doesn't like baseball and would like to spend his afternoons drawing still lifes. That woman who fixes cars and grows daffodils.

Today a girl our age comes in and orders coffee and vanilla in a dish. She's glad it's spring and vears red and black striped tights. I begin to tell Emma about this girl's feelings for the weather when Emma says, "Wait. Can I tell you about her?"

Emma starts with the quiet whisper we're used to, so the customers won't hear. "You're right, he's glad it's spring. She can finally open the windows for a few hours in the day and air out her attic partment. The apartment's small and she wants to paint over the chipped green walls, but she never has he time. In fact, I don't know how she found the time to come here today. She woke up at five o'clock o make tea for her grandmother Kata, who told the girl her dream. "I dreamt I was nineteen and in Spain again during the war. It was exactly like it had been. I stood next to Lexa and Francisco singing nd holding our guns over our heads while the troops shot. Line after line of our dead bodies but none of s shot back. 'Come to us,' we called to them, until they put down their guns and came."

"Kata said this happened, but the girl isn't sure. She sat at the big wooden table, placing piece fter piece of cut glass into lead, another piece of glass, another strip of lead, blue white, the full figure f the Virgin Mary, holding a child, and then she soldered it together. She's afraid she'll get lead oisoning, but Kata's hands are too tired to work any more, so the girl must do it all.

"Since Kata stopped working, she's been dreaming of Spain, telling stories of Spain, even hinking she's there. 'We are finally free,' she says, over and over, until she starts crying.

"One day Kata pulled the shades and they sat in darkness all day. The girl kept quiet and tretched piece after piece of lead until she had enough for two windows. Kata spoke in a quiet voice Don't worry Terecina, we will get out of here,' and she hummed a lullaby. Terecina is the girl's mother.

"All the girl remembers about her mother is the drive they took in a blue station wagon. They rove for hours, eating marshmallows and sandwiches, looking out the windows. At night they got to the house of a large woman. The house was small and cold and her mother cooked fish and potatoes. They slept on the bedroom floor for two nights until the woman started moaning and Terecina told the girl, get this, do that, hold her hand, watch. An hour later a baby came out from the large woman.

"When they left, they went to a stream, a small trickle of water. 'This is where the Mississippi starts' her mother said. The girl walked across it. Then they drove back to the city.

"Sometimes when the girl can't sleep, she catches the last bus to the University, walks down to the river, and waits there until sunrise."

Emma's eyes are closed. We didn't notice the girl leave and the ice cream mixing too long. I'm jealous of Emma's story. It's not like my stories. It's more like Emma. It's real. The buzzer goes off for the oven and Emma puts down her cold coffee. We've fallen behind in our work, but we split a hot cinnamon roll before returning.

The girl with the black and red tights comes in again and Emma tells me more story.

"Today the girl finished the Virgin Mary and Child window. It was fifteen feet by seven and she was packing it in a wooden crate to send off to Wisconsin when Kata whispered 'Come here'.

"The girl went over and sat at the foot of the bed. Kata said, 'your mother left you here when you were five. That's what I told you, that she left you, but it's not true.'

'I didn't think she left, ' the girl said quietly, 'but I don't remember.'

'She was taken. They came and took her because she was right. She wanted freedom and they always do anything to take that from us. I want to see her again before I die. I need to know they didn't break her.'

"The girl was afraid of Kata dying. She didn't know what to do. She comes here, hoping to make friends. Like us, she doesn't have any. She wants to stay up until three in the morning talking about changing the world. She wants to plant gardens on the rooftops of abandoned buildings, run along the tops of parked train cars, and play hopscotch in the rain like she did when she was ten and Kata drew hopscotch boards on the sidewalk in colored chalk.

"The girl has dreams where her mother is walking through a forest of oak trees holding a picnic basket and calling her name until her voice is hoarse and she can't talk any more. In her dream, she thinks the forest is beautiful, but when she enters it, she sees the trees are planted in straight lines.

"She is writing down her dreams, trying to get her memory back. She sleeps very little so she'll have time to make windows, take care of Kata, and write her memories. See the ink on her hand? She's writing about the time she had to change schools because she told Kata that every day in the room the other girls would corner her and chant 'Your mom kills babies. Why didn't she kill you?'"

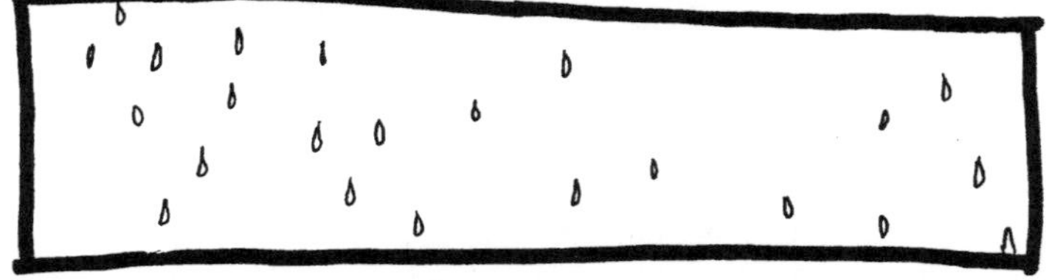

A few days ago, Tommy came in. His name really is Tommy. While I was fixing him a dish of bubble gum ice cream he told me he was new in the city and asked me what places to see. I didn't know what to say. He asked me out and I said yes. I should have known better.

He's from Tucson," I told Emma after he left, "and when he's home alone he plays his grandfather's accordion and dances jigs, he has five cats and listens to albums of tropical rain forests when he's trying to fall asleep. Every night he dreams about his seven brothers and sisters."

We went to a club. He didn't know how to dance and was mad that I did. We went to the park and sat on a bench. He told me he was from Oregon, likes windsurfing and doesn't have any pets. He tried to kiss me. I walked home.

I told Emma this. She said, "Did you really expect him to be from Tucson and all that?"

"I don't know," I said. I thought she would understand, but we haven't talked much since.

I don't have any friends and I like it that way. They're confusing and take too much time. They never call and don't know how to cook or make beautiful things. And then they always leave. Yesterday, I went to the airport to watch the planes come in. I saw a young boy with roller-skates and a woman with a goat bone necklace. There was a woman with a statue of Elvis and one with a Peter Pan hat. I followed the woman with the hat and almost asked her if I could have it. Then I went home.

At home I thought about the girl with the black and red tights. I could see every freckle on her face, the ink on her hand. I thought about this girl; how I would like to sit across from her and listen to her write, refill her coffee cup when she needed it. I wouldn't mind at all if she chose to talk. I thought about her small apartment, the colors of glass, Spain and her dreams. And when I slept I dreamt I was holding her hand on the front lines of a war.

It's Tuesday and not very busy. Emma makes blueberry muffins while I put together our new espresso machine. Emma seems sad lately. I don't particularly care, but business is slow and I fix her a dish of vanilla with colored sprinkles. When I give it to her I think she'll cry. I hate tears. I don't cry.

A couple comes in and they split a hot fudge sundae and a large cappuccino. The first coffee I've made with our new machine turns out fine. I go into the kitchen and tell Emma about them.

"They got married last week in Vegas by an Elvis impersonator. She wears rings on every finger to disguise that one, then they lost thirty dollars on slot machines and listened to tapes of Liberace while the sun set. He's a bartender and doesn't like sports, and she has a closet full of clothes that are green and black. She doesn't dress up. In the winter they go to the river and picnic behind the frozen falls. She likes tuna fish and red wine. He likes celery with peanut butter. She dreams in vivid colors and talks in her sleep, and her toenails are painted gold.

Emma smiles but doesn't stop greasing the two twelve by eight pans for the brownies. I turn off the mixer, scoop the ice cream into buckets, and start up a batch of lemon. I go back to my stool behind the ice cream counter.

The woman with the black and red tights comes in. She orders tea and strawberry coffee cake, and sits down with her notebook. She's been in five times since Emma told her stories, but I never told Emma she was here.

"The girl with the grandmother is here," I say.

"I'll be right out."

I watch the girl write. She has thin hands that move fast, then slow. They stop. She looks out the window. If she would dictate, I would write for her.

Emma comes out and sits on her stool next to mine. She has her floured board with her and is kneading cinnamon bread. She watches the girl for a while and doesn't say anything.

"Tell me about her friends." I say.

"I told you, she doesn't have time for friends. She has to make windows, buy groceries, pay rent, cook. When she was twelve she had a friend. He was fifteen and lived in the house below the attic. He still lives there but they never talk. They used to take walks around the lake, chase ducks, watch the stars, talk. She wanted to marry him someday, until her pulled her into a little closet. He said his mother told him to stop hanging around her because she was bad and bound to be a slut because her mom was in jail and her grandfather had been hung. "I'll get you started," he said. He put his hand tight over her mouth and raped her. She didn't make a sound. Afterward she bled and wished her mother would come back."

The buzzer rings. Emma goes into the kitchen and doesn't come back. I want to sit down with the girl and follow her home. I want to hold her hand and walk around the lake late at night and listen to her. If she were my friend I'd tell her that I'm afraid of Christmas. I'd show her my collages and my shelf of special things. No one's seen these things. I'd have her over to my house and cook soup. We'd eat by candlelight and laugh until morning. My cats would like her. I'd help her take care of Kata and she'd teach me to cut glass. But I can't sit down with her. Emma would say, "Did you really expect her to be that way?"

The girl leaves and Emma comes back and sits beside me. I give her coffee with a scoop of cinnamon.

"I'd be her friend if I could," I say.

Emma says "Me too."

It's been three days since Emma's come in. She called and said there was a family emergency, but Joe doesn't believe her. He told her not to bother coming back. He's mad, works all day and night, swears every time he makes caramel rolls. I try to defend Emma, but I don't know what to say. Joe works with me all day, but he doesn't sit next to me on Emma's stool. His hands knead bread to a different rhythm than the ice cream mixer. I can't go into the kitchen and tell him that Jonas just walked in with eyes red from crying, that his grandmother talked to him in a dream. Joe wouldn't know what I meant. I can't tell him I got another letter from Neigre, that she might come visit, and I'm afraid. The girl with red and black tights comes in and Joe doesn't have a story about her. It's lonely and I think that's weird.

The girl with the blue hair comes in and asks me if I'd like to go swimming with her on Tuesday. I say I'm busy. I lie. I know it's of no use to even try. She'd be an only child and hate poetry. She drinks her coffee and leaves.

I haven't seen Emma for two weeks. Joe hired a new baker, Jonathon, and his hands are tanner than Emma's. He doesn't like cinnamon ice cream in his coffee and he talks too much.

The girl with the black and red tights comes in again, wearing green tights for the first time. She orders coffee and a caramel roll and sits down at a table and writes. I watch her and every time she brings her cup up to her lips, I drink from mine. She reminds me of Emma and it hurts my stomach. When we're done with our coffee I offer her more. She accepts, and while I pour I try to read what she's writing in her black leather notebook. I ask her and she looks at me with heavy brown eyes. "Articles for this newsletter I work with." I look closely at her hands. They are not full of little glass cuts. She is not writing dreams and memories. I tell Jonathon I'm going outside for a bit.

I think of Emma and can picture everything about her, her hands when she would wash them after kneading dough, they're strong, scratched like mine from my cats, only her cuts are deeper.

Joe comes in at five to take over. Jonathon offers to walk me home, but I tell him I'm going to visit a friend and this is not a lie. I walk uptown and down to the lake, then around it until I get to a large blue and grey house. There are stairs up the back to the attic apartment, open windows.

I usually avoid stairs. When I was little I fell down them five times and got stitches under my chin, my lip, head. You can't see any of the scars, but I walk up these stairs slowly. A woman my mother's age – she has thick black hair and a face like Emma's – steps out the door.

"Is Emma home?"

"You must be Polly. I'm Emma's mom."

She shows me in. Emma is holding Kata in her arms, calming her, Terecina takes over. "It's me. It's fine," she says softly.

I give Emma the cup of coffee with cinnamon ice cream I brought for her.

"How did you find me?" she asks, her eyes swollen.

"I looked up your address."

"I didn't think you'd come."

"I told you I'd be that girl's friend." I take her hands, this girl whose life I never cared to make stories about.

Everything goes the right speed on my rollerskates, and I feel like I'm just pulling my awkward body along, up hills through Vallejo, to a big empty fountain with a sign that says "no wading". The water is clear. There is no one to wade in it, just one old lady and me.

We left Berkeley at four o'clock, sped through rush hour traffic and arrived at the junkyard three hours late. "Maybe he'll show up after he eats dinner", Chris says, "We can wait here all night if we have to. I need that car!"

Chris had told us earlier that it would be a two hour trip, but I'm learning to expect delays. And really, what reason is there to go back? In the parkinglot behind the junkyard is an abandon foldout bed. So we head into town. Mani street is empty and closed down except for one thrift store, where I find rollerskates. we get beer at the liquor store and new red shoelaces. I think maybe we should move here, all of us together, when I skate by the boarded up storefronts with "for rent" signs. I tell this to Jason and he rolls his eyes. I am always looking for someplace more deserted to live, and I try my hardest to convince them. Caty doesn't take any convincing at all.

"We could take the ferry across the Bay when we wanted to! We could live by this clock and always know the time!"

"There's no reason for time" Jason says, "Not in this town".

I look down the street and I know it's true, but to me the clock is reason enough to move here. It's this big monument that they brought here from S.F. when the people wanted to tear it down to build something new. It's a memorial to some old bank robber or something, and it takes up half the sidewalk, says 3:15 when it's 8:00.

Me and Caty needed a vacation, but we didn't expect it to be in Vallejo. The four of us sitting on one caving in bed. The parkinglot is sketchy, like someplace we should have known better than to hang out in. It's freezing and windy and all we have to keep us warm is a few pieces of rotten fabric we found in a dumpster and some cardboard. We huddle together and drink beer. It gets darker and windier, colder and more ominous. We decide to take turns staying awake and keeping watch. Or maybe we should all sleep locked up in the car. We're debating these choices when cars start pulling up. We prey that they can't see us. We lay low.

There's six cars, two guys to a car. They get out slowly and move suspiciously. Is it some huge drug deal? Oh fuck, it looks bad. They start pulling out guns. I don't want to die in Vallejo. We watch them walking in formations, go back to their cars and start again. We watch them for an hour and finally they speed away. SWAT team maybe, practicing? I don't know.

The junkyard night watchman's dog starts barking and the guy comes out and finds us there, cold and shivering. He says he has a fire going and invites us in through the gate. We cook hotdogs and marshmallows, slumped back in his broken chairs, listening to the radio playing oldies.

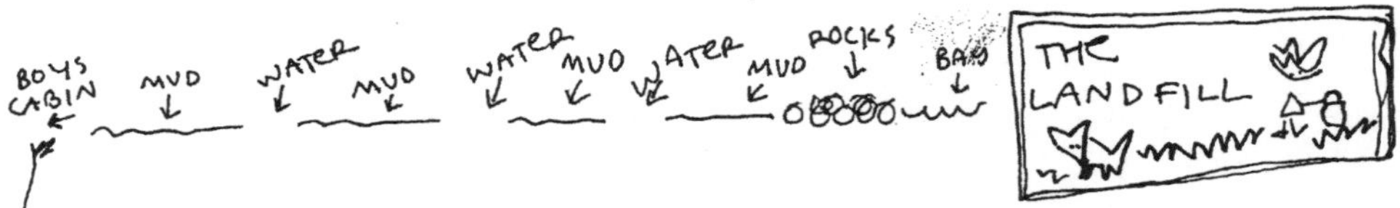

I complained a lot about living in a tent when it rained every day and I had to wade a mile through the mud to get home. Never seemed to be able to get dry. wet dog wet tent wet shoes wet blankets wet clothes. I'd go to the laundrymat where they had 25¢ hotchocolate and burn my tounge. watch the sheets and the shirts and the jackets spin around. change in the bathroom, I'd be warm for a minute, but it never lasted long.

We'd steal cake from the cake shop and drink coffee for hours in the back, sloshing past the fancy customers, me and Caty in our ratty yellow rain gear. our dog outside, lonely and wet.
"Goddamn" the boys would say when I ran into them at Safeway, "another fucking beautiful fucking day!" We'd all walk home together. They lived in the cabin next to the tent. They had a propane stove and a table where we'd play cards by candlelight. Sometimes Kerb would read stories outloud.
We had to haul water out in 2 gallon containers, and 2 gallons is heavier than you'd think. It runs out quick - cooking pasta, washing dishes, washing the mud off our hands. coffee, tea, brushing teeth, and the boys had to shave. Too much whiskey, too much wine, we were always dehydrated with all that water around. ocean, rain, puddles of mud. It didn't seem right. why couldn't we just absorb water through our skins? We were soaked enough. Jesuschrist, what the hell were we doing, living out there, in the middle of a landfil? I complained about it, but I loved that tent, and our fucked up family living hidden in the fennel plants. In the morning I'd wake up to the boys swearing and stumbling around. I'd put on my fur lined slippers and make a beeline to their cabin. We listened to the traffic radio station; every 20 minutes it would give the weather report. Every 20 minutes it always said "more rain".

There were floods in the valleys,monsoons in the mountains, they declared the whole area a disaster zone. That was fine with us, we were disasters already. The boys would unload and reorganize their backpacks. Everything had its own seperate plastic bag. One for pens, one for paper. letters, wallets, misc. junk, Plastic bags were the only thing keeping our lives from complete ruin. Ziplocks were a prized commodity. One day Mike sunk up to his knees on the mud path. Brad had to pry him out. He almost lost his shoes. One day Brad unzipped my tent after I'd only slept 2 hours. "Phone's for you" he said. I sat up and reached out and grabbed the coffee cup he was holding, spilling coffee on myself, but still asleep. I had the warm cup tagainst my cheek and was saying "hello" before I woke up enough to realize what was going on.

One day they taught me how to shoot a slingshot. One night Ewan came and taught us to play hearts. One time we sat up talking nonstop for six hours. I found my golashes and then the rain stopped. The ground dried up and we stuck around more. Fires and fireworks and barbecues. We still drank too much and fought sometimes, but we all agreed on one this, this disaster was our home!

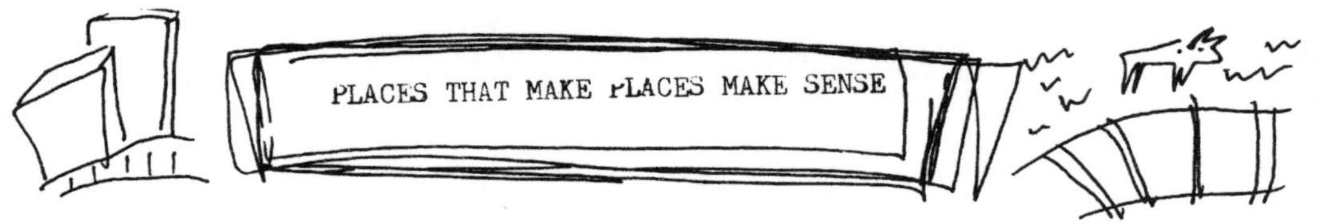

In SanFrancisco it was Jimmy's junk shop, stuck in that no-man's-land, that strange spot on Market between downtown and the Castro. He hauled junk for a living and dumped it where he could, kept whatever might possibly sell. Bikes and clothes and old photo albums, phonographs that played only 78's, records, dog tags, cords and knick-knacks. He rented out a basement apartment that wasn't zoned for commercial use, so he pretended like he lived there and put a big garage sale sign out front, and pretended like that was all his stuff. The room was so packed you could hardly move in it, and Jimmy would be down there with those eyelashes of his, and that voice. He gave me darts for my dartboard, and I bought a pocket watch. Sasha wanted a stack of old photos, and he went through them and said "you can have all these for 10¢ each, but this one", he said, holding on in his hand, "this one's a dollar". We looked at him strange and he laughed and said that he liked that picture and it's hard to let the things he likes go.

In Chattanooga there's Mick's diner, where they're always out of biscuits and gravy, and the waitresses call you sweetheart and the sky is always grey when you're looking out the window and you can sit there for hours watching the traffic jam on I24. Or the shows at the IBP (Instant Beer Pleasure), where even when it's just us and our friends, there's bodies being lifted up and tossed around the room. Dancing and raised fists and everyone gathered around the microphone, shouting out the best lines of the songs.

In Minneapolis, hardly anything made sense, except for theMayDay parade. It was big puppets with a political theme, and everyone else parading behind. politicians, Robert Bly freaks trying to get their manhood back, the American Indian Movement patrol, and us anarchists too, we had tiny black flags made out of chopsticks with fabric stapled to them, and flyers explaining the history of mayday and the distortion of anarchist ideas. We passed them all out, and you'd see kids for weeks riding bikes and waving their black flags proudly.

In Vermont there was the bridge after Peter risked his life to find out if it was safe to jump off or not. After that, everyone was always up there and I could watch them from my porch, people getting up their guts and jumping. Here,it's that burnt brick building on the tracks where you can sit and drink coffee out of a thermos or wind out of a jug, and look over the rubble past the tracks and up the hill and watch the goat wander around, watch the sun go down, watch the trains go by. I don't know. It makes sense to me.

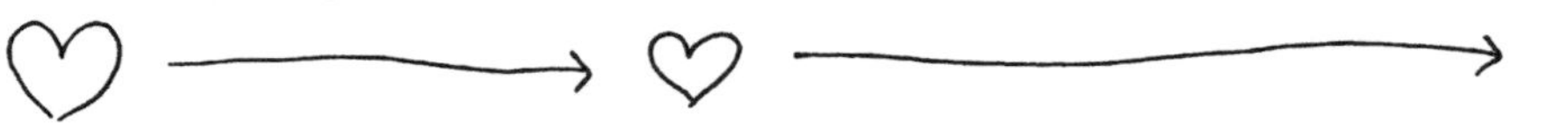

In the diner near 5th avenue that was the taxi drivers pick of the week; 8 tables, no bathroom, we both got BLT's. He has always had a lulling voice, but he tells me now that he quit writing years ago, because he read so much Rilke and poets like that and he saw how much time and work it would take to get that good, so what was the point? But now he regrets it, thinks it was a stupid reason to stop, but he doesn't know how to start again.

I remember him with his poems spread out on the floor in Park Slope, 1989, house-sitting Andrea's house; waking up there half in love and seeing how good his life looked; him crouched on the floor, weeding through the lines.

I should have told him, in that diner. Should have said Write, just start again. But who am I to tell him that, even if it's true. I wanted to describe the feel of it, the way he looked, the necessity, but who am I to say, what if his poems did suck? So I am quiet, as always, and mad at him for quitting, and later regretful, when Aaron sums it up so nicely, says "I would rather read anyone writing from Brooklyn right now, in these days, our times, than any poems by the traditional greats."

V E G E T A B L E S O L S T D
O C G H B A A N N A L L K T D
C S A G G O N O R O H E A M U
A M R E P Q A O K T L E L I C
B O L J O L N C F I J K E L K
U N I O T I A E H C S U C K Y
L P C X A G O N R H H E V D I
A W T F T O A S T O I U Y V R
R A E S O H O N L K T F R D E
Y H E F A L U M P E T K E S O
S O M U S C R U M M Y V S O A
A L B A T R O S S B D S I U E
E Y D G G A T H C I T T M P H
P M O L E P T T M O J A C K R
P A O O O P E I D E A R W A X
A C M O C Y N H R N O H S H I
N K Q M U G H S P H O H O H C
S E B C F M Q H N O H D M O E
R R K A L L O O H B U C K Y C
A E E U B X H H E F G N L S R
G L V C O G H M E G A O S I E
U K I P E Y E Y H E N H T A A
S Y N E T K L G C B N Q M Z M
J O Z N J S L O R G A N I Z E
A M A J R O O D E N A M R E H

crummy
shitty
rotten
albatross
crappy
sucky
ducky
vegetables
eggplant
banana
bagel
goner
sugarsnappeas
artichoke
moe
leek

potato
anna
garlic
kale
vocabulary
yuck
ugh
ohmeohmy
ohoh
ohno
ohfuck
ohshit
ohgeez

ohho
ohhell
organize
ocean
earwax
milkduds
kevin
soup
rats
ack
holymackerel
hefalump
toast
herman
anna
doorjam
icecream
doom
gloom
misery

Woodtics
AT MY SISTERS FARM THERE ARE MANY MANY WOODTICS. THIS TENDS TO MAKE PEOPLE FROM STRANGE PLACES LIKE CALIFORNIA FREEK OUT
HELP! TIC! GET IT OFF!
ME TOO! I GOT ONE! HELP!
BUT I AM HERE TO TELL YOU...
Just because an insect is trying to dig a hole through your skin isn't necessarily something to worry about
HAVE YOU EVER BEEN SNIPE HUNTING?
IT IS AN OLD TRADITION IN MINNESOTA THAT TAKES ON MANY FORMS. IT IS A GAME PARENTS PLAY AGAINST THEIR KIDS TO TRY + GAIN A LITTLE PEICE OF MIND. SIMILAR TO THE
why don't you kids go play on Highway seven
EXCEPT THAT SNIPE HUNTING ACTULLY WORKS.
IN OUR FAMILY, SNIPES WERE A BIRD THAT COULD NOT FLY, WAS MOSTLY BLIND, HAD A LONG beak + slept IN BUSHES.
THE PARENTS WOULD TAKE US OUT TO THE WOODS AT NIGHT AND GIVE EACH OF US A PAPER BAG. THEY WOULD ARRANGE US IN A SEMICIRCLE WITH OUR BAGS OPEN, HELD TO THE GROUND, FACING AWAY FROM US.
THEN THE PARENTS WOULD GO "BEAT THE BUSHES" ABOUT ONE MILE AWAY IN AN OPPOSITE SEMI CIRCLE TO WAKE UP + STARTLE THE SNIPES WHO WOULD THEN RUN RIGHT INTO OUR AWAITING BAGS
HEAR THAT?
WHAT?
WE WERE STUBBORN + WOULD SIT FOR HOURS SCARING EACHOTHER + NO ONE WANTED TO BE THE FIRST TO ADMIT DEFEAT. FINALLY WE WOULD FIND OUR WAY HOME
CATCH ANY?
yes! 7 OF THEM
3 HOURS IN THE WOODS MEANS WE WOULD ALL HAVE AT LEAST 30 WOODTICS. IT WAS FUN CUZ YOU HAD TO CHECK EVERYWHERE. BETWEEN TOES, ARMPITS, BACK. TAKE STOCK OF EVERY INCH OF SKIN.
I HAVE HAD AT LEAST 10,000 WOOD TICS + THE ONLY SCARY ONE WAS WHEN I WAS 8 + HAD ONE IN MY EAR FOR DAYS + IT WAS HARD TO GET FINGERS IN TO PULL IT OFF
IF A WOODTIC IS BITEING YOU, PINCH IT WHERE IT CONNETS TO THE SKIN + IT SHOULD PULL SKIN OFF WITH IT. IT DOESN'T HURT
OK
THEY SAY THAT IF YOU JUST PULL THE BODY it could SEPERATE FROM THE HEAD + THE HEAD WILL CONTINUE TO EAT YOU + IT WILL GET INFECTED + GROSS BUT I HAVE NEVER SEEN THIS HAPPEN
so... if something is trying to bore a hole into you, do not freek, remember this is a common, human experience + proceed with logic, caution + humor.
SODE

Doris #18: I was not sure I should write it. I thought I should write a comic book instead, called How To Not Deal With Your Mother's Death, complete with ytrue life examples of how to fuck fuck up your life completely. But honestly, it is not funny, and trying to laugh only makes me mad.

birds dog

here start here. here on the front step. Anna laying on the sidewalk. "There are so many birds" John says. So many strange birds here, us from the MidWest. He says

"there was a woodpecker in that tree with a red head". I say "redheaded woodpecker." I am looking at the dove, those dove grey birds that are as common as pidgeons here. Are they pidgeons? I feel dumb. I want to look and see again. I want to see and feel. I have been something I dislike, turning back.

I want things to be beautiful now, after seeing Sean's house and how he took the walls out and rebuilt it. He took out the walls and built a kitchen, carefully unnailing solid passets and building slatwood walls at angles and straight, And there are beautiful scavenged windows. He took out one whole wall practically, all windows now, looking down the hill, looking down the landscape.

How did he know where the structure was? What could go?

September

When mom died, every small thing turned huge. I was living in New York and still got lost easily. I hadn't figured out a way to slip into the city. I thought at first I would become a dog hawker. I had seen it one afternoon down at Union Square park, ten dogs tied to the fence on short leashes, big

and small, and each dog with a person sitting next to it, petting, talking into ears, keeping the sweet things calm. And there was a woman yelling like a carnival barker, about neglected dogs, please adopt or donate, we need money for food, poor dogs to feed. She was jangling her bucket.

I thought dog hawking would be funny, a good thing to write home about, and I would become a public fixture, calmer of the biggest dog of the day. And also in the park, I had seen a girl typing on her portable blue manual typewriter, and at first I looked at her and thought - god, she must think she's some hot shit - and then, quickly, I was embarrassed at myself. What the fuck had happened to me that I would think that, instead of looking and wishing I had my typewriter too.

I had given up something vital, given up the things that gave me life, the things I did for myself, not for show; or for both sometimes but in a laughing way, showing up in life full of color, embracing, because I had to or because I could.

I was embarrassed at myself, and I wished then that I hadn't given up my ways, and I knew I would be less lost if I hadn't learned scorn, stupid thing. I had lost myself, huge chunks, huge defining things, like riding my bike in the sun, typewriter in basket; or working hard for what I believed in, working with other people, not just alone, by myself.

But dog hawking? Would it fill my heart and make me feel useful? Or just drown me, overrun me; the carnival voice, men's stares, and the noise of the street there in the busyness. I was not sure I could take the noise.

In the building where I lived (a squat, it was very exciting for me), there was heavy construction next door. Early in the morning, when we'd only been asleep a few hours, they would start, and it sounded like they were drilling their building directly into ours. It was a very flat faced building, designed by a Russian architect, very strangely flat with two round windows near the top. And outside, on the sidewalk next to it, there were always two or three guys, day or night, sitting on lawn chairs, washing in the fire hydrant, sitting on buckets, drinking beer sometimes. And when it rained, there was a tarp they stretched from the tree to I can't remember what, to form a little roof. That was for when it was raining not too hard.

It seemed like we should be friendly, but they scowled. And they told on us when someone from our house spraypainted the new building. I heard the men were hired or at least had some agreement with the construction company to be guardian angels of this building that was going over what had, for years, been a community garden.

When my mom died, I walked too fast down the street. I could feel the ends of my skin. My depth perception was bad, there was tingling in my head. I was in shock, I know. I couldn't remember anything. I couldn't remember where Charas was, even though I walked by it most days. I was trying to meet Mary. I didn't know what she looked like. I was late. The message on the answering machine, before the message about my mom, was from Mary, saying could I please meet her at 6 to give her a key to the building, she had just gotten back to town and had all her stuff and was locked out. But here it was, 7 already, wand when I finally found Charas, she was not on the steps. I went inside, looking. There was an IWW movie showing that I had originally wanted to see. It was old footage on the screen, the movie itself, a sad looking woman and the loud persistant clack clascking of looms. I wanted to sit down, even though I couldn't consintrate enough to pick out the muddled, accented words. I wanted to sit down and watch weavers and the noise, if only that noise would just, please, go on forever.

But I didn't sit. I looked for Mary. I asked women alone if they were her. I asked the guy at the literature table - I was supposed to meet someone named Mary, did he know who she was? - And the more I tried to explain, the more everyone was disturbed by me, like I was crazy, and so I went home to wait. I remember now. It has been four months and already my mind is fogging over the facts, not the feeling so much as the placement of events. That day was not the day my mom died, it was the day I heard she was sick and could go at any minute, although it was possible she would be ok. In my heart I knew she wouldn't, and I went home to wait.

Round White Cookies

I cup butter
½ cup powdered sugar
I 3/4 cup bread flour
I cup nuts (walnuts)
I tsp vanilla

mix butter and sugar, then mix in the rest (the nuts should be chopped). chill. roll into balls that would take two bites to eat. cook at 350 degrees for I2 minutes. they should not be brown, except for a little tan on the bottom. roll in powdered sugar when they are still warm, and then again when they are cool.

Ginger Snaps

3/4 cup butter
I/2 cup sugar
mix these then add
2 tsp baking soda
2 cup flour
¼ cup molasses

I egg
¼ tsp cloves
½ tsp ginger
I tsp cinnamin
½ tsp salt

chill

roll into balls. roll in sugar. squish slightly. bake 7-10 minutes at 350°

letters

Dear Cindy,

today I am at Essex St. Market, buying carrot juice and thinking a lot while my laundry spins its heart out around the corner. There's some kind of exhibit here "the history of the market", and it's chock full of useful information. It's cool cause it's all related to Latino culture. Did you know that coffee is a cure for conjunctivitus (pink eye)? You wipe your eyelid and lashes with strong black coffee. And I always thought "cupping" was exclusively Chinese. But in Latin America (it doesn't say where) they have "ventosa" which is said to cure back pain by removing air pockets in your back. You light a candle and put a cup over it, after a nice massage with coconut oil to loosen it all up.

So, I got back from Europe alive. I started writing you a letter that didn't make any fucking sense but I'm still deliberating over whether or not to send it.

Prague gave me perspective on ugliness and beauty. In DC, when I went to jail for living in an abandoned building, my last bastions of the friendly Cop daydream went flying out the window. I realized that the job of a police officer is not to help any individual human beings, but to destroy with physical and emotional violence anyone percieved as a threat to capitolism, racism, sexism. I mean, I wasn't totally asleep before that, but in DC I was witness to ugly violence, scary lies, and insane conspiratorial puppetish doughboys that made me think I could never trust any white man again. What I saw in DC terrified me too much to figure out. It was all so weird, twisted, unexplainable (seemingly). Turns out it was just language.

As soon as I got to Berlin, I breathed out a breath that had been building in my chest for years. It was great. Everywhere I went I couldn't understand a thing. Until just a few days before I left (when I started to speak and understand more German) I was totally unaffected by advertising and "soft" street harassment.

In Prague I was surrounded by some really amazing people. I learned how to do cool two and three person acrobatic tricks by walking up to some folks who were practicing on the sidewalk. Everywhere I went there were revolutionaries looking for the same places as me. I couldn't get out of the net and I didn't want to. It was warm and easy. If I wanted food I went to the kitchen or asked someone where the HareKrishna place was. If I needed a place to stay that night, I could ask 2-3 people. If I needed to organize a group tof womyn to confront a guy who'd made a sexist banner, I just put up a sign that stated the meeting place. On top of facing every day knowing I could rally the support, creativity, and commitment to direct action of about I2,000 people, I was enourmously rich! The exchange rate there is crazy. $100 turns into 4,000 crohns. I found a place where you could get a small ice cream cone for 6 crohns. That's less than a penny I think. A bagel at the yuppie Australian coffee shop was anywhere from 20-I00 crohns, but when you have 4,000 of them, come ON!!

Police were everywhere, hunting like dogs. They'd stand on a bridge, in uniform, taking our pictures or videotaping everyone who walked by. They filled the subway stations we used most, setting up random checkpoints where you had to show your saved subway ticket and passport. No passport? No ticket? You went to jail. Sometimes that meant sitting in a waiting room for 6-I2 hours while they did who knows what with your passport, sometimes it meant starving in jail for 5-I0 days, and too often, like in this guy Yoshua's case and the case of an Austrian women I've never met, it meant several broken bones, being thrown out of police station windows, chained to a wall and slapped over and over in the face while cops yell "Jew! fucking Jew!" and of course having every cop in the world come by and take your photo for their own personal collection, sometimes while you were nude. Mirjam was made to wear her clothes in "anarchist" styles, like hood up, cloth over face, so the cops could photograph her. Two of my friends and I were walking right in front of the building I was staying in when suddenly we were surrounded by police. I'd forgot that there was a station right there. They would say nothing but "Passports". We handed them over, I had stupidly stuffed my passport into my jeans pocket along with a bunch of leaflets and crap, so this card with lawyers numbers andCzech writing had gotten wedged into the passport. He put them all in his pocket and said "this way", leading us to the station doors. When we saw he was trying to take us in, I started playing Dumb Outraged American Tourist. I was yelling "mlwite angliski?"

We knew they spoke English but were faking, and we were lucky to a ssume what I know as a fact now, that theCzech cops were very hesitant to do anything in public. They wanted to grab activists as quick as possible and then almost kill them in jail for revenge. We were surrounded in broad daylight with lots of people walking by, and I was being LOUD, asking everyone on the street if they spoke english. The cop looked nervous and simply disappeared into the station for 45 minutes with our passports. We were really lucky.
The day of was amazing. There were I2,000 of us, split into 3 groups. Yellow, pink and blue. Radical Cheerleaders decided to go with blue, since all our friends were there. It was becoming known as the anarchist march.

I saw molotov cocktail being thrown for the first time. It was pretty violent in general, but so exciting. No matter how many times I got hit by a rock or concussion grenade, the whole time I was smiling (sometimes maniacally laughing) it was the first time I'd seen an all-out peoples war being waged against a system that was oppressing humans all over the world. Two moments stood out as permanently beautiful to me; One, in which a woman wearing a long ornate skirt, black bra, and gas mask, threw rocks at the police right in the front lines, and Two, in which the entire crowd acted suddenly, as if one tactical mind, and began to tear down this huge fence and all the billboards andbegin to put up barricades, like this: Some would tear down the fences and prop them while others dug rock after rock out of the sidewalk, (which are made of stones). Everything was lined up as if people had some kind of orders, but no one was giving orders. It just happened.

At the same time, a train had pulled up next to us. We were defending out group from the advancing police and at the same time trying to continue the blockade of the Conference Center, which is where the I.M.F. meetings were being held. So when this train pulled up, a group of people all got an idea and ran over to it. They randomly turned [illegible] wheels to let some air out, and took huge rocks to literally break the train with. More and more people ran over to it, detaching cars and breaking off handles and weird train parts. Within maybe 5 minutes (I swear) the train was so fucked up it was going to be disabled for days.

So me and Famous had some words about violence against cops. I have years of thinking to do about my true feelings, beyond anger and sympathy. But I just wanted you to know that stuff happened, cops were set on fire and stuff.

I saw for the first time total fear in cops eyes... fear of people and their power in numbers and drive. I wish I could talk to you in person... I wish we could look over the photos and go back and forth over ideologies.

... there is still so much to tell

-love, Mary Xmas

When my mom was probably dieing, I didn't want to go. I thought - what if I spend all the money to go out there, and then she doesn't die - and so I come back and then she dies and I have to go out there again. It was a terrible feeling to think. I also thought - I am sick of this shit. Sick of having to think about her, haven't I done enough already, taken care of her. I don't care anymore. I don't want to think about it. I don't want to go.

But if you had ever seen my mother, you would know how much I love her. I went, and she didn't die, and I came back and later she died and I borrowed money and went again.

TOFFEE BARS

I/2 lb sweet butter
I cup light brown sugar
I egg yolk
2 cups unbleached flour
Itsp vanilla
I2 oz semisweet chocolat chips
I cup walnuts or pecans, choped

preheat oven to 350, grease a 9byI2 baking pan
Cream butter and sugar, add egg yolk.
stir in flour, mix well, add vanilla. Spread in pan and bake 25 minutes. Cover cak
Cover it with chocolate chips and bake again 3-4 minutes.
Remove from oven, spread melted chips evenly
sprinkle with nuts. Cool completely
(they actually are better cool, trust me)

309

You should see next door, with the transmission on the diningroom table, Tim and Joe rebuilding it, and rebuilding it because it's so damn interesting, their eyes with real joy in them, like kids I guess you could say, kids with a new toy, except I think this is not kid like at all - joy and excitement and wonder - not kid qualities only.

They are fixing it because they want to, and because they can, not like the way I started learning to fix cars, with this dogma, this language that said something along the lines of "we have become dependent on machines that we don't understand, a mechanized, alienation by the products in our lives and we must demystify the inner workings or crush them". either that or "we must break down the class division between the people who use machines and the people who fix them". Whatever. There's some validity in there, but I like the joy and curiosity better.

Transmission on the table, and in one room, someone learning, alone, how to fix coaster breaks. In another room the tapping of typewriter keys. in one pen on paper. These are my neighbors. some of them. One of them is learning to build a banjo. He says he'll make me one next if he ever really does it, and me, I have just been learning to play.

Underneath the sad and feeling of never quite enough, of incompletion, this is more than I ever would have expected I could get. Here in my house with the rotting floorboards. we wheatpasted the walls from floor to cealing, pictures of trees like Minnesota in the winter, a world map (black and white), Ho Chi Minh in '46 at the First National Assembly of the Democratic Republic of Vietnam, seagulls, world leaders. and it is unfortunate that the backyard doesn't get any sun, so whatever I plant only germinated, never grows, but soon I will be back in the mountains. Back to Caty's farm.

IN FL. THE TREES HAVE FLOWERS INSTEAD OF LEAVES. THE TRAINS RIDE BY
SKRINK
SKRINK
SKRINK
hey listen
my wheel
has been making this skrinky noise
do you think if I dip it in oil it will fix it up?
SLOW ENOUGH TO GET ON (I HAVEN'T YET)
AND A ONE SPEED BIKE IS ALL YOU NEED TO GET AROUND. NO HILLS.
LOOKS LIKE LOOSE SPOKES
TO TIGHTEN SPOKES, ALL YOU NEED IS A FORK. JUST JAM THE SPACE BETWEEN THE TONGS ON TO THE LITTLE END SPOKE PART AND TURN RIGHT.
AND IF YOU ARE LIKE ME YOU CAN SPEND ALL DAY ON THE PORCH WITH YOUR BIKE + FORK
WATCHING THE SUN GO AND RAIN COME IN. ALL DAY ON THE PORCH BEFORE REALIZING IT WOULD HAVE BEEN A LOT FASTER THE REGULAR WAY. TAKING OFF THE TIRE + TIGHENING IT ALL UP WITH A REGULAR OLD SCREWDRIVER.

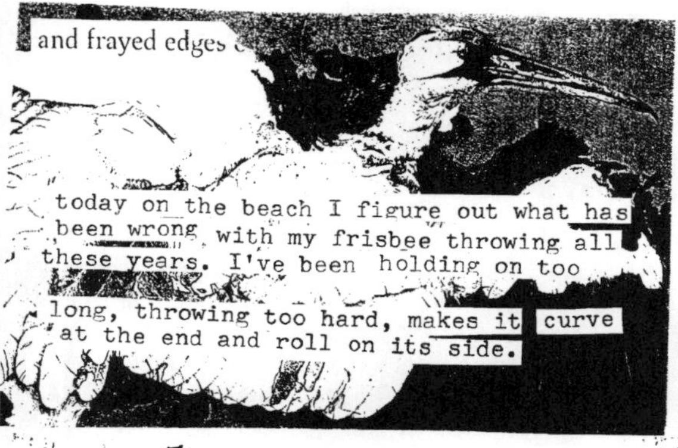

and frayed edges
today on the beach I figure out what has been wrong with my frisbee throwing all these years. I've been holding on too
long, throwing too hard, makes it curve at the end and roll on its side.

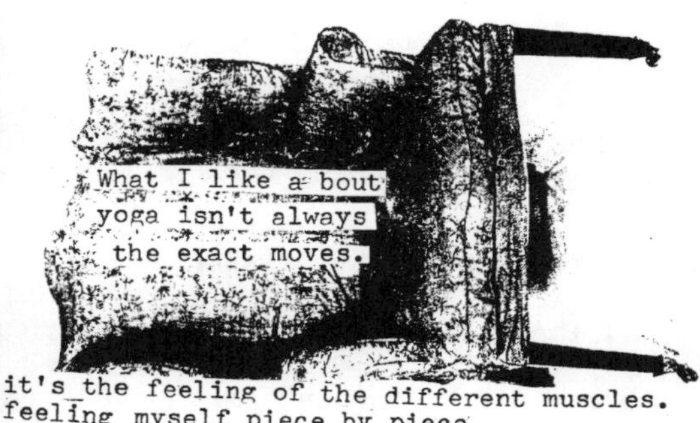

What I like a bout yoga isn't always the exact moves.
it's the feeling of the different muscles. feeling myself piece by piece.

Waking up alone, with no voices, no ones needs.
My fingers on typewriter keys, on the coffee button, on the mailbox flag.

It's Florida, the first warm day and I need beach, blue sky, white sand, the taste, the sound, what I'm here for and never get.

wind vento vent viento
whale
balena
baleine
ballena
So I drive and here it is, empty, cold wind on my bare arms bare legs, but the sun high enough, hot enough to soak in.

I try cartwheels and it stretches too fast, too quickly.

So I stretch my own stretches, twirl and feel the gravity shooting out my fingers.

あらら こと

Anna plays fetch with the waves, dropping the frisbee in and letting the ocean carry it out and back in. and she brings it to me, and absentmindedly, I learn to throw.

ProAbortion before pro choice.

I never really know what is common knowledge and what is not. What history is washed away or watered down, like this: the abortion history.

Before Roe vs Wade, women were fighting for the repeal of all laws having to do with abortion. They saw it as a women's rights issue- that women had the absolute right to control her own body, no matter what. and they placed it in a larger struggle for reproductive freedom. Repeal. Free abortion on demand. Of course, the liberals thought this was too much to ask for, and they started lobbying heavily for legalization- pushing the debate into the private realm. Saying it was a 4th amendment thing - it was a privacy issue - abortion was a private decision made between a woman and her doctor, and that's what the court decisions were based on.

There has been a steady chipping away of the right to abortion - parental consent, 24 hour waiting periods, laws against third term, doctors and clinics being so terrorized they are forced to quit, close down, they're killed.

Only 12% of ob/gyn residency programs require training in first trimester abortions, even though it is the most common ob/gyn surgical procedure in the U.S. (and only 75 require training in second term. I can't remember the statistic for the number that offer it, but it's really, really low!)

94% of non metropolitan areas don't have abortion providers, and one forth of women getting abortions have to travel over 50 miles from home to get one. There is so little funding that even though it's legal, it is often inaccessible just because it's expensive.

And now that Bush's people are in power, the health department is reconsidering the 'safty' of RU486, and a law was passed, in South Carolin and I think North Dakota, that says all clinics that provide abortion must meet hospital regulations, the the doors have to be the size of hospital doors - just rediculous shit which will effectively shut them all down.

The gag rule has been reinstated. They don't even have to overturn Roe vs Wade to make it so abortions are practically impossible to get (except for the rich.)

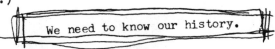

We need to know our history.

There was Jane, an abortion service in the late 60's early 70's (when abortion was illegal). Jane started out as a referal service, women would call them and they would find them a doctor and provide emotional support before and after. But it was still pretty expensive, and eventually the Jane women got to watch the procedure and saw how simple it was, and they learned to do it themselves. They did over 11,000 abortions, sliding scale, they never turned anyone away for lack of funds, and it was done in a very supportive atmosphere. (When I first read about Jane I couldn't believe it -

they just did that? They just up and learned it?! It seemed so impossible to me. abortion still so scary. and then I learned about the selfcare movement - that this was still going on. women learning all about their bodies, how to do self exams and menstrual extraction! That it wasn't just history. Important still, going on now) So I tell you here - please learn the history, learn about your body, fight the laws that are coming so quickly. Fight on every level.

My Mobil Home

Caty won't let me call my new home my RV, because of when we lived in Vermont and she'd walk down Route 2 to go to work washing dishes by hand at Maple Valley General Store and Cafe, the tourists on their way to Bangor Maine or up to look at the leaves, the tourists in RVs wizzed by on that road with nearly no shoulder, sped by one after the other in a steady stream, and almost blew Caty over. Then later, down by Lake Tahoe, she was broadsided by one when she was driving a small car and she had to be pulled out by the jaws of life. Broken ribs, bleeding kidney, I got the phone call and went into shock I guess, cuz I drove 5 hours in the wrong direction to be by her side. Didn't realize what was happening until I saw that mountain, the one below Portland on I-5.

figure 1

In the hospital parkinglot, I'd fix her tea on the camp stove and sneak it in through her window at night. "No herbal medicine" the docs said, and then later "We've never seen anything like this - 3 broken ribs and not a bit of bruising".

and says:

CAN'T YOU NAME IT OR CALL IT SOMETHING OTHER THAN "THE RV"?

she sighs at me now

YOU DON'T RECREATE IN THERE! YOU LIVE!

and she's right I don't know how it slips out - RV when I mean to say Mobile Home

figure 2 - brasicas

I was driving to Caty's new farm with Jody, driving in her truck because the road is something else. You have to drive straight through a creek, no bridge. "It's hardly bigger than a puddle" Caty says, but I'm not so sure, and the road it ruts and rocks.

Jody says - how is it? Living in that thing? (I should describe it to you now so you don't get the wrong impression. It's a long van with a high roof. some wild man cut the back off and welded on an extra section. It is like nothing Iever seen before.) I say to Jody - it's great, it'snice, except that my tire blew up, it ripped a big hole in the floor and the wood back there was rotten anyway and the rail comes up now through the hole and it's wet and moldy.

How did a tire rip a hole in the floor? she says.

Well, it was ripped and rusted already, and patched back together...with spray insulation. I say and laugh.

She says - I would have used duct tape, layer after layer of duct tape. or chewing gum. Once I patched the holes in my truck with chewing gum.

I believe her.

At the farm, we skin the greenhouse. How you do this is you have the frame built already out of wood and plastic pipe, and the skin is just a giant piece of plastic. Everyone pulls it tight as can possibly be, and the other people nail it on there quick.

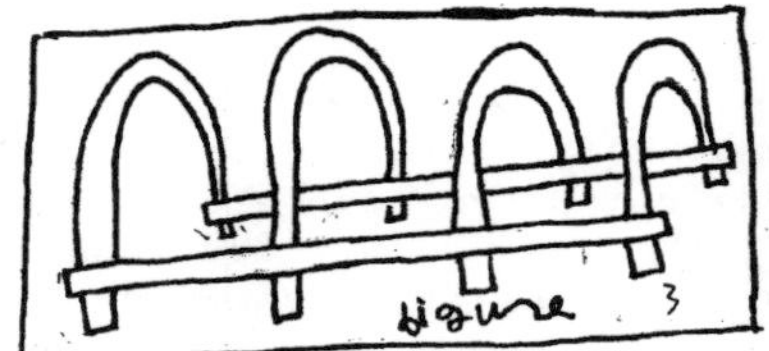

In Caty's house I bake banana bread. Talk to the dogs and the hikers who hike by. I lay down to sleep and hear Caty upstairs, awake still and talking to the cat. I say "Goodnight Miss", tired my s's slurr, my lisp. The stars are bright and I grow restless, growing into my new lives, happy and restless.

dear Mary,

I am under 100 blankets trying to keep warm. what's the deal? I thought this was Spring! I want to go to the beach beforeI leave! I turned off the heat a month ago and if I try to relight it I'll risk blowing my face up like last time.

I'm sick. sick since you left practically, which is no real excuse for not writing, but it's my lame excuse for an excuse.

What was I going to so urgently tell you? I have not figured out any great thesis about the subject - just that those things struck a cord in me - the bonding with people about how fucked up we are and what a strong bond that makes, and what to do when you're not feeling fucked. How to bond? How hard it is. And also this romanticizing fucked-up-ness.

That was this huge issue I was trying to write about in the Snarla story, but it was too complicated, so I just touched the bare bones - but I know. It was/is hard.

There was something really great about the whole movement to romanticize fucked-up-ness, because, for me, it let me finally accept these ways I felt. It was validating. Finally it was clear that I was fucked up because the world was fucked, where as before I was fucked up because I couldn't 'get over it'. There was something really great about diving into it, and thinking it was fucked up that everyone wasn't fucked up. Like if we could just pull the fucked-up-ness out of each person and into the open, there would be total world change. Better than world change. It would be something way beyond what we could dream.

But for me, there was something really dangerous about it too- because the coping mechanisms I had developed are important. And it's not really that embracing fucked-up-ness made it so hard to live in this world - it's more about this; that it was keeping me from all these other very real parts of me, and keeping me from other things I wanted to be doing. It kept me from the sort of stupid pure hope that's core in me, and from a conscious mental, psychological, political, social growth.

It sounds weird articulated like that, but you know what I mean. It kept me from being able to write. Most of what I did was reaction, and I didn't want IT, THEM to have that much say over my life.

I didn't mean to go on so much, I just wanted to say that I know - it is so hard to form bonds that aren't about being fucked up, but they're there, they take a hell of a lot longer, years, but they're there and good.

I love you

cindy

STAY

When I first met Issac, one of the first days, he pulled me under the pine tree outside the International House, he sat me down and told me that his mom had died a few months before. I am not sure what I said, but I think I took it to mean: stay away from the subjects of mothers and death. I didn't know how to deal with it. ~~What~~ do you do when someone's mother dies?

I will write this, but I know the people around me will disagree. I will write this, but I know they will say - but we did that - but we didn't know.

When my mom died I felt so alone. I was in NYC and hadn't figure my way into the city yet, but I loved it there. I would do my shift at the women's collective bookstore, and we were all a little nervous there, like we were playing a game, given this big thing. And when someone came in just to get coffee, we had to read the instructions about how to make it. And when the French woman came in and asked me if there were any magazines about feminism, and I tried to help, but really there aren't any; political, radical feminism, not cultural, is what she meant, and I felt ashamed of myself.

When mom died, I understood the traditions of what people some places do after death, how people bring them food, flowers, talk about the deceased, wear black so everyone, even strangers, are especially respectful, reverent even, tender, without you yourself having to explain.

I remember having times of being glad that it was out of my mind. being relieved for other thoughts, like spark plugs, petty things. But for the most part, I never got to talk about it enough. I turned down invitations from acquaintances but it was becaused they were offered as distractions, and I couldn't be around groups of people, I had no extra energy to extend. I didn't want to hear or see other people's projects or hear their problems. I didn't trust myself to get on the subway and ever get off.

I know people don't know what to do, and that is why I am telling you this.

That, and really, what else can I do.

When my mom died, I felt like an alien, like a leper. I am telling you, don't shy away. Mothers die. It is an interesting subject. Ask questions and keep your opinions to yourself. I felt like I needed very little, or a lot, but simple things. To be cooked for, to talk, flowers, sympathy, some distraction, some small talk, but mostly to be held.

I wanted to be held close, to feel it in my chest, held and brought to tears. Or if crying already, brought to sobs. Or maybe just held in my anger, held while I said cynical things, held while I dismissed it all. What I wanted most was to be held.

I wanted to tell stories. Wanted to explain what it was like; tell the childhood stories that I used to hold such stake in, used to think those stories held the key to anyone truly understanding me, and I wanted true understanding, believed it was possible and good. I told the stories obsessively, not obsessively but with calculated precision. If I got the right response, I would open myself up more. I would let myself care more. But it was tricky because even I did not know what the right reaction was.

Later I decided these stories were not so important. I had grown up and had plenty of other things under my belt that had made me. But when my mother died, I wanted to tell the stories.

I wanted to be asked "what was she like?" and I was asked this question I suppose, though I couldn't say for sure. I was cooked for and held, but it was so constant, so heavy, always there.

Asked the wrong question would have been better than none.

Every morning I cried, and frustrated crying because I did not know if I was still crying for her, or crying because I did not know how to get what I needed.

Now it has been four months, and the shock is finally starting to wear away, and I feel like I'm just now starting the hard part. It is like one of Caty's farmers market customers said. The customers, they seem to have known more about death and how to be supportive than anyone else did. One of them brought pictures. Another said this: It is going to be hard, hard for a really long time. Long after everyone else has forgotten all about it, it's still going to be really hard for you.

and this is true.

the end

Outroduction

How could I have left you with that hard end, when there is happy ending all around me: wood stove, mountains, empty roads, empty house. I put the headphones of my borrowed four-track and practice singing, trying to hit different notes instead of just belting it all out. I learn how electrical wiring works and how to do minor plumbing. Tomorrow I start building my sister a greenhouse. My sister! She's moving back to me! I haven't the slightest idea how to build, but I have books from the library; I have memories of watching my Spillcorn friends build their structures; I have a telephone, I can call people and ask questions. I have learned finally, how to stop always going in the same circles, repeating the same mistakes.

This house I am renting from my friend Amy, and it came with two cats - little hunter cats that can survive on their own just fine when I leave for a weekend, a week, a month - but who will also follow me on long hikes in the woods. I talk to them. touch their faces, sing to them.

One time, Amy's new house had some mice, and she asked to borrow the cats for a week. I carried them into my sister's truck, and they tried to jump out of the broken window. When we got to the grocery store, I stood outside the truck, blocking their escape, whispering comfort.

My sister and I look insane. Me with two orange braids sticking out of my head, striped shirt, plaid skirt, striped socks, boots, whispering into the window. Her with a tiny mohawk, button-up, sptr spraypainted on shirt, suspenders holding up her petticoats, rummaging through her bag, swearing, looking for her wallet.

A teenaged boy comes up to us and asks if we'll buy him cigerettes. Caty takes his money, finds her wallet, goes inside, and I am left in the parkinglot, making small talk. He is cleancut, not too shy, not too outgoing, with a McDonalds hat on so I assume he must work there. "Old enough for early enlistment but still illegal to smoke," he says, and then starts talking about the truck - an old Chevy diesel - a friend of his used to have one just like it. He talks truck talk for awhile before he realizes I have no idea about any of it.

The silence comes and then becomes uncomfortable, and I think - What the hell? I am trying to learn to talk to people, aren't I? I say "Have you ever heard about running diesels off of used vegetable oil?" He laughs at me. I laugh at myself. "I'm serious," I say, and I explain the little that I know about how it works, and that my sister and her friend drove across the country like that, fueled on grease from restaurants.

"I can see it, I can see how that would work," he says, and he points due North, "I bet the guys up there are hoping that news doesn't get out!"

We stand around, quiet again, but a more peaceful kind of quiet this time, watching the cats who have given up trying to escape and are sleeping now. Watching the people load up their cars with groceries and the grocery store worker wheeling back the empty carts. The clouds move thickly, slowly across the sky. The sky is a deep, dark, resonant blue.

"See that?" he says, pointing up to where I'm looking. "See how blue that blue is? When the sky turns that color, you know that fall is coming."

So, fall was here, and now it's winter: snow falling thickly on the world around me. Do you believe in happy endings? Because sometimes they do happen. Something inside shifts, something outside comes together, and your fight becomes more purposeful, your rest becomes actually restful, your hurt becomes something you can bear, and your happiness becomes something that shines out with ease, not in lightning manic bursts that fill and then drain you, but something else, something steady, somthing you can almost trust to stay there.

CREDITS

Page I and 3 have drawings by Caty Crabb

Page 42 is a letter from someone, I think Christine

Page 49 has a poem by Sandra Cisneros, from her book Loose Woman

Page 6I is a drawing by an old friend

Page 7I has a flyer by Lelia

Page 90 and 9I had imput from my roomates Megan, Caty Carolyn, Aaron, and a Canadian whose name I can't remember

Page 97 has a letter from Sam

Page I33-I35 has drawings by Eric Drooker, from his graphic novel, I think it might be called Rain

Page I46 has questions from the book Courage To Heal

Page I47 has reprinted part of the zine "Mr. Dog"

Page 222 has an old AWOL flyer

Pages 244, and 247-249 are by Caty

Page 247 has a recipe by Adam Sellers

Page 268 has part of a block print by Sarah Danforth

Page 292-294 is a letter from Mary X-mas

Page 304 is a block print by Shari Rother

there are other graphics taken from places I can't recal